Cognitive Behaviora.
for Medical Settings

This book offers specific evidence based behavioral treatment plans for the most commonly observed symptoms seen in medical and clinical settings. It will address the needs of therapists who work in fast-paced clinics and are often mandated to provide time-limited and effective treatment. Intended for early career clinicians as well as experienced psychotherapists, clear goal-directed protocols are outlined in a specific manner to assist the clinician in treating frequently reported pain complaints, somatic illnesses, anxiety, sleep difficulties, panic, agitation, anger management, and more. A brief review of symptoms is followed by specific cognitive behavioral treatment strategies, quantitative treatment tracking tools, and methods to address obstacles and facilitate progress. This clinician-friendly manual will guide research based interventions and documentation needs, while also showing how the intervention can best be used to avoid common pitfalls in treatment.

Jennifer LaBuda, PhD, is a rehabilitation neuropsychologist and clinical psychologist. She is a national consultant for chronic pain treatment and frequent lecturer to professional organizations on behavioral and cognitive behavioral treatment.

Bradley N. Axelrod, PhD, is a clinical psychologist who has expertise in clinical neuropsychology. Well published in the fields of neuropsychological and psychological assessment, he has been clinical staff at the John D. Dingell Department of Veterans Affairs Medical Center in Detroit since 1990.

James Windell, MA, is an author and college instructor. As a limited-licensed psychologist, he specialized in work with families and children. He has been recognized as a parenting and discipline expert and for many years worked as a court clinical psychologist. In private practice as a family therapist, he frequently worked with both juvenile and adult offenders.

Cognitive Behavioral Protocols for Medical Settings

A Clinician's Guide

Jennifer LaBuda,
Bradley N. Axelrod,
and James Windell

Routledge
Taylor & Francis Group

NEW YORK AND LONDON

First published 2018
by Routledge
711 Third Avenue, New York, NY 10017

and by Routledge
2 Park Square, Milton Park, Abingdon, Oxon, OX14 4RN

Routledge is an imprint of the Taylor & Francis Group, an informa business

Library of Congress Cataloging-in-Publication Data
Title: Cognitive behavioral protocols for medical settings : a clinician's guide /
by Jennifer La Buda, Bradley N. Axelrod, and Jim Windell.
Description: New York, NY : Routledge, 2018. | Includes bibliographical
references. Identifiers: LCCN 2017047143 (print) | LCCN 2017047923
(ebook) | ISBN 9781315282411 (ebk) | ISBN 9781138223615 (hbk) |
ISBN 9781138223646 (pbk)
Subjects: | MESH: Cognitive Therapy | Mental Disorders—therapy |
Pain Management—psychology
Classification: LCC RC489.C63 (ebook) | LCC RC489.C63 (print) |
NLM WM 425.5.C6 | DDC 616.89/1425—dc23
LC record available at https://lccn.loc.gov/2017047143

ISBN: 978-1-138-22361-5 (hbk)
ISBN: 978-1-138-22364-6 (pbk)
ISBN: 978-1-315-28241-1 (ebk)

Typeset in Baskerville
by Florence Production Ltd., Stoodleigh, Devon, UK

To those from whom we have learned: our supervisors, clients, and students.

Contents

Section Four: Interpersonally Disruptive Symptoms   **295**

Introduction

What is the best way to treat someone with sleep problems? What is the best approach to treating a person with chronic pain? What are the steps to treating a person who has a panic disorder?

These kinds of questions were a primary motivation for us as we thought about the challenges we faced with treating people we encountered in hospitals and clinics over the course of our careers. We frequently thought that there must be a manual for treating individuals experiencing white coat anxiety or being preoccupied with thinking that they had a fatal form of cancer. Despite searching for those manuals and guidelines, we found very few. Certainly, there were guidelines for treating depression or anger problems, but those books and manuals were devoted to one treatment approach for a specific diagnosis or problem. Not one book containing separate chapters and protocols for each of several conditions one might encounter in a hospital or medical setting was found. With that motivation guiding us, we set out to fill that gap. The result is the book you are now holding in your hands.

Our focus is on nine problems for diagnoses frequently presented by people coming to a medical clinic or hospital. Those conditions are: pain, sleep difficulties, depression, anger-management problems, white coat hypertension or anxiety, illness anxiety, panic disorder, agitation and disruptive behavior, and pragmatics. In reviewing the research about each of these disorders, many of them had a history of being treated with medication. Unfortunately, medications alone were not always successful in treating the conditions, or they included too many negative side effects to maintain compliance by the patients.

However, the treatment approach that had some relevance for all of them, or was clearly well researched, was cognitive behavioral treatment. Thus, our focus is on treatments that are cognitive behavioral in nature. In other words, we wanted to develop an approach that best addressed the treatment of the most salient symptoms. Again, that turned out to be cognitive behavioral therapy. Treatments that focus on identifiable symptoms, specific goals, monitoring of symptoms, and a way that can objectively indicate if the treatment works to reduce those symptoms.

Our aim was to merge the model with the conditions, offering specific treatment protocols that can be readily applied in the clinical setting. What you will find in this book is that we have created treatment manuals that can be used as is, or that can be modified for similar populations.

Before those treatment chapters are mentioned, we would like to guide you through the contents of this book. The first part of the book presents a summary of the nine conditions we are addressing in terms of symptoms, etiologies, assessment, and treatments. We then offer principles of psychotherapy in general, and in particular, cognitive behavioral therapy, and evidence-based treatments. These initial three chapters give a relatively in-depth look at the nine conditions, principles of psychotherapy that can be applied in treating these nine problems, and then devoting a chapter to evidence-based treatment. Among the principles discussed in Chapter 2 are those that state some of our beliefs informing this book. For instance, our guiding principles include the proposition that treatment should be goal-directed, that treatment should combine both patient education and therapist–client collaboration, that treatment be structured to a limit of twelve sessions, and that patients are taught in treatment to learn to adjust to the presence of their symptoms rather than be focused on eliminating their symptoms.

In Chapter 3, research demonstrating the efficacy of cognitive behavioral therapy over medication for physical, mood, anxiety, and disruptive disorders will be discussed. Furthermore, the authors review effective treatment interventions for mood issues prevalent in medical patients. These treatment interventions will focus on areas such as behavioral activation/pleasurable activity, cognitive distortions, utilization of alternate behavioral responses, and environmental management.

The second part of this book, starting with Chapter 4, begins to look at each condition offering a protocol for treatment for each one. Starting with the treatment management of pain in Chapter 4, we offer a complete guideline or manual for a clinician to provide appropriate intervention. In each treatment chapter, we present a short-term approach for treatment, ranging from six to ten sessions. Before the directions and instructions for each session, there is an agenda that outlines what will be covered in that session, the materials needed for the session, and the protocol for the session. That protocol spells out what the therapist will discuss and how they should interact with the client or patient. Finally, at the end of each session is a homework or practice assignment for the patient.

The focus of Chapter 4 is on pain and chronic pain. After the agenda and the assessment materials needed during the sessions, a protocol for successful intervention is provided. Techniques described in the ten sessions include patient pain education (neurobiology of pain, gate control theory, and fear/threat response), setting appropriate movement goals, addressing fear of movement, increasing behavioral activation, and challenging thinking distortions.

Chapter 5 has to do with sleep difficulties, including insomnia. Patient education regarding sleep (i.e., the sleep drive), stimulus control (of the sleep environment), anxiety management, and sleep restriction are of considerable importance in treatment and included here primary to therapy.

Chapter 6 shifts to treating a mood disorder—depression. The target is mild to moderate depression. Specific techniques, such as behavioral activation, identification of prototypical distortions, cognitive reframing, and mindfulness are all a part of a seven-session treatment protocol. Clinicians will learn how to select appropriate activities for the depressed patient to generate momentum, and they will learn how to rapidly identify inaccurate thoughts and assist patients in overcoming those thought patterns.

Anger management is the focus of Chapter 7, where anger is introduced as a learned response or habit. The treatment protocol is seven sessions where interventions like cue identification; trigger awareness; and utilization of alternate physiological, cognitive, and behavioral responses are discussed. Therapists will learn how to help patients identify anger before the feelings escalate, and then change their responses, and assessing how well change has worked.

Beginning in Chapter 8, three protocols are offered over the next chapters for anxiety-related conditions. Chapter 8, specifically, is aimed at helping those clients who suffer from anxiety related to the medical setting. Common anxieties in this area include "white coat" anxiety, fear of needles, and difficulties with having blood drawn. Behavioral techniques (i.e., exposure hierarchies), coupled with cognitive instruction and physiological responses (relaxation), are presented to guide clinicians to help these patients function better in medical settings while overcoming their fears.

Illness anxiety is the target condition in Chapter 9. This chapter addresses the persistent anxiety about illnesses and diseases as well as other anxious behaviors in patients who frequently seek medical intervention. Intervention is predicated upon acceptance by the clinician of subjective symptom reports and not challenging patient's physical symptoms. The goal of treatment in these sessions is to increase habituation and functional adaptation. Techniques to facilitate this include patient education about unexplained medical symptoms and the role of the stress response in augmenting symptoms. Behavioral avoidance is explicitly addressed via graded exposure. Cognitive techniques to address how patients process symptoms will be taught to patients so that progress continues after the sessions are concluded.

Since panic disorder is one of the conditions that frequently brings patients to emergency departments and doctor's offices, Chapter 10 is devoted to its treatment. This chapter discusses a model of panic that includes physical sensation, hypersensitivity to bodily responses, catastrophic thinking, and the escape/avoidance paradigm. These sessions review common panic triggers and outline how to teach patients to habituate to these triggers via exposure and altering catastrophic thinking patterns. Clinicians can learn to identify, explain, and treat panic with clear and well-validated techniques.

The final section of protocols, chapters 11 and 12, provide guidelines for treating agitation. Verbal and physical agitation is a behavioral difficulty that is troublesome both to families and to caregivers and often leads to the prescription of psychotropic medication, especially in the elderly. Chapter 11 is unique among all the protocol chapters in this book in that treatment is conducted with the caregiver, rather than the patient. Caregivers are taught to identify behavioral triggers (like stimulation, confusion, anxiety, and physical sensations) and about the factors that maintain disruptive behaviors. Various environmental interventions are presented so that caregivers develop new approaches to making changes to reduce agitated behaviors.

Finally, the last protocol chapter is Chapter 12 which addresses the problem of adults who have pragmatic impairments. While this may not always be a psychological symptom, sometimes it is. Thus, various types of pragmatic impairments will be discussed. However, since adults with pragmatic difficulties usually have deficits in social interaction, clinicians will be taught to improve patient's verbal and nonverbal communication in order to help patients develop appropriate social interaction skills, and to help them learn to understand and use figurative language to communicate effectively.

This book concludes with a final chapter that sums up the book and the behavioral interventions discussed in the book. Final thoughts and ideas about cognitive behavioral treatment are presented and concluding comments regarding treatment effectiveness will be discussed.

Our hope is that you find this book to be a practical, results-oriented book for treating patients who come to hospitals and other medical settings with the symptoms that we have selected for the treatment protocols.

Part I

General Principles and Evidence-Based Treatment

Chapter 1

Common Conditions Significant in Medical Settings

If you are a psychologist or a clinician in a hospital or medical clinic, there are a number of physical conditions and symptoms which you will likely encounter with surprising regularity. In this book, we have selected nine of these common physical conditions because these are the ones most often seen by clinicians.

In this initial chapter, those nine conditions and symptoms will be described in detail. While the core of this book will provide treatment protocols for each of the nine conditions, this chapter may be regarded as the background you will need prior to beginning treatment. Each condition or symptom will be described in terms of epidemiology, prevalence, symptoms, interrelationship with other symptoms, misdiagnosis, assessment, treatment, and relapse potential. In later chapters, the recommended treatment, based on the research and evidence, will be presented.

The conditions and symptoms covered in this chapter and in this book are:

- pain
- sleep difficulties
- depression
- anger dysregulation
- anxiety about the medical setting and treatment
- illness anxiety
- "anxiety attacks" (panic)
- agitation (confusion)
- pragmatic difficulties.

Pain

Of all the physical conditions and symptoms, pain affects more Americans than any other disease, symptom, or condition. According to the American Academy of Pain Medicine, more people in this country are affected by pain than by diabetes, heart disease, and cancer combined.

Pain is commonly defined as an unpleasant sensory and emotional experience associated with actual or potential tissue damage, or described in terms of such damage (International Association for the Study of Pain, 2015). Acute pain is often associated directly with underlying tissue damage; it fades as tissues heal. Most often, acute pain is associated with an identified cause (such as injury or disease), and usually responds well to treatment. Pain becomes chronic if it continues after the expected healing time. The cause of the pain *may not* be identifiable in chronic pain, and usually persists despite treatment. Pain is generally classified as "chronic" if it persists more than 3 months after the identifiable medical event (Smith et al., 2001).

There may be as many as 116 million Americans who suffer from chronic pain (Jensen and Turk, 2014). The risk of pain increases with age, with some estimates suggesting that 25 percent or more of people older than 50 years experience chronic pain at any one time (Johannes et al., 2010). Although pervasive, certain groups report more difficulties with pain. For instance, women are more likely than men to have chronic pain, as are older adults, Caucasians, people who did not graduate from high school, as are adults who are obese, who describe their overall health as fair or poor, and who have been hospitalized in the past year (Kennedy et al., 2014).

A survey conducted by the National Institute of Health Statistics indicated that lower back pain was the most common pain (27 percent), followed by severe headache or migraine pain (15 percent), neck pain (15 percent), and facial ache or pain (4 percent) (American Academy of Pain Medicine, 2016). Importantly, when an individual's movements are limited by their discomfort, their ability to work, perform daily tasks around the home, and engage socially can all be disrupted. Consequently, their lives can become more restricted both in terms of the way they spend their time as well as their financial stability in light of reduced income from changes in employment. Whether pain is acute or chronic, pain robs people of their productivity, their well-being, and, some individuals suffering from extended illness, their very lives. The financial toll of what might be labeled as an epidemic is tremendous. A report funded by the Institute of Medicine pegs the cost in the neighborhood of $600 billion a year (Gaskin and Richards, 2011). This cost does not even begin to take into account the challenges one person's pain presents to family, friends, and health care providers who often offer comfort to that individual.

More recently, the cost of pain has been directly associated with the a rising opioid abuse epidemic in the United States. Many opioid abusers are introduced to narcotics in their doctor's office, as treatment for chronic pain. In fact, opioids are now the most commonly prescribed medication in the United States for pain (National Institute on Drug Abuse, 2015). Prescription opioid misuse is the fastest growing form of drug misuse, and is now the leading cause of accidental overdoses and mortality in the United States (American Society of Addiction Medicine, 2016).

Chronic pain is often associated with comorbid mental health conditions. Typically, as pain gets worse, depression, anxiety, and posttraumatic stress disorder (PTSD) symptoms may worsen. Conversely, as mental health conditions worsen, pain also worsens, along with increased emotional distress. It is estimated that the overlap between depression and pain is as much as 66 percent, and for PTSD, there is a high co-occurrence as well (Bair et al., 2003). More recently, associations between chronic pain and mental health disorders in general have been found, especially concerning PTSD (Bosco et al., 2013). One of the most frequently reported symptoms of U.S. service members returning from operations in Iraq and Afghanistan is pain. Along with pain, many servicemen returning from these two countries report persistent post-concussive syndromes, and PTSD or posttraumatic symptoms (Bosco et al., 2013).

As simple as it sounds, pain is anything but simple. Pain is a multidimensional perceptual experience that includes not only the physical injury but also consequences that are not physiologic at all. Think about the last time you hurt yourself—not only did you feel the sensory (ouch!), but you also had a behavioral reaction (maybe you moved away from something), you had a thought ("I can't believe I did that."), an image or memory (the last time you did it), an emotion (anxiety, irritation), and a social experience (sympathy). Each one of these is like a river that feeds into the pool of pain. Because there are so many channels, people's experience of pain is unique to them—and those who appear to have identical injuries or illnesses can have very different pain experiences! We have all heard emergency room stories about people with terrible injuries (like a knife still in the body) and felt nothing (how can this be?), or conversely had small injuries (ever had a paper cut?) that caused big pain. A person's experience of pain is determined by sensory, emotional, cognitive, behavioral, and social factors.

The multifactorial presentation of a pain experience can make the diagnosis and assessment of pain especially challenging. Acute pain—associated with tissue damage or disease—is typically assessed in a primary care medical or hospital setting. Comprehensive medical evaluations (including imaging, blood work, physical examination, symptom review) are conducted in order to find the cause of pain. When the cause is identified, it can be treated, healing occurs, and the pain abates.

Chronic pain, in contrast, occurs long after tissue healing has ended. It is dissociated from acute damage and often not linked to an identifiable cause. It is instead maintained by the nervous system. The assessment focus is therefore targeted at factors that impact the nervous system, the subjective magnitude of the pain, and the daily consequences of pain.

Assessment of Chronic Pain

Comprehensive pain assessment must include both unidimensional and multidimensional tools, as well as a review of the patient's pain and medical history. A comprehensive assessment should include an individual's unique pain story.

Unidimensional tools are accurate, simple, quick, and both easy to use and easy to understand, and are commonly used for both acute and postoperative pain assessment. Measuring pain allows the clinician to assess the degree of a patient's pain, and, according to Melzack and Katz (2013), it is a patient's self-report of his or her pain that provides the most valid measurement of the pain experience. Unidimensional pain intensity scales used most often in the clinical setting are Pain Numeric Rating Scale (PNRS), also known as the Numerical Pain Intensity Scale (NPIS); Visual Analog Scale (VAS); Subjective Units of Distress Scale (SUDS), and Verbal Descriptor Scale (VDS).

There are multidimensional pain assessment tools which are also available. These tools help identify the many factors that have an effect on the subjective pain experience (Herr et al., 2006). Multidimensional instruments look at the emotional responses to the pain, how the person thinks about the pain, activity levels, subjective pain descriptors, and behavioral history. The most common multidimensional assessment tools include the McGill Pain Questionnaire, Brief Pain Inventory, and the Memorial Pain Assessment Card.

Treatments for Pain

The treatments for pain are as diverse as the causes. The many approaches to pain range from over-the-counter and prescription drugs to mind/body techniques to acupuncture. However, no single approach or technique is guaranteed to produce complete pain relief. As many patients discover, relief may be found only by using a combination of treatment methods.

Several medications have been shown in research studies to be effective. The most effective pain medications include anticonvulsants, which are used to treat trigeminal neuralgia, postherpetic neuralgia, glossopharyngeal neuralgia, and posttraumatic neuralgia (Aiello-Laws et al., 2009). In addition, antidepressants, used in treating neuropathic pain, pain from surgical trauma, postherpetic neuralgia, radiation therapy, chemotherapy, or malignant nerve infiltration, serotonin-norepinephrine reuptake inhibitors (SNRIs), and tramadol are often effective in treating pain (Tauben, 2015).

Some doctors now prescribe exercise as part of the treatment regimen for patients with pain. Since there is a known link between many types of chronic pain and tense, weak muscles, exercise—even light to moderate exercise such as walking or swimming—can contribute to an overall sense of well-being by improving blood and oxygen flow to muscles (Landmark et al., 2013). Just as we know that stress contributes to pain, we also know that exercise, sleep, and relaxation can all help reduce stress, thereby helping to alleviate pain (Mork et al., 2013).

Psychological treatment, however, provides safe, nondrug methods that can treat pain directly by reducing high levels of stress that often aggravate pain. Psychological treatment also helps improve the indirect consequences of pain by helping patients learn how to cope with the many problems associated with pain. Some forms of psychological treatment help establish an internal locus of control about the client's ability to manage the pain. This leads to the client believing that they have some control over their pain. A large part of psychological treatment for pain is education, which helps patients acquire skills to manage what is a very difficult problem. Education can also assist with increasing and changing movement and activity patterns, which in turn reduces pain-related fear of movement. Cognitive behavioral therapy (CBT) utilizes a wide variety of coping skills and relaxation methods to help clients cope with pain. But, along with CBT, some frequently effective treatments include relaxation techniques, meditation, guided imagery, biofeedback, and hypnosis (National Sleep Foundation, 2016). Relaxation techniques, such as meditation and yoga, have been found to help alleviate discomfort related to chronic pain and to reduce stress-related pain when these techniques are practiced regularly (Kwekkeboom and Gretarsdottir, 2006; Zeidan et al., 2011).

There is little scientific evidence supporting current complementary and alternative medicine approaches to pain that have become popular in recent years. These approaches include acupuncture, massage, chiropractic and osteopathic manipulation therapies, herbal therapies, dietary approaches, and nutritional supplements. Despite the lack of documented support, some methods may nonetheless offer temporary relief for many individuals. However, if these methods—or almost any method—generate no long-term benefit, continuation of such treatments is not justified.

The goal of pain management and most treatment approaches is to improve the patient's functioning, enabling them to work, attend school, or participate in other day-to-day activities and promote long-term adaptation to pain. While clients and their therapists have a number of options for the treatment of pain, some are more effective than others. In Chapter 3, you can read about research related to the effectiveness of CBT for pain, and in Chapter 4, you can learn about effective treatment protocols for pain.

Sleep Difficulties

Although everyone needs a good night's sleep, far too many Americans fall short of the 7 or 8 hours of sleep most people need to thrive. It is estimated that 50 to 70 million Americans suffer from a chronic sleep disorder, according to the Institute of Medicine (National Academy of Sciences, 2006). Many adults report at least occasional difficulty sleeping, but the National Institutes of Health reports that chronic and severe forms of insomnia affects one in five (National Institutes of Health, 2011).

Each year, the cost of sleep disorders, sleep deprivation, and sleepiness, according to the National Center for Sleep Disorders Research, is estimated to be $15.9 million in direct costs and $50 to $100 billion a year in indirect and related costs (National Center on Sleep Disorders Research, 2015). And according to the National Highway Traffic Safety Administration, falling asleep while driving is responsible for at least 83,000 crashes, 37,000 injuries, and 886 deaths each year in the United States (National Highway Traffic Safety Administration, 2016).

What Keeps People from Getting All the Sleep They Need?

For most people, the barrier to sound sleep comes down to sleep disorders. Surveys conducted by the National Sleep Foundation reveal that at least 40 million Americans suffer from more than 70 different sleep disorders and 60 percent of adults report having sleep problems a few nights a week or more (American Psychological Association, 2016). Sleep disorders and sleep disturbances comprise a broad range of problems, including sleep apnea, narcolepsy, insomnia, jet lag syndrome, and disturbed biological and circadian rhythms (Sateia, 2014).

Psychologists and other scientists who study the causes of sleep disorders have shown that sleep problems can be related—directly or indirectly—to abnormalities in the following systems:

- brain and nervous system
- cardiovascular system
- metabolic functions
- immune system.

Furthermore, unhealthy conditions, disorders, and diseases can also cause sleep problems, including:

- pathological sleepiness, insomnia, and accidents
- hypertension and elevated cardiovascular risks (heart attack, stroke)
- emotional disorders (depression, bipolar disorder)
- obesity, metabolic syndrome, and diabetes
- alcohol and drug abuse (Dinges, 2004).

What Causes Us to Sleep?

Sleep is a complex phenomenon, best understood as the product of two intertwined biological systems: the "sleep drive" and the "circadian alerting system." The sleep drive is our biological "need for sleep." The sleep drive can be thought of as a tank that empties and fills throughout the course of a day, like the gas tank in a car. When you sleep at night, the tank is "filled" with sleep. You awaken in the morning, refueled, and ready to "drive through the day." The longer you "drive" through the day, the more the tank depletes. By bedtime, the tank is on "E"; it is empty and you must sleep to replenish it. The sleep drive forces sleep, so that your tank can be refilled and your biological sleep need is met.

The circadian alerting system is like the on-off switch or biological clock. Simply put, it tells your brain when to stay awake and when to sleep. It switches the brain into "alert" mode during the day and "sleep" mode at night. This system responds to light. It triggers the release of neuromodulators that fluctuate in accordance with light levels. Chief among these neuromodulators is adenosine. Adenosine is an alertness blocker which is low first thing in the morning as the light levels rise, making you alert for the day. It remains low during the day—but rises gradually as the day goes on and gets darker. When it is dark, it "blocks" alertness. It blocks alertness strongly enough at bedtime so that you feel sleepy. It "switches" your brain into sleep mode. When you wake up in the morning, adenosine is low again, and the cycle repeats.

The alerting system and the sleep drive operate in a complementary and homeostatic way. The alerting system turns you off so you can meet your sleep drive at night, and turns you on in the morning when your sleep has been replenished. It keeps you awake during the day as your sleep tank empties and makes you sleepy at night so you can refill it. Sleep disorders happen when the systems do not work in homeostasis.

What are Sleep Disorders?

Sleep itself can be divided into two types: rapid eye movement (REM) sleep and non-rapid eye movement (NREM) sleep. NREM sleep has four stages of increasingly deep sleep. Stage 1 sleep is the lightest, while Stage 4 the deepest.

During normal sleep, you cycle through these types and stages of sleep. In total, individuals spend 20 percent of their sleep in REM sleep, with Stage 2 sleep the next amount of time during sleep (50 percent) (Carskadon and Dement, 2011). But if your sleep is repeatedly interrupted and you cannot cycle normally through REM and NREM sleep, you may feel tired, fatigued, and have trouble concentrating and paying attention while awake. People who have one or another of the typical sleep disorders may have one of the following sleep problems:

- *Circadian rhythm disorders*: This is a disruption of the arousal or circadian alerting system. As previously stated, the sleep of most people is driven by an internal "clock." This clock is a small part of the brain called the suprachiasmatic nucleus of the hypothalamus, which produces neurotransmitters that regulate the sleep-wake cycle (Carskadon and Dement, 2011). It sits just above the nerves leaving the back of our *eyes*. Light and exercise "reset" the clock and can move it forward or backward. Abnormalities related to this clock are called circadian rhythm disorders (Sack et al., 2007). Circadian rhythm disorders include jet lag, adjustments to shift work, delayed sleep phase syndrome (falling asleep too late and waking up too late), and advanced sleep phase syndrome (falling asleep too early and waking up too early) (Sack et al., 2007).

- *Insomnia*: People who have insomnia not only do not feel as if they get enough sleep at night, but they may have trouble falling asleep or may wake up frequently during the night or too early in the morning. Insomnia is considered a problem if it affects your daytime activities. It can be caused by disruptions of the alerting system, poor regulation of the sleep drive, and poor sleep habits (Ancoli-Israel and Roth, 1999). It can be linked to stress, anxiety, depression, circadian rhythm disorders (such as jet lag), and taking certain medications (Ancoli-Israel and Roth, 1999).

- *Snoring*: Although many adults snore, snoring can be a problem simply because of the noise it causes. It may also indicate a more serious sleep problem called sleep apnea. Sleep apnea occurs when the upper airway becomes completely or partially blocked, interrupting regular breathing for short periods of time—which then wakes the individual up (Somers et al., 2008). This prevents individuals from obtaining all but the lightest levels of sleep, missing essential restorative (stages 3 and 4) and REM sleep. Not only can apnea cause severe daytime sleepiness, but if left untreated, severe sleep apnea may be associated with high blood pressure and the risk of stroke and heart attack (Somers et al., 2008).

- *Nightmares*: Nightmares are frightening dreams that arise during REM sleep. Although there is no clear cause of nightmares, they may be related to stress, anxiety, and some drugs.

- *Depression:* Depression is one of the most common mental illnesses and more than 16 percent of Americans experience major depressive disorder during their lifetime, according to the National Institute of Mental Health (2016a). However, sleep problems and depression often go together. Sometimes people who are depressed sleep more than usual; insomnia is also common in people experiencing depression. Although some people may be depressed first and then develop sleep problems, others develop sleep difficulties first and then go on to suffer from depression.

Assessing Sleep Disorders

One of the methods of assessing sleep is polysomnography, a method that combines an all-night recording of a multiple-lead electroencephalogram with measures of muscle tone and eye movements (Chesson et al., 1997). The recordings are scored using standardized criteria to categorize whether the individual is awake or in stages 1, 2, 3, 4 or REM sleep during each 30-second interval (Chesson et al., 1997).

Wrist actigraphy can also provide an objective assessment of sleep duration and fragmentation. Actigraphy monitors are devices about the size of a wristwatch that use sensitive accelerometers to count wrist movements. Although wrist actigraphy does not differentiate REM from non-REM sleep, it does provide a fairly accurate estimate of sleep patterns (Pollak et al., 2001).

Also, there are a number of validated self-report questionnaires to assess sleep duration and quality. Sleep diaries are self-report inventories where individuals report daily sleep habits, sleep and wake times, and amount of sleep. Other measures examine the severity of sleep difficulties and sleep quality, and can be used to assess progress. The most commonly used is the Pittsburgh Sleep Quality questionnaire, the Insomnia Severity Index, the Berlin Questionnaire, and the G.A.S.P.

Treating Sleep Disorders

In some cases, doctors will prescribe medicines for the treatment of sleep disorders. In most instances, research suggests that medications could be used as a stand-alone solution; however, other research indicates that better long-term outcomes are produced with combination therapies, including sleep education, good sleep practices, and/or behavioral treatments (Bloom et al., 2009).

The types of medications used to treat sleep disorders include anti-parkinsonian drugs, used to treat REM and movement disorders, such as Larodopa, Sinemet, Parlodel, Requip, Permax, and Mirapez. Antipsychotics like Seroquel are sometimes used to treat nightmares. The so-called hypnotic medications, including benzodiazepines like Klonopin, Valium, Restoril, Xanax, and Ativan, are often used to force sleep. Various non-benzodiazepine hypnotics include Ambien, Sonata, and Lunesta. In addition, antidepressant medications with sedation profiles are also used for hypnotic effect, such as trazodone. Finally, anticonvulsants, like Tegretol, Carbatrol, Depakene, Depakote, and Neurontin, can be useful to treat some sleep problems (Placidi et al., 2000).

Some treatments for sleep disorders that do not rely on medications include the following:

*   relaxation training
*   cognitive therapy
*   stimulus control
*   sleep restriction therapy
*   sleep hygiene.

While all of these approaches to treating sleep disorders have shown some success, CBT may work better than alternative treatments. In a 2001 study published in the *Journal of the American Medical Association*, Jack Edinger and colleagues found that CBT worked better than either progressive muscle relaxation or a placebo treatment for people with insomnia (Edinger et al., 2001). Another *JAMA* study 2 years earlier by psychologist Charles Morin found that behavioral and pharmacological therapies, alone or in combination, are effective in the short-term management of late-life insomnia (Morin et al., 1999). Morin reported that those who received CBT had the best long-term results and the participants rated the behavioral therapy as more effective and satisfying. A 2001 German study by Jutta Backhaus and colleagues found that the benefits of short-term CBT had long-term effects. After therapy, the participants in the study showed improvement in their total sleep time and sleep efficiency, and they reduced their negative sleep-related cognitions (Backhaus et al., 2001), and those improvements were sustained during the 3-year follow-up period. More recently, Trauer and his associates published a meta-analysis showing that CBT is an effective treatment for insomnia (Trauer et al., 2015).

In Chapter 5, you can learn about effective treatment protocols for sleep disorders.

Depression

Sadness is an emotion central to human experience. For most people, it is an appropriate and adaptive response to loss, perceived failure, or rejection. It can be especially important when it informs us that something is amiss in our lives that we may need to address. Ideally, it is a transient emotional experience that fades as circumstances change or evolve. For some individuals, however, sadness persists for weeks, months, or years, regardless of the situation or time. It is this persistence that helps define depression. But depression also exists on a continuum involving severity, chronicity, and subtype.

Major depression is the most serious and severe of the depressive mood disorders, affecting an estimated one in fifteen adults—nearly 7 percent of all adults—in any given year (National Institute of Mental Health, 2016a). And one in six people (about 16 percent) will experience depression at some time in their life (National Institute of Mental Health, 2016a). Although depression can strike at any time, typically depressive symptoms first appear during the late teens to the mid-20s. The mean age of onset is 30, although 10 percent of individuals will have their first onset after the age of 55 (Blanco et al., 2010). Women are more likely than men to experience depression, and some studies show that one in eight women will experience a major depressive episode in their life-time (Mental Health America, 2016). Interestingly, prior to puberty, the gender divide does not exist; however, after puberty, the base rate for women rises substantially. This finding has been replicated across cultures (Albert, 2015).

Acute depression causes significant symptoms that affect how people feel, think, and handle daily activities, such as sleeping, eating, or working. Symptoms can be classified as vegetative (physical), cognitive (thinking), or emotional (sadness, lack of joy). To be diagnosed with major depression, an individual must have some of the following symptoms for at least 2 weeks:

- persistent sad, anxious, or "empty" mood
- feelings of hopelessness, or pessimism
- irritability
- feelings of guilt, worthlessness, or helplessness

- loss of interest or pleasure in hobbies and activities
- decreased energy or fatigue
- moving or talking more slowly
- feeling restless or having trouble sitting still
- difficulty concentrating, remembering, or making decisions
- difficulty sleeping, early-morning awakening, or oversleeping
- appetite and/or weight changes
- thoughts of death or suicide, or suicide attempts
- aches or pains, headaches, cramps, or digestive problems without a clear physical cause and/or that do not ease even with treatment (American Psychiatric Association, 2013).

Research suggests that the vegetative, or physical, symptoms are the cardinal symptoms that can discriminate a more serious depressive episodes from milder forms (Kessler et al., 2009; National Institute of Mental Health, 2016a).

The length of depressive episodes can vary from weeks to years. The mean duration is 4 to 5 months (Boland and Keller, 2010). Remission often occurs in the first year; however, if it does not remit entirely, then the risk is increased for future relapse and poor prognostic recovery (Boland and Keller, 2010).

For most individuals, depression is not a single episode lifetime occurrence, but instead a relapsing disorder. Longitudinal studies have indicated that the majority of individuals who have a major depressive episode are likely to evidence a subsequent episode or relapse (Fekado et al., 2009). The median number of lifetime episodes is four to seven (Kendler et al., 2000). Relapse is thus a major risk factor in persons with histories of depression, and an important consideration for diagnosticians and therapists.

Depression can be conceptualized on the basis of severity and chronicity. Remitting forms of depression include major depression, psychotic depression, and in some cases postpartum depression (U.S. Department of Health and Human Services, National Institutes of Health, National Institute of Mental Health, 2015). Seasonal affective disorder is time-limited but generally not as severe (U.S. Department of Health and Human Services, 2015). Depression that is chronic is classified as dysthymia, and is defined by a milder symptomatic presentation (Mayo Clinic, 2016a). "Double depression" describes underlying dysthymia with superimposed discrete major depressive episodes (Harvard Mental Health Letter, 2016).

More specific definitions of these types of depression are the following:

- *Persistent depressive disorder (also called dysthymia)*: A depressed mood that lasts for at least 2 years. A person diagnosed with persistent depressive disorder generally has symptoms that are less debilitating than a major depressive episode.
- *Perinatal depression*: This form of depression is much more serious than the "baby blues"—relatively mild depressive and anxiety symptoms that

typically go away within 2 weeks after delivery—that many women experience after giving birth. Women with perinatal depression may experience full-blown major depression during pregnancy or after delivery. This is generally diagnosed as postpartum depression, but is recognized by feelings of extreme sadness, anxiety, and exhaustion that make it difficult for these new mothers to complete daily care activities for themselves and/or for their babies (Rosenberg et al., 2004).

- *Psychotic depression*: This form of depression occurs when a person has severe depression plus some form of psychosis, such as having disturbing false-fixed beliefs (delusions) or hearing or seeing upsetting things that others cannot hear or see (hallucinations). Delusions may take several forms, but often relate to guilt, poverty, or illness. Importantly, in this condition, delusions or hallucinations are mood congruent, which means that they are highly correlated with negative mood and thinking (i.e., voices making critical comments, delusions of somatic decay). When delusions are mood incongruent (i.e., grandiose), this is often an indicator of a much more serious and potentially incipient thought disorder (Goes et al., 2007).

- *Seasonal affective disorder*: This kind of depression is characterized by the onset of depression during the winter months, when there is less natural sunlight. It often lifts during spring and summer, only to return during the next winter season accompanied by social withdrawal, increased sleep, and weight gain. A hallmark of this condition to is that symptoms represent an excess (overeating and oversleeping) rather than the deficit observed in major depression (loss of appetite and sleep) (Saeed and Bruce, 1998).

- *Bipolar disorder*: Although different from depression, people with bipolar disorder usually experience episodes of extremely low moods that are likely to be diagnosed as major depression. The key difference between bipolar disorder and major depression is that the individual with bipolar disorder also experiences extreme highs that result in a euphoric mood or "mania" (National Institute of Mental Health, 2016b).

Depression, it should be noted, also is associated with medical or organic conditions, such as endocrine and neurodegenerative conditions. In addition, it can be observed in dementia and strokes, and is common in Parkinson's disease (Engmann, 2011). Also, depression can be found in hypothyroidism and Cushing's disease, both of which are endocrine disorders (Musselman and Nemeroff, 1996).

Causes of Depression

Depression is caused by the interaction of inherited vulnerability and problems external to the person, like severe stress, trauma, or social challenges. This interaction may best be explained by the "cracked egg" analogy. Vulnerability risk factors produce a crack that may or may not develop into depression. Inherent vulnerability risk factors include genetics, the individual stress response, and female gender. These vulnerability factors, or "cracks," are also called diathesis. Depression happens when external stressors force the crack "open." The external factors include stress, reduced social support, and painful or traumatic experiences. An egg that is already cracked requires much less force to rupture. So it is with the person who has multiple risk factors—the "crack" that will require much less force to open up and result in depression. In contrast, a person with low inherent vulnerability has a smooth surface, and will be able to withstand much greater external stress before "cracking" and before depression occurs. The cracked egg analogy of interaction is also called the "the diathesis stress model of depression" (Banks and Kerns, 1996). Understanding diathesis stress enables a clinician to better assess a person's depression and risk profile. It may be well to keep in mind that diathesis stress can also be applied to a variety of the disorders we will be talking about in this book.

Primary among vulnerability risk factors is genetics, because genetics play a role in increasing a person's chances of depression (Hettema, 2010). Depression is two to three times more likely to occur in the relatives of persons with depression than in persons with histories of depression (Levinson, 2009). Twin studies have found concordance rates as high as 35 percent among identical twins and 26 percent among fraternal twins (Kendler and Prescott, 1999). Interestingly, there are also gender differences in the heritability of depression, with indications that this disorder is much more heritable in women than in men (40 percent heritability in women and 20 percent in men) (Bierut et al., 1999).

There is also research that suggests that depression results from a chronically heightened nervous system stress response. The "stress hypothesis" of depression proposes that depression results from a sensitized and overactive endocrine stress response system (called the Corticotropin Releasing Factor System or CRF) (Nemeroff, 1996). Stress, via the hypothalamic pituitary axis, causes the pituitary to release cortisol into the bloodstream. For some individuals, this system is easily triggered and hard to inhibit, resulting in excessive and chronic release of cortisol in the blood. Consistent with this, depressed individuals demonstrate elevated blood cortisol and resistance to cortisol lowering drugs (Oquendo et al., 2003). This means that the stress response remains chronically "stuck." The prolonged cortisol elevation produced by stress has a neurotoxic effect on brain structures specific to emotion and memory (hippocampus; limbic system) (Lupien et al., 2009). Depressed individuals demonstrate marked changes or reductions in the hippocampus, with positive changes when the mood disorder has abated.

External factors, like stressful life events, have been shown to precipitate depression. Research demonstrates a relatively consistent relationship between difficult life events and the onset of depression (Monroe and Reid, 2009). The more severe or traumatic a life event is, the more likely it is to lead to depression. Severe events (losing a job, a loved one, a home) are most predictive of an initial episode (Lewinsohn et al., 1999). Social support appears to mitigate this risk, however, particularly for women (Kendler et al., 2005).

Finally, neurotransmitter systems are implicated in depression and are the basis of pharmacotherapy. The neurotransmitter serotonin (5HT), which has been linked with mood lability and impulsivity, is reduced in the brains of depressed individuals. This neurotransmitter acts in concert with other neurotransmitters, so medication intervention often addresses serotonin and other neurotransmitters, including norepinephrine.

It is important for the clinician to observe that major depression or depressive symptoms share a very high co-occurrence with anxiety disorders, particularly panic disorder (Gorman, 1996). The "stress response" hypothesis of depression also appears to create a biological framework for anxiety. Careful assessment of co-occurring conditions is also important, as they can exacerbate depression if not addressed. Co-occurring disorders require careful evaluation and diagnosis by a trained and experienced psychologist.

Assessment of Depression

Most often, adults with symptoms of depression are first treated for "sadness" or mild symptoms, and usually by their primary care physician—not a psychologist or psychiatrist. One consequence of this is that a formal diagnosis of more significant depression is not made. A meta-analysis of more than forty studies found that among all of the patients with a depressive disorder, general practitioners identified depression in approximately 50 percent of them (Mitchell et al., 2009). Other studies have found similar statistics. However, it is good to remember that diagnosing depression in the context of chronic medical conditions is complex and primary care physicians are generally untrained in making psychiatric diagnoses.

In order to properly make a diagnosis of depression, screening tools are fairly quick and reliable tools to use in the first step of depression assessment. However, an initial screen must be followed by a clinical interview to finally make the diagnosis of depression. *Diagnostic and Statistical Manual of Mental Disorders, Fifth Edition (DSM-5)* criteria for major depression are reviewed below.

At least five of the following symptoms have been present during the same 2-week period, represent a change from previous functioning, and include either depressed mood or loss of interest or pleasure:

- depressed mood
- marked diminished interest or pleasure
- significant weight loss or weight gain
- insomnia or hypersomnia

- psychomotor agitation or retardation
- fatigue or loss of energy
- feelings of worthlessness or excessive guilt
- diminished ability to concentrate
- recurrent thoughts of death or suicidal ideation (American Psychiatric Association, 2013).

There are several self-report screening tools for depression, all of which involve the client answering a questionnaire that is then scored. The most commonly used depression screening devices include the following measures:

- *Beck Depression Inventory–Second Edition (BDI-II)*: The BDI-II produces a single score indicating the intensity of the depressive symptoms. It takes 5 to 10 minutes to administer, but it often requires longer for patients with severe depression or obsessional disorders.
- *Center for Epidemiological Studies Depression Scale (CES-D)*: The CES-D consists of twenty items and takes 5 to 10 minutes to complete. The CES-D was actually developed for use in studies of the epidemiology of depressive symptomatology in the general population.
- *Geriatric Depression Scale (GDS)*: The GDS consists of thirty items and takes 10 to 15 minutes to complete. There is a shorter version of the GDS which consists of fifteen items and takes 5 to 10 minutes to complete. The items included in the GDS were selected from previously published scales. It is easy to administer, uses a Yes/No answer format, and is easily understood by patients who might be confused.
- *Major Depression Inventory (MDI)*: The MDI is a self-report mood questionnaire developed by the World Health Organization's Collaborating Center in Mental Health. It consists of twelve items which generally takes less than 10 minutes to complete.
- *Zung Self-Rating Depression Scale (Zung SDS)*: The Zung SDS consists of twenty items and takes 5 to 10 minutes to complete. The twenty items of the scale address each of the four most commonly found characteristics of depression: the pervasive effect, the physiological equivalents, other disturbances, and psychomotor activities (Bienenfeld and Stinson, 2016).

In addition to patient self-report questionnaires, there are also interviewer-administered assessment tools. These instruments involve the patient answering questions posed by the interviewer. The most widely used assessments administered by interviewers are:

- *Cornell Scale for Depression in Dementia (CSDD)*: The CSDD is a nineteen-item instrument that uses information from interviews with both the patient and a nursing staff member, and is thus appropriate for use with patients who have cognitive deficits. It takes about 10 minutes to complete with the patient or about 20 minutes with both the patient and the caregiver.

• *Hamilton Depression Rating Scale (HDRS)*: The HDRS has proven useful for many years as a way of determining a patient's level of depression before, during, and after treatment. It is a seventeen or twenty-one item (the original version was seventeen items) scale which is administered by a clinician and generally takes 20 to 30 minutes to complete (Ramos-Brieva and Cordero-Villafafila, 1988).

It is important to be aware that certain medications and some medical conditions, such as viruses or a thyroid disorder, can cause the same symptoms as depression. A physician can help rule out physical or medical conditions by doing a physical examination, conducting an interview, and ordering laboratory tests. Once medical or physical conditions have been ruled out, a psychologist, with the use of screening devices and other tests, along with a clinical interview can make the diagnosis of depression. A clinical interview should include a discussion of the family history of depression or other mental disorders, along with a complete history of the symptoms.

Treating Depression with Medications and Supplements

In general, depression can be effectively treated; however, the earlier depression treatments begin, the more effective they are likely to be.

The most common depression treatments are medication and psychotherapy. Antidepressants primarily work on the brain's neurotransmitters, especially serotonin and norepinephrine, although there are some antidepressants that work on the neurotransmitter dopamine. Some of the most popular antidepressants are called selective serotonin reuptake inhibitors (SSRIs), which include fluoxetine (Prozac), sertraline (Zoloft), escitalopram (Lexapro), paroxetine (Paxil), and citalopram (Celexa). SNRIs, which are similar to SSRIs, include venlafaxine (Effexor) and duloxetine (Cymbalta).

SSRIs and Serotonin and norepinephrine reuptake inhibitors (SNRI) tend to have fewer side effects than do older antidepressants, but they sometimes produce side effects of headaches, nausea, jitters, or insomnia when people first start to take them (Sindrup et al., 2005)—although these symptoms tend to fade with time. Some people also experience sexual problems with SSRIs or SNRIs, which may be helped by adjusting the dosage or switching to another medication (Montgomery et al., 2002).

Almost all antidepressants must be taken for at least 4 to 6 weeks before they have a full effect. Antidepressants should be stopped only under a doctor's supervision. Some antidepressant medications need to be gradually stopped to give the body time to adjust, but suddenly stopping an antidepressant can cause withdrawal symptoms or lead to a relapse of the depression (Melfi et al., 1998).

Antidepressant therapy as a stand-alone intervention, however, has a much higher rate of relapse than psychotherapy or combined medication with therapy. One study estimated that the relapse rate for medication alone after 1 year of treatment was 77 percent (Melfi et al., 1998). In contrast, CBT produced a much lower relapse rate of 30 percent (Hollon et al., 2006).

Research funded by the National Institute of Mental Health has shown that people who did not get well after taking a first medication increased their chances of beating the depression after they switched to a different drug, or added another medication to their existing one (FDA, 2016). Sometimes stimulants, antianxiety medications or other drugs are used together with an antidepressant, especially if a person has a coexisting illness. Importantly, neither antianxiety medications nor stimulants are effective depression treatments when taken alone.

It is necessary that all patients prescribed antidepressants should be closely monitored, especially during the initial weeks of treatment. Possible side effects that need to be looked for and addressed are worsening depression; suicidal thinking or behavior; or any unusual changes in behavior, such as sleeplessness, agitation or withdrawal from normal social situations (Olfson et al., 2002).

Some patients will want to avoid medication and may ask about "natural" products or herbal remedies. One of the more common herbs that has been used, especially in Europe, to treat mild to moderate depression is St. John's wort. Although it is one of the top-selling botanical products in the United States, one research study found that St. John's wort was no more effective than a placebo in treating depression (National Center for Complementary and Integrative Health, 2016). In addition, St. John's wort can interact with other medications, including those used to control HIV infection. In 2000, the FDA issued a Public Health Advisory letter stating that the herb may interfere with certain medications used to treat heart disease, depression, seizures, certain cancers, and those used to prevent organ transplant rejection (FDA, 2000). The herb also may interfere with the effectiveness of oral contraceptives.

Treating Depression with Psychotherapy

There are several types of psychotherapy that provide an alternative to medication and have been found helpful for depressed people. The two effective types are CBT and interpersonal therapy (IPT).

IPT is structured, time-limited therapy aimed at addressing issues related to interpersonal role changes and loss. It focuses on four primary areas: dealing with interpersonal roles, adjusting to the loss of a relationship, acquiring a new relationship, and identifying and correcting social skills deficits (deMello et al., 2005).

CBT helps people with depression restructure negative thought patterns, so they can interpret their environment and interactions with others in a positive and realistic way (Jacobson et al., 2001). It may also help people recognize things that may be contributing to the depression and help them change behaviors that may be making the depression worse. The behavioral aspect of CBT, which involves getting individuals to engage in activity they value or enjoy, is a key ingredient for the success of this treatment (National Institute of Mental Health, 2016c).

Studies have confirmed that for mild to moderate depression, psychotherapy may be the best option. However, for severe depression or for certain people, psychotherapy may not be enough. That is, a combination of medication and psychotherapy may be the most effective approach to treating major depression and reducing the chances of it coming back (National Institute of Mental Health, 2016c).

As indicated, CBT aims to help people identify and change negative, self-destructive thought patterns. And although it does not work for everyone with depression, data shows that it is effective with a great many depressed patients (Forman et al., 2007).

CBT encompasses a range of psychotherapies, all based on the premise that people with depression have excessively negative, and often inaccurate, beliefs about themselves and the world. This approach to psychotherapy is designed to equip patients with the skills they need to critically examine their negative beliefs. The theory behind CBT is that by correcting the way a person thinks and by changing their behaviors, depression will dissipate.

There are many studies that show CBT results in less depression as well as less negative thinking (Hollon et al., 2006). In CBT, therapists typically ask their patients to monitor their own thoughts, and that once they have learned these skills, they can use them for the rest of their lives. This may explain why the benefits of CBT last even after the treatment has ended.

Other research suggests that those individuals with personality disorders in addition to depression tend to do better with antidepressant medications than with cognitive therapy, and married people seem to benefit more from cognitive therapy than from medication (Hamilton and Dobson, 2002).

In Chapter 6, you can learn about effective treatment protocols for depression.

Emotional Dysregulation

Emotional dysregulation refers to the inability of a person to control or regulate their emotional responses to provocative stimuli. It can also be termed "emotional hyper reactivity." Carolyn Daitch, in her book *Affect Regulation Toolbox*, adopts the term "over-reactivity" to describe "affect dysregulation" (Daitch, 2007).

Typically, an individual with emotional dysregulation responds in an emotionally exaggerated manner to all sorts of environmental and interpersonal challenges. This over-reactivity includes bursts of anger, crying, accusing, passive-aggressive behaviors, or the creation of chaos or conflict among others. Some clinicians see this set of features as part of a high conflict personality. However, affective or emotional instability, bursts of anger, intense efforts to avoid real or perceived abandonment, and unstable interpersonal relationships point to underlying psychological issues intertwined with emotional dysregulation.

A growing body of research focuses on the development and correlates of emotional dysregulation, including deficits in the ability to regulate intense and shifting emotional states (Gratz and Roemer, 2004). There is research supporting the conceptualization of emotional dysregulation as a distinct and clinically meaningful construct associated with psychiatric distress (Bradley et al., 2011). However, emotional dysregulation is a key component in a range of psychiatric symptoms and disorders and a core target for psychopharmacologic and psychosocial treatment interventions (Bradley et al., 2011).

Emotional regulation difficulties are also strongly associated with childhood trauma, and in turn, may be a particularly important factor related to dissociative symptoms (Cook et al., 2005). In addition, it has been associated with PTSD, panic disorder, obsessive-compulsive disorder, and mood disorders, such as bipolar disorder and depression (Cook et al., 2005). Patients with alcoholism or chemical dependency may also struggle with emotional dysregulation (Stasiewicz et al., 2012). Likewise, traumatic brain injury, especially injuries with frontal lobe disorders, is characterized by emotional dysregulation (Warriner and Velikonja, 2006).

While emotional dysregulation is a feature in a large percentage of psychological or psychiatric disorders in the *DSM-5*, there are certain psychological illnesses that involve emotional dysregulation as a prominent characteristic. This is particularly observed in the group of characterological or personality disorders called "Cluster B" disorders (histrionic, narcissistic, antisocial, and borderline). For example, Borderline Personality Disorder (BPD) has been referred to as emotional dysregulation disorder, emotional regulation disorder, emotional instability disorder, emotion-impulse regulation disorder, or emotionally unstable personality disorder (Lieb et al., 2004). Marsha Linehan (1993) proposes that emotion dysregulation is one of the central features of BPD and underlies many of the associated behaviors of this disorder, including deliberate self-harm (a behavior thought to serve an emotion-regulating function). Her conceptualization of self-harm as an emotion regulation strategy is supported by both empirical and theoretical literature on the function of this behavior (Gratz and Roemer, 2004).

Emotional dysregulation affects anywhere from 1 percent to 3 percent of people in the United States (Grant et al., 2008). Some studies suggest that up to 30 percent of people who require mental health services have at least one personality disorder—characterized by abnormal and maladaptive inner experience and behavior, including emotional dysregulation (Grant et al., 2008).

Causes of Emotional Dysregulation

The causes of emotional dysregulation may involve diathesis-stress, and may include heritability as well as environmental stressors like trauma or childhood adversity. Affective instability appears to be a heritable trait, in addition to impulsivity, both of which drive the behavioral reactions associated with dysregulation (Henry et al., 2001). Trauma stressors can include histories of childhood abuse, neglect, separation, and loss.

PTSD can also be associated with emotional dysregulation. In PTSD, hyperarousal often occurs related to minor stimuli, exhibited as exaggerated startle responses, vivid intrusive thoughts, and flashbacks and nightmares related to past traumatic events (Taylor, 2006). Persons with PTSD, for instance veterans who have served in war zones, display emotional dysregulation characterized by excessive fear, anxiety, anger, or sadness (Taylor, 2006).

Assessment of Emotional Regulation Problems

Despite the clinical usefulness of assessing difficulties in emotion regulation, there are few measures of emotional regulation or dysregulation in adults. The most commonly used measure of emotional regulation is the Generalized Expectancy for Negative Mood Regulation Scale (NMR) (Catanzaro and Mearns, 1990). The NMR measures beliefs that some behavior or cognition will alleviate a negative state or induce a positive one, emphasizing the elimination and avoidance of negative emotions (as opposed to the ability to act in desired ways in the presence of these emotions) (Catanzaro and Mearns, 1990). Many items on the NMR refer to particular emotional regulation strategies that people may use to modulate emotional arousal.

Another measure used to assess emotional regulation is the Trait Meta-Mood Scale (TMMS) (Salovey et al., 1995). The TMMS assesses "individual differences in the ability to reflect upon and manage one's emotions." Patients rate the degree to which they endorse a series of statements regarding their attitudes toward, and experience of, their emotions. The TMMS assesses some aspects of emotional regulation that are absent from the NMR, such as emotional awareness and understanding of emotions (Salovey et al. 1995).

The Difficulties in Emotion Regulation Scale (DERS) was developed to assess emotional dysregulation more comprehensively than existing measures. The DERS items were chosen to reflect difficulties within the following dimensions of emotion regulation: (a) awareness and understanding of emotions; (b) acceptance of emotions; (c) the ability to engage in goal-directed behavior, and refrain from impulsive behavior, when experiencing negative emotions; and (d) access to emotion regulation strategies perceived as effective (Bardeen et al., 2016).

Treating Emotional Dysregulation

Psychological treatment is an appropriate option when a patient exhibits uncontrolled anger or rage, irritability, sadness, or other manifestation of emotional instability. However, since emotional dysregulation is often a part of a psychological condition, the prognosis for persons experiencing emotional dysregulation varies, depending on the severity of their underlying issues.

Dialectical Behavioral Therapy (DBT) has produced excellent results in helping persons with emotional dysregulation (Lynch et al., 2006). DBT typically includes weekly counseling and group training sessions on skills such as distress tolerance, interpersonal effectiveness, emotion regulation, and mindfulness skills. DBT teaches patients how to learn to take control of their life, their emotions, and themselves through self-knowledge and cognitive restructuring (Lynch et al., 2006). However, DBT is an intensive, relatively long-term treatment that may be less suitable for many clinicians in a medical setting. A recognized alternative is STAIR group therapy.

STAIR, which stands for Skills Training in Affect and Interpersonal Regulation, is an evidence-based CBT for individuals with affect dysregulation and interpersonal difficulties. Originally developed to help people, especially military veterans, suffering from PTSD and co-occurring disorders, STAIR has been found effective for anyone with emotional regulation problems (Jackson et al., 2010).

STAIR is a twelve-session group therapy program that helps patients become more aware of their emotions and learn to regulate their emotions while also developing skills to better handle interpersonal relationships (Ford et al., 2005).

In Chapter 7, you can learn about an effective treatment protocol for emotional dysregulation.

Anxiety

Anxiety is an adaptive emotional response that informs us when something is wrong or potentially harmful. Simply put, it alerts us to situations that require our attention and that may represent a threat. It can be said that without the protective effect of anxiety, we would not survive our natural environment.

Anxiety is accompanied by a physiological response through the activation of "stress" or the functioning of the sympathetic nervous system. This system causes changes in attention, respiration, digestion, muscle tension, and blood flow. The stress response is inhibited by the "soothing nervous system" or the parasympathetic system. This system causes slower breathing, relaxed musculature, digestion, and diffuse attention. The parasympathetic nervous system is what is active when we feel relaxed, when we are sleeping, having sex, or even going to the bathroom. The stress response system alternates with the soothing nervous system interchangeably, in response to situational demands requiring anxiety or relaxation. Anxiety, however, "switches on" the stress nervous system. The stress nervous system is in turn "switched off" by the soothing nervous system and relaxation, and the cycle repeats.

Anxiety becomes a problem only when it is disproportionate to the situation, occurs too frequently, or is chronic. For a person with an anxiety disorder, the anxiety is not contextually appropriate and does not remit in the way it is expected to; the feeling and the physiological stress response become more intense, chronic, and problematic. When anxiety is chronic, it interferes with daily activities, such as job performance, school, work, and social relationships.

There are several different types of anxiety disorders. The most common disorders associated with anxiety are generalized anxiety disorder (GAD), panic disorder, and social anxiety disorder:

- *Generalized anxiety disorder*. Perhaps the most frequent anxiety disorder is generalized anxiety disorder. People with GAD display excessive anxiety or worry for months and face several anxiety-related symptoms (Rowa and Antony, 2008). The anxiety does not occur in response to a specific situation, but is instead "free floating" or "general." GAD symptoms encapsulate the effects of a sympathetic nervous system chronically stuck in the "on" position, and includes symptoms such as:
  - restlessness or feeling wound-up or on edge
  - being easily fatigued
  - difficulty concentrating or having their minds go blank
  - irritability
  - muscle tension
  - difficulty controlling the worry
  - sleep problems (difficulty falling or staying asleep or restless, unsatisfying sleep).
- *Panic disorder*. Another very common type of anxiety disorder is panic disorder. Panic disorder is differentiated from general anxiety disorder in that it is characterized by discrete and intense episodes of fear. It is estimated that one out of every ten people suffers from panic disorder, and in a given year, nearly 30 percent of people will have at least one panic attack (Kessler et al., 2006). A panic attack is an intensely uncomfortable combination of physical symptoms, fear, fatalistic thinking, and avoidant behaviors. These panic attacks are diagnosed as panic disorder when they occur repeatedly.

  Panic disorder is caused by erroneous symptom interpretation, a highly sensitized stress and fear response, and behavioral avoidance (Austin and Richards, 2001). For the person with a panic disorder, common physical symptoms, such as palpitations, sweating, nausea, suffocation/choking, and lightheadedness/dizziness, are interpreted in a frightening way—for instance, life-threatening medical events. This, in turn, triggers anxiety and the stress nervous system. The stress response exacerbates physical symptoms, which may increase fatalistic thinking. Nonetheless, the flight or fight system is triggered and it tends to override other behavioral responses. At this point, the individual will seek to escape the situation they are in, to reduce their fear. When they escape, the fear drops and symptoms resolve. This kind of resolution provides relief which is powerfully reinforcing, and cements "escape" and "avoidance" as the primary coping tools. That leads people to begin to avoid situations where they may have physical symptoms of panic, and soon they are avoiding more and more "dangerous" situations. This is called generalization. Many people fear that they are "going crazy" when this happens.

- *Social anxiety disorder:* Distinct from panic disorder. At the core of social anxiety disorder (sometimes called "social phobia") is a fear of being negatively evaluated or judged by other people. Attributions about poor social judgment cause anxiety and initiate the stress response. When this happens, people may blush, sweat, tremble, have a tremulous voice, etc.— all of which increase perceived awkwardness and judgment fears. People start to avoid situations where there are other people—so that they do not have to experience uncomfortable anxiety and the perceived judgments of others. Every time they avoid a social situation, they feel better. Just like the immediate relief experienced by escaping situations, as noted when generalized anxiety disorder was discussed, the avoidance of interactions in social anxiety escalates and continued evasion of social settings becomes the hallmark of this disorder. Common triggers of social anxiety include talking to other people, speaking in front of groups, activities in the presence of others, and meeting new people or going to a new social setting.

How Common is Anxiety?

According to the National Institute of Mental Health, anxiety disorders are the most common mental illness in the United States, affecting 40 million adults aged 18 and older—or about 18 percent of the population (National Institute of Mental Health, 2016d).

Anxiety disorders cost the United States more than $42 billion a year, which amounts to nearly one-third of the country's $148 billion total mental health bill (Kroenke et al., 2007). People with anxiety disorders seek relief for symptoms that at times mimic physical illnesses, and as a result, may frequently utilize health care services (Health care costs, 1995). Patients with an anxiety disorder are three to five times more likely to go to the doctor and six times more likely to be hospitalized for psychiatric disorders than those who do not suffer from anxiety disorders (Facts and Statistics, 2016).

Causes and Risk Factors

In general, it can be said that anxiety disorders develop from a complex set of risk factors, including genetics, brain chemistry, personality, and life events.

Researchers are finding that genetic and environmental factors, frequently in interaction with one another, are risk factors for anxiety disorders (Hettema et al., 2005). However, some of the specific factors for developing an anxiety disorder include:

- shyness, or behavioral inhibition, in childhood
- being female
- having few economic resources
- being divorced or widowed
- exposure to stressful life events in childhood and adulthood
- anxiety disorders in close biological relatives
- parental history of mental disorders
- elevated afternoon cortisol levels in the saliva (specifically for social anxiety disorder)
- depression (Merikangas and Pine, 2002).

Assessment of Anxiety Disorders

Since many patients express concern about an anxiety disorder to their primary care provider, that is where the evaluation typically begins. Since some physical health conditions, such as an overactive thyroid or low blood sugar, imitate or worsen an anxiety disorder, it is well for a patient to have a thorough physical examination. However, a mental health evaluation is also helpful because anxiety disorders often coexist with other related conditions, such as depression or obsessive-compulsive disorder (Simon, 2009). Evaluating an anxiety disorder by both mental health and primary care clinicians is important since a reliable diagnosis and assessment can help guide the type and frequency of the therapeutic intervention. In addition, accurate assessment of anxiety in the beginning provides a benchmark for evaluating the effectiveness of treatment.

The most commonly used assessment tools to measure anxiety are the GAD-7, the PC-PTSD, the Hamilton Anxiety Rating Scale (HAM-A), the Generalized Anxiety Disorder Severity Scale (GADSS), the State-Trait Anxiety Inventory (STAI), the Beck Anxiety Inventory (BAI), and the Hospital Anxiety and Depression Rating Scale-Anxiety (HADS-A).

The GAD-7 is a seven-question screening tool that identifies whether a complete assessment for anxiety is indicated. Research indicates that the GAD-7 is a valid and efficient tool for screening GAD and assessing its severity in clinical practice and research (Spitzer et al., 2006). The PC–PTSD is a four-item questionnaire designed for use in primary care and other medical settings to screen for PTSD. It is currently used by the Department of Veterans Affairs medical centers to screen veterans (Ouimette et al., 2008).

Another widely used assessment tool is the HAM-A, which assesses several of the associated symptoms of GAD. The HAM-A features items that address the more subjective cognitive and affective components of anxious experience, such as anxious mood, tension, fears, and difficulty concentrating (Hamilton, 1986).

A more recently developed questionnaire is the GADSS. The GADSS was designed to be a specific measure of the severity of GAD (Shear et al., 2006). It addresses types of worry as well as some of the symptoms defining GAD. Research has shown that the GADSS has good reliability, validity, and treatment sensitivity (Shear et al., 2006).

Also widely used is the STAI, which measures the presence and severity of current symptoms of anxiety and a generalized propensity to be anxious (Julian, 2011). The two subscales within the STAI are the State Anxiety Scale (S-Anxiety), which evaluates the current state of anxiety, and the Trait Anxiety Scale (T-Anxiety), which evaluates relatively stable aspects of "anxiety proneness," including general states of calmness, confidence, and security (Julian, 2011).

The BAI is also a frequently used and brief measure of anxiety. Focusing on somatic symptoms of anxiety, it is a twenty-one-item questionnaire that is useful for discriminating anxiety and depression (Julian, 2011). Finally, the HADS-A is a popular assessment inventory developed as a brief measure of generalized symptoms of anxiety and fear (Julian, 2011). The purpose of the seven-item HADS is to screen for clinically significant anxiety and depressive symptoms in medically ill patients. It includes specific items that assess generalized anxiety, such as tension, worry, fear, panic, difficulties in relaxing, and restlessness.

Treating Anxiety Disorders with Medications

Although medication does not cure anxiety disorders, it often helps to relieve symptoms. However, although medication for anxiety can be easily provided by medical practitioners, there is a high relapse rate when medication is used alone (Mandos et al., 2009).

The most common classes of medications used to combat anxiety disorders are antidepressants, antianxiety drugs, and beta-blockers (National Institute of Mental Health, 2016e). Antidepressants are used to treat depression, but they also are helpful for treating anxiety disorders (National Institute of Mental Health, 2016e). Antidepressants take several weeks to start working and may cause side effects such as headache, nausea, or difficulty sleeping (National Institute of Mental Health, 2016e).

Antianxiety drugs, also known as tranquilizers, help in relieving anxiety by slowing down the central nervous system. Benzodiazepines, such as Xanax, Valium, Klonopin, and Ativan, are the most common types of antianxiety drugs. Benzodiazepines are fast acting—typically bringing relief within 30 minutes to an hour (Rivas-Vazquez, 2003). Although they are effective for acute anxiety, the antianxiety medications tend to be ineffective in treating chronic or recurring anxiety conditions (Rivas-Vazquez, 2003). Some arguments against prescribing medications for anxiety include concerns about medications reinforcing behavioral avoidance, medications allow patients to "escape" anxiety symptoms rather than learning to "ride them out" and learn to eliminate them, and the addiction possibilities with antianxiety medications (Ashton, 1994). Finally, another disadvantage of medication to treat anxiety is that some people develop a physical tolerance for the drugs and the dosages may need to be increased in order to achieve the same effect (Ashton, 1994).

Another type of medication used to treat anxiety is beta-blockers, which are often used to treat blood pressure and heart problems. Beta-blockers work by blocking the effects of norepinephrine, a stress hormone involved in the fight-or-flight response. By blocking the effects of norepinephrine, physical symptoms like rapid heart rate, a trembling voice, sweating, dizziness, and shaky hands are brought under control. Beta-blockers have been most successfully used to treat phobias, particularly social phobia and performance anxiety (National Institute of Mental Health, 2016e). Beta-blockers, such as propranolol (Inderal) and atenolol (Tenormin), frequently produce side effects, including light-headedness, sleepiness, nausea, and slow pulse (Nordqvist, 2015).

Treating Anxiety Disorders with Psychotherapy

While anxiety disorders are very treatable, only about one-third of those suffering from anxiety actually receive treatment (Facts and Statistics, 2016). Anxiety disorders are most effectively treated with psychotherapy, or combined medication and psychotherapy treatment. For instance, CBT has been found to be especially helpful for people with anxiety disorders. CBT teaches a patient different ways of thinking, behaving, and reacting to anxiety-producing and fearful situations. CBT is predicated upon teaching clients how to re-appraise anxiety-provoking situations, how to control the physiological stress response, and how to approach and habituate to fear-producing stimuli (Bearman and Weisz, 2012). For some disorders, patients are instructed in skills (i.e., social skills) and asked to practice them in feared situations. Exposure to anxiety-provoking situations is often an integral component of CBT for anxiety.

Exposure therapy focuses on confronting the fears underlying an anxiety disorder in order to help the patient engage in activities they have been avoiding. Exposure therapy uses systematically structured in vivo or imaginal activity (which is least anxiety-provoking to most patients) called a hierarchy. This is used concurrently with relaxation and cognitive restructuring. Relaxation and stress management techniques and meditation can help people with anxiety disorders calm themselves and may enhance the effects of therapy.

In Chapter 8, you can learn about an effective treatment protocol for anxiety.

Anxiety about Medical Settings and Treatment

It is often referred to as "white coat syndrome," "white coat anxiety," or "white coat hypertension." For a great many Americans, there is real fear and anxiety about going to see a doctor (Epstein, 2000). Although this anxiety may only result in an elevated blood pressure reading for some people, for others there is a phobic response to medical procedures—especially when blood, injection, or injury is involved.

While it is probably the rare individual who looks forward to visiting a doctor, still most people handle such trips to the doctor with relative calmness and without a racing pulse. But there are those whose fear and anxiety actually reach such levels that they may even avoid getting vital health care.

White coat hypertension was first reported in 1896 by a doctor who described this phenomenon as an increase in blood pressure experienced only during a physician's visit (Cobos et al., 2015). This event was researched until the 1980s, but by then, it was confirmed that the appearance of a physician was accompanied by an immediate increase in a patient's blood pressure and heart rate (Cobos et al., 2015).

A 2013 European report indicates that the overall prevalence of white coat anxiety is about 13 percent (Cobos et al., 2015). However, a recent review reported that 30 percent to 40 percent of patients who are diagnosed with hypertension on the basis of their office blood pressure measurement alone have normal out-of-office blood pressure (Cobos et al., 2015). Other reports contend that as many as one-fifth of the population suffers from white coat hypertension (Pickering, 1998).

The extreme anxiety related to having blood withdrawn or receiving an injection is more common than many people might think. Importantly, this reaction poses significant barriers to medical care for some (Cobos et al., 2015). A 2006 study showed that 15 million adults and 5 million children reported high discomfort or phobic behavior when faced with a needle (Sokolowski et al., 2010). Nearly one quarter of those 15 million adults said they refused to allow their blood to be drawn or refused a recommended injection because of fear (Sokolowski et al., 2010). White coat anxiety is the only phobia during which many patients fear fainting (Wright et al., 2009). Although rare, fainting can take place for some patients. A fainting event is caused by the rapid activation of the sympathetic nervous system (fear response) and an attendant parasympathetic response. Together, they cause a drop in heart rate and blood pressure.

The problems associated with white coat anxiety have increased in importance with medicine's increasing emphasis on preventive care in recent years. Screenings such as mammograms, colorectal exams, cholesterol checks, and digital rectal exams can save lives, but only if people are willing to submit to uncomfortable procedures and do not experience anxiety which prevents them from participating in such screenings.

Causes and Risk Factors

Some research has shown that females, especially those older than 50 years, are more likely to experience white coat hypertension (Franklin et al., 2013).

Other studies indicate that high perceived stress levels in women are associated with white coat hypertension more than in men (Franklin et al., 2013). It is possible that women may experience a different stress response to medical clinic visits than men, as evidenced by their blood pressure measurements. According to some research, this might explain the high percentage of women experiencing white coat hypertension (Pickering et al., 1999). In addition, the diagnosis of white coat anxiety has been shown to significantly increase with age, and this could be a result of an age-related increase in arterial stiffness (Pickering et al., 1999).

Of the known fears and phobias of specific triggers, blood injection fears are the most highly heritable (Van Houtem et al., 2013). It appears to run in families, as it is estimated that 30 percent to 40 percent of first-degree relatives of phobic patients have phobias themselves (Van Houtem et al., 2013). Like many phobias, this disorder often starts in childhood, with nine being the median age of onset (Becker et al., 2007). Many people with this phobia also have other comorbid phobias (Becker et al., 2007).

Assessment of Anxiety of Medical Procedures

Diagnosing white coat anxiety may be most effectively done with ambulatory monitoring. Ambulatory monitors are small, portable electrocardiograph machines that are able to record the heartbeat, and doctors use ambulatory monitors to assess a patient's heartbeat over a period of time. This can confirm whether patients are persistently hypertensive or experiencing white coat syndrome (Stergiou et al., 1998). When blood pressure is measured in the office or clinic, having the patient in a quiet room may help reduce the difference between out-of-the office and office blood pressure. One method of measuring and studying white coat hypertension has been with the use of microneurography, which measures the muscles and skin of the sympathetic nerve traffic (Mancia et al., 2011). Results from a study researching white coat hypertension used this technique and found that pronounced activation of skin nerves and associated sympathetic inhibition of muscle nerve-traffic were demonstrated by participants when physicians either took blood pressure measurements or were present during these measurements (Grassi et al., 1999).

Blood-injection-injury phobia may be assessed with the use of a simple questionnaire which identifies the severity of the fear response. Called "The Severity Measure for Specific Phobia—Adult Version," it is a ten-item questionnaire that asks the individual to rate the degree of reaction they have to the phobic stimulus (Craske et al., 2013).

Although there are effective methods for relieving fear of doctors and white coat anxiety, it is important first for the patient to recognize and acknowledge his or her anxiety. Some people may mask their fears and anxieties by saying they do not have the time for a doctor's visit or by speaking disparagingly about the medical profession.

After recognizing their fear and anxiety, there must be adequate communication between physician and patient. White coat hypertension may be initially addressed through the development of a therapeutic and trusting relationship between the doctor and the patient. Effective communication and relationship building can help reduce the patient's anxiety about their illness and about their interaction with medical staff. Effective communication, in and of itself, will not necessarily reduce the patient's blood pressure. But, a physician's overall attention to effective communication and empathy may increase trust and reduce the patient's anxiety (Cobos et al., 2015).

Efforts to deal with patients' fears and anxieties should focus on providing information and reducing stress before the patient shows up in the office or clinic. Some methods to improve patient communication, for example, have involved waiting room interventions by health educators who can discuss medical procedures and coach participants to ask questions and to talk openly about concerns.

One of the techniques that has been found most useful in relieving patient anxiety about doctor visits and/or medical procedures is CBT. By reframing a patient's state of mind and teaching coping techniques, this form of therapy has been shown to relieve white coat anxiety sometimes in only a few sessions.

Needle and injection phobias are treated like most phobias with a combination of exposure, cognitive reframing, and relaxation management of the stress response. The exposure hierarchy can be either or both imaginal (talking about needles, for instance) and in vivo—as the procedure is actually carried out.

In Chapter 9, you can learn about an effective treatment protocol for white coat anxiety or other anxieties related to the medical setting and procedures.

Illness Anxiety Disorder

Illness anxiety disorder, once known as hypochondriasis or health anxiety, is characterized by an excessive anxiety or fear about having a serious disease. This disorder is often encountered in hospitals or medical clinics, with some estimates in primary care settings as high as 7 percent (Creed and Barsky, 2004).

Illness anxiety disorder is a type of somatic disorder whose cardinal feature is anxiety or worry about disease and repeated requests for medical reassurance. It is unlike panic and phobic disorders in that the intense fear and fight/flight reaction is absent. Instead, it is a "worry" disorder. Most often, individuals with this disorder ruminate about catastrophic outcomes for common physical symptoms. And frequently visit the doctor for reassurance. Unfortunately, this produces only temporary relief because the worry persists, often developing into conviction of underlying disease. For instance, a person with a headache thinks it is indicative of a brain tumor. Or an individual with a cough sees it as a sign of lung cancer. Patients who experience illness anxiety disorder may spend an excessive amount of time on these symptoms; by over-researching their symptoms; scheduling multiple doctor appointments; or seeking assurance from physicians, relatives, and friends.

Illness anxiety disorder usually begins in early or middle adulthood and may get worse with age (Reuman and Abramowitz, 2015). Frequently, for some older patients, their health-related anxiety may focus on the fear of losing their memory (Reuman and Abramowitz, 2015).

The causes of illness anxiety disorder also appear to fall along the diathesis-stress model, with vulnerabilities including heritability, enhanced sensitivity to illness symptoms, cognitive style, and family modeling of illness behavior (Reuman and Abramowitz, 2015). For many people, a difficult life event or stressor often precipitates the development of this disorder. For example, a person with illness anxiety may notice a symptom (like shoulder pain) and focus on it. The more they focus attention on it, the worse it feels, and because of their elevated arousal or anxiety, they may interpret this symptom as a "threat" due to a catastrophic thinking style. This will lead to more anxiety and eventually to scheduling doctor's appointments in order to be reassured they do not have cancer or some other life-threatening ailment. Illness anxiety disorder can run in families, but may not entirely be for genetic reasons. Some people experiencing illness anxiety disorder have had parents who worried too much about their own health or about their children's health (Mayo Clinic, 2016b). In addition, some patients with illness anxiety may have had a traumatic experience with serious illness during childhood and, as a result, most physical sensations are frightening to them.

Assessment of Illness Anxiety Disorder

Diagnosing illness anxiety disorder will often require physical examinations and medical tests to rule out medical conditions. A psychological evaluation may also be part of the assessment process and will usually include a clinical interview and psychological tests. The psychological examiner, during the clinical interview, will likely ask the patient about their symptoms, stressful situations, family history, fears and concerns, relationship problems, and other issues affecting their life. The *DSM-5*, published by the American Psychiatric Association, emphasizes these points in the diagnosis of illness anxiety disorder:

- a preoccupation with having or getting a serious illness;
- being easily alarmed about their personal health status;
- physical symptoms are either nonexistent or only mild;
- when there is another medical condition or a strong family history of a medical condition, the preoccupation about this is excessive;

- the patient performs excessive health-related behaviors, such as repeatedly checking their body for signs of disease, or they avoid medical appointments for fear of being diagnosed with a serious illness;
- the illness preoccupation has lasted for at least 6 months, even though the specific illness that is feared may have changed during that time;
- the illness preoccupation is not better explained by another mental disorder, such as somatic symptom disorder, panic disorder, or GAD (American Psychiatric Association, 2013).

Treating Illness Anxiety Disorder

Treatment can include simple explanatory intervention, CBT and exposure therapy, as well as medication.

The goal of treatment for illness anxiety disorder is to improve the patient's symptoms and his or her ability to function in daily life. In general, psychotherapy can be helpful for illness anxiety disorder, although sometimes medications are prescribed. CBT and exposure therapy are found to be the most effective types of psychotherapy for most anxiety disorders, including illness anxiety disorder (Mayo Clinic, 2016b).

CBT can be effective in teaching patients skills to manage this disorder. CBT is also useful in helping patients identify fears and beliefs about having a serious medical disease. At the same time, CBT will help the individual learn alternate ways of viewing their body sensations by working to change unhelpful thoughts. In addition, people suffering from illness anxiety disorder can, through CBT, become more aware of how their worries affect them and then learning skills to cope with and tolerate anxiety and stress.

Exposure therapy is any treatment that encourages the systematic approach to feared stimuli (Kaplan and Tolin, 2011). The aim of exposure therapy is to reduce the person's fearful reaction to the stimulus. In imaginal exposure, the patient is asked to vividly imagine and describe the feared stimulus (in the case of illness anxiety disorder, that might mean imaging certain physical sensations), usually using present tense language and including details about various kinds of cues, for example, feelings and sensations. Furthermore, imaginal exposure can also be useful for confronting fears of worst-case scenarios (for instance, a patient imagining that they actually have the feared disease or condition). Exposure therapy can also involve having the patient recreate their symptoms by focusing on them in the office setting itself. In this way, patients' learn that they have control over their symptoms.

Some research suggests that "explanatory therapy" (Kroenke et al., 2007) may also be an effective intervention for a portion of individuals with illness anxiety. Explanatory therapy is a patient-education-centered therapy. The clinician provides a detailed explanation of the patient's symptoms and causes, in a supportive setting. Kroenke and his colleagues (2007) demonstrated significant reduction in complaints after 6 months compared to controls who did not receive explanations.

In terms of the utility of prescription medications, antidepressants, such as SSRIs, may be helpful for some patients with illness anxiety disorder (Medication, 2016).

The prognosis for illness anxiety disorder is usually long term and chronic, unless psychological factors are addressed in treatment (Illness Anxiety Disorder, 2016).

See Chapter 8 for specific guidelines for treating illness anxiety disorder.

Panic Disorder

Another type of anxiety disorder is panic disorder. People with panic disorder have recurrent unexpected panic attacks, which are sudden periods of intense fear that may include palpitations, pounding heart, or accelerated heart rate; sweating, trembling or shaking; sensations of shortness of breath, smothering, or choking; and nausea (Craske and Waikar, 1994). Thoughts of impending doom, dying, and going insane or crazy are common (Craske and Waikar, 1994). The fear is so intense that most individuals experiencing a panic attack leave the situations they are in in order to relieve their feelings (Craske and Waikar, 1994). Panic is unique from other phobic or anxiety disorders in that it reflects a fear response that is triggered by internal bodily sensations and the catastrophic interpretation of these sensations. People with panic attacks or a panic disorder are acutely attuned to their bodily responses and notice physical sensations and changes that others might not (i.e., heart rate increase). They are prone to a catastrophic thinking style and interpret their sensations as having a dangerous or malignant cause (i.e., increased heart rate equals heart attack or numb feeling in fingers equals a stroke). This sets off a fear response, and with it, a rapid increase in breathing. Increased breathing leads to a drop in blood carbon dioxide, and with it a panoply of other symptoms and sensations (trembling, sweating, shortness of breath, dizziness, numbness/tingling, etc.). The symptoms, in turn, increase the "volume" of the panic. Once the panic attack occurs, it becomes associated with the places it happens in (stores, theaters, etc.). People begin to fear that they will have another panic attack and often begin to think that they will experience the panic attack in a place where they will not be able to leave; this leads to avoiding leaving home (Craske and Waikar, 1994).

There is, thus, a cyclical pattern of anxiety symptoms. Anxiety leads to more symptoms; more symptoms lead to avoidance of many places and situations (driving, shopping, going to a show). In some individuals, this cycle develops into a more generalized fear of open places or crowds, which is referred to as agoraphobia (Craske and Waikar, 1994).

Studies have found that the prevalence of panic disorder in the United States in people aged 15 to 54 years is about 2.5 percent (Eaton et al., 1994). However, the prevalence of panic disorder among primary care patients is approximately twice as high as in the general population with rates of 4 percent to 6 percent (Kroenke et al., 2007). Panic attacks, which can occur in disorders other than panic disorder, are much more common than panic disorder, occurring in up to one-third of individuals at some point in their lifetime (Roy-Byrne, 2016). Panic disorder has a median age of onset of 24 years and is approximately twice as common in women as among men (Roy-Byrne, 2016). Panic disorder shares a very high comorbidity with depression, with some estimates suggesting lifetime prevalence rates for both as high as 60 percent to 70 percent (Olfson et al., 1997). It is important for clinicians to be aware of this co-occurrence, as many individuals who report depression may also be experiencing panic episodes, and vice versa.

Assessment of Panic Disorder

Assessing for panic disorder is largely a diagnosis of exclusion and there are few, if any, standard assessment instruments to help identify the disorder. However, a physical examination is essential to begin the process of ruling out other physical reasons for panic attacks or other symptoms.

An understanding of panic disorder is particularly important for emergency physicians and others working in a medical clinic or hospital because patients with this condition frequently present to an emergency department or their primary physician with various somatic complaints (Fleet et al., 1998). Many of the symptoms of an anxiety attack correspond with the symptoms found in life-threatening medical disorders, such as myocardial infarction and pulmonary embolus, which may appear with anxiety or panic disorder as a primary symptom (Fleet et al., 1998). Approximately 25 percent of patients who show up at an emergency department with chest pain have panic anxiety disorder (Fleet et al., 1998).

Some other medical conditions which may be diagnosed along with panic attacks or panic disorders include:

- angina and myocardial infarction (e.g., dyspnea, chest pain, palpitations, diaphoresis)
- cardiac dysrhythmias (e.g., palpitations, dyspnea, syncope)
- mitral valve prolapse
- pulmonary embolus (e.g., dyspnea, hyperpnea, chest pain)
- asthma (e.g., dyspnea, wheezing)
- hyperthyroidism (e.g., palpitations, diaphoresis, tachycardia, heat intolerance)
- hypoglycemia

- pheochromocytoma (e.g., headache, diaphoresis, hypertension)
- hypoparathyroidism (e.g., muscle cramps, paresthesias)
- transient ischemic attacks
- seizure disorder (Fleet et al., 1998).

In general, panic disorder symptoms can be easily assessed by a mental health professional. Many people who have panic attacks are very aware that they have some sort of "anxiety attacks." A simple query about whether a client has ever had an anxiety attack or a problem with anxiety or "nerves" is a natural beginning. If the client indicates any difficulty with anxiety, it is important for the clinician to closely evaluate the physiological, cognitive, behavioral, and situational elements of the anxiety episodes.

Panic can be easily discriminated from most anxiety disorders by the physical symptoms of the fear response. Questions related to palpitations, shortness of breath, nausea, dizziness, sweating, numbness, and tingling should be asked. Key cognitive features are a sense of foreboding doom and thoughts about dying or even "going crazy." Behaviorally, the escape/avoidant response needs to be evaluated. Does the client feel the intense urge to leave the situation that they are in? If they do, does the anxiety dissipate once they leave? Do they then avoid that place and others like it? Then, specific situational triggers should be evaluated. Frequently, individuals report intense anxiety in situations that they think they will not be able to get out of easily. This means that auditoriums, crowds, stores, movie theaters, and concerts are often avoided because of fear of panic and concerns about their ability to escape. Driving can also become problematic, as can riding on elevators or escalators. Concern about public scrutiny during a panic attack can lead to avoidance of situations where other people are present, including standing in line at stores.

It is important for the clinician to observe that for many panic patients talking about panic is profoundly anxiety provoking. Many panic patients fear that by talking about it a panic attack will be triggered. Therefore, many panic patients would rather talk about anything else other than panic. It is important for the provider to reassure the patient that talking about panic, even during assessment, will help to begin to reduce it (for the clinician, this is the first step in exposure therapy). Avoiding discussion and evaluation only makes the panic and fear of it stronger. Instead of making panic worse, talking about it can begin to dissipate it. On rare occasions, some clients may experience panic attack during an initial session or an evaluation. It is important for the clinician to remain with the client until it has subsided. If the clinician does not remain with the client for the duration of the episode, the clinician may be associated with the panic attack and avoided in the future.

One tool for assessing panic disorder is the Panic Assessment Scale. However, diagnostic criteria, as listed in the *DSM-5*, published by the American Psychiatric Association, are also important:

- has frequent, unexpected panic attacks;
- at least one of the attacks has been followed by 1 month or more of ongoing worry about having another attack; continued fear of the consequences of an attack, such as losing control, having a heart attack or "going crazy"; or significantly changing their behavior, such as avoiding situations that you think may trigger a panic attack;
- the panic attacks are not caused by drugs or other substance use, a medical condition, or another mental health condition, such as social phobia or obsessive-compulsive disorder (American Psychiatric Association, 2013).

Treating Panic Disorder

Panic disorder is generally treated with psychotherapy, medication, or both (Gould et al., 1995). Among physicians and psychiatrists, the most commonly prescribed medications for panic disorder are antianxiety medications and antidepressants, including:

- SSRIs, such as Paxil, Prozac, or Zoloft
- benzodiazepines, such as Ativan, Valium, or Xanax
- antidepressants with mixed neurotransmitter effects, such as Effexor
- tricyclic antidepressants, such as Anafranil, Norpramin, or Tofranil
- monoamine oxidase inhibitors, such as Marplan, Nardil, or Parnate (Star, 2016).

However, most specialists agree that a combination of cognitive and behavioral therapies is the best treatment for panic disorder (National Institute of Mental Health, 2016f). And among various treatment approaches, CBT is especially useful for treating panic disorder (Otto and Deveney, 2005). In general, when CBT is used, the first part of therapy is largely informational. That is, many people are greatly helped by simply understanding exactly what panic disorder is, and how many others suffer from it (Pollack et al., 2003). By helping to change the way a patient thinks about their panic attacks, a first step is taken toward replacing their worst thoughts with more realistic, positive ways of viewing the attacks.

Furthermore, CBT can help the patient identify possible triggers for the attacks. A trigger in this disorder could be something like a thought, a situation, or something as subtle as a slight change in heartbeat. Once the patient understands that the panic attack is separate and independent of the trigger, that trigger begins to lose some of its power to induce an attack (Sanderson, 2015).

The behavioral components of CBT usually consist of a type of exposure treatment. Similar to the systematic desensitization used to treat phobias, the exposure phase focuses on the actual physical sensations that the patient experiences during a panic attack.

Finally, relaxation techniques can further help the individual "flow through" an attack. Since often people with panic disorder have somewhat higher breathing rates, by using breathing retraining and positive visualization, the patient learns to slow down their breathing which help them deal more effectively with their panic attack while working to prevent future attacks.

See Chapter 9 for specific guidelines for treating panic disorder.

Agitation Secondary to Confusion

When a loved one begins resisting care, becomes physically combative, disruptive, and verbally abusive, it often comes as an unwelcome surprise. However, it is also difficult to manage.

Unfortunately, it is also a fairly common occurrence in certain organic and medical conditions. For example, changes in behavior or personality can herald or accompany dementia and approximately 60 percent to 80 percent of patients with dementia have neuropsychiatric symptoms that include agitation (Lyketsos et al., 2001). Some studies estimate that as much as 24 percent of a community sample of elderly patients evidenced agitated behavior and aggression (Steffens et al., 2015). Yet, agitation can also be associated with delirium (resulting from medical illness), medication side effects, and substance use withdrawal (Steffens et al., 2015).

Problematic behaviors during agitation can be classified into two categories: aggression and primary agitation. Aggression includes resistance to care, combativeness, physical aggression, and verbal aggression. Primary agitation is defined by excessive activity, psychomotor or verbal (Richmond et al., 2012). This kind of activity can include walking aimlessly, wandering, pacing, trailing, perseverative repetitive actions, dressing, and undressing (Richmond et al., 2012). In addition, it can also include verbally disruptive behaviors.

The cost of these behaviors is enormous. They are associated with excess morbidity and mortality (Wancata et al., 2003) and increased hospitalization times (Wancata et al., 2003). These behaviors are also a primary reason for nursing home placement (Lyketsos et al., 2002). Rarely do families seek nursing home placement for memory loss or disorientation, but they do seek nursing home care when the family member is difficult to manage (Buhr et al., 2006). The burden on caregivers is high. Trying to manage the agitated and aggressive patient can negatively impact caregiver employment and caregiver emotional functioning. It is estimated that as much as 30 percent of costs of dementia care is related to behavioral disturbance (Beeri et al., 2002).

In the acute care setting, emergency department staff frequently encounter agitated patients, which is why studies have documented that at least 25 percent of emergency department staff feel unsafe at work (Kansagra et al., 2008). A 2010 Emergency Nurses Association study on violence in the workplace reported that more than half of emergency nurses had been verbally or physically threatened at work within the preceding 7 days (The American Nurse, 2016). Such assaults are typically a direct result of patient agitation.

Agitation can be a sign of disease or medical illness. For instance, when it occurs with a change in alertness (i.e., altered arousal), it can indicate delirium, which almost always has a medical cause. Among the many causes of organic agitation are:

- alcohol intoxication or withdrawal
- allergic reaction
- caffeine intoxication
- certain forms of heart, lung, liver, or kidney disease
- intoxication or withdrawal from drugs of abuse (such as cocaine, marijuana, hallucinogens, PCP, or opiates)
- hospitalization (older adults often have delirium while in the hospital)
- hyperthyroidism (overactive thyroid gland)
- infection (especially in elderly people)
- nicotine withdrawal
- poisoning (e.g., carbon monoxide poisoning)
- theophylline, amphetamines, steroids, and certain other medicines
- trauma
- vitamin B6 deficiency (American Psychiatric Association, 2013).

In addition, agitation can occur with brain and mental health disorders, such as:

- anxiety
- dementia (such as Alzheimer disease)
- depression
- mania
- schizophrenia (American Psychiatric Association, 2013).

Agitation and aggression that persist without an identified medical condition often have an internal or external cause. That is, agitated and aggressive behaviors can be generated by environmental conditions or by internal factors within the individual.

Internal triggers can be negative emotional states such as anxiety, anger, confusion, helplessness, or loneliness (Leger et al., 2000). Physical pain can also contribute to behavioral difficulty (Desai and Grossberg, 2001). The external or environmental causes can include things such as excess sensory stimulation (noise, movement, light), too little stimulation (boredom), changes in routine, or caregiver behaviors (Desai and Grossberg, 2001).

Agitation may persist because it serves several functions for the individual. For instance, agitation and aggressiveness may bring about escape or termination of something the patient wishes to avoid. In addition, combativeness and agitation can stop what is upsetting to the patient. And for some people, agitation and aggression may reflect a need to assert autonomy and identity in the face of increasing dependency and feelings of powerlessness (Lantz et al., 1997). In this regard, it becomes a power struggle between a care provider and a patient who is struggling against loss of independence. Agitation can also be a powerful reinforcer for someone who is seeking interpersonal connection or feels ignored or isolated because it generates attention, albeit often negative attention. It can be a way of reducing boredom when it provides stimulation.

Assessment of Agitation

Assessment of behavioral agitation starts with identification of the etiology or cause. It is essential initially to determine if the agitation is connected to a reversible cause. This can be determined via a careful interview with collateral informants or staff to assess the timeline of the behavior change. If the behavior change represents an abrupt change from the person's baseline, it is essential to consider a new or underlying medical etiology. It should be noted that the goal of a psychological assessment is not necessarily to obtain a definitive diagnosis, but instead the goal should be to establish a reasonable differential diagnosis, identify issues related to safety of the patient and others, and develop a suitable treatment and disposition plan.

A reversible etiology, such as delirium, can be assessed with the utilization of the Confusion Assessment Method (CAM). This is a quick instrument that can be given at bedside or in primary care settings. The CAM is a simple rating scale that assesses arousal, attention, speech organization, disorientation, perceptual disturbance, psychomotor agitation or retardation, and sleep-wake disruption (Cerejeira and Mukaetova-Ladinska, 2011).

Referral to a primary care practitioner for a delirium work up and medication review is an important next step, following a positive finding on the CAM.

Some tests that may be ordered or considered during the assessment period may include:

- blood studies (e.g., blood count, infection screening, thyroid tests, or vitamin levels)
- head CT or head MRI scan
- lumbar puncture (spinal tap)
- urine tests (for infection screening, drug screening)
- vital signs (temperature, pulse, breathing rate, blood pressure) (Cerejeira and Mukaetova-Ladinska, 2011).

Once reversible causes have been excluded, it is important to observe or ascertain when the behaviors happen, what time of day they occur, the circumstances, or people present. This can be done by speaking with caregivers, or direct observation. It is important to note the consequences of the behavior, or what happens after it has occurred. This assessment can sometimes be complicated by the intermittent nature of the behavior and if not directly observed, reliance on collateral informant report. However, collateral informants may at times be inaccurate, subject to opinion, bias or limited expertise of the particular individual.

Behavioral agitation can be evaluated more objectively with several instruments that can be rapidly administered. These include the Overt Behavior Scale (OBS) and the Agitated Behavior Scale. The Agitated Behavior Scale is a ten-item rating scale that can be given consecutively to assess the level of agitation, and it has been found helpful in identifying behaviors and tracking overall agitation over time (Corrigan and Bogner, 1994). The OBS for Agitation is a more comprehensive rating instrument, which can be useful in identifying the types of agitated or disruptive behavior (Kelly et al., 2005). There are nine categories of behavior in the OBS: verbal aggression, physical aggression against objects, physical acts against the self, physical aggression against other people, inappropriate sexual behaviors, perseveration and repetitive behaviors, wandering/absconding, inappropriate social behavior, and lack of initiation (Kelly et al., 2005).

Treating Agitation

Pharmacologic strategies for the treatment of agitation and aggression include tranquilizing medications for short-term management and antipsychotics for long-term management. Antipsychotics have now become so widely utilized for the management of agitation and behavioral symptoms that more than 70 percent of antipsychotic prescriptions are for off-label purposes (Glick et al., 2001). Some studies have demonstrated that almost a third of nursing home resident are on antipsychotics (Chen et al., 2010), with the majority of these prescriptions for agitation or aggression. This is concerning, however, particularly for elderly or demented individuals because studies suggest that conventional and atypical antipsychotics are associated with significantly higher 12-month mortality rate than other psychotropics (Desai and Grossberg, 2001).

Strategies for agitation management can be divided into two categories: immediate and preventative. Immediate interventions are those that are used when the individual is already agitated and de-escalation is needed. Preventative strategies are implemented to preempt or reduce early signs of agitation, before a high level of distress occurs.

Immediate strategies have the intent of addressing acute and high levels of agitation. These strategies capitalize on modifying the caregiver approach, reducing stimulation (internal or external), and allowing the individual to de-escalate in a safe and peaceful environment. Body language in these settings is important, as even impaired patients may respond to nonverbal cues. Power struggles between caregivers and patients are often observed in escalated agitation, and it is important for care providers to become comfortable with retreating in these moments (although being clear that they will later return, so as not to reinforce the agitation).

Preventative strategies include learning to identify signaling behaviors (early indicators of agitation), discerning triggers, and modifying them. Such strategies can also involve managing the approach by reducing potential for patient surprise/disruption and increasing patient control by providing them with opportunities for autonomous choice. More specific strategies include:

- creating a calm environment;
- removing stressors; this may involve moving the person to a safer or quieter place, or offering a security object, rest, or privacy;
- avoiding excessive stimulation: noise, light, movement, and activity (such as regulating the type of program on television or reducing the volume);
- reducing boredom (too little stimulation), increasing activity levels with valued activity based on the person's past interests;
- reducing physical discomfort—checking for pain, hunger, thirst, constipation, full bladder, fatigue, infections, and skin irritation;
- simplifying tasks and routines, to limit frustration;
- providing an opportunity for exercise, such as going for a walk;
- exposing individuals to the natural light cycle whenever possible, particularly in cases of day/night confusion;
- providing calming music can also help;
- providing reassurance; staff should use calming phrases such as "You're safe here," "I'm sorry that you are upset," and "I will stay until you feel better" (Desai and Grossberg, 2001).

See Chapter 11 for specific guidelines for treating agitation.

Social Communication Disorder (Pragmatic Difficulties)

The ability to intentionally influence others and also be affected by them in return is basic to social living. This aspect of social living is the domain of the area of linguistics and philosophy known as pragmatics (Leech, 1983). In its broadest sense, pragmatics is the study of the use of language for the purpose of communication (Ninio and Snow, 1999). When people have language deficits, their ability to communicate effectively and appropriately is usually reduced, but it is also the case that when individuals have poor social skills, their ability to communicate is affected. The pragmatic difficulties discussed in this section are those for whom interventions are needed because of their social (pragmatic) communication difficulties.

In 2013, when the American Psychiatric Association issued a newly revised edition of the *DSM-5*, a new diagnostic category was included: social communication disorder (SCD) (American Psychiatric Association, 2013). This diagnostic category is intended to recognize individuals who have significant problems in using verbal and nonverbal communication in their social interactions. Such problems can interfere with interpersonal relationships, academic achievement, and occupational performance. Problems with social communication are common in those patients with cognitive limitations, autism and related disorders, and a variety of other psychiatric conditions (Drake, 2016). Patients who have difficulties in their use of language in social contexts but do not have autism, Asperger's syndrome or cognitive limitations have been variously diagnosed and inconsistently treated. Often they are simply considered maladroit, eccentric, or inattentive and, many times not treated at all. The new diagnosis from the American Psychiatric Association is intended to remedy this problem.

A specific cause for SCD has not been discovered, but it has been suggested by various experts that a genetic predisposition and environmental influences or a disturbance of development around the time of language acquisition may lead to SCD (Drake, 2016). Between 30 percent and 60 percent of children with speech or language disabilities have a parent or sibling who is similarly affected (US Department of Education, 2005). Choudhury and Benasich (2003) estimated the incidence of specific language impairment in families with a history of such disorders to be 20 percent to 40 percent. Among families with a child having a disorder in the autistic spectrum, the chance of having another affected child is 2 percent to 8 percent, which is greater than it is for the general population (Muhle et al., 2004).

Diagnostic Criteria

Since SCD is a newly defined disorder, its incidence and prevalence cannot yet be determined (American Psychiatric Association, 2013). It is likely to be substantial, particularly among children in school, because communication disorders are estimated to be among the most common disabilities in the United States. Approximately 6.1 million children in public schools received services under the Individuals with Disabilities Education Act (IDEA) in 2003, of these 24.1 percent (about 1.5 million) had speech or language disorders (US Department of Education, 2005). Estimates of language disabilities in preschool children range from 2 percent to 19 percent (US Department of Education, 2005). Similarly, wide-ranging estimates of the prevalence of autistic spectrum disorder have been published (less than 1 to 1,300 per 10,000 individuals) (Charman, 2002), and many SCD sufferers have been incorrectly diagnosed with this or with the miscellaneous subcategory of pervasive developmental disorder (18 to 60 per 10,000 prevalence) (Drake, 2016). The diagnosis of Asperger's syndrome, in which disturbed social communication predominates but is accompanied by restricted and repetitive behavior and interests, has been withdrawn from the *DSM-5*, which attempts to replace imprecise diagnoses. However, the prevalence of Asperger's syndrome has been estimated at anywhere between 2 and 97 cases per 10,000 (Fombonne, 2005). Given these wide-ranging estimates, it cannot be predicted as to how many adult patients with SCD will show up in a medical clinic.

According to the *DSM-5*, diagnosis of SCD involves observing persistent difficulties in verbal and nonverbal communication in social settings, manifested by all of the following:

- Deficits in social communication, such as greeting or sharing information in an appropriate manner.
- Difficulty with changing communication to match the listener (e.g., an adult versus a child) or the context (e.g., social versus business).
- Stereotypic or formal language may be inappropriately used for informal conversation.
- Difficulty with the rules governing conversation, such as speaking in turn, repeating information if not clearly understood, and regulating conversation in response to verbal and nonverbal information from others.
- Inference of what is not explicitly stated may not be made, or language with ambiguous meaning may not be correctly interpreted, such as metaphors or jokes.
- These problems must cause functional limitations in effective communication, social participation, relationships and academic or occupational performance, either individually or in combination.
- The symptoms must begin in the early developmental period, when language is usually acquired, and must not be better accounted for by another mental disorder or a general medical or neurological condition. In particular, cognitive impairment causing low abilities in the domains of word structure and grammar cannot be the cause, and developmental delay, intellectual disability and autism spectrum disorder (ASD) must be excluded (American Psychiatric Association, 2013).

Given that impairments in social communication are a hallmark feature of ASD, overlap in the symptomatology of SCD and ASD is expected. Specifically, patients with ASD who have adequate structural language abilities may have pragmatic difficulties such as verbosity, overly formal speech, and trouble taking turns in conversation (Swineford et al., 2014). These specific pragmatic deficits are expressed in the context of a larger constellation of ASD symptoms, which may include impairments in social reciprocity and the presence of restricted interests and repetitive behaviors. On the other hand, it is important to note that pragmatic language deficits have been reported to occur without the impairing social deficits and repetitive behaviors indicative of ASD, suggesting that two distinct patterns of symptoms exist (Swineford et al., 2014).

Some studies that have investigated more broadly defined pragmatic language impairments have reported that many individuals with pragmatic language impairments did not meet the *DSM-IV* criteria for autistic disorder (Swineford et al., 2014). It is less clear whether such individuals will meet the *DSM-5* ASD criteria. For example, the inclusion of patient history rather than just present symptoms in the *DSM-5* criteria for ASD may mean that some individuals who currently have only deficits of social communication would still receive an ASD diagnosis because they had a history of repetitive behavior/restricted interests. Stereotyped language is now part of the repetitive and restrictive behavior domain for ASD (Swineford et al., 2014). Thus, stereotyped language would now also count as one of the two required symptoms of repetitive and restrictive behavior for an ASD diagnosis. Given the mutual exclusivity of ASD and SCD, the presence of stereotyped language in the restrictive and repetitive behavior domain may have significant impact on who is considered for a possible diagnosis of SCD.

Pragmatic language difficulties have been described in a variety of psychiatric and neurodevelopmental disorders, including schizophrenia, bipolar disorder, and attention deficit hyperactivity disorder, among others (Swineford et al., 2014). With respect to attention deficit hyperactivity disorder, it has been hypothesized that the primary symptoms of the disorder (i.e., impulsiveness, inattention, hyperactivity) may cause impairments in social communication, which result in additional limitations on communication, social participation, and academic achievement (Bellani et al., 2011).

Assessment of SCD

There are two standardized measures to assess SCD: Test of Pragmatic Language and Comprehensive Assessment of Spoken Language. The Test of Pragmatic Language is a norm-referenced measure for children between 6 and 18 years of age which measures several aspects of pragmatic communication including physical setting, audience, topic, purpose, visual gestural cues, and abstraction (WPS, 2016). The Comprehensive Assessment of Spoken Language is an omnibus test of expressive language including four subtests to measure pragmatics for individuals between 3 and 21 years of age (Pearson Clinical, 2016). Specific areas of pragmatics measured on the Comprehensive Assessment of Spoken Language include pragmatic judgment, idiomatic language, nonliteral language, and inferencing. Although both of these measures capture aspects of pragmatic language related to SCD, the scoring systems of both make it difficult to measure the quality of pragmatic language.

Pragmatic tools typically identify and measure single cognitive processes underlying a range of communication behaviors.

Although profiling specific pragmatic strengths and weaknesses leads to identification of processes involved in communication, it does not outline the consequences of the communication deficit in individuals' daily interactions. For such evaluation, functional assessments may be used to measure a person's ability to communicate efficiently in real-life situations (Rad, 2014). Examples of such tests are Functional Communication Profile (FCP) and Functional Assessment of Communication Skills (FACS) for adults.

Among all the introduced instruments, most commonly used checklists designed for adult pragmatic and functional assessments are the Discourse Comprehension Test (DCT); Pragmatic Protocol (PP); Profile of Communicative Appropriateness (PCA); Assessment Protocol of Pragmatic-Linguistic Skills; Discourse Abilities Profile; the revised version of Edinburgh FCP; Communicative Abilities in Daily Living (CADL); Communication Competence Self-Report; the Expression, Reception and Recall of Narrative Instrument; and the Verbal Pragmatic Rating Scale (Rad, 2014). Following are capsule reviews of these instruments:

- DCT is a well-controlled measure of narrative processing that taps comprehension of implied information as well as explicitly conveyed information. DCT permits sensitive and reliable measurement of changes in both listening and reading comprehension of discourse over time, and provides information useful for planning treatment and for counseling communication partners (Rad, 2014).
- PP is a general observation profile based on speech act theory. All pragmatic parameters in PP checklist are assigned to three aspects:
    - verbal behaviors such as speech acts, message specificity, cohesion and topic selection, initiation and maintenance
    - paralinguistic behaviors including fluency, prosody, vocal quality, and speech intelligibility
    - nonverbal behaviors such as facial expressions, eye gaze, and gestures (Rad, 2014).
- PCA consists of various parameters that are grouped in five sections: (a) response to interlocutor, (b) control of semantic content, (c) cohesion-fluency, (d) sociolinguistic sensitivity, and (e) nonverbal communication (Rad, 2014).
- CADL is a pragmatic instrument based on speech act theory, like PP, that makes use of role playing and uses everyday social situations (Rad, 2014).
- FCP rates the effectiveness of communicative behavior in an informal conversation. The FCP checklist consists of forty-five items divided into five areas: Movement, Speaking, Understanding, Reading, and Other activities (Rad, 2014).

- FACS is an adult assessment tool available from the American Speech-Language Hearing Association. FACS scores 43 communicative abilities in four domains: Social communication; Communication of basic needs; Reading, Writing and Number concepts: and Daily planning (Rad, 2014).

Treating SCD

Although medical treatment of developmental disorders has been found to be essentially ineffective, some psychostimulants have been used to control impulsivity and hyperactivity, and atypical antipsychotic drugs have been indicated as a means to lessen some of the behavioral disturbances of autism (Rezaei et al., 2010; Strock, 2007). In general, however, there have been no studies of drug treatment for the communication disorders.

Speech and language professionals recommend the early assessment of cognition, language, hearing, and speech in children with social interaction problems (Drake, 2016). There is a general agreement that the educational and occupational prognosis is poor for patients who receive no intervention (Drake, 2016). There is, however, no high-level evidence from controlled clinical trials treatment in adults with pragmatics deficits. Treatment approaches that have been used include augmentative and alternative communication (AAC), computer-based instruction, and video-based instruction (Drake, 2016). AAC involves supplementation of speech communication with symbols or tangible objects, which may require a transmission device, or with unaided gestures and manual signing that may enhance communication. Computer-based instruction uses programs designed to teach social skills and understanding, while video-based instruction, also called video-modeling, uses videotaped interactions to practice communication skills (Drake, 2016).

Behavioral interventions that are supported by some research include applied behavioral analysis (ABA), functional communication training (FCT), incidental teaching, milieu therapy, and pivotal response training (PRT) (Drake, 2016). ABA is based on behavioral theory and utilizes observation of social interactions to make modifications in the environment to facilitate social communication. FCT involves the assessment of the communicative function of maladaptive behavior in order to teach alternative responses to bring about more effective communication. Incidental teaching and milieu therapy are carried out through-out the day and not just in "therapy" periods. Incidental teaching offers reinforcement for more effective communication and adaptive behaviors, while milieu therapy attempts to integrate communication training into other activities during the day. PRT attempts to teach "pivotal" skills that are needed for effective social interactions, such as the ability to respond appropriately to multiple cues, initiate social contact, and self-regulate impulses (Drake, 2016).

Positive behavior support (PBS) is an approach that uses the functional assessment of problem behaviors to target the relationship between challenging behavior and communication. PBS integrates the principles of applied behavior analysis with person-centered values to foster skills that replace challenging behaviors through positive response/support (Carr et al., 2002).

CBT has been used with individuals with pragmatics deficits. The underlying assumptions of CBT—that an individual's behavior is mediated by cognitive events and that changes in thinking or cognitive patterns can lead to changes in behavior—have been used to improve social communication (ASHA, 2016).

See Chapter 11 for specific guidelines for treating pragmatic difficulties and SCD.

References

Aiello-Laws, L., Reynolds, J., Deizer, N., Peterson, M., Ameringer, S., and Bakitas, M. (2009). Putting evidence into practice: What are the pharmacologic interventions for nociceptive and neuropathic cancer pain adults? *Clinical Journal of Oncology Nursing*, 13(6), 649–655.

Albert, P.R. (2015). Why is depression more prevalent in women? *Journal of Psychiatry Neuroscience*, 40(4), 219–221.

American Academy of Pain Medicine. (2016). Facts and figures on pain. American Academy of Pain Medicine [Online]. Available: www.painmed.org/patientcenter/facts_on_pain.aspx#incidence

American Psychological Association. (2016). Why sleep is important and what happens when you don't get enough? Available: www.apa.org/topics/sleep/why.aspx

American Society of Addiction Medicine. (2016). Opioid addiction: 2016 facts and figures. [Online]. Available: www.asam.org/docs/default-source/advocacy/opioid-addiction-disease-facts-figures.pdf

American Speech-Language-Hearing Association. (ASHA). (2016). Social communication disorders in school-age children [Online]. Available: www.asha.org/PRPSpecific Topic.aspx?folderid=8589934980&section=Treatment

Ancoli-Israel, T., and Roth, M. (1999). Characteristics of insomnia in the United States: Results of the 1991 National Sleep Foundation Survey. I. *Sleep*, 22(Suppl. 2), 347–353.

Ashton, H. (1994). Guidelines for the rational use of benzodiazepines. *Drugs*, 48(1), 25–40.

Austin, D.W., and Richards, J.C. (2001). The catastrophic misinterpretation model of panic disorder. *Behaviour Research and Therapy*, 39(11), 1277–1291.

Backhaus, J., Hohagen, F., Voderholzer, U., and Riemann, D. (2001). Long-term effectiveness of a short-term cognitive behavioral group treatment for primary insomnia. *European Archives of Clinical Neuroscience*, 251, 35–41.

Bair, M.J., Robinson, R.L., Katon, W., and Kroenke, K. (2003). Depression and pain comorbidity: A literature review. *Archives of Internal Medicine*, 163(20), 2433–2435.

Banks, S.M., and Kerns, R.D. (1996). Explaining high rates of depression in chronic pain: A diathesis-stress framework. *Psychological Bulletin*, 119(1), 95–110.

Bardeen, J.R., Fergus, T.A., Hannan, S.M., and Orcutt, H.K. (2016). Addressing psychometric limitations of the difficulties in Emotion Regulation Scale through item modification. *Journal of Personality Assessment*, 98(3), 298–309.

Bearman, S.K., and Weisz, J.R. (2012). Cognitive Behavior Therapy: An introduction. In E. Szigethy, J.R. Weisz, and R.L. Findling (Eds.), *Cognitive-Behavior Therapy for children and adolescents* (pp. 1–28). Washington, D.C.: American Psychiatric Publishing.

Becker, E.S., Rinck, M., Turke, V., Kause, P., Goodwin, R., Neumer, S., and Margraf, J. (2007). Epidemiology of specific phobia subtypes: Findings from the Dresden Mental Health Study. *European Psychiatry*, 22(2), 69–74.

Beeri, M.S., Werner, P., Davidson, M., and Noy, S. (2002). The cost of behavioral and psychological symptoms of dementia (BPSD) in community dwelling Alzheimer's disease patients. *International Journal of Geriatric Psychiatry*, 17, 403–408.

Bellani, M., Moretti, A., Perlini, C., and Brambilla, P. (2011). Language disturbances in ADHD. *Epidemiological Psychiatric Science*, 20, 311–315. DOI: 10.1017/S2045796 011000527

Bienenfeld, D., and Stinson, K. (2016). Screening tests for depression. Mesdcape. Available: http://emedicine.medscape.com/article/1859039-overview

Bierut, L.J., Heath, A.C., Bucholz, K.K., Dinwiddie, S.H., Madden, P.A., Statham, D.J., and Martin, N.G. (1999). Major depressive disorder in a community-based twin sample: Are there different genetic and environmental contributions for men and women? *Archives of General Psychiatry*, 56(6), 557–563.

Blanco, C., Okuda, M., Markowitz, J.C., Liu, S., Grant, B., and Hasin, D.S. (2010). The epidemiology of chronic major depressive disorder and dysthymic disorder: Results from the National Epidemiologic Survey on Alcohol and Related Conditions. *Journal of Clinical Psychiatry*, 71(12), 1645–1656.

Bloom, H.G., Ahmed, I., Alessi, C.A., Ancoli-Israel, S., Buysse, D.J., Kryger, M.H., Phillips, B.A., Thorpy, M.J., Vitiello, M.V., and Zee, P.C. (2009). Evidence-based recommendations for the assessment and management of sleep disorders in older persons. *Journal of the American Geriatric Society*, 57(5), 761–789.

Boland, R.J., and Keller, M.B. (2010). Course and outcome of depression. In I.H. Gotli and C.L. Hammen (Eds.), *Handbook of depression* (2nd ed., pp. 23–43). New York: Guilford.

Bosco, M.A., Gallinati, J.L., and Clark, M.E. (2013). Conceptualizing and treating comorbid chronic pain and PTSD. *Pain Research and Treatment* 2013, Article ID 174728. DOI: 10.1155/2013/174728

Bradley, B., DeFife, J.A., Guarnaccia, C., Phifer, J., Fani, N., Ressler, K.J., and Westen, D. (2011). Emotion dysregulation and negative affect: Association with psychiatric symptoms. *Journal of Clinical Psychiatry*, 72(5), 685–691.

Buhr, G.T., Kuchibhatla, M., and Clipp, E.C. (2006). Caregivers' reasons for nursing home placement: Clues for improving discussions with families prior to the transition. *The Gerontologist*, 46(1), 52–61.

Carr, E.G., Dunlap, G., Horner, R.H., Koegel, R.L., Turnbull, A.P., Sailor, W., Anderson, J.L., Albin, R.W., Koegel, L.K., and Fox, L. (2002). Positive behavior support: Evolution of an applied science. *Journal of Positive Behavior Interventions*, 4(1), 4–16.

Carskadon, M.A., and Dement, W.C. (2011). Monitoring and staging human sleep. In M.H. Kryger, T. Roth, and W.C. Dement (Eds.), *Principles and practice of sleep medicine* (5th ed., pp. 16–26). St. Louis: Elsevier Saunders.

Catanzaro, S.J., and Mearns, J. (1990). Measuring generalized expectancies for negative mood regulation: Initial scale development and implications. *Journal of Personality Assessment*, 54(3–4), 546–563.

Cerejeira, J., and Mukaetova-Ladinska, E.B. (2011). A clinical update on delirium: From early recognition to effective management. *Nursing Research and Practice*, 2011. DOI: http://dx.doi.org/10.1155/2011/875196

Charman, T. (2002). The prevalence of autism spectrum disorders. *European Child & Adolescent Psychiatry*, 11(6), 249–256.

Chen, Y., Briesacher, B.A., Field, T.S., Tjia, J., Lau, D.T., and Gurwitz, J.H. (2010). Unexplained variation across US nursing homes in antipsychotic prescribing rates. *Archives of Internal Medicine*, 170(1), 89–95.

Chesson, A.L., Ferber, R.A., Fry, J.M., Grigg-Damberger, M., Hartse, K.M., Hurwitz, T.D., Johnson, S., Littner, M., Kader, G.A., Rosen, G., Sangal, R.B., Schmidt-Nowara, W., and Sher, A. (1997). Practice parameters for the indications for polysomnography and related procedures. *Sleep*, 20, 406–422.

Choudhury, N., and Benasich, A.A. (2003). A family aggregation study: The influence of family history and other risk factors on language development. *Journal of Speech, Language, and Hearing Research*, 46, 261–272.

Cobos, B., Haskard-Zolnierek, K., and Howard, K. (2015). White coat hypertension: Improving the patient–health care practitioner relationship. *Psychology Research and Behavior Management*, 8, 133–141.

Cook, A., Spinazzola, J., Ford, J., Lanktree, C., Blaustein, M., Cloitre, M., DeRosa, R., Hubbard, R., Kagan, R., Liautaud, J., Mallah, K., Olafson, E., and van der Kolk, B. (2005). Complex trauma in children and adolescents. *Psychiatric Annals*, 30(5), 390–398.

Corrigan, J.D., and Bogner, J.A. (1994). Factor structure of the agitated behavior scale. *Journal of Clinical and Experimental Neuropsychology*, 16(3), 386–392.

Craske, M., and Waikar, S.V. (1994). Panic disorder. In M. Hersen and R.T. Ammerman (Eds.), *Handbook of prescriptive treatments for adults* (pp. 135–155). New York: Springer.

Craske, M., Wittchen, U., Bogels, S., Stein, M., Andrews, G., and Lebeu, R. (2013). Severity measure for social anxiety disorder (social phobia)—Adult. Available: www.psychiatry.org/practice/dsm/dsm5/online-assessment-measures

Creed, F., and Barsky, A. (2004). A systematic review of the epidemiology of somatisation disorder and hypochondriasis. *Journal of Psychosomatic Research*, 56(4), 391–408.

Daitch, C. (2007). *Affect regulation toolbox*. New York: Norton.

deMello, M., Mari, J.D., Bacaltchuk, J., Verdeli, H., and Neugebauer, R. (2005). A systematic review of research findings on the efficacy of interpersonal therapy for depressive disorders. *European Archives of Psychiatry and Clinical Neuroscience*, 255(2), 75–82.

Desai, A.K., and Grossberg, G.T. (2001). Recognition and management of behavioral disturbances in dementia. *Primary Care Companion: Journal of Clinical Psychiatry*, 3(3), 93–109.

Dinges, D.F. (2004). Sleep debt and scientific evidence. *Sleep*, 27, 1–3.

Drake, M.E. (2016). Social (Pragmatic) Communication Disorder DSM-5 315.39. Theravive [Online]. Available: www.theravive.com/therapedia/social-(pragmatic)-communication-disorder-dsm--5-315.39-(f80.89)

Eaton, W.W., Kessler, R.C., Wittchen, H.U., and Magee, W.J. (1994). Panic and panic disorder in the U.S. *American Journal of Psychiatry*, 151, 413–420.

Edinger, J.D., Wohlgemuth, W.K., Radke, R.A., Marsh, G.R., and Quillian, R.E. (2001). Cognitive behavioral therapy for treatment of chronic primary insomnia: A randomized controlled trial. *Journal of the American Medical Association*, 289(14), 1856–1864.

Engmann, B. (2011). Bipolar affective disorder and Parkinson's disease. *Case Reports in Medicine*, 2011, Article ID 154165. Available: http://dx.doi.org/10.1155/2011/154165

Epstein, R.H. (2000, October 31). Major medical mystery: Why people avoid doctors. *The New York Times*. Available: www.nytimes.com/2000/10/31/health/major-medical-mystery-why-people-avoid-doctors.html?_r=0

Facts and Statistics. (2016). Anxiety and Depression Association of America. Available: www.adaa.org/about-adaa/press-room/facts-statistics

FDA. (2000). Drugs: Risk of drug interactions with St. John's wort. Federal Food & Drug Administration. Available: www.fda.gov/Drugs/DrugSafety/PostmarketDrug SafetyInformationforPatientsandProviders/ucm052238.htm#

FDA. (2016). Understanding antidepressant medication. U.S. Federal Food & Drug Administration. Available: www.fda.gov/forconsumers/consumerupdates/ucm095 980.htm

Fekado, A., Wooderson, S.C., Markopoulo, K., Donaldson, C., Papadopoulos, A., and Cleare, A.J. (2009). What happens to patients with treatment-resistant depression? A systematic review of medium to long term outcome studies. *Journal of Affective Disorders*, 116(1–2), 4–11.

Fleet, R.P., Marchand, A., Dupuis, G., Kaczorowski, J., and Breitman, B.D. (1998). Comparing emergency department and psychiatric setting patients with panic disorder. *Psychosomatics*, 39(6), 512–518.

Fombonne, E. (2005). Epidemiology of autistic disorder and other pervasive developmental disorders. *Journal of Clinical Psychiatry*, 36, 272–281.

Ford, J.D., Courtois, C.A., Steele, K., Hart, O.D., and Nijenhuis, E.R.S. (2005). Treatment of complex posttraumatic self-dysregulation. *Journal of Traumatic Stress*, 18(5), 437–447.

Forman, E.M., Herbert, J.D., Moitra, E., Yeomans, P.D., and Geller, P.A. (2007). A randomized controlled effectiveness trial of acceptance and commitment therapy and cognitive therapy for anxiety and depression. *Behavior Modification*, 31(6), 772–799.

Franklin, S.S., Thijs, L., Hansen, T.W., O'Brien, E., and Staessen, J.A. (2013). White-coat hypertension: New insights from recent studies. *Hypertension*, 62(6). DOI: http://dx.doi.org/10.1161/HYPERTENSIONAHA.113.01275

Gaskin, D.J., and Richards, P. (2011). The economic costs of pain in the United States. In *Institute of Medicine (US) Committee on Advancing Pain Research, Care, and Education. Relieving pain in America: A blueprint for transforming prevention, care, education, and research*. Washington, D.C.: National Academies Press (US). Appendix C. Available: www.ncbi.nlm.nih.gov/books/NBK92521/

Glick, I.D., Murray, S.R., Vasudevan, P., Marder, S.R., and Hu, R.J. (2001). Treatment with atypical antipsychotics: New indications and new populations. *Journal of Psychiatric Research*, 35(3), 187–191.

Goes, F.S., Zandi, P.P., Miao, K., McMahon, F.J., Steele, J.W., Mackinnon, D.F., Mondimore, F.M., Schweizer, B., Nurnberger, J.I., Rice, J.P., Scheftner, W., Coryell, W., Berrettini, W.H., Kelsoe, J.R., Byerley, W., Murphy, D.L., Gershon, E.S., Depaulo, J.R., McInnis, M.G., and Potash, J.B. (2007). Mood-incongruent psychotic features in bipolar disorder: Familial aggregation and suggestive linkage to 2p11-q14 and 13q21–33. *American Journal of Psychiatry*, 164(2), 236–247.

Gorman, J.M. (1996). Comorbid depression and anxiety spectrum disorders. *Depression and Anxiety*, 4(4), 160–168.

Gould, R.A., Otto, M.W., and Pollack, R.A. (1995). A meta-analysis of treatment outcome for panic disorder. *Clinical Psychology Review*, 15(8), 819–844.

Grant, B.F., Chou, S.P., Goldstein, R.B., Huang, B., Stinson, F.S., Saha, T.D., Smith, S.M., Dawson, D.A., Pulay, A.J., Pickering, R.P., and Ruan, W.J. (2008). Prevalence, correlates, disability, and comorbidity of DSM-IV Borderline Personality Disorder: Results from the Wave 2 National Epidemiologic Survey on Alcohol and Related Conditions. *Journal of Clinical Psychiatry*, 69(4), 533–545.

Grassi, G., Turri, C., Vailati, S., Dell-Oro, R., and Mancia, G. (1999). Muscle and skin sympathetic nerve traffic during the "white-coat" effect. *Circulation*. DOI: http://dx. doi.org/10.1161/01.CIR.100.3.222

Gratz, K.L., and Roemer, L. (2004). Multidimensional assessment of emotion regulation and dysregulation: Development, factor structure, and initial validation of the difficulties in Emotion Regulation Scale. *Journal of Psychopathology and Behavioral Assessment*, 26, 41–54.

Hamilton, K.E., and Dobson, K.S. (2002). Cognitive therapy of depression: Pretreatment patient predictors of outcome. *Clinical Psychology Review*, 22(6), 875–893.

Hamilton, M. (1986). The Hamilton Rating Scale for depression. In N. Sartorius and T.A. Ban (Eds.), *Assessment of depression* (pp. 143–152). New York: Springer Berlin Heidelberg.

Harvard Mental Health Letter. (2016). Managing chronic depression. Available: www.health.harvard.edu/newsletter_article/managing-chronic-depression

Health care costs associated with depressive and anxiety disorders in primary care. (1995). *American Journal of Psychiatry*, 152(3), 352–357.

Henry, C., Mitropoulou, V., New, A.S., Koenigsberg, H.W., Silverman, J., and Siever, L.J. (2001). Affective instability and impulsivity in borderline personality and bipolar II disorders: Similarities and differences. *Journal of Psychiatry Reports*, 35(6), 307–312.

Herr, K., Coyne, P.J., McCaffery, M., Manwarren, R., and Merkel, S. (2006). Pain assessment in the patient unable to self-report: Position statement with clinical practice recommendations. *Pain Management Nursing*, 7(2), 44–52.

Hettema, J.M. (2010). Genetics of depression. *Focus*, 8, 316–322.

Hettema, J.M., Prescott, C.A., Myers, J.M., Neale, M.C., and Kendler, K.S. (2005). The structure of genetic and environmental risk factors for anxiety disorders in men and women. *Archives of General Psychiatry*, 62(2), 182–189.

Hollon, S.D., Stewart, M.O., and Strunk, D. (2006). Enduring effects for cognitive behavior therapy in the treatment of depression and anxiety. *Annual Review of Psychology*, 57, 285–315.

Illness Anxiety Disorder. (2016). A.D.A.M. Adam.com. Available: http://pfizer.adam. com/content.aspx?productId=101&pid=1&gid=001236

International Association for the Study of Pain. (2015). IASP Taxonomy. IASP [Online]. Available: www.iasp-pain.org/Taxonomy

Jackson, C., Nissonson, K., and Cloitre, M. (2010). Treatment for complex PTSD. In D. Sookman and R.L. Leahy (Eds.), *Treatment resistant anxiety disorders: Resolving impasses to symptom remission*. New York: Routledge.

Jacobson, N.S., Martell, C.R., and Dimidjian, S. (2001). Behavioral activation treatment for depression: Returning to contextual roots. *Clinical Psychology: Science and Practice*, 8(3), 255–270.

Jensen, M.P., and Turk, D.C. (2014). Contributions of psychology to the understanding and treatment of people with chronic pain: Why it matters to ALL psychologists. *American Psychologist*, 69, 105–118.

Johannes, C.B., Le, T.K., Zhou, X., Johnston, J.A., and Dworkin, R.H. (2010). The prevalence of chronic pain in United States adults: Results of an Internet-based survey. *Journal of Pain*, 11(11), 1230–1239.

Julian, L.J. (2011). Measures of anxiety: State-Trait Anxiety Inventory (STAI), Beck Anxiety Inventory (BAI), and Hospital Anxiety and Depression Scale-Anxiety (HADS-A). *Arthritis Care & Research*, 63(Suppl. S11), S467–S472.

Kansagra, S.M., Rao, S.R., Sullivan, A.F., Gordon, J.A., Magoid, D.J., Kaushal, R., Camargo, C.A., and Blumenthal, D. (2008). A survey of workplace violence across 65 U.S. emergency departments. *Academy of Emergency Medicine*, 20(12), 1268–1274.

Kaplan, J.S., and Tolin, D.F. (2011, September 6). Exposure therapy for anxiety disorders. *Psychiatric Times*. Available: www.psychiatrictimes.com/anxiety/exposure-therapy-anxiety-disorders

Kelly, G., Todd, J., Simpson, G., Kremer, P., and Martin, C. (2005). The overt behaviour scale (OBS): A tool for measuring challenging behaviours following ABI in community settings. *Brain Injury*, 20(3), 309–319.

Kendler, K.S., Kuhn, J.W., Vittum, J., Prescott, C.A., and Riley, B. (2005). The interaction of stressful life events and a serotonin transporter polymorphism in the prediction of episodes of major depression: A replication. *Archives of General Psychiatry*, 62(5), 529–535.

Kendler, K.S., and Prescott, C.A. (1999). A population-based twin study of lifetime major depression in men and women. *Archives of General Psychiatry*, 56(1), 39–44.

Kendler, K.S., Thornton, L.M., and Gardner, C.O. (2000). Stressful life events and previous episodes in the etiology of major depression in women: An evaluation of the "Kindling" Hypothesis. *American Journal of Psychiatry*, 157(8), 1243–1251.

Kennedy, J., Roll, J.M., Schraudner, T., Murphy, S., and McPherson, S. (2014). Prevalence of persistent pain in the U.S. adult population: New data from the 2010 National Health Interview Survey. *Journal of Pain*, 15(10), 979–984.

Kessler, R.C., Chiu, W.T., Jin, R., Ruscio, A.M., Shear, K., and Walters, E.E. (2006). The epidemiology of panic attacks, panic disorder, and agoraphobia in the National Comorbidity Survey Replication. *Archives of General Psychiatry*, 63(4), 415–424.

Kessler, R.C., deJong, P., Shahley, P., van Loom, M.V., Wang, P.S.-E., and Wilcox, M.A. (2009). Epidemiology of depression. In I.H. Gotlieb and C.L. Hammen (Eds.), *Handbook of depression* (3rd ed., pp. 7–25). New York: Guilford.

Kroenke, K., Spitzer, R.L., Williams, J.B.W., Monahan, P.O., and Löwe, B. (2007). Anxiety disorders in primary care: Prevalence, impairment, comorbidity, and detection. *Annals of Internal Medicine*, 146, 317–325.

Kwekkeboom, K.L., and Gretarsdottir, E. (2006). Systematic review of relaxation interventions for pain. *Journal of Nursing Scholarship*, 38(3), 269–277.

Landmark, T., Romundstad, P.R., Borchgrevink, P.C., Kaasa, S., and Dale, O. (2013). Longitudinal associations between exercise and pain in the general population—The HUNT Pain Study. PloS One, 8(6). DOI: 10.1371/journal.pone.0065279

Lantz, M.S., Buchalter, E.N., and McBee, L. (1997). The Wellness Group: A novel intervention for coping with disruptive behavior in elderly nursing home residents. *The Gerontologist*, 37(4), 551–557.

Leech, G. (1983). *Principles of pragmatics*. New York: Routledge.

Leger, J.M., Moulias, R., Vellas, B., Monfort, J.C., Chapuy, P., Robert, P., Knellesen, S., and Gerard, D. (2000). Causes and consequences of elderly's agitated and aggressive behavior. *Encephale*, 26(1), 32–43.

Levinson, D.F. (2009). Genetics of major depression. In I.H. Gotleib and C.L. Hammen (Eds.), *Handbook of depression* (2nd ed., pp. 165–186). New York: Guilford.

Lewinsohn, P.M., Rohde, P., Klein, D.N., and Seeley, J.R. (1999). Natural course of adolescent major depressive disorder: I. Continuity into young adulthood. *Journal of the American Academy of Child & Adolescent Psychiatry*, 38(1), 56–63.

Lieb, K., Zanarini, M.C., Schmahl, C., Linehan, M.M., and Bohus, M. (2004). Borderline personality disorder. *The Lancet*, 364(9432), 453–461.

Linehan, M. (1993). *Cognitive behavioral treatment of Borderline Personality Disorder*. New York: Guilford.

Lupien, S.J., McEwen, B.S., Gunnar, M.R., and Heim, C. (2009). Effects of stress throughout the lifespan on the brain, behaviour and cognition. *Nature Reviews Neuroscience*, 10, 434–445.

Lyketsos, C.G., Sheppard, J.M.E., Steinberg, M., Tschanz, J.A.T., Norton, M.C., Steffens, D.C., and Breitner, J. (2001). Neuropsychiatric disturbance in Alzheimer's disease clusters into three groups: The Cache County study. *International Journal of Geriatric Psychiatry*, 16(11), 1043–1053.

Lynch, T.R., Chapman, A.L., Rosenthal, M.Z., Kuo, J.R., and Linehan, M.M. (2006). Mechanisms of change in dialectical behavior therapy: Theoretical and empirical observations. *Journal of Clinical Psychology*, 62(4), 459–480.

Mancia, G., Bombelli, M., Sweravelle, G., and Grassi, G. (2011). Diagnosis and management of patients with white-coat and masked hypertension. *Nature Reviews Cardiology*, 8, 686–693.

Mandos, L.A., Reinhold, J.A., and Rickels, K. (2009). Achieving remission in generalized anxiety disorder. *Psychiatric Times*, 26(2), 38.

Mayo Clinic. (2016a). Persistent depressive disorder. Available: www.mayoclinic.org/diseases-conditions/persistent-depressive-disorder/home/ovc-20166590

Mayo Clinic. (2016b). Illness anxiety disorder. Available: www.mayoclinic.org/diseases-conditions/illness-anxiety-disorder/basics/causes/con-20124064

Medication. (2016). Anxiety and Depression Association of America. Available: www.adaa.org/finding-help/treatment/medication

Melfi, C.A., Chawla, A.J., Croghan, T.W., Hanna, M.P., Kennedy, S., and Sredl, K. (1998). The effects of adherence to antidepressant treatment guidelines on relapse and recurrence of depression. *Archives of General Psychiatry*, 55(12), 1128–1132.

Melzack, R., and Katz, J. (2013). Pain. *Cognitive Science*, 4(1), 1–15.

Mental Health America. (2016). Depression in women. Available: www.mentalhealthamerica.net/conditions/depression-women

Merikangas, K.R., and Pine, D. (2002). Genetic and other vulnerability factors for anxiety and stress disorders. In K.L. Davis, D. Charney, J.T. Coyle, and C. Nemeroff (Eds.), *Neuropsychopharmacology: The fifth generation of progress*. New York: Lippincott, Williams and Wilkins.

Mitchell, A.J., Vaze, A., and Rao, S. (2009). Clinical diagnosis of depression in primary care: A meta-analysis. *The Lancet*, 374(9690), 609–619.

Monroe, S.M., and Reid, M.W. (2009). Life stress and major depression. *Current Directions in Psychological Science*, 18(2), 68–72.

Montgomery, S.A., Baldwin, D.S., and Riley, A. (2002). Antidepressant medications: A review of the evidence for drug-induced sexual dysfunction. *Journal of Affective Disorders*, 69(13), 119–140.

Mork, P.J., Holtermann, A., and Nilsen, T.I.L. (2013). Physical exercise, body mass index and risk of chronic arm pain: Longitudinal data on an adult population in Norway. *European Journal of Pain*, 17(8). DOI: 10.1002/j.1532.2149.2013.00298

Morin, C.M., Hauri, P.J., Espie, C.A., Spielman, A.J., Buysse, D.J., and Bootzin, R.R. (1999). Nonpharmacologic treatment of chronic insomnia: An American Academy of Sleep Medicine review. *Sleep*, 22(8), 1134–1156.

Muhle, R., Trentacoste, S.V., and Rapin, I. (2004). The genetics of autism. *Pediatrics*, 113(5), e472–e486.

Musselman, D.L., and Nemeroff, C.B. (1996). Depression and endocrine disorders: Focus on the thyroid and adrenal system. *British Journal of Psychiatry Supplement*, 30, 123–128.

National Academy of Sciences. (2006). Sleep disorders and sleep deprivation: An unmet public health problem. Available: www.nationalacademies.org/hmd/Reports/2006/Sleep-Disorders-and-Sleep-Deprivation-An-Unmet-Public-Health-Problem.aspx

National Center for Complementary and Integrative Health. (2016). St. John's wort and depression: In depth. National Institute of Health. Available: https://nccih.nih.gov/health/stjohnswort/sjw-and-depression.htm

National Center for Sleep Disorders Research. (2015). National Institutes of Health [Online]. Available: www.nhlbi.nih.gov/about/org/ncsdr/

National Highway Traffic Safety Administration. (2015). Research on drowsy driving. Available: www.nhtsa.gov/Driving+Safety/Drowsy+Driving/scope-of-the-problem

National Institute on Drug Abuse (2015). Prescription and over-the-counter medications. [Online]. Available: www.drugabuse.gov/publications/drugfacts/prescription-over-counter-medications

National Institute of Mental Health. (2016a). Major depression among adults. Available: www.nimh.nih.gov/health/statistics/prevalence/major-depression-among-adults.shtml

National Institute of Mental Health. (2016b). Bipolar disorder. Available: www.nimh.nih.gov/health/topics/bipolar-disorder/index.shtml

National Institute of Mental Health. (2016c). Psychotherapies. Available: www.nimh.nih.gov/health/topics/psychotherapies/index.shtml

National Institute of Mental Health. (2016d). Any anxiety disorder among adults. Available: www.nimh.nih.gov/health/statistics/prevalence/any-anxiety-disorder-among-adults.shtml

National Institute of Mental Health. (2016e). Anxiety disorders. Available: www.nimh.nih.gov/health/topics/anxiety-disorders/index.shtml#part_145338

National Institute of Mental Health. (2016f). Panic disorder: When fear overwhelms. Available: www.nimh.nih.gov/health/publications/panic-disorder-when-fear-overwhelms/index.shtml

National Institutes of Health. (2011). Updated NIH sleep disorders research plan seeks to promote and protect sleep health. Available: www.nhlbi.nih.gov/news/press-releases/2011/updated-nih-sleep-disorders-research-plan-seeks-to-promote-and-protect-sleep-health

National Sleep Foundation. (2016). Insomnia. National Sleep Foundation [Online]. Available: https://sleepfoundation.org/insomnia/content/treatment

Nemeroff, C.B. (1996). The corticotropin-releasing factor (CRF) hypothesis of depression: New findings and new directions. *Molecular Psychiatry*, 1, 336–342.

Ninio, A., & Snow, C. (1999). The development of pragmatics: Learning to use language appropriately. In W.C. Ritchie and T.K. Bhatia (ed.). *Handbook of child language acquisition.* pp.: 347-383. San Diego, CA: Academic Press.

Nordqvist, C. (2015). Beta-blockers: Types, side effects, interactions. *Medical News Today*, 27/07/2015. Available: www.medicalnewstoday.com/articles/173068.php

Olfson, M., Fireman, B., Weissman, M.M., Leon, A.C., Sheehan, D.V., Kathol, R.G., Hoven, C., and Farber, L. (1997). Mental disorders and disability among patients in a primary care group practice. *The American Journal of Psychiatry*, 154(12), 1734–1740.

Olfson, M., Marcus, S.C., Druss, B., Elinson, L. Tanielian, T., and Pincus, H.A. (2002). National trends in the outpatient treatment of depression. *JAMA*, 287(2), 203–209.

Oquendo, M.A., Echavarria, G., Galfalvy, H.C., Grunebaum, M.F., Burke, A., Barrera, A., Cooper, T.B., Nalone, K.M., and Mann, J.J. (2003). Lower cortisol levels in depressed patients with comorbid post-traumatic stress disorder. *Neuropsychopharmacology*, 28(3), 591–598.

Otto, M.W., and Deveney, C. (2005). Cognitive-Behavioral Therapy and the treatment of panic disorder: Efficacy and strategies. *Journal of Clinical Psychiatry*, 66(Suppl. 4), 28–32.

Ouimette, P., Wade, M., Prins, A., and Schohn, M. (2008). Identifying PTSD in primary care: Comparison of the primary care-PTSD screen (PC-PTSD) and the General Health Questionnaire-12 (GHQ). *Journal of Anxiety Disorders*, 22(2), 337–343.

PearsonClinical. (2016). Comprehensive Assessment of Spoken Language. Available: www.pearsonclinical.com/language/products/100000605/comprehensive-assessment-of-spoken-language-casl.html

Pickering, T.G. (1998). White coat hypertension: Time for action. *Circulation*, 98(18). DOI: http://dx.doi.org/10.1161/01.CIR.98.18.1834

Pickering, T.G., Coats, A., Mallion, J.M., Mancia, G., and Verdecchia, P. (1999). Task force V: White-coat hypertension. *Blood Pressure Monitoring*, 4(6), 333–342.

Placidi, F., Diomedi, M., Scalise, A., Marciani, M.G., Romini, A., and Gigli, G.L. (2000). Effects of anticonvulsants on nocturnal sleep in epilepsy. *Neurology*, 54(2) (5 Suppl. 1), 25–32.

Pollack, M.H., Simon, N.M., and Otto, M.W. (2003). *Social anxiety disorder: Research and practice.* New York: Professional Publishing Group.

Pollak, C.P., Tryon, W.W., Nagaraja, H., and Dzwonczyk, R. (2001). How accurately does wrist actigraphy identify the states of sleep and wakefulness? *Sleep*, 24(8), 956–965.

Rad, D.S. (2014). A review on adult pragmatic assessments. *Iran Journal of Neurology*, 13(3), 113–118; PMCID: PMC4240926. Department of Speech Therapy, School of Rehabilitation, Tehran University of Medical Sciences, Tehran, Iran

Ramos-Brieva, J.A., and Cordero-Villafafila, A. (1988). A new validation of the Hamilton Rating Scale for depression. *Journal of Psychiatric Research*, 22(1), 21–28.

Reuman, L., and Abramowitz, J.S. (2015). Illness anxiety disorders. In K.A. Phillips and D.J. Stein (Eds.), *Handbook of obsessive-compulsive and related disorders* (pp. 225–266). Washington, D.C.: American Psychiatric Press.

Rezaei, V., Mohammadi, M.R., Ghanizadeh, A., Sahraian, A., Tabrizi, M., Rezazadeh, S.A., and Akhondzadeh, S. (2010). Double-blind, placebo-controlled trial of risperidone plus topiramate in children with autistic disorder. *Progress in Neuro-Psychopharmacology and Biological Psychiatry*, 34(7), 1269–1272.

Richmond, J.S., Berlin, J.S., Fishkind, A.B., Holloman, G.H., Zeller, S.L., Wilson, M.P., Rifai, M.A., and Ng, A.T. (2012). Verbal de-escalation of the agitated patient: Consensus statement of the American Association for Emergency Psychiatry Project BETA De-escalation Workgroup. *Western Journal of Emergency Medicine*, 13(1), 17–25.

Rivas-Vazquez, R.A. (2003). Benzodiazepines in contemporary clinical practice. *Professional Psychology: Research and Practice*, 34(3), 324–328.

Rosenberg, R., Greening, D., and Windell, J. (2004). *Conquering postpartum depression: A proven plan for recovery*. New York: Da Capo Press.

Rowa, K., and Antony, M.M. (2008). Generalized anxiety disorder. In W.E. Craighead, D.J. Miklowitz, and L.W. Craighead (Eds.), *Psychopathology: History, diagnosis, and empirical foundations* (pp. 78–114). New York: Wiley.

Roy-Byrne, P.P. (2016). Panic disorder in adults: Epidemiology, pathogenesis, clinical manifestations, course, assessment, and diagnosis. UptoDate.com. Available: www.uptodate.com/contents/panic-disorder-in-adults-epidemiology-pathogenesis-clinical-manifestations-course-assessment-and-diagnosis

Sack, R.L., Auckley, D., Auger, R., Carskadon, M.A., Wright, K.P., Vitiello, M.V., and Zhdanova, I.V. (2007). Circadian rhythm sleep disorders: Part II, advanced sleep phase disorder, delayed sleep phase disorder, free-running disorder, and irregular sleep-wake rhythm: An American Academy of Sleep Medicine Review. *Sleep*, 30(11), 1484–1501.

Saeed, S.A., and Bruce, T.J. (1998). Seasonal affective disorders. *American Family Physician*, 57(6), 1340–1346, 1351–1352.

Salovey, P., Mayer, J.D., Goldman, S.L., Turvey, C., and Palfai, T.P. (1995). Emotional attention, clarity, and repair: Exploring emotional intelligence using the Trait Meta-Mood Scale. *Emotion, Disclosure, and Health*, 125, 154.

Sanderson, W.C. (2015). Panic disorder and agoraphobia. Academy of Cognitive Therapy [Online]. Available: www.academyofct.org/panic-disorder/

Sateia, M.J. (2014). International classification of sleep disorders (3rd ed.): Highlights and modifications. *Chest*, 146(5), 1387–1394.

Shear, K., Belnap, B.H., Mazumdar, S., Houck, P., and Rollman, B.L. (2006). Generalized anxiety disorder severity scale (GADSS): A preliminary validation study. *Depression and Anxiety*, 23(2), 77–82.

Simon, M.N. (2009). Generalized anxiety disorder and psychiatric comorbidities such as depression, bipolar disorder, and substance abuse. *Journal of Clinical Psychiatry*, 70(Suppl. 2), 10–14.

Sindrup, S.H., Otto, M., Finnerup, N.B., and Jensen, T.S. (2005). Antidepressants in the treatment of neuropathic pain. *Basic & Clinical Pharmacology & Toxicology*, 96(6), 399–409.

Smith, B.H., Elliott, A.M., Chambers, W.A., Smith, W.C., Hannaford, P.C., and Penny, K. (2001). The impact of chronic pain in the community. *Family Practice*, 18(3), 292–299.

Sokolowski, C.J., Giovannitti, J.A., and Boynes, S.G. (2010). Needle phobia: Etiology, adverse consequences, and patient management. *Dental Clinics of North America*, 54(4), 731–744.

Somers, V.K., White, D.P., Amin, R., Abraham, W.T., Costa, F., Culebras, A., Daniels, S., Floras, J.S., Hunt, C.E., Olson, L.J. and Pickering, T.G., (2008). Sleep apnea and cardiovascular disease: An American Heart Association/American College of Cardiology Foundation Scientific statement from the American Heart Association Council for High Blood Pressure Research Professional Education Committee, Council on Clinical Cardiology, Stroke Council, and Council on Cardiovascular Nursing In Collaboration With the National Heart, Lung, and Blood Institute National Center on Sleep Disorders Research (National Institutes of Health). *Journal of the American College of Cardiology*, 52(8), 686–717. DOI: 10.1016/j.jacc.2008.05.002

Spitzer, R.L., Kroenke, K., and Williams, W.J.B. (2006). A brief measure for assessing general anxiety. *Archives of Internal Medicine*, 166(10), 1092–1097.

Star, K. (2016). Medications for panic disorder. Verywell.com. Available: www.verywell.com/panic-disorder-treatment-a2-2584309

Stasiewicz, P.R., Bradizza, C.M., Gudleski, G.D., Coffey, S.F, Schlauch, R.C., Bailey, S.T., Bole, C.W., and Gulliver, S.B. (2012). The relationship of alexithymia to emotional dysregulation within an alcohol dependent treatment sample. *Addictive Behaviors*, 378(4), 469–476.

Steffens, D.C., Blazer, D.G., and Thakur, M.E. (Eds.). (2015). *The American Psychiatric Publishing textbook of geriatric psychiatry* (5th ed.). Washington, D.C.: American Psychiatric Publishing.

Stergiou, G.S., Zourbaki, A.S., Skeva, I.I., and Mountokalakis, T.D. (1998). White coat effect detected using self-monitoring of blood pressure at home: Comparison with ambulatory blood pressure. *American Journal of Hypertension*, 11(7), 820–827.

Strock, M. (2007). *Autism spectrum disorders (pervasive developmental disorders)*. Bethesda, MD: National Institute of Mental Health (NIMH).

Swineford, L.B., Thurm, A., Baird, G., Wetherby, A.M., and Swedo, S. (2014). Social (pragmatic) communication disorder: A research review of this new DSM-5 diagnostic category. *Journal of Neurodevelopmental Disorders*, 6(1), 41–46.

Tauben, D. (2015). Nonopioid medications for pain. *Physical Medicine Rehabilitation Clinics of North America*, 26(2), 219–248.

Taylor, S. (2006). *Clinician's guide to PTSD*. New York: Guilford.

The American Nurse. (2016). Workplace violence against emergency nurses remains high. American Nurses Association [Online]. Available: www.theamericannurse.org/2011/12/05/workplace-violence-against-emergency-nurses-remains-high/

Trauer, J.M., Qian, M.Y., Doyle, J.S., Rajaratnam, S.M., and Cunnington, D. (2015). Cognitive Behavioral Therapy for chronic insomnia: A systematic review and meta-analysis. *Annals of Internal Medicine*, 163(3), 191–204.

U.S. Department of Education. (2005). To assure the free appropriate public education of all Americans: Twenty-seventh annual report to Congress on the implementation of the Individuals with Disabilities Education Act. [Online]. Available: www.ed.gov/about/reports/annual/osep/2005/index.html.

U.S. Department of Health and Human Services, National Institutes of Health, National Institute of Mental Health. (2015). *Depression* (NIH Publication No. 15–3561). Bethesda, MD: U.S. Government Printing Office.

Van Houtem, C.M.H.H., Laine, M.L., Boomsma, D.I., Ligthart, L., Van Wijk, A.J., and DeJongh, A. (2013). A review and meta-analysis of the heritability of specific phobia subtypes and corresponding fears. *Journal of Anxiety Disorders*, 27(4), 379–388.

Volkow, N.D. (2014). America's addiction to opioids: Heroin and prescription drug abuse. National Institute on Drug abuse [Online]. Available: www.drugabuse.gov/

about-nida/legislative-activities/testimony-to-congress/2016/americas-addiction-to-opioids-heroin-prescription-drug-abuse

Wancata, J., Musalek, M., Alexandrowicz, R., and Krautgartner, M. (2003). Number of dementia sufferers in Europe between the years 2000 and 2050. *European Psychiatry*, 18(6), 306–313.

Warriner, E.M., and Velikonja, D. (2006). Psychiatric disturbances after traumatic brain injury: Neurobehavioral and personality changes. *Current Psychiatry Reports*, 8(1), 73–80.

WPS. (2016). Test of pragmatic language, second edition (TOPL-2). WPS [Online]. Available: www.wpspublish.com/store/p/3057/test-of-pragmatic-language-second-edition-topl-2

Wright, S., Yelland, M., Heathcote, K., and Ng, S. (2009). Fear of needles: Nature and prevalence in general practice. *Australian Family Physician*, 38(3), 172–176.

Zeidan, F., Martucci, K.T., Kraft, R.A., Gordon, N.S., McHaffie, J.G., and Coghill, R.C. (2011). Brain mechanisms supporting the modulation of pain by mindfulness meditation. *Journal of Neuroscience*, 31, 5540–5548.

Chapter 2

General Principles of Psychological Interventions

The purpose of this chapter is to outline therapeutic principles that appear to be shared by many psychotherapists. And while what constitutes psychotherapy may differ markedly among therapists and clinicians, the principles we discuss in this chapter may share a greater consensus.

One way of starting our discussion would be to refer back to Jerome Frank and the four therapeutic components he identified (Frank, 1985). Those four components are the following: (1) an emotionally charged, confiding relationship with a helping person; (2) a healing setting; (3) a rationale, conceptual scheme, or myth; and (4) a ritual. These components seem basic to the psychotherapeutic process; however, we think there are a number of other components or processes that should be discussed and which we believe are essential for the therapeutic protocols that form the basics of Part II of this book.

The principles we propose are the following:

- treatment approaches involve well-validated techniques;
- treatment is goal-directed;
- patient education and collaboration are important to success;
- treatment is structured to be limited to a maximum of twelve sessions;
- patients are taught in treatment to adjust to the presence of their symptoms rather than be focused on eliminating their symptoms;
- therapeutic interventions involve skill instruction leading to generalizability;
- treatment is graded activity that always features achievable goals;
- there is an ongoing assessment of treatment progress;
- after treatment ends, there may be booster sessions and future inoculation.

Treatment Approaches Involve Well-Validated Techniques

There are many theories of psychotherapy and many different approaches to treating clients and patients. Although almost all of these theories and approaches have adherents, some have only proven to be effective with the originator of the approach. And some have not been tested at all. Some transfer well to other clinicians; some do not. Some are grounded in sound theory; some are not so grounded.

However, it is our position that a specific approach to treatment should not be promoted unless there is scientific evidence of its effectiveness. That means that there has been research conducted with control groups to demonstrate that the approach helps people and that the approach can be taught to other therapists. Therefore, the therapeutic protocols described in Part II will be those that have been shown through research to work with certain disorders.

For the most part, the approach for nearly every disorder covered in this book will be cognitive behavioral therapy (CBT) or some variant of CBT. In contrast to some other forms of psychotherapy, CBT is a solution-focused approach to treatment that focuses on solving problems and helping clients learn new skills. The goal of CBT is to help people get better and stay better. Its effectiveness has been demonstrated in many clinical trials for a great many psychiatric disorders since it was developed by Dr. Aaron T. Beck in the 1960s (Butler et al., 2006; Nathan and Gorman, 2015).

In CBT, the client and therapist collaborate to identify and solve problems. The therapist's particular role is to help clients overcome their difficulties by changing their thinking, behavior, and emotional responses (Kuyken et al., 2008). This approach has been shown to be effective either as the sole therapeutic approach or in combination with medication in treating serious mental disorders, such as bipolar disorder and schizophrenia. Not only can CBT be used in the treatment of clients of all ages as well as with couples and families, but it has been found to be a therapy that can be adapted for treatment of conditions such as irritable bowel syndrome, chronic fatigue syndrome, hypertension, fibromyalgia, diabetes, and migraine (Hassett and Gevirtz, 2009). In addition, it has been shown effective in the conditions and disorders that commonly show up in medical settings and which are the focus of this book.

A variety of cognitive and behavioral strategies are utilized in cognitive therapy. The cognitive techniques are designed to address the patient's specific misconceptions and maladaptive assumptions. The CBT approach consists of specific methods and approaches aimed at teaching the patient the following operations: (1) to monitor his negative, automatic thoughts (cognitions); (2) to recognize the connections between cognitions, affect, and behavior; (3) to examine the evidence for and against his distorted automatic thoughts; (4) to substitute more reality-oriented interpretations for these biased cognitions; and (5) to learn to identify and alter the dysfunctional beliefs which predispose him to distort experiences (Beck et al., 1979).

Treatment is Goal-Directed

If you believe that goal-directed therapy is a principle just recently invented or proposed, think again. In fact, one of the pioneering psychoanalysts, Alfred Adler, felt that the therapeutic relationship would be enhanced by goal setting and that therapy was essentially a collaboration between therapists and clients (Dinkmeyer et al., 1987).

More recently than Alfred Adler's day (Adler lived from 1870 to 1937) is a study that demonstrates the importance of goal setting. In this 1983 study, clients who dropped out of therapy after one session were compared to those who stuck with therapy for a longer period of time (Epperson et al., 1983). One component of this research was the recognition that clients who stayed in therapy were likely to be those who believed that the therapist clearly understood their problems. A valuable aspect of goal setting is to assure clients that the therapist understands why the client has come to therapy and projects an understanding of what that client hopes to achieve.

Cormier and Cormier (1991) suggested the following purposes of goals in therapy:

1.   They provide a direction for therapy.
2.   They allow therapists to evaluate their own skills and competence.
3.   They facilitate performance because they are mentally rehearsed and call attention to useful strategies.
4.   They suggest effective therapeutic strategies and allow the therapist to choose the best strategies and resources for the client.
5.   They allow both the therapist and the client to track the client's progress.
6.   They are self-motivating, emphasizing to both therapist and client that what they are doing is worthwhile.

The basic components related to goal-directed psychotherapy include (1) selection of a meaningful goal, (2) analysis of baseline performance, (3) intervention/practice regimen, and (4) evaluation of the outcome (Kleinke, 1994).

The goal-setting process is essential because it directly influences the therapeutic approach. When the client actively participates in meaningful, purposeful, and focused goals, the therapist then can choose the most relevant treatment approach. While all, or at least most, clients come to psychotherapy with wishes for the therapeutic outcome, clients often need help transforming their wishes into treatment goals. McLellan (1997) points out that goals need to be "SMART." To McLellan that means they must be Specific, Measurable, Attainable, Realistic, and Time specified. Goal-directed approaches to psychotherapy provide an initial boost toward SMART goal setting.

An aspect of SMART goal setting (which will be discussed in more detail later in this chapter) is the therapist and client carrying on a discussion of who will do what, where, and when. Each must play a role, but how, when, and where those roles are played comes about in appropriate goal setting.

Patient Education and Collaboration Are Important to Success

Since something over 10 million Americans receive psychotherapy every year, clearly, then, psychotherapy is an established practice in the United States (Olfson et al., 2002; Wang et al., 2005). Not only is psychotherapy widely used, it is effective. That is, those people who receive psychotherapy achieve much better outcomes than they would have had they not received psychotherapy (Lambert, 2005; Wampold, 2001, 2007). In various studies, psychotherapy comes off well in treating depression, anxiety, marital dissatisfaction, substance abuse, health problems (including smoking, pain, and eating disorders) and sexual dysfunction, and with children, adolescents, adults, and elders (Chambless and Hollon, 1998).

If it is so effective, the more complex question is this: What factors make psychotherapy effective?

This is a question that arouses considerable debate. While the results of research do not produce clear findings, in general, it can be said that the psychotherapist is tremendously important to producing the benefits (Flückiger et al., 2010).

What the research strongly suggests about psychotherapists is that effective therapists are able to form a working alliance with their clients. This alliance involves the therapeutic bond and that includes the essential agreement as to the task of goal setting in therapy. The working alliance is typically described as collaborative, purposeful work on the part of the client and the therapist (Bordin, 1994).

So, collaboration is extremely important. And it is a collaborative relationship that leads to a trusting, working relationship. Initially, it is the client's trust and belief in the therapist that facilitates this alliance and the collaborative spirit becomes solidly established early in therapy.

Although building a working and trusting relationship is important, the therapist—in order to offer effective assistance—must provide an acceptable and helpful explanation for the client's distress. Most patients desire an explanation of his or her symptoms or problems. There are at least four considerations involved in providing such an explanation. First, the explanation must be psychological in nature. The client is coming for psychotherapy, therefore, the explanation must be relevant to the therapy offered. Second, the explanation must be acceptable and accepted by the client. That necessarily involves an explanation that is compatible with the clients' attitudes, values, culture, and worldview. Third, the explanation must be therapeutically useful. That is, the explanation must provide a means by which the client can overcome his or her problems. This suggests that the therapist has positive expectations that the client can overcome his or her difficulties. Fourth, the explanation does not have to be scientific or technical in order to be accepted by the client. But, the explanation not only has to be relevant to the particular patient but it must lead to purposeful collaborative work too. This involves the education part of the psychotherapeutic relationship, which is quite important to a successful outcome.

Treatment is Structured to be Limited to a Maximum of Twelve Sessions

Given the restrictions imposed by health insurance requirements, short-term therapies are now the treatments of choice for many therapists and patients. Short-term therapies may be best described as "time-limited psychotherapy." Be that as it may, research nonetheless has found increasing evidence of the effectiveness of such time-limited approaches as interpersonal psychotherapy, CBT, and solution-focused therapy.

In all of the short-term approaches, both the therapist and the client have to make active use of the time available to them. Therefore, a focus is created at a very early stage, and the client plays an active role in addressing the problems and the goals.

One of the most prominent of the time-limited therapies is CBT, which focuses on illogical thoughts as the main driver of emotional difficulties. Illogical thoughts, such as, "Everything I attempt inevitably fails," are considered a cause of emotional states like depression or hopelessness. The therapist actively collaborates with the patient to determine which faulty cognitions are currently accepted by the patient as true. The client and therapist discover these cognitions and together explore the evidence for and against them. Relief of symptoms comes from replacing unfounded cognitions with more reality-based thoughts. CBT has been shown effective in numerous research reports, particularly for depression and anxiety disorders (Butler et al., 2006).

Over the past few decades, research has fueled interest in briefer therapies. For interest, some studies found that much of the identifiable change in psychotherapy occurred within the first ten sessions (Howard et al., 1986). In addition, other research found that more sessions were not associated with better outcome than were fewer sessions.

But other practical considerations bolstered the increasing interest in time-limited therapy. One concern was related to how to make psychotherapy available to larger segments of society and at the same time meet the needs for psychological services. In order to meet the demands of therapy, economic considerations became more central. Briefer therapies almost always are less expensive. With briefer therapies more "symptomatic treatments," short-term therapy involves problem-solving strategies focused on specific treatment goals rather than focused on change of basic personality patterns or traits.

Patients Are Taught in Treatment to Adjust to the Presence of Their Symptoms Rather than be Focused on Eliminating Their Symptoms

In the paradoxical approach to treatment, it is assumed that all aspects of a person have value—even his or her symptoms (Yapko, 2003). By using paradoxical approaches, the therapist is not trying to get rid of or eliminate symptoms, instead the therapist is attempting to help the patient accept and develop experiences. Most clients work to stop or devalue anxiety, for instance, rather than accept the anxiety and develop it more fully.

It is in acceptance and commitment therapy (ACT), however, that clients are encouraged to take action without first changing or eliminating feelings. Rather than fighting the feeling attached to a behavior, ACT principles state that a person can observe himself as having the feeling but still act (Mattaini, 1997). Acceptance-based approaches (Hayes and Wilson, 1994) postulate that instead of opting for change alone, the most effective approach may be to accept and change.

ACT is one of the contemporary short-term interventions that has been used frequently in the past two decades. In the ACT approach, it is suggested that both behavior and emotion can exist simultaneously and independently. For that reason, acceptance has been described as the "missing link in traditional behavior therapy" (Jacobson and Christensen, 1996). But, ACT is part of a larger movement in the behavioral and cognitive realm, which includes the mindfulness approaches (Hayes, 2005).

Steven Hayes (1994, 2005), along with his colleagues (Hayes et al., 2006), has been credited as the founder of ACT as a contextual approach to treatment. He explores the paradoxes of context, such as separating words and actions, and distinguishing clients' sense of self from their thoughts and behavior. For example, when a person does not go to work because of anxiety related to a possible confrontation with their boss, it is encouraged that the person think about going to work while feeling anxious.

It has been suggested by Hayes that ACT is born from the behavioral school of therapy. However, Hayes sees behavior therapy as divided into three generations: traditional behaviorism, CBT, and the current "third generation" or contextual approaches to behavior (Hayes, 2005). In the third wave of behaviorism, Hayes offers as a premise that suffering is a basic characteristic of human life and is a dramatic change from traditional behaviorism and CBT because of the inclusion of acceptance and mindfulness-based interventions.

Similar to CBT, ACT is based on the belief that a client's life can be improved by overcoming negative thoughts and feelings. The main goal of ACT, though, is to help clients consistently choose to act effectively in the face of difficult or problematic cognitive or psychological events. The acronym ACT may be used to describe what takes place in therapy: accept the effects of life's hardships, choose directional values, and take action (Dewane, 2008).

While articles about ACT have been appearing in the literature for nearly three decades, only more recently has it been tested empirically. That testing suggests that it could be beneficial for a variety of populations, including sexual abuse survivors, at-risk adolescents, and patients with substance abuse or mood disorders (Wilson et al., 1996). It has also been proposed for trauma work as well as for those with phobias and obsessive behavior (Twohig et al., 2006). The use of ACT with victims of trauma seems particularly pertinent, especially for those who suffer from posttraumatic stress and are likely to benefit from being helped to accept the experience without resigning themselves to its negative consequences.

Therapeutic Interventions Involve Skill Instruction Leading to Generalizability

How do you bridge the gap between what a patient learns in therapy sessions and using that new learning in real life?

It turns out that such a question reflects a core belief of CBT. CBT believes there should be efforts to program a transfer of learning from the therapeutic environment to the world outside of the clinic or hospital. While skills are being built in the treatment sessions, there should be a step-by-step sequencing of those skills along with rehearsal of new behavior patterns that can lead to new behavior patterns in the client's real-world experiences.

In helping the client transition from what is learned in therapy to using the skills in firing-line situations, therapists must ask what obstacles the client might anticipate in using the new skills and how can he or she remember to put those new skills to work in daily life.

Treatment is Graded Activity that Always Features Achievable Goals

In order for therapy to be successful, it must involve change. We already stated that therapy should start with goal setting. But those goals must not only be realistic and achievable, but they must be measureable too. Typically, that means breaking the goals down into manageable chunks. If the client sets a goal to "Be happy," the therapist and client must figure out what exactly this equates to in measureable terms. For example, does it mean the client wants to feel more energetic? Enjoy sex again? Socialize more? Start to play the guitar again? Begin going back to the gym and engaging in more exercise? Or, does it mean she wants to sleep better?

Once there is an understanding of what the goal is, and both therapist and patient agree that it can be accomplished in a series of steps, it is time to start working to achieve those goals.

But it is often necessary to have sub-goals. Breaking each main goal into smaller, achievable sub-goals may not only make them more measurable, but it may help the client to feel optimistic about achieving each one.

In general, the following goal-setting approach is based on the methods used in CBT:

1.   identify the goal;
2.   identify the start point;
3.   specify the steps or the sub-goals;
4.   rank the steps from easiest to most difficult;
5.   get started.

The acronym SMART, mentioned earlier in this chapter, is helpful in identifying goals and steps:

Specific: The more specific the goal, the easier it is to attain. For example, if the client's goal is to be more social, the specific goal of having coffee with one friend each week is easier to check off as an accomplished goal.

Measureable: If a goal is measureable, it means it can be tracked over time. The goal of running 1 mile three times a week is measureable; "getting more exercise" is not.

Achievable: A client's goal to stop and talk with three people at work each week is much more achievable than to "Have many friends at work."

Relevant: Make sure the goal is relevant for the client's issues. Losing 25 pounds is a worthwhile goal for many people, but it would be irrelevant if the major issue for the client is to cope more effectively with chronic pain.

Timely: The goal must be important and relevant at the present time. Learning to be less depressed might be useful but may not be timely if the client's mother just died unexpectedly.

There is Ongoing Assessment of Treatment Progress

Barlow et al. (1984) highlight three key reasons why therapists should measure their clients' progress during treatment: (1) to improve treatment; (2) to help therapists become aware of effective treatment techniques; and (3) to provide accountability to themselves, their agency, and to third-party payers.

By regularly assessing change during therapy, it allows both the therapist and the patient to discuss modifying the treatment approach to better enhance positive results and to make sure there is continual progress toward the established goals.

Research has shown that tracking clients' progress can improve outcome (Lambert et al., 2003). For instance, setting aside time each week for a brief progress update would be an efficient and easily manageable way to assess client improvement or relapse regularly. Changes from the previous week could be used as a tool in the session to either investigate what worked well over the week or to make adjustments when client efforts were thwarted. However, one of the primary difficulties in utilizing written and/or scored assessments in clinical sessions is the time required to administer, score, and interpret such assessments.

After Treatment Ends, There Should Be Booster Sessions and Future Inoculation

Many patients are concerned that they will not be able to manage future psychological problems or psychosocial stressors without the aid of ongoing therapy. But, in planning for the end of treatment, the therapist and the patient can anticipate potential stressors and symptoms, and plan together as to how the client can continue to implement tools and techniques that were learned in therapy or when he or she might need to return to therapy or contact another mental health professional for additional assistance. Preparing for inevitable difficulties is empowering and encouraging for patients.

But it may be particularly encouraging for clients if they know that future booster sessions can be scheduled following the end of treatment and then whenever they might be needed. The client can be told that during a booster session, they can discuss their progress in self-management of symptoms and stressors and that they can refresh any skills previously learned in therapy.

In short, knowing that they can call at any time in the future for booster sessions for a sort of "tune-up" to help them stay on track and continue to use the skills they have learned in therapy will, in many cases, help maximize their long-term benefit from therapy.

The Therapeutic Relationship

Although the principles just explored are important to successful therapy outcomes, there is no denying that positive therapeutic outcomes are related to the therapeutic relationship.

Yalom stated a maxim that is learned by most, if not all, therapists at some point in their training. That maxim is this: It is the relationship that heals (Yalom, 1980). Hans Strupp (1982) said that the goal of the therapeutic relationship is not to impose change on the client, but to create a condition that allows change within the client to occur. And Carl Rogers (1961) said it this way: "One brief way of describing the change which has taken place in me is to say that in my early years I was asking the question, How can I treat, or cure, or change this person? Now I would phrase the question in this way: How can I provide a relationship which this person may use for his own personal growth?" (p. 32).

Research indicates that the quality of the working alliance is related to therapeutic outcome (Horvath and Symonds, 1991). A good working alliance requires a bond between therapist and client that reinforces collaboration toward agreed-upon tasks and goals (Bordin, 1979). In developing a good working alliance, the therapist is challenged to win the client's trust and to communicate to the client a feeling of competence, acceptance, and respect (Kleinke, 1994).

Other research finds strong consensus in the conclusion that the relationship is central to therapeutic change (Beitman et al., 1989; Lambert and Bergin, 1992; Safran et al., 1990). In an analysis of nine major review studies of relationship variables, Patterson (1984) concluded that the evidence in favor of the "necessity if not sufficiency" (p. 437) of positive relationship conditions was as strong as any in the field of psychology. In a comprehensive review of the literature, Orlinsky et al. (1994) looked at more than 2,300 empirical studies and concluded that the most important determinant of a positive outcome is the quality of patient participation in therapy. Further, the therapeutic relationship is a significant mediating link in the process and outcome interaction. Therapist warmth, empathy, and a positive relationship bond are most strongly associated with treatment outcome when the patient's perceptions of these qualities are considered (Lambert and Bergin, 1994; Orlinsky et al., 1994). Even in specific behavioral therapies, patients who view their therapist as warm and empathetic will be more involved in their treatment and, ultimately, have a better outcome (Holtzworth-Munroe et al., 1989; Miller et al., 1980; Williams and Chambless, 1990).

Therapists contribute to a successful relationship by engaging the patient with empathic, affirming, and collaborative interactions that incorporate the skillful application of potent interventions (Orlinsky et al., 1994). In an article in *Cognitive and Behavioral Practice*, the authors considered the importance of the therapeutic relationship in CBT (Wright and Davis, 1994). They concluded that the therapeutic relationship is an essential, interactive component of CBT. Wright and Davis (1994) stated that cognitive behavioral therapists need to be sensitive to both the general and idiosyncratic expectations of their patients, without compromising the necessary limits or boundaries of the relationship.

Helping Clients Change

As we have pointed out in this chapter, clients come to therapy with goals in mind. And these goals invariably involve change. They want to sleep better, be less depressed, cope with chronic pain, have fewer panic attacks, or be free of anxiety. Although the therapist often has to help them come up with realistic and achievable goals, the basic idea is to help them change in some way.

The process of helping clients change involves four basic principles: (1) clients must work at their own pace, (2) the client is the agent of change, (3) change requires action, and (4) change involves risks (Kleinke, 1994). But change is not easy to bring about. And, therein lies the requirement for the skill and training of the therapist.

Because clients must take risks and they must actually take some form of action, there is frequently resistance. Resistance is often defined as client behaviors that interfere with successful progress and desired changes (Kleinke, 1994). When there is too much resistance to change, noncompliance with treatment homework and tasks can lead to failure.

There are many strategies for dealing with client resistance and noncompliance and these will be explored in each chapter in Part II. However, some aspects of treatment already discussed in this chapter will facilitate better compliance and help reduce resistance. These strategies include SMART goal setting and a positive therapeutic alliance.

References

Barlow, D.H., Hayes, S.C., and Nelson-Gray, R.O. (1984). *The scientist practitioner: Research and accountability in clinical and educational settings* (Vol. 128). New York: Pergamon.

Beck, A.T., Rush, A.J., Shaw, B.F., and Emery, G. (Eds.). (1979). *Cognitive therapy of depression.* New York: Guilford.

Beitman, B.D., Goldfried, M.R., and Norcross, J.C. (1989). The movement toward integrating the psychotherapies: An overview. *American Journal of Psychiatry,* 146(2), 138–147.

Bordin, E.S. (1979). The generalizability of the psychoanalytic concept of the working alliance. *Psychotherapy: Theory, Research & Practice,* 16(3), 252.

Bordin, E.S. (1994). Theory and research on the therapeutic working alliance: New directions. In A.O. Horvath and L.S. Greenberg (Eds.), *The working alliance: Theory, research, and practice* (pp. 13–37). New York: Wiley.

Butler, A.C., Chapman, J.E., Forman, E.M., and Beck, A.T. (2006). The empirical status of cognitive-behavioral therapy: A review of meta-analyses. *Clinical Psychology Review,* 26(1), 17–31.

Chambless, D.L., and Hollon, S.D. (1998). Defining empirically supported therapies. *Journal of Consulting and Clinical Psychology,* 66(1), 7.

Cormier, W.H., and Cormier, L.S. (1991). *Interviewing strategies for helpers.* Pacific Grove, CA: Brooks/Cole Publishing.

Dewane, C. (2008). The ABCs of ACT—Acceptance and commitment therapy. *Social Work Today,* 8(5), 34.

Dinkmeyer, D.C., Dinkmeyer, D.C., Jr., and Sperry, L. (1987). *Adlerian counseling and psychotherapy.* Princeton, NC: Merrill Publishing.

Epperson, D.L., Bushway, D.J., and Warman, R.E. (1983). Client self-terminations after one counseling session: Effects of problem recognition, counselor gender, and counselor experience. *Journal of Counseling Psychology,* 30(3), 307–315.

Flückiger, C., Wüsten, G., Zinbarg, R., and Wampold, B. (2010). *Resource activation: Using clients' own strengths in psychotherapy and counseling.* Boston, MA: Hogrefe Publishing.

Frank, J.D. (1985). Therapeutic components shared by all psychotherapies. In M.J. Mahoney and A. Freeman (Eds.). *Cognition and psychotherapy.* pp: 49–79. New York: Springer.

Hassett, A.L., and Gevirtz, R.N. (2009). Nonpharmacologic treatment for fibromyalgia: Patient education, cognitive-behavioral therapy, relaxation techniques, and complementary and alternative medicine. *Rheumatic Disease Clinics of North America*, 35(2), 393–407.

Hayes, S.C. (Ed.). (1994). *Acceptance and change: Content and context in psychotherapy*. Oakland, CA: Context Press.

Hayes, S.C. (2005). *Get out of your mind and into your life: The new acceptance and commitment therapy*. Oakland, CA: New Harbinger Publications.

Hayes, S.C., Luoma, J.B., Bond, F.W., Masuda, A., and Lillis, J. (2006). Acceptance and commitment therapy: Model, processes and outcomes. *Behaviour Research and Therapy*, 44(1), 1–25.

Hayes, S.C., and Wilson, K.G. (1994). Acceptance and commitment therapy: Altering the verbal support for experiential avoidance. *The Behavior Analyst*, 17, 289–303.

Holtzworth-Munroe, A., Jacobson, N.S., DeKlyen, M., and Whisman, M.A. (1989). Relationship between behavioral marital therapy outcome and process variables. *Journal of Consulting and Clinical Psychology*, 57(5), 658.

Horvath, A.O., and Symonds, B.D. (1991). Relation between working alliance and outcome in psychotherapy: A meta-analysis. *Journal of Counseling Psychology*, 38(2), 139.

Howard, K.I., Kopta, S.M., Krause, M.S., and Orlinsky, D.E. (1986). The dose–effect relationship in psychotherapy. *American Psychologist*, 41(2), 159.

Jacobson, N.S., and Christensen, A. (1996). *Acceptance and change in couple therapy: A therapist's guide to transforming relationships*. New York: W.W. Norton & Company.

Kleinke, C.L. (1994). *Common principles of psychotherapy*. Pacific Grove, CA: Brooks/Cole Publishing.

Kuyken, W., Padesky, C.A., and Dudley, R. (2008). *Collaborative case conceptualization: Working effectively with clients in cognitive-behavioral therapy*. New York: Guilford.

Lambert, M.J. (2005). Early response in psychotherapy: Further evidence for the importance of common factors rather than "placebo effects". *Journal of Clinical Psychology*, 61(7), 855–869.

Lambert, M.J., and Bergin, A.E. (1992). Achievements and limitations of psychotherapy research. In D.K. Freedheim, H.J. Freudenberger, J.W. Kessler, S.B. Messer, D.R. Peterson, H.H. Strupp, and P.L. Wachtel (Eds.), *History of psychotherapy: A century of change* (pp. 360–390). Washington, D.C.: American Psychological Association, xxxiii, 930 pp. http://dx.doi.org/10.1037/10110–010

Lambert, M.J., Whipple, J.L., Hawkins, E.J., Vermeersch, D.A., Nielsen, S.L., and Smart, D.W. (2003). Is it time for clinicians to routinely track patient outcome? A meta-analysis. *Clinical Psychology: Science and Practice*, 10(3), 288–301.

Mattaini, M.A. (1997). *Clinical practice with individuals*. Washington, D.C.: NASW.

McLellan, D.L. (1997). Introduction to rehabilitation. In B.A. Wilson and D.L. McLellan (Eds.), *Rehabilitation studies handbook* (pp. 1–20). Cambridge, UK: Cambridge University Press.

Miller, W.R., Taylor, C.A., and West, J.C. (1980). Focused versus broad-spectrum behavior therapy for problem drinkers. *Journal of Consulting and Clinical Psychology*, 48(5), 590.

Nathan, P.E., and Gorman, J.M. (Eds.). (2015). *A guide to treatments that work*. New York: Oxford University Press.

Olfson, M., Marcus, S.C., Druss, B., Elinson, L., Tanielian, T., and Pincus, H.A. (2002). National trends in the outpatient treatment of depression. *JAMA*, 287(2), 203–209.

Orlinsky, D.E., Grawe, K., and Parks, B.K. (1994). Process and outcome in psychotherapy: Noch einmal. In A.E. Bergin and S.L. Garfield (Eds.), *Handbook of psychotherapy and behavior change* (4th ed., pp. 270–376). Oxford, UK: Wiley.

Patterson, C.H. (1984). Empathy, warmth, and genuineness in psychotherapy: A review of reviews. *Psychotherapy: Theory, Research, Practice, Training*, 21(4), 431.

Rogers, C.R. (1961). The characteristics of a helping relationship. On becoming a person: A therapist's view of psychotherapy (pp. 39–58). Boston, MA: Houghton Mifflin.

Safran, J.D., Crocker, P., McMain, S., and Murray, P. (1990). Therapeutic alliance rupture as a therapy event for empirical investigation. *Psychotherapy: Theory, Research, Practice, Training*, 27(2), 154.

Strupp, H.H. (1982). *The outcome problem in psychotherapy: Contemporary perspectives.* Washington, D.C.: American Psychological Association.

Twohig, M.P., Hayes, S.C., and Masuda, A. (2006). Increasing willingness to experience obsessions: Acceptance and commitment therapy as a treatment for obsessive-compulsive disorder. *Behavior Therapy*, 37(1), 3–13.

Wampold, B.E. (2001). Contextualizing psychotherapy as a healing practice: Culture, history, and methods. *Applied and Preventive Psychology*, 10(2), 69–86.

Wampold, B.E. (2007). Psychotherapy: The humanistic (and effective) treatment. *American Psychologist*, 62(8), 857.

Wang, P.S., Lane, M., Olfson, M., Pincus, H.A., Wells, K.B., and Kessler, R.C. (2005). Twelve-month use of mental health services in the United States: Results from the National Comorbidity Survey Replication. *Archives of General Psychiatry*, 62(6), 629–640.

Williams, K.E., and Chambless, D.L. (1990). The relationship between therapist characteristics and outcome of in vivo exposure treatment for agoraphobia. *Behavior Therapy*, 21(1), 111–116.

Wilson, K.G., Follette, V.M., Hayes, S.C., and Batten, S.V. (1996). Acceptance theory and the treatment of survivors of childhood sexual abuse. *National Center for PTSD Clinical Quarterly*, 6(2), 34–37.

Wright, J.H., and Davis, D. (1994). The therapeutic relationship in cognitive-behavioral therapy: Patient perceptions and therapist responses. *Cognitive and Behavioral Practice*, 1(1), 25–45.

Yalom, I.D. (1980). *Existential psychotherapy.* New York: Basic Books.

Yapko, M.D. (2003). *Trancework: An introduction to the practice of clinical hypnosis.* New York: Psychology Press.

Chapter 3

Evidence-Based Research for Psychological Interventions

If clinicians are sometimes confused about psychotherapy, it is no wonder. There are more than 250 different psychotherapeutic approaches and well over 10,000 books describing or discussing those competing approaches (Wampold, 2001). In addition, Wampold estimates that there are tens of thousands of books, book chapters, and articles that describe research aimed at better understanding of psychotherapy as well as to test whether the different psychotherapeutic approaches work (Wampold, 2001).

Despite the complexities of sorting through the research and trying to find relevant research and studies that may be important to a clinician looking for help with treatment, it seems especially important to discover evidence regarding treatment approaches for specific disorders or diagnoses.

In general, when meta-analyses of numerous outcomes studies are reviewed, the conclusion is that psychotherapies typically have good outcomes for clients (Grissom, 1996; Lipsey and Wilson, 1993). However, in reviewing the evidence about the effectiveness of various psychotherapeutic approaches, Wampold (2001) could only conclude that most, if not all, psychotherapies work and they all seem to work almost equally well.

Nonetheless, there has been a growing emphasis on using research to guide clinical practice, which is best exemplified by the empirically supported treatment (EST) movement. The EST movement began in 1993 with Division 12 of the American Psychological Association's (APA) Task Force on Promotion and Dissemination of Psychological Procedures (1995). The purpose of this task force, and subsequent updates and refinements (Chambless et al., 1998), was to identify and disseminate information about treatments that have been demonstrated, through solid research, to be effective treatments for specific disorders (Wampold and Bhati, 2004). Although the criteria for identifying such treatments have been modified over the years to address various concerns and to account for developments in research design, the essence of the criteria are based on the U.S. Food and Drug Administration (FDA) criteria for approving drugs.

Essentially, FDA rules for approving drugs are based on the randomized, double-blind placebo control group design (Wampold and Bhati, 2004). Drugs are typically approved by the FDA if they can be shown in a number of trials to be much better than a placebo, and placebos are designed to be indistinguishable from the active medication. Wampold and Bhati (2004) point out that the reasoning behind this approach is that the specific ingredients of the active medication should be shown to be responsible for benefits over and above psychological effects such as hope and expectation. Although the origins of this design go back to the 1950s, it was not until 1980 that such designs were required by the FDA for drug approval (Shapiro and Shapiro, 1997). While psychotherapy research uses the basic design, beginning in the 1970s, meta-analysis was popularized and began to also be used to examine the efficacy of psychotherapy (Hunt, 1997).

Evidence-Based Practice

In the 1980s and 1990s, the term "evidence-based medicine" came into use and referred to a process that involves "the conscientious, explicit, judicious use of current best evidence in making decisions about the care of individual patients" (Sackett et al., 1996, p. 71). Later, this phrase would be changed slightly to evidence-based practice (EBP) and, as noted by Eddy (2005), EBP suggests somewhat different meanings in different professional disciplines. In some professions, it might refer to normative guidelines, while in others, it means combining hard scientific evidence with clinical expertise (McKibbon, 1998). In psychology, according to the APA, EBP is the integration of the best available research with clinical expertise in light of patient characteristics, culture, and preferences (Policy Statement on Evidence-Based Practice in Psychology, 2005).

Does EBP Matter?

A motivating force behind EBP was the urge to improve the quality of health care services. The enhancement of the quality of health care services was highlighted by Wennberg and Gittelsohn (1973) and by Wennberg and associates in 2004 (Wennberg et al., 2004). In general, it seems that the emphasis is on using scarce health care dollars only on treatments of demonstrated worth. However, clinicians themselves, along with the clinics, hospitals, and agencies employing them also want to use the most effective and most powerful treatment approaches. Most psychotherapeutic approaches in the Unites States have become more short term and focused—undoubtedly due to the influence of third-party payers and managed care providers.

The Results of Empirical Research

In general, according to a review of research studies conducted by the APA, research results show that psychotherapy is effective, helps reduce the overall need for health services, and produces long-term health improvements (Recognition of Psychotherapy Effectiveness, 2012).

The general effectiveness of psychotherapy was given recognition in an APA resolution in 2012 (Recognition of Psychotherapy Effectiveness, 2012). Among the points made in this resolution were some of the following:

- The general effects of psychotherapy are found to be significant and, sometimes, large (Chorpita et al., 2011; Smith et al., 1980; Wampold, 2001). These significant effects of psychotherapy are quite constant across most diagnostic conditions.
- The results of psychotherapy, compared to psychopharmacologic treatment, tend to last longer and be less likely to require additional treatment. For example, in the treatment of depression and anxiety disorders, the clients treated with psychotherapy develop various skills they can continue to use after treatment has ended, and in some cases, clients continue to improve even after the termination of treatment (Hollon et al., 2006; Shedler, 2010).
- Clinical research studies suggest that a variety of psychotherapies are effective with children, adults, and older adults. Generally, these studies show large, positive effects for psychotherapy when compared to no treatment (Beutler, 2009; Beutler et al., 2003; Lambert and Ogles, 2004; McMain and Pos, 2007; Shedler, 2010; Thomas and Zimmer-Gembeck, 2007; Verheul and Herbrink, 2007; Wampold, 2001).
- Different forms of psychotherapy typically produce relatively similar outcomes. These findings indicate that most well-known and valid psychotherapies are about the same in effectiveness and that it is often therapist and client characteristics that affect the results (Castonguay and Beutler, 2006; Livesley, 2007; Miklowitz, 2008; Norcross, 2011).
- In many studies looking at the effectiveness of psychotherapy, clients often report that the benefits of treatment not only last but help lead to continued improvement well into the future (Abbass et al., 2006; Anderson and Lambert, 1995; de Maat et al., 2009; Grant et al., 2012; Leichsenring and Rabung, 2008; Leichsenring et al., 2004; Shedler, 2010).
- Psychotherapy research shows that psychotherapy is an effective treatment with most clients who are experiencing conditions such as depression and anxiety disorders. Clients experiencing these conditions typically attain or return to a level of functioning, following brief therapy, that is very much like the general population (Baldwin et al., 2009; Minami et al., 2009; Stiles et al., 2008; Wampold and Brown, 2005).
- There is considerable scientific evidence supporting the links between mental and physical health. A number of therapeutic approaches support the effectiveness of psychotherapy being offered within the primary health care system (Alexander et al., 2010; Felker et al., 2004; Roy-Byrne et al.,

2003). It is, in fact, seen that early mental health treatments tend to reduce overall medical expenses, simplify and provide better access to appropriate services and care, and improve patient's ability seek and find treatment.

• Significant evidence supports psychotherapy as a front-line intervention for older adults, older adults with medical illnesses, older adults who are at low income, and older adults who have co-occurring mild cognitive impairments. Also, increasing evidence has found that older adults respond well to a variety of psychotherapeutic approaches and that they respond to such approaches just as well as younger adults. Finally, many older adults prefer psychotherapy to antidepressants, and psychotherapy is an important treatment option for older adults who are taking other medications for management of chronic conditions (Alexopoulos et al., 2011; American Psychological Association, 2004; Areán, Ayalon et al., 2005; Areán, Gum et al., 2005; Areán et al., 2007; Areán et al., 2010; Arnold, 2008; Gum et al., 2007; Cuijpers et al., 2006; Kazdin et al., 2010; Kaslow et al., 2012).

Despite the APA's endorsement of psychotherapy, some authorities argue that in the clinical field, there is a gap between practice and research in psychotherapy (Beutler et al., 1995; Boisvert and Faust, 2006; Castonguay et al., 2013; Wilson et al., 2009). Psychologists and other mental health clinicians sometimes feel that research findings do not reflect their practice realities and, thus, they may not consistently use research to inform their practices (Recognition of Psychotherapy Effectiveness, 2012).

As an example of the failure of many clinicians to use research findings, surveys have demonstrated that clinicians do not typically rely on research to determine their interventions with clients (Tobin et al., 2007; Von Ranson et al., 2013). Although research may have great potential in helping clinicians, clinicians may not view rigorous research studies as relevant to their practice realities (Westen et al., 2004).

In this book, our goal is to present the research and the treatment protocols for commonly observed problems in medical settings so that clinicians do see the relevance for their practice and they have at their disposal a practical guide to inform their direct treatment of clients.

The Results of Outcome Studies of Cognitive Behavioral Therapy

The popularity of cognitive behavioral therapy (CBT) is indicated by the number of research articles devoted to CBT. Hofmann and associates (2012) identified 269 meta-analytic studies and out of that number chose 106 meta-analyses examining CBT for several problems including the following: substance use disorder, schizophrenia and other psychotic disorders, depression and dysthymia, bipolar disorder, anxiety disorders, insomnia, anger and aggression, general stress, distress due to general medical conditions, and chronic pain and fatigue. Other meta-analytic reviews examined the efficacy of CBT for various problems in children and elderly adults. Most of this does not concern us in this book, but Hoffmann et al. (2012) indicated that the strongest support for CBT was in relationship to the treatment of anxiety disorders, somatoform disorders, bulimia, anger control problems, and general stress.

Brief therapies in general, but especially CBT, have accumulated ongoing evidence of their effectiveness (Butler et al., 2006; Hudson-Allez, 1997). And, as it turns out, CBT is one of the most extensively researched forms of psychotherapy. More than 120 controlled clinical trials were added to the literature in the 8 years between 1986 and 1993 (Hollon and Beck, 1994) and this proliferation continued into 2001 (Dobson, 2009). Then, from 2001 to 2006, there were more than 325 published outcome studies on cognitive behavioral interventions as seen in a meta-analysis conducted by Butler and his colleagues (2006). This growth is due in part to the application of CBT to a wide range of disorders and problems (Butler et al., 2006; Salkovskis, 1996).

Findings of the 2006 meta-analysis (Butler et al, 2006) suggest that CBT is highly effective for adult unipolar depression, generalized anxiety disorder, panic disorders, and social phobia. It is less effective in treating anger and several chronic pain variables (i.e., pain expression behavior, activity level, social role functioning and cognitive coping and appraisal), and CBT is somewhat better than antidepressants in the treatment of adult unipolar depression (Butler et al., 2006).

Does the effect of CBT last beyond the end of treatment? Butler and his associates (2006) examined this, and their meta-analysis strongly indicated that across many disorders, the effects of CBT are maintained for significant periods beyond the termination of treatment. More importantly for the purposes of this book, evidence suggests that there is long-term effectiveness for depression, generalized anxiety, panic, and social phobia.

CBT and Common Conditions

The common conditions on which we focus in this book are reviewed in the following paragraphs in terms of the empirical evidence for using CBT to address these frequently encountered conditions and disorders.

Pain and CBT

Chronic pain is often difficult to treat because it frequently occurs alongside other symptoms such as sleep disturbance, anxiety, and depression (Attal et al., 2011). These other symptoms and disorders may increase pain severity and lead to further reductions in quality of life and physical functioning (Bair et al., 2003; Beesdo et al., 2009; Gupta et al., 2007; McCracken and Iverson, 2002).

Anxiety and sleep disturbance co-occur in up to 45 percent and 53 percent of individuals with chronic pain, respectively (Kroenke et al., 2013; Tang et al., 2007; Taylor et al., 2007). In addition, depression has been shown to be associated with increased pain severity in more than 50 percent of cases (McWilliams et al., 2004; Poole et al., 2009). Given these comorbidities, management of chronic pain can be challenging. Typically, first-line treatments for chronic pain include tricyclic antidepressants and combined serotonergic and noradrenergic antidepressants (Dworkin et al., 2010; Park and Moon, 2010), but meta-analyses suggest that only about half of patients experience clinically meaningful pain relief from pharmacological therapies (Bjordal et al., 2007; Finnerup et al., 2010; Machado et al., 2015). Furthermore, many patients discontinue pharmacological therapy due to burdensome side effects, fear of addiction, or lack of efficacy (Broekmans et al., 2010; McNicol et al., 2013). With this low efficacy of pharmacological approaches to pain management, multidimensional approaches that include both pharmacological and nonpharmacological treatments are frequently recommended to more effectively manage chronic pain and the associated comorbid conditions accompanying pain (AAPM Facts and Figures on Pain, 2013; Chou et al., 2009; Practice Guidelines for Chronic Pain Management, 2010).

CBT for chronic pain can be delivered via individual or group counseling sessions that occur over several weeks (Ehde et al., 2013). Research indicates that CBT reduces pain perception and psychological distress by improving an individual's ability to cope with their pain (Ehde et al., 2013; Kerns et al., 2011). Cognitive behavioral strategies for pain include, but are not limited to, cognitive restructuring, relaxation techniques, time- or quota-based activity pacing, and sleep hygiene. Cognitive restructuring involves identifying and reframing automatic negative thoughts, and their resulting behaviors in an effort to develop more adaptive coping thoughts and behaviors (Kerns et al., 2011). Relaxation training includes strategies such as deep breathing, progressive muscle relaxation, and visualization to reduce muscle tension and alter the perception of physical pain (Kerns et al., 2011). Activity pacing is a behavioral strategy used to help individuals schedule their activities based on time or quotas (rather than based on pain) to maximize their functionality despite persistent pain (Kerns et al., 2011). In addition, sleep hygiene refers to a variety of sleep scheduling, dietary, environmental, and activity strategies to improve sleep onset, maintenance, and quality (McCurry et al., 2007). A meta-analysis published by Morley et al. (1999) reviewed twenty-five trials in which the effectiveness of cognitive treatments for pain (excluding headache) was compared to alternative control conditions. They found that CBT was significantly superior to a waiting list on all domains measured (including pain experience, mood, etc.) with the exception of the expression of pain behavior. When CBT was compared to a heterogeneous collection of alternative treatments, it was found to be superior in reducing pain experience, increasing positive cognitive coping and appraisal, and reducing behavioral expression of pain (Butler et al., 2006).

The CBT approach to helping clients deal with pain more effectively is based on the Gate Control Theory of Pain (Melzack and Wall, 1967). According to the Gate Control Theory, descending modulation from areas in the brain that govern thought (frontal cortex), emotions (limbic system), and regulatory processes (i.e., hypothalamus) influence pain transmission in the dorsal horn of the spinal cord via neurotransmitters, endogenous opiates, and hormones such as cortisol. Moreover, as an update to the Gate Control Theory, Neuromatrix Theory (Melzack, 1999) suggests that multiple sensory, cognitive, visual, and emotional inputs may disrupt the homeostasis-regulation patterns of the brain's built-in matrix of neurons (the neuromatrix), producing a prolonged stress response (i.e., cortisol release). Due to this prolonged stress response, there may be an increase of muscle, bone, and neural tissue destruction that creates the conditions necessary for varying chronic pain conditions (Melzack, 1999). Preliminary evidence from functional magnetic resonance imaging trials suggest that CBT-induced structural changes in the prefrontal cortex may lead to the release of pain-inhibiting neurotransmitters which "gate" or block pain impulse transmission from the spinal cord to the brain (Jensen et al., 2012; Seminowicz et al., 2013). Thus, CBT-mediated descending inhibitory mechanisms result in decreased pain perception (Turk et al., 1983).

While there is strong evidence in the literature (Hoy et al., 2012) that CBT is effective for chronic pain compared with other forms of treatment, some researchers suggest that more information is needed about whether CBT's efficacy varies based on (a) the underlying pain etiology (such as cancer versus low back pain), (b) "dose" (duration of therapy in weeks and number of hours) or delivery method, and (c) additional pain-related outcomes in individuals with chronic pain (Bernardy et al., 2013; Eccleston et al., 2014; Ehde et al., 2013; Hoy et al., 2012; Macea et al., 2010).

Sleep Problems and CBT

Among the various forms of cognitive therapy for insomnia are those therapies that involve didactic focus, paradoxical intention, distraction and imagery techniques, and cognitive restructuring. In most cognitive approaches to sleep disorders, there is an attempt to alter beliefs about sleep (Sharma and Andrade, 2012). But, cognitive therapy can also address catastrophizing about the consequences of poor sleep. Overall, in cognitive approaches to sleep problems, clients are helped to reconceptualize the realities of their beliefs. By doing this, anxiety that interferes with sleep may be reduced—particularly just before bedtime (Perlis et al., 2005).

CBT for sleep disorders, such as insomnia, refers to a combination of behavioral techniques and conventional cognitive restructuring, and has evolved into a treatment approach with several components (Sharma and Andrade, 2012). Those components usually include psychoeducation, behavioral strategies, cognitive therapy, and relaxation training (Pigeon, 2010). Although pharmacotherapy has been found to be useful for acute insomnia, psychological interventions which mainly include cognitive and behavioral interventions are considered better choices for primary insomnia, chronic insomnia, and insomnia comorbid with other psychological disorders and medical conditions (Morgenthaler et al., 2006; Morin et al., 2006; Pigeon et al., 2007; Stepanski and Rybarczyk, 2006).

CBT, which often combines different behavioral and cognitive therapy techniques, has emerged as a preferred treatment for insomnia. Although some medications for insomnia may have immediate benefits, those typically have side effects that will be objectionable to many clients (Jacobs et al., 2004; Morin and Benca, 2012). Relaxation therapy for insomnia has been shown to be effective in research studies (Morin et al., 1994; Morgenthaler et al., 2006; Murtagh and Greenwood, 1995). But the single most effective treatment for chronic insomnia is stimulus control therapy, according to the American Academy of Sleep Medicine (Morgenthaler et al., 2006; Riedel et al., 1998).

Does CBT work equally well in research studies and applied settings? Studies of both found strong support for CBT (Babson et al., 2010). Many studies have demonstrated that CBT is very reliable across different measures of sleep disturbance (Malaffo and Espie, 2007), although the individual components of CBT (such as psychoeducation, behavioral strategies, cognitive therapy, and relaxation training) can be used as single-approach treatments. However, combining several components of CBT is often most effective (National Institutes of Health, 2005). Compared to pharmacological treatments, CBT is demonstrated to be effective in the short term and more effective in the long term (Morin et al., 2006; Jacobs et al., 2004; Omvik et al., 2006; Smith et al., 2002).

In summary, for the millions of people who suffer from chronic insomnia or other sleep disorders, the research suggests that CBT can help many of them get a good night's sleep. CBT works better than other approaches to treatment and CBT does not lead to side effects as does pharmacological therapies. Finally, a 2001 study by Jutta Backhaus and colleagues found that the benefits of short-term CBT had long-term effects. After therapy, the participants improved their total sleep time and sleep efficiency and reduced their negative sleep-related cognitions, and those improvements were sustained during the 3-year follow-up period (Backhaus et al., 2001).

Depression and CBT

CBT is among the most extensively tested psychotherapeutic treatments for depression. By 2000, there were more than eighty controlled research studies testing the effectiveness of CBT with depression (American Psychiatric

Association, 2000). The results of these studies show that CBT is as effective as well-administered antidepressant medications as a treatment for depression. And some meta-analytic reviews suggest that CBT is slightly better than antidepressant medications in alleviating depressive symptoms (Segal et al., 2001). Meta-analyses published since the 1980s (Cuijpers et al., 2008; Dobson, 1989; Gloaguen et al., 1998; Hollon et al., 1991; Wampold et al., 2002) have concluded that CBT has high treatment efficacy when used with depressed clients (Johnsen and Friborg, 2015).

In the original formulation for CBT in the treatment of depression, Beck (1967) theorized that it is a person's depressive mood that causes various depressive cognitions. These cognitions include seeing the self as inadequate, believing the world is not reinforcing, and viewing the future as devoid of hope. These cognitions lead to CBT encouraging depressed individuals to reflect on the contents of their cognitions, identify beliefs, and to modify any unrealistic views or beliefs. The client is then trained to practice cognitive techniques by themselves to modify their depression-causing beliefs. Beck proposes that by changing those beliefs, the depressive mood improves (Beck et al., 1979).

Some studies indicate that CBT may change brain functioning. For instance, Mayberg and her collaborators (2004) had depressed adults participate in a study during which they had fifteen to twenty sessions of CBT. The researchers used positron emission tomography (PET) to record the metabolic activity of the participants' brains at the beginning of the treatment program and again at the end. Those results were then compared to the brain activity of a similar group of patients who were treated for 6 weeks with the selective serotonin reuptake inhibitor "paroxetine" (marketed as Paxil). Comparing results of PET scans, the CBT patients showed decreased overactivity in the medial frontal cortex, an area of the brain implicated in self-monitoring and self-assessment (Mayberg et al., 2004). Those individuals who took paroxetine showed no such changes in this area of the brain, although both groups did report decreases in their depressive symptoms (Mayberg et al., 2004).

In 1989, Dobson reported the first meta-analysis on this topic and found CBT to be superior to untreated controls, wait-list, pharmacotherapy, behavior therapy, and a variety of other therapies (Dobson, 1989). Gloaguen et al. (1998), after an extensive meta-analysis on CBT with depression, found that CBT was superior when compared with waiting list or placebo controls. Gloaguen and colleagues (1998), comparing CBT to a group of miscellaneous therapies found that CBT was somewhat superior. Wampold et al. (2002), pointing out that some of the therapies in the Gloaguen et al. (1998) study's miscellaneous category did not represent comprehensive treatments for depression, further categorized these miscellaneous therapies into bona fide and non-bona fide therapies for depression. Comparing CBT to the bona fide group of therapies, Wampold and his associates found that CBT was, in fact, somewhat superior (Wampold et al., 2002).

When CBT is compared directly to psychodynamic therapy in the treatment of depression, CBT and psychodynamic treatment are nearly the same or CBT comes out ahead. For instance, in an initial study comparing CBT and psychodynamic therapy, conducted in the 1980s in the Treatment of Depression Collaborative Research Project (TDCRP), the results show CBT and interpersonal therapy to be roughly equivalent (Elkin et al., 1989). In this TDCRP study, however, CBT did not fare quite as well as interpersonal therapy or antidepressant medication among the more severely depressed patients. In another major study, done in the 1990s, Shapiro et al. (1994) compared CBT and psychodynamic therapy. Results showed, as in the previous research, that the two approaches to treatment were equally effective (Shapiro et al., 1994). However, 1 year after completing treatment, patients who had received CBT were faring better than those patients who had received psychodynamic therapy.

In the United States, antidepressant medication is the most widely used form of treatment for depression (Olfson and Klerman, 1993). When CBT was compared to antidepressant medication, however, CBT was significantly better (Gloaguen et al., 1998). Other favorable comparisons between CBT and pharmacotherapy include a 2005 study reported by DeRubeis et al. (2005). DeRubeis and his associates compared CBT with a commonly prescribed serotonin reuptake inhibitor (paroxetine). It was found that CBT was equally effective for the initial treatment of moderate to severe major depression (DeRubeis et al., 2005). However, in the community, depression treatment often combines CBT and medication. In their review, Hollon and Beck (1994) reported that the combination of CBT and pharmacotherapy has usually been associated with a small advantage over either modality alone. This is particularly true with severely depressed patients where the evidence indicates that CBT and antidepressant medication leads to significantly better outcomes (Thase et al., 1997).

Studies have also been conducted to determine which approach to the treatment of depression prevents relapse. In a meta-analysis testing the effectiveness of CBT in preventing relapse, Gloaguen et al. (1998) concluded that CBT was more likely to be associated with preventing a depression relapse. Gloaguen and colleagues found that on average, only 29.5 percent of CBT patients relapsed versus 60 percent of patients treated with antidepressants. Paykel et-al. (1999) also found that combining CBT with patients who had partial responses to pharmacotherapy were lower than for medication alone. In another study, CBT demonstrated an ongoing effect for moderate-to-severely depressed patients and CBT was shown to be just as effective as continuing patients on antidepressant medication (Hollon et al., 2005). Even patients who had withdrawn from CBT were significantly less likely to relapse during a 12-month follow-up period than patients withdrawn from medications (DeRubeis et al., 2005).

Anger and CBT

Anger is an important, but sometimes troublesome, human emotion. Anger may lead to useful discussion and productive outcomes when it is expressed in a constructive, nonhostile manner, as it may help identify problems, pinpoint concerns, and motivate positive behavior (Frost and Averill, 1982; Novaco, 1975). However, when anger is intense and bitterly displayed in hostile or aggressive ways, then it is often indicative of a major problem (Deffenbacher, 1992). Anger is often associated with various other problems, such as domestic violence, child abuse, and family conflict. Furthermore, anger and hostility frequently contribute to serious health problems, especially cardiovascular disease (Brosschot and Thayer, 1998).

The research on anger reduction has not kept pace with the research on other emotional problems, such as anxiety and depression, still studies show that CBT is an empirically supported intervention. In 1998, Beck and Fernandez reviewed fifty outcome studies on anger and found that the average CBT patient did better than 76 percent of untreated subjects in terms of anger reduction (Beck and Fernandez, 1998).

But, almost all approaches to counseling and psychotherapy have a positive effect on anger (Wampold, Lichtenberg et al., 2002). In addition to the research findings of Beck and Fernandez (1998), other studies, including Jacobson and Truax (1991), show that there is at least a moderate effect for CBT interventions for anger reduction in adults. As suggested by an accumulation of studies on CBT in the treatment of anger problems, research points to four specific CBT interventions (relaxation, cognitive, skill building, and their combinations) that are most effective in dealing with anger problems. These studies have focused predominantly on Novaco's (1975) adaptation of Meichenbaum's stress inoculation training (SIT) initially developed for the treatment of anxiety (Meichenbaum, 1975). Using a coping skills approach, SIT interventions are typically structured into three phases: cognitive preparation, skill acquisition, and application training (Kelly, 2007). During this treatment, the client is exposed to cognitive reframing, relaxation training, imagery, modeling, and role playing to enhance ability to cope with problem situations in daily life.

During SIT in the treatment of anger problems, clients start by identifying situational "triggers" which precipitate the onset of the anger response. After identifying these triggers or cues, they rehearse self-statements intended to reframe the situation and facilitate healthy responses (e.g., a healthy response might be: "Relax, it's not worth it to blow up over that insult"). The second phase of SIT requires the acquisition of relaxation skills. The cognitive self-statements can then be coupled with relaxation as the client learns to mentally and physically soothe themselves while exposed to anger triggers. Finally, in the rehearsal phase, clients are exposed to anger-provoking situations during the session utilizing imagery or role-plays. They practice the cognitive and relaxation techniques until the mental and physical responses can be achieved automatically and on cue. This basic treatment approach of SIT can be supplemented with alternative techniques such as problem-solving, conflict management, and social skills training as indicated in the social cognitive model of Lochman and Lenhart (1993).

DiGiuseppe and Tafrate (2003) performed a meta-analytic review of anger-management treatment interventions for adults. The results of their review showed that individuals who received the various anger-management interventions showed improvement with respect to anger-related concepts when compared to control groups and pretest measures. This review also found that anger treatments produced moderate to large improvements on anger self-reports, aggressive behavior measures, measures of positive non-angry behviors, cognitions, and physiological measures. According to DiGiuseppe and Tafrate's (2003) study, anger-management treatments often led to reductions in the affect of anger, reductions in aggressive behaviors, and increases in positive behaviors in response to anger-provoking situations in adults.

It has been found in other studies that anger control is aided by the usual types of skills taught in CBT—the use of relaxation techniques and social skills training. For example, when Deffenbacher et al. (1994) studied the use of social skills training and cognitive-relaxation coping skills training, those individuals receiving social skills training and coping skills training showed significant anger reduction. There were also positive changes for trait anger, general anger, and anger across situations. And anger expression also showed consistent improvement. Deffenbacher et al. (1994) found that those who were taught relaxation techniques had fewer negative expressions of anger, but it was the social skills training group that demonstrated the greatest progress in lowering day-to-day anger. In a different research project by Deffenbacher et al. (1995), it was shown that even after 15 months after CBT training, those clients reported lower trait anger, lower general anger, less anger across situations, and reduced anger-related physiological arousal. Furthermore, Deffenbacher and his associates (1995) found that CBT clients demonstrated greater calm and more controlled expression of anger than those in control groups.

In summary, research shows that the use of CBT techniques is an effective treatment approach for anger and aggression (Kellner et al., 2002; Linkh and Sonnek, 2003; Tang, 2001).

Anxiety and CBT

Cognitive and behavioral interventions are the most widely studied psycho-therapeutic interventions for addressing anxiety disorders (Olatunji et al., 2010). The effectiveness of CBT for generalized anxiety disorder was investigated in 1997 in a meta-analysis by Gould, Otto et al. (1997). The results of this meta-analysis found that CBT was found to be significantly better than wait-list or no-treatment controls, nondirective therapy, or pill placebo. Gould, Otto et al. (1997) indicated in their results that CBT and pharmacotherapy showed similar levels of improvement from pretreatment to posttreatment for anxiety disorder.

Gould and his colleagues also reported in two studies (Gould, Buckminster et al., 1997; Gould, Otto et al., 1997) that CBT treatment effects for anxiety disorder were maintained through at least 6 months following the termination of treatment. In a similar study from DeRubeis and Crits-Cristoph's (1998) review of general anxiety disorder clinical trials, it was reported that the effects of CBT persisted for more than 3, 6, and 12 months after treatment ended. In 2003, a study by Durham et al. indicated that the treatment effects of CBT were still evident 8 to 10 years after treatment. CBT has demonstrated stronger long-term effects compared to other treatments (Borkovec and Costello, 1993).

Older adults with anxiety, also, benefit from CBT (Stanley et al., 2004). Stanley and associates (2004) reported on a "new" version of CBT for anxiety disorders among older patients in primary care. This new version included such treatment components as motivation and education, relaxation skills, cognitive therapy, problem-solving-skills training, exposure exercises, and sleep-management-skills training. Results of studies related to this version of CBT with older adults suggested significant improvements in the key features of generalized anxiety disorder: worry and anxiety, depression, and quality of life. The improvements reported in the studies were maintained or enhanced over 6 to 12 month follow-ups (Stanley et al., 2004).

A number of controlled studies have reported that CBT is effective in reducing symptoms of psychopathology, and stronger effects are often reported for the treatment of anxiety disorders relative to other conditions (Olatunji et al., 2010). In a meta-analysis examining a total of sixty-five CBT and pharma-cological studies for generalized anxiety disorder, Mitte (2005) found substantial effect size for CBT compared with wait-list and psychological/pill placebo. In Mitte's findings, symptoms improved with both anxiety and depression versus psychological treatment and pill placebo (Mitte, 2005). When CBT was directly compared to pharmacotherapy, CBT was shown to be more effective.

More recently, Hunot and colleagues (2007) conducted a thorough examin-ation of the generalized anxiety disorder treatment outcome literature and found that 46 percent of patients assigned to CBT showed a positive response after treatment ended, while the positive response was only 14 percent in wait-list/treatment-as-usual groups. Hunot and colleagues also reported that those patients receiving CBT were more likely to show reductions in anxiety and depression symptoms than those undergoing analytic therapy at posttreatment and at 6 months follow-up. It was concluded that the literature suggested that CBT was more effective than non-CBT approaches in maximizing treatment gains (Hunot et al., 2007).

Siev and Chambless (2007) examined the question of the specificity of treatment effects of CBT and relaxation training for generalized anxiety disorder. Their findings indicated that there was almost equally significant change after treatment for both CBT and relaxation training. Meta-analytic investigations have also looked at the efficacy of CBT for chronic worry among patients with generalized anxiety disorder. For example, Covin and colleagues (2008) found a large effect size when comparing CBT with a control group, and they also found that positive treatment outcomes made by patients of all ages after CBT were largely maintained for up to 1 year after treatment ended.

Panic Disorder and CBT

When CBT is used to treat panic disorder, therapists typically focus on education about the nature and physiology of the panic response. In addition, CBT therapists use cognitive therapy techniques designed to modify the common client misinterpretations of panic symptoms and their consequences. In some approaches to the treatment of panic disorder by CBT clinicians, there is gradual exposure to panic-related body sensations and to situations patients have come to avoid. And some CBT approaches also include arousal-reduction techniques, such as diaphragmatic breathing or progressive muscle relaxation.

How Effective is CBT for Treating Panic Disorder?

The outcome research of Gould et al. (1995) consistently supported the use of CBT for panic disorder. Gould and his associates found that more than twenty comparative studies conducted with control groups had demonstrated the efficacy of CBT in treating panic disorder. Conducting a meta-analysis comparing CBT interventions with exposure treatments and various control conditions, Gould et al. (1995) found that those CBT treatments combining cognitive restructuring with interoceptive exposure (exercises that bring about the physical sensations of a panic attack) had the strongest effect. It was also found that CBT was better than pharmacological treatments (Gould et al., 1995). Also, CBT treatment showed almost no return of symptoms after 1 year following treatment. Oei et al. (1999) compared panic disorder patients' scores at the end of treatment and at follow-up against community norms. Oei and associates (1999) found that CBT reduced symptoms to levels near or below those found in the general population by end of treatment and these treatment gains were maintained over time.

Several meta-analyses have examined the relative efficacy of CBT for treating panic disorder. For instance, Siev and Chambless (2008) looked at the effects of CBT and relaxation training for patients with panic disorder. In five such studies, they discovered that CBT was superior on a range of outcomes (Siev and Chambless, 2008). More CBT patients (77 percent) than those who had received relaxation training (53 percent) no longer experienced panic attacks (Siev and Chambless, 2008). In general, these studies indicate that CBT is an effective treatment for panic disorder and that relaxation training, by itself, is less effective.

Mitte (2005) also examined studies of CBT used with panic disorder patients. When compared with no-treatment and placebo psychotherapy control groups, CBT showed significantly greater improvement on measures of anxiety, depression, and quality of life for such patients. Mitte (2005) concluded that a combined CBT approach (using cognitive and behavioral techniques) is a preferred treatment for panic disorder.

In summary, the research strongly suggests that CBT is the preferred method of treating panic disorder and that this approach produces consistently positive results over a relatively long period of time following the end of treatment.

Phobias and CBT

As Hood and Anthony (2012) have pointed out, given the importance of cognitions in the maintenance of specific phobias (Thorpe and Salkovskis, 1995), CBT, either alone or in combination with exposure, has been considered as a viable treatment option. Researchers and clinicians see CBT as potentially valuable in the treatment of phobias because this approach involves challenging the patient's beliefs, expectations, and/or predictions about the likelihood or consequences of harm related to encountering the feared object or situation. However, studies regarding the efficacy of CBT for specific phobias are mixed, although CBT appears to be more effective than no treatment or wait-list controls in reducing self-reported fear and avoidance (Hood and Anthony, 2012). But, it is less effective than in vivo exposure (Craske and Rowe, 1997). As a supplementary treatment, cognitive strategies may enhance the effects of exposure for some individuals, particularly in the treatment of claustrophobia (Booth and Rachman, 1992).

A review of the literature by Choy et al. (2007) and a meta-analysis by Wolitzky-Taylor et al. (2008) both concluded that the use of CBT provides little added benefit over and above exposure alone. In vivo exposure seems to be a particularly powerful form of learning in which maladaptive beliefs are modified without the need for additional or alternative strategies that directly target such beliefs. This would suggest that although CBT is very effective for other anxiety disorders, it is not the treatment of choice for specific phobias.

When CBT has been studied as a treatment for specific phobia (Craske and Rowe, 1997) either alone (Booth and Rachman, 1992; De Jongh et al., 1995; O'Donohue and Szymanski, 1993) or in combination with exposure-based treatments (Kamphuis and Telch, 2000; Koch et al., 2004), the results tend to be mixed. The addition of cognitive strategies enhances some treatment outcomes, but some research tends to favor exposure with a cognitive augmentation strategy (e.g., Kamphuis and Telch, 2000; Sloan and Telch, 2002) and some lean toward other approaches (e.g., Szymanski and O'Donahue, 1995). But, Paquette et al. (2003) did find that CBT is an effective therapy approach for reducing the symptoms of specific phobias (Antony and Swinson, 2000; Öst, 1989, 1996).

When using CBT for specific phobias, exposure to the phobia-relevant stimuli appears to be important. Exposure may be conducted either in vivo (i.e., direct confrontation with actual phobic stimuli/situations) or imaginal (i.e., imagery-based representations) (Olatunji et al., 2010). Technological advances now allow for the use of virtual reality exposures to phobic stimuli that were once difficult—or impossible—to create in the standard treatment setting.

In conclusion, it should be pointed out that while CBT remains an option for treating specific phobias, treatment outcomes are not yet convincing that CBT is the superior approach (Olatunji et al., 2010). However, the effectiveness of CBT can be enhanced with the inclusion of in vivo exposure along with other cognitive techniques.

Agitation and CBT

With increased longevity, the number of people with dementia is rising. Although dementia's core symptom is cognitive decline, agitation is common, persistent, and distressing for caregivers. Nearly half of all people with dementia have agitation symptoms every month, including 30 percent of those living at home (Ryu et al., 2005). Four-fifths of those with clinically significant symptoms remain agitated over 6 months and 20 percent of those who may not have shown agitation at first gradually develop agitation over a 2-year period (Savva et al., 2009). Not only is agitation distressing for family members and caregivers, but it is associated with a poor quality of life (Wetzels et al., 2010).

Reviews published up to 2004 did not consider whether treatments and approaches were effective only during the intervention or whether the effect lasted longer; the settings in which the intervention had been shown to be effective (e.g., in the community or in care homes); or whether the intervention reduced levels of agitation symptoms and was preventive or treated clinically significant agitation (Livingston et al., 2014).

When Livingston et al. (2014) reviewed a number of studies, they found that direct behavioral management therapies applied to patients experiencing dementia and agitation, along with specific staff education had lasting effects. However, research has not been able to pinpoint which symptoms (for instance, agitation) actually improve given different approaches to management (Livingston et al., 2014).

In past years, psychiatric medication was routinely used to treat agitation, but now tends to be discouraged since benzodiazepines and antipsychotics increase cognitive decline (Bierman et al., 2007), and antipsychotics cause excess mortality and are of limited efficacy (Maher et al., 2011).

Spector et al. (2012) reported that individuals with dementia have diminished cognitive resources, but there is evidence that they can learn and develop skills—even when somewhat cognitively impaired. This suggests that CBT, perhaps in an adapted form, could be used with adult patients with dementia. Paukert et al. (2010) developed Peaceful Mind, a CBT intervention for anxiety and dementia, finding reductions in anxiety, depression, and caregiver distress in a study with a limited number of families. This study, among others (Spector et al., 2012), suggest that CBT in people with dementia is feasible, although specific approaches to treating agitation are limited.

Brodaty and Arasaratnam (2012) reported that nonpharmacological interventions delivered by family caregivers have the potential to reduce the frequency and severity of behavioral and psychological symptoms of dementia. They pointed out that successful interventions generally lasted nine to twelve sessions tailored to the needs of the person with dementia as well as with the caregiver, and could be delivered over 3 to 6 months with periodic follow-up. Kong et al. (2009) conducted a systematic review and found that among seven types of nonpharmacological interventions available for agitation in older adults with dementia, only sensory interventions had efficacy in reducing agitation.

Cohen-Mansfield (2001) reports on various approaches using behavioral interventions. Her review of many studies indicates that a majority of the studies reported a reduction in problem behavior. She writes (2001) that most staff training programs focus on understanding inappropriate behaviors, improving verbal and nonverbal communications with persons suffering from dementia, and improving methods of addressing their needs. Cohen-Mansfield's findings suggest that repeated ongoing training is needed to affect staff behavior. As an example of programs in her report, the CARE program (Calming Aggressive Reactions in the Elderly) (Mentes and Ferrario, 1989) involved six staff-training sessions that emphasized risk factors for aggression, preventive and calming techniques, and protective intervention. Sessions utilized videotaped vignettes, discussions, and role-play, and they emphasized nonverbal communications. This program led to a decrease in staff abuse reports (Mentes and Ferrario, 1989). The NACSP (Nursing Assistant Communication Skill Program) taught nursing assistants to communicate more effectively with nursing home residents with dementia (McCallion et al., 1999). The program, which consisted of five group-training sessions and four individual conferences with nursing assistants, emphasized enhancing residents' ability to use sensory input, effective and ineffective communication styles, utilization of memory aids, and addressing residents' needs. The program resulted in a significant decrease in verbal agitation and in physically nonaggressive behaviors at the end of 3 months (McCallion et al., 1999).

Pragmatics/Social Communication Problems and CBT

The underlying assumption of CBT is that an individual's behavior is mediated by cognitive events and that a change in thinking or cognitions can lead to changes in behavior. But, how does that square with pragmatics problems, or as the new *Diagnostic and Statistical Manual of Mental Disorders, Fifth Edition* (*DSM-5*) calls it, Social Communication Disorder?

In the *DSM-5*, Social Communication Disorder is defined by a primary deficit in the social use of verbal and nonverbal communications (APA, 2013). Some of the characteristics of what was formerly called pragmatic difficulties are difficulties in using language for social purposes, in appropriately matching communication to the social context, in following rules of the communication context, in understanding nonliteral language (such as jokes and idioms), and in integrating language with nonverbal communicative behaviors (Swineford et al., 2014). As has been pointed out throughout this chapter, CBT has been shown to be a powerful therapeutic tool for things such as pain management, depression, phobias, and anxiety. However, the question is, can CBT exert an influence in improving Social Communication Disorder?

The best answer to that question is that at this point the research is scarce. As indicated earlier in this chapter, there has been research directed at comparing CBT with other forms of treatment for various disorders. And various authors have conducted meta-analyses to show the effectiveness of CBT and other therapies, especially when used with other common disorders. But, to date, there has been no research to show that CBT is a useful approach to treating patients with Social Communication Disorder.

The only caveat is that if Social Communication Disorder also involves social anxiety or social phobia, then CBT has already been examined as a treatment approach. For instance, Butler et al. (2006) has reported on two meta-analyses related to social phobia. The first was by Feske and Chambless (1995), and that review was replicated by Gould, Buckminster et al., (1997). In both reviews of the treatment literature, it was found that CBT was superior to wait-list and pharmacology placebo control groups.

Social anxiety disorder, also known as social phobia, is an anxiety disorder in which there is an excessive and unreasonable fear of social situations. Usually, an individual with this disorder is anxious and fearful about making mistakes, looking bad, or being embarrassed or humiliated in front of others. The fear may be made worse by a lack of social skills or experience in social situations. Typically, patients who experience social anxiety disorder suffer from distorted thinking, which might include false beliefs about social situations and the negative opinions of others; thus, it is fairly easy to see why CBT could be a preferred treatment for this disorder.

Summary

In summary, CBT has demonstrated across many studies to be an effective treatment for most, if not all, of the common disorders featured in this book. In Part II, we discuss and illustrate treatment approaches for each of the common conditions.

References

AAPM Facts and Figures on Pain. (2013). American Academy of Pain Medicine. Available: www.painmed.org/patientcenter/facts-on-pain/

Abbass, A., Kisely, S., and Kroenke, K. (2006). Short-term psychodynamic psychotherapy for somatic disorders: Systematic review and meta-analysis of clinical trials. *Psychotherapy and Psychosomatics*, 78, 265–274. DOI: 10.1159/000228247

Alexander, C.L., Arnkoff, D.B., and Glass, C.R. (2010). Bringing psychotherapy to primary care. *Clinical Psychology: Science and Practice*, 17, 191–214. DOI: 10.1111/j.1468 –2850.2010.01211.x

Alexopoulos, G.S., Raue, P., Kiosses, D.N., Mackin, R.S., Kanellopoulos, D., McCulloch, C., and Areán, P.S. (2011). Problem-solving therapy and supportive therapy in older adults with major depression and executive dysfunction: Effect on disability. *Archives of General Psychiatry*, 63, 33–41. DOI: 10.1001/archgenpsychiatry.2010.177

American Psychiatric Association. (2000). *Diagnostic and Statistical Manual of Mental Disorders* (4th ed.). Washington, D.C.: American Psychiatric Association Press.

American Psychological Association. (2004). Guidelines for psychological practice with older adults. *American Psychologist*, 59, 236–260.

American Psychiatric Association. (2013). *Diagnostic and statistical manual of mental disorders* (5th ed.). Washington, D.C.: American Psychiatric Association Press.

Anderson, E.M., and Lambert, M.J. (1995). Short-term dynamically oriented psychotherapy: A review and meta-analysis. *Clinical Psychology Review*, 15, 503–514. DOI: 10.1016/0272–7358(95)00027-M

Antony, M.M., and Swinson, R.P. (2000). *Phobic disorders and panic in adults: A guide to assessment and treatment*. Washington, D.C.: American Psychological Association.

Areán, P.A., Ayalon, L., Hunkeler, E.M., Tang, L., Unutzer, J., Lin, E., Harpole, L., Williams, J., and Hendrie, H. (2005). Improving depression care in older minority primary care patients. *Medical Care*, 43, 381–390. DOI: 10.1097/01.mlr.0000 156852.09920.b1

Areán, P.A., Gum, A., McCulloch, C.E., Bostrom, A., Gallagher-Thompson, D., and Thompson, L. (2005). Treatment of depression in low-income older adults. *Psychological Aging*, 20, 601–609. DOI: 10.1037/0882–7974.20.4.601

Areán, P.A., Gum, A.M., Tang, L., and Unutzer, J. (2007). Service use and outcomes among elderly persons with low incomes being treated for depression. *Psychiatric Services*, 58, 1057–1064. DOI: 10.1176/appi.ps.58.8.1057

Areán, P.A., Raue, P., Mackin, R.S., Kanellopoulos, D., McCulloch, C., and Alexopoulos, G.S. (2010). Problem-solving therapy and supportive therapy in older adults with major depression and executive dysfunction. *American Journal of Psychiatry*, 167, 1391–1398. DOI: 10.1176/appi.ajp.2010.09091327

Arnold, M. (2008). Polypharmacy and older adults: A role for psychology and psychologists. *Professional Psychology: Research and Practice*, 9(3), 283–289.

Attal, N., Lanteri-Minet, M., Laurent, B., Fermanian, J., and Bouhassira, D. (2011). The specific disease burden of neuropathic pain: Results of a French nationwide survey. *Pain*, 152(12), 2836–2843.

Babson, K.A., Feldner, M.T., and Badour, C.L. (2010). Cognitive behavioral therapy for sleep disorders. *Psychiatric Clinics of North America*, 33, 630–640.

Backhaus, J., Hohagen, F., Voderholzer, U., and Riemann, D. (2001). Long-term effectiveness of a short-term cognitive-behavioral group treatment for primary insomnia. *European Archives of Psychiatry & Clinical Neuroscience*, 251(1), 35–41.

Bair, M.J., Robinson, R.L., Katon, W., and Kroenke, K. (2003). Depression and pain comorbidity: A literature review. *Archives of Internal Medicine*, 163(20), 2433–2445.

Baldwin, S.A., Berkeljon, A., Atkins, D.C., Olsen, J.A., and Nielsen, S.L. (2009). Rates of change in naturalistic psychotherapy: Contrasting dose-effect and good-enough level models of change. *Journal of Consulting and Clinical Psychology*, 77, 203–211. DOI: 10.1037/a0015235

Beck, A. (1967). *Depression: Clinical, experimental, and theoretical aspects*. New York: Hoeber.

Beck, A.T., Rush, A.J., Shaw, B.F., and Emery, G. (1979). *Cognitive therapy of depression*. New York: Guilford.

Beck, R., and Fernandez, E. (1998). Cognitive-behavioral therapy in the treatment of anger: A meta-analysis. *Cognitive Therapy and Research*, 22(1), 63–74.

Beesdo, K., Hoyer, J., Jacobi, F., Low, N.C., Höfler, M., and Wittchen, H.U. (2009). Association between generalized anxiety levels and pain in a community sample: Evidence for diagnostic specificity. *Journal of Anxiety Disorders*, 23(5), 684–693.

Bernardy, K., Klose, P., Busch, A.J., Choy, E.H.S., and Häuser, W. (2013). Cognitive behavioural therapies for fibromyalgia. *Cochrane Database of Systematic Reviews*, Issue 9. Art. No.: CD009796. DOI: 10.1002/14651858.CD009796.pub2

Beutler, L.E. (2009). Making science matter in clinical practice: Redefining psychotherapy. *Clinical Psychology: Science and Practice*, 16, 301–317. DOI: 10.1111/j.1468-2850.2009.01168.x

Beutler, L.E., Malik, M.L, Alimohamed, S., Harwood, T.M., Talebi, H., and Nobel, S. (2003). Therapist variables. In M.J. Lambert (Ed.), *Handbook of psychotherapy and behavior change* (5th ed., pp. 227–306). New York: Wiley.

Beutler, L.E., Williams, R.E., Wakefield, P.J., and Entwistle, S.R. (1995). Bridging scientist and practitioner perspectives in clinical psychology. *American Psychologist*, 50(12), 984–994.

Bierman, E.J., Comijs, H.C., Gundy, C.M., Sonnenberg, C., Jonker, C., and Beekman, A.T. (2007). The effect of chronic benzodiazepine use on cognitive functioning in older persons: Good, bad or indifferent? *International Journal of Geriatric Psychiatry*, 22, 1194–2000.

Bjordal, J.M., Klovning, A., Ljunggren, A.E., and Slørdal, L. (2007). Short-term efficacy of pharmacotherapeutic interventions in osteoarthritic knee pain: A meta-analysis of randomised placebo-controlled trials. *European Journal of Pain*, 11(2), 125–138.

Boisvert, C.M., and Faust, D. (2006). Practicing psychologists' knowledge of general psychotherapy research findings: Implications for science-practice relations. *Professional Psychology: Research and Practice*, 37(6), 708–716.

Booth, R., and Rachman, S. (1992). The reduction of claustrophobia—I. *Behaviour Research and Therapy*, 30(3), 207–221.

Borkovec, T.D., and Costello, E. (1993). Efficacy of applied relaxation and cognitive behavioral therapy in the treatment of generalized anxiety disorder. *Journal of Consulting and Clinical Psychology*, 61, 611–619.

Brodaty, H., and Arasaratnam, C. (2012). Meta-analysis of nonpharmacological interventions for neuropsychiatric symptoms of dementia. *American Journal of Psychiatry*, 169, 946–953.

Broekmans, S., Dobbels, F., Milisen, K., Morlion, B., and Vanderschueren, S. (2010). Pharmacologic pain treatment in a multidisciplinary pain center: Do patients adhere to the prescription of the physician? *The Clinical Journal of Pain*, 26(2), 81–86.

Brosschot, J.F., and Thayer, J.F. (1998). Anger inhibition, cardiovascular recovery, and vagal functioning: A model of the link between hostility and cardiovascular disease. *Annals of Behavioral Medicine*, 20(4), 326–332.

Butler, A.C., Chapman, J.E., Forman, E.M., and Beck, A.T. (2006). The empirical status of cognitive-behavioral therapy: A review of meta-analyses. *Clinical Psychology Review*, 26(1), 17–31.

Castonguay, L.G., Barkham, M.L.W., and McAleavey, A.A. (2013). Practice-oriented research: Approaches and application. In *Bergin and Garfield's Handbook of Psychotherapy and Behavior Change* (6th ed., pp. 85–133). New York: Wiley.

Castonguay, L.G., and Beutler, L.E. (2006). *Principles of therapeutic change that work*. New York: Oxford University Press.

Chambless, D.L., Baker, M.J., Baucom, D.H., Beutler, L.E., Calhoun, K.S., and Daiuto, A. (1998). Update on empirically validated therapies, II. *The Clinical Psychologist*, 51, 3–16. DOI: 10.1037//0022–006X.66.1.53

Chorpita, B.F., Daleiden, E.L., Ebesutani, C., Young, J., Becker, K.D., Nakamura, B.J., Phillips, L., Ward, A., Lynch, R., Trent, L., Smith, R.L., Okamura, K., and Starace, N. (2011). Evidence-based treatments for children and adolescents: An updated review of indicators of efficacy and effectiveness. *Clinical Psychology: Science and Practice*, 18, 154–172. DOI: 10.1111/j.1468–2850.2011.01247.x

Chou, R., Baisden, J., Carragee, E.J., Resnick, D.K., Shaffer, W.O., and Loeser, J.D. (2009). Surgery for low back pain: A review of the evidence for an American Pain Society Clinical Practice Guideline. *Spine*, 34(10), 1094–1109.

Choy, Y., Fyer, A.J., and Lipsitz, J.D. (2007). Treatment of specific phobia in adults. *Clinical Psychology Review*, 27(3), 266–286.

Cohen-Mansfield, J. (2001). Nonpharmacologic interventions for inappropriate behaviors in dementia: A review, summary, and critique. *American Journal of Geriatric Psychiatry*, 9(4), 361–381.

Covin, R., Ouimet, A.J., Seeds, P.M., and Dozois, D.J. (2008). A meta-analysis of CBT for pathological worry among clients with GAD. *Journal of Anxiety Disorders*, 22(1), 108–116.

Craske, M.G., and Rowe, M.K. (1997). A comparison of behavioral and cognitive treatments of phobias. In G.C.L. Davis (Ed.). *Phobias—A handbook of theory, research and treatment*, (pp. 247–280). New York: Wiley.

Cuijpers, P., van Straten, A., Andersson, G., and van Oppen, P. (2008). Psychotherapy for depression in adults: A meta-analysis of comparative outcome studies. *Journal of Consulting & Clinical Psychology*, 76, 909–922. DOI: 10.1037/a0013075

Cuijpers, P., van Straten, A., and Smit, F. (2006). Psychological treatment of late-life depression: A meta-analysis of randomized clinical trials. *International Journal of Geriatric Psychiatry*, 21, 1139–1149. DOI: 10.1002/gps.1620

Deffenbacher, J.L. (1992). Trait anger: Theory, findings, and implications. *Advances in Personality Assessment*, 9, 177–201.

Deffenbacher, J.L., Oetting, E.R., Huff, M.E., and Thwaites, G.A. (1995). Fifteen-month follow-up of social skills and cognitive-relaxation approaches to general anger reduction. *Journal of Counseling Psychology*, 42(3), 400–405.

Deffenbacher, J.L., Thwaites, G.A., Wallace, T.L., and Oetting, E.R. (1994). Social skills and cognitive-relaxation approaches to general anger reduction. *Journal of Counseling Psychology*, 41(3), 386–396.

De Jongh, A.D., Muris, P., Ter Horst, G., Van Zuuren, F., Schoenmakers, N., and Makkes, P. (1995). One-session cognitive treatment of dental phobia: Preparing dental phobics for treatment by restructuring negative cognitions. *Behaviour Research and Therapy*, 33(8), 947–954.

DeRubeis, R.J., and Crits-Christoph, P. (1998). Empirically supported individual and group psychological treatments for adult mental disorders. *Journal of Consulting and Clinical Psychology*, 66(1), 37–52.

DeRubeis, R.J., Hollon, S.D., Amsterdam, J.D., Shelton, R.C., Young, P.R., Salomon, R.M., O'Reardon, J.P., Lovett, M.L., Gladis, M.M., Brown, L.L., and Gallop, R. (2005). Cognitive therapy vs medications in the treatment of moderate to severe depression. *Archives of General Psychiatry*, 62(4), 409–416.

DiGiuseppe, R., and Tafrate, R.C. (2003). Anger treatment for adults: A meta-analytic review. *Clinical Psychology: Science and Practice*, 10(1), 70–84.

Dobson, K.S. (1989). A meta-analysis of the efficacy of cognitive therapy for depression. *Journal of Consulting and Clinical Psychology*, 57(3), 414–419.

Dobson, K.S. (Ed.). (2009). *Handbook of cognitive-behavioral therapies*. New York: Guilford Press.

Durham, R.C., Chambers, J.A., Macdonald, R.R., Power, K.G., and Major, K. (2003). Does cognitive-behavioural therapy influence the long-term outcome of generalized anxiety disorder? An 8–14 year follow-up of two clinical trials. *Psychological Medicine*, 33(03), 499–509.

Dworkin, R.H., O'Connor, A.B., Audette, J., Baron, R., Gourlay, G.K., Haanpää, M.L., Kent, J.L., Krane, E.J., LeBel, A.A., Levy, R.M., Mackey, S.C., Mayer, J., Miaskowski, C., Raja, S.N., Rice, A.S.C., Schmader, K.E., Stacey, B. Stanos, S., and Wells, C.D. (2010, March). Recommendations for the pharmacological management of neuropathic pain: An overview and literature update. In *Mayo Clinic Proceedings*, 85(3), pp. S3–-S14.

Eccleston, C., Palermo, T.M., Williams, A.C.D.C., Lewandowski Holley, A., Morley, S., Fisher, E., & Law, E. (2014). Psychological therapies for the management of chronic and recurrent pain in children and adolescents. *The Cochrane Library*, May 5, (5):CD003968.

Eddy, D.M. (2005). Evidence-based medicine: A unified approach. *Health Affairs*, 24(1), 9–17.

Ehde, D.M., Kratz, A.L., Robinson, J.P., and Jensen, M.P. (2013). Chronic pain. *Multiple sclerosis rehabilitation: From impairment to participation*. New York: Taylor & Francis.

Elkin, I., Shea, M.T., Watkins, J.T., Imber, S.D., Sotsky, S.M., Collins, J.F., Glass, D.R., Pilkonis, P.A., Leber, W.R., Docherty, J.P., Fiester, S.J., and Parloff, M.B. (1989). National Institute of Mental Health treatment of depression collaborative research program: General effectiveness of treatments. *Archives of General Psychiatry*, 46(11), 971–982.

Felker, B.L., Barnes, R.F., Greenberg, D.M., Chancy, E.F., Shores, M.M., Gillespie-Gateley, L., Buike, M.K., and Morton, C.E. (2004). Preliminary outcomes from an integrated mental health primary care team. *Psychiatric Services*, 55, 442–444. DOI: 10.1176/appi.ps.55.4.442

Feske, U., and Chambless, D.L. (1995). Cognitive behavioral versus exposure only treatment for social phobia: A meta-analysis. *Behavior Therapy*, 26(4), 695–720.

Finnerup, N.B., Sindrup, S.H., and Jensen, T.S. (2010). The evidence for pharmacological treatment of neuropathic pain. *Pain*, 150(3), 573–581.

Frost, W.D., & Averill, J.R. (1982). Differences between men and women in the everyday experience of anger. In J.R. Averill (Ed.). *Anger and aggression* (pp. 281–316). New York: Springer.

Gloaguen, V., Cottraux, J., Cucherat, M., and Blackburn, I.M. (1998). A meta-analysis of the effects of cognitive therapy in depressed patients. *Journal of Affective Disorders*, 49(1), 59–72.

Gould, R.A., Buckminster, S., Pollack, M.H., and Otto, M.W. (1997). Cognitive-behavioral and pharmacological treatment for social phobia: A meta-analysis. *Clinical Psychology: Science and Practice*, 4(4), 291–306.

Gould, R.A., Otto, M.W., & Pollack, M.H. (1995). A meta-analysis of treatment outcome for panic disorder. *Clinical Psychology Review*, 15(8), 819–844.

Gould, R.A., Otto, M.W., Pollack, M.H., and Yap, L. (1997). Cognitive behavioral and pharmacological treatment of generalized anxiety disorder: A preliminary meta-analysis. *Behavior Therapy*, 28(2), 285–305.

Grant, P.M., Huh, G.A., Perivoliotis, D., Solar, N., and Beck, A.T. (2012). Randomized trial to evaluate the efficacy of cognitive therapy for low-functioning patients with schizophrenia. *Archives of General Psychiatry*, 69, 121–127. DOI: 10.1001/archgenpsychiatry.2011.129

Grissom, R.J. (1996). The magical number: Meta-analysis of the probability of superior outcome in comparisons involving therapy, placebo, and control. *Journal of Consulting and Clinical Psychology*, 64(5), 973–982.

Gum, A.M., Areán, P.A., and Bostrom, A. (2007). Low-income depressed older adults with psychiatric comorbidity. Secondary analyses of response to psychotherapy and case management. *International Journal of Geriatric Psychiatry*, 22, 124–130. DOI: 0.1002/gps.1702

Gupta, A., Silman, A.J., Ray, D., Morriss, R., Dickens, C., MacFarlane, G.J., and McBeth, J. (2007). The role of psychosocial factors in predicting the onset of chronic widespread pain: Results from a prospective population-based study. *Rheumatology*, 46(4), 666–671.

Hofmann, S.G., Asnaani, A., Vonk, I.J., Sawyer, A.T., and Fang, A. (2012). The efficacy of cognitive behavioral therapy: A review of meta-analyses. *Cognitive Therapy and Research*, 36(5), 427–440.

Hollon, S.D., and Beck, A.T. (1994). Cognitive and cognitive-behavioral therapies. In A.E. Bergin and S.L. Garfield (Eds.), *Handbook of psychotherapy and behavior change* (4th ed., pp. 428–466). Oxford, UK: Wiley.

Hollon, S.D., Jarrett, R.B., Nierenberg, A.A., Thase, M.E., Trivedi, M., and Rush, A.J. (2005). Psychotherapy and medication in the treatment of adult and geriatric depression: Which monotherapy or combined treatment? *Journal of Clinical Psychiatry*, 66(4), 455–468.

Hollon, S.D., Shelton, R.C., and Loosen, P.T. (1991). Cognitive therapy and pharmacotherapy for depression. *Journal of Consulting and Clinical Psychology*, 59(1), 88–99.

Hollon, S.D., Stewart, M.O., and Strunk, D. (2006). Enduring effects for cognitive behavior therapy in the treatment of depression and anxiety. *Annual Review of Psychology*, 57, 285–315. DOI: 10.1146/annurev.psych.57.102904.190044

Hood, H.K., and Antony, M.M. (2012). Evidence-based assessment and treatment of specific phobias in adults. In T.E. Davis, T.H. Ollendick, and L.G Öst (Eds.), *Intensive one-session treatment of specific phobias* (pp. 19–42). New York: Springer.

Hoy, D., Bain, C., Williams, G., March, L., Brooks, P., Blyth, F., Woolf, A., Vos, T., and Buchbinder, R. (2012). A systematic review of the global prevalence of low back pain. *Arthritis & Rheumatism*, 64(6), 2028–2037.

Hudson-Allez, G. (1997). *Time-limited therapy in a general practice setting: How to help within six sessions*. New York: Sage.

Hunot, V., Churchill, R., Teixeira, V., and Silva de Lima, M. (2007). Psychological therapies for generalised anxiety disorder. *Cochrane Database of Systematic Reviews*, (1).

Hunt, M. (1997). *How science takes stock: The story of meta-analysis*. New York: Russell Sage Foundation.

Jacobs, G.D., Pace-Schott, E.F., Stickgold, R., and Otto, M.W. (2004). Cognitive behavior therapy and pharmacotherapy for insomnia: A randomized controlled trial and direct comparison. *Archives of Internal Medicine*, 164, 1888–1896.

Jacobson, N.S., and Truax, P. (1991). Clinical significance: A statistical approach to defining meaningful change in psychotherapy research. *Journal of Consulting and Clinical Psychology*, 59(1), 12–19.

Jensen, K.B., Kosek, E., Wicksell, R., Kemani, M., Olsson, G., Merle, J.V., and Ingvar, M. (2012). Cognitive behavioral therapy increases pain-evoked activation of the prefrontal cortex in patients with fibromyalgia. *Pain*, 153(7), 1495–1503.

Johnsen, T.J., and Friborg, O. (2015). The effects of cognitive behavioral therapy as an anti-depressive treatment is falling: A meta-analysis. *Psychological Bulletin*, 141(4), 747–768.

Kamphuis, J.H., and Telch, M.J. (2000). Effects of distraction and guided threat reappraisal on fear reduction during exposure-based treatments for specific fears. *Behaviour Research and Therapy*, 38(12), 1163–1181.

Kaslow, N.J., Broth, M.R., Smith, C.O., and Collins, M.H. (2012). Family-based interventions for child and adolescent disorders. *Journal of Marital and Family Therapy*, 38, 82–100. DOI: 10.1111/j.1752–0606.2011.00257.x

Kazdin, A.E., Hoagwood, K., Weisz, J.R., Hood, K., Kratochwill, T.R., Vargas, L.A., and Banez, G.A. (2010). A meta-systems approach to evidence-based practice for children and adults. *American Psychologist*, 65, 85–97. DOI: 10.1037/a0017784

Kellner, M.H., Bry, B.H., and Colletti, L.A. (2002). Teaching anger management skills to students with severe emotional or behavioral disorders. *Behavioral Disorders*, 400–407.

Kelly, J.R. (2007). Mindfulness-based and cognitive-behavior therapy for anger-management: An integrated approach. *PCOM Psychology Dissertations*. Paper 68. Available: http://digitalcommons.pcom.edu/cgi/viewcontent.cgi?article=1067&context=psychology_dissertations

Kerns, R.D., Sellinger, J., and Goodin, B.R. (2011). Psychological treatment of chronic pain. *Annual Review of Clinical Psychology*, 7, 411–434.

Koch, E.I., Spates, C.R., and Himle, J.A. (2004). Comparison of behavioral and cognitive-behavioral one-session exposure treatments for small animal phobias. *Behaviour Research and Therapy*, 42(12), 1483–1504.

Kong, E.H., Evans, L.K., and Guevara, J.P. (2009). Nonpharmacological intervention for agitation in dementia: A systematic review and meta-analysis. *Aging and Mental Health*, 13, 512–520.

Kroenke, K., Outcalt, S., Krebs, E., Bair, M.J., Wu, J., Chumbler, N., and Yu, Z. (2013). Association between anxiety, health-related quality of life and functional impairment in primary care patients with chronic pain. *General Hospital Psychiatry*, 35(4), 359–365.

Lambert, J.J., and Ogles, B.M. (2004). The efficacy and effectiveness of psychotherapy. In M.J. Lambert (Ed.), *Bergin and Garfield's Handbook of psychotherapy and behavior change* (5th ed., pp. 139–193). New York: Wiley.

Leichsenring, F., and Rabung, S. (2008). Effectiveness of short-term psychodynamic psychotherapy: A meta-analysis. *Journal of the American Medical Association*, 200, 1551–1565. DOI: 10.1001/jama.300.13.1551

Leichsenring, F., Rabung, S., and Leibing, E. (2004). The efficacy of short-term psychodynamic psychotherapy in specific psychiatric disorders: A meta-analysis. *Archives of General Psychiatry*, 61, 1208–1216. DOI: 10.1001/jama.290.18.2428

Linkh, D.J., and Sonnek, S.M. (2003). An application of cognitive-behavioral anger management training in a military/occupational setting: Efficacy and demographic factors. *Military Medicine*, 168(6), 475–478.

Lipsey, M.W., and Wilson, D.B. (1993). The efficacy of psychological, educational, and behavioral treatment: Confirmation from meta-analysis. *American Psychologist*, 48(12), 1181–1209.

Livesley, W.J. (2007). An integrated approach to the treatment of personality disorder. *Journal of Mental Health*, 16, 131–148. DOI: 10.1080/09638230601182086

Livingston, G., Kelly, L., Lewis-Holmes, E., Baio, G., Morris, S., Patel, N., Omar, R.Z., Katona, C., and Cooper, C. (2014). A systematic review of the clinical effectiveness and cost-effectiveness of sensory, psychological and behavioural interventions for managing agitation in older adults with dementia. *Health Technology Assessment, No. 18.39*. Available: www.ncbi.nlm.nih.gov/books/NBK262105/

Lochman, J.E., and Lenhart, L.A. (1993). Anger coping intervention for aggressive children: Conceptual models and outcome effects. *Clinical Psychology Review*, 13(8), 785–805.

de Maat, S., de Jonghe, F., Schoevers, R., and Dekker, J. (2009). The effectiveness of long-term psychoanalytic therapy: A systematic review of empirical studies. *Harvard Review of Psychiatry*, 17, 1–23. DOI: 10.10880/16073220902742476

Macea, D.D., Gajos, K., Calil, Y.A.D., and Fregni, F. (2010). The efficacy of web-based cognitive behavioral interventions for chronic pain: A systematic review and meta-analysis. *The Journal of Pain*, 11(10), 917–929.

Machado, G.C., Maher, C.G., Ferreira, P.H., Pinheiro, M.B., Lin, C.W.C., Day, R.O., McLachlan, A.J. and Ferreira, M.L., (2015). Efficacy and safety of paracetamol for spinal pain and osteoarthritis: Systematic review and meta-analysis of randomised placebo controlled trials. *British Medical Journal*, 350, h1225.

Maher, A.R., Maglione, M., Bagley, S., Suttorp, M., Hu, J.H., Ewing, B., and Shekelle, P.G. (2011). Efficacy and comparative effectiveness of atypical antipsychotic medications for off-label uses in adults: A systematic review and meta-analysis. *Journal of the American Medical Association*, 306(12), 1359–1369.

Malaffo, M., and Espie, C.A. (2007). Current issue Minerva Psichiatrica. *Minerva Psichiatrica*, 48(3), 313–327.

Mayberg, H.S., Goldapple, K., Segal, Z., Garson, C., Lau, M., Bieling, P., and Kennedy, S., (2004). Modulation of cortical-limbic pathways in major depression: Treatment-specific effects of cognitive behavior therapy. *From the Rotman Research Institute at Baycrest Centre (Ms Goldapple and Dr Mayberg) and Department of Psychiatry, Centre for Addiction and Mental Health (Drs Segal, Lau, Bieling, Kennedy, and Mayberg and Ms Garson), University of Toronto, Toronto, Ontario. Archives of General Psychiatry*, 61(1), 34–41. DOI: 10.1001/archpsyc.61.1.34

McBride, C., Atkinson, L., Quilty, L.C., and Bagby, R.M. (2006). Attachment as moderator of treatment outcome in major depression: A randomized trial of inter-personal psychotherapy versus cognitive behavior therapy. *Journal of Consulting and Clinical Psychology*, 74, 1041–1054. DOI: 10.1037/0022–006X.74.6.1041

McCallion, P., Toseland, R.W., Lacey, D., and Banks, S. (1999). Educating nursing assistants to communicate more effectively with nursing home residents with dementia. *The Gerontologist*, 39(5), 546–558.

McCracken, L.M., and Iverson, G.L. (2002). Disrupted sleep patterns and daily function-ing in patients with chronic pain. *Pain Research and Management*, 7(2), 75–79.

McCurry, S.M., Logsdon, R.G., Teri, L., and Vitiello, M.V. (2007). Evidence-based psychological treatments for insomnia in older adults. *Psychology and Aging*, 22(1), 18–27.

McKibbon, K.A. (1998). Evidence-based practice. *Bulletin of the Medical Library Association*, 86(3), 396–401.

McMain, S., and Pos, A.E. (2007). Advances in psychotherapy of personality disorders: A research update. *Current Psychiatry Reports*, 9, 46–52. DOI: 10.1007/s11920–007–0009–7

McNicol, E.D., Midbari, A., and Eisenberg, E. (2013). Opioids for neuropathic pain. *Cochrane Database Syst Rev*, Aug 29;(8):CD006146.

McWilliams, L.A., Goodwin, R.D., and Cox, B.J. (2004). Depression and anxiety associated with three pain conditions: Results from a nationally representative sample. *Pain*, 111(1), 77–83.

Meichenbaum, D. (1975). A self-instructional approach to stress management: A pro-posal for stress inoculation training. *Stress and Anxiety*, 1, 237–263.

Melzack, R. (1999). From the gate to the neuromatrix. *Pain*, 82, S121–S126.

Melzack, R., and Wall, P.D. (1967). Pain mechanisms: A new theory. *Survey of Anesthesiology*, 11(2), 89–90.

Mentes, J.C., and Ferrario, J. (1989). Calming aggressive reactions: A preventive program. *Journal of Gerontological Nursing*, 15, 22–27.

Miklowitz, D.J. (2008). Adjunctive psychotherapy for bipolar disorder: State of the evidence. *American Journal of Psychiatry*, 165, 1408–1419. DOI: 10.1176/appi.ajp.2008.08040488

Minami, T., Davies, D., Tierney, S.C, Bettmann, J., McAward, S.M., Averill, L.A., Huebner, L.A., Weitzman, L.M., Benbrook, A.R., Serlin, R.C., and Wampold, B.E.

(2009). Preliminary evidence on the effectiveness of psychological treatments delivered at a university counseling center. *Journal of Counseling Psychology*, 56, 309–320. DOI: 10.1037/a0015398

Mitte, K. (2005). Meta-analysis of cognitive-behavioral treatments for generalized anxiety disorder: A comparison with pharmacotherapy. *Psychological Bulletin*, 131, 785–795. DOI: 10.1037/0033–2909.131.5.785

Morgenthaler, T., Kramer, M., Alessi, C., Friedman, L., Boehlecke, B., Brown, T., Coleman, J., Kapur, V., Lee-Chiong, T., Owens, J., Pancer, J., and Swick, T. (2006). Practice parameters for the psychological and behavioral treatment of insomnia: An update. An American Academy of Sleep Medicine report. *Sleep*, 29(11), 1415–1419.

Morin, C.M., and Benca, R. (2012). Chronic insomnia. *The Lancet*, 379(9821), 1129–1141.

Morin, C.M., Bootzin, R.R., Buysse, D.J., Edinger, J.D., Espie, C.A., and Lichstein, K.L. (2006). Psychological and behavioral treatment of insomnia: Update of the recent evidence (1998–2004). *Sleep*, 29(11), 1398–1414.

Morin, C.M., Culbert, J.P., and Schwartz, S.M. (1994). Nonpharmacological interventions for insomnia. *American Journal of Psychiatry*, 151(8), 1172–1180.

Morley, S., Eccleston, C., and Williams, A. (1999). Systematic review and meta-analysis of randomized controlled trials of cognitive behaviour therapy and behaviour therapy for chronic pain in adults, excluding headache. *Pain*, 80(1), 1–13.

Murtagh, D.R., and Greenwood, K.M. (1995). Identifying effective psychological treatments for insomnia: A meta-analysis. *Journal of Consulting and Clinical Psychology*, 63(1), 79–89.

National Institutes of Health. (2005). State-of-the-Science Conference. Statement on manifestations and management of chronic insomnia in adults. *NIH Consensus & State-of-the-Science Statem*, 22, 1–30.

Norcross, J.C. (Ed.). (2011). *Psychotherapy relationships that work: Evidence-based responsiveness* (2nd ed). New York: Oxford University Press.

Novaco, R.W. (1975). *Anger control: The development and evaluation of an experimental treatment*. New York: Lexington.

O'Donohue, W., and Szymanski, J. (1993). Change mechanisms in cognitive therapy of a simple phobia: Logical analysis and empirical hypothesis testing. *Journal of Rational-Emotive and Cognitive-Behavior Therapy*, 11(4), 207–222.

Oei, T.P.S., Llamas, M., and Devilley, G.J. (1999). *Behavioural and Cognitive Psychotherapy*, 27(1), 63–88.

Olatunji, B.O., Cisler, J.M., and Deacon, B.J. (2010). Efficacy of cognitive behavioral therapy for anxiety disorders: A review of meta-analytic findings. *Psychiatric Clinics of North America*, 33(1), 557–577.

Olfson, M., and Klerman, G.L. (1993). Trends in the prescription of antidepressants by office-based psychiatrists. *American Journal of Psychiatry*, 150, 571.

Omvik, S., Pallesen, S., Havik, O.E., Kvale, G., & Nordhus, I.H. (2006). Cognitive behavioral therapy vs zopiclone for treatment of chronic primary insomnia in older adults: A randomized controlled trial. *Journal of the American Medical Association*, 295(24), 2851–2858.

Öst, L.G. (1989). One-session treatment for specific phobias. *Behaviour Research and Therapy*, 27(1), 1–7.

Öst, L.G. (1996). One-session group treatment of spider phobia. *Behaviour Research and Therapy*, 34(9), 707–715.

Paquette, V., Lévesque, J., Mensour, B., Leroux, J.M., Beaudoin, G., Bourgouin, P., and Beauregard, M. (2003). Change the mind and you change the brain: Effects of cognitive-behavioral therapy on the neural correlates of spider phobia. *Neuroimage*, 18(2), 401–409.

Park, H.J., and Moon, D.E. (2010). Pharmacologic management of chronic pain. *The Korean Journal of Pain*, 23(2), 99–108.

Paukert, A.L., Calleo, J., Kraus-Schuman, C., Snow, L., Wilson, N., Petersen, N.J., Kunek, M.E., and Stanley, M.A. (2010). Peaceful mind: An open trial of cognitive-behavioral therapy for anxiety in persons with dementia. *International Psychogeriatrics*, 22(6), 1012–1021.

Paykel, E.S., Scott, J., Teasdale, J.D., Johnson, A.L., Garland, A., Moore, R., Jenaway, A., Cornwall, P.L., Hayhurst, H., Abbott, R., and Pope, M. (1999). Prevention of relapse in residual depression by cognitive therapy: A controlled trial. *Archives of General Psychiatry*, 56(9), 829–835.

Perlis, M.L., Jungquist, C., Smith, M.T., and Posner, D. (2005). *Cognitive behavioral treatment of insomnia: A session-by-session guide* (Vol. 1). New York: Springer Science & Business Media.

Pigeon, W.R. (2010). Treatment of adult insomnia with cognitive-behavioral therapy. *Journal of Clinical Psychology*, 66(11), 1148–1160.

Pigeon, W.R., Crabtree, V.M., and Scherer, M.R. (2007). The future of behavioral sleep medicine. *Journal of Clinical Sleep Medicine*, 3(1), 73–79.

Policy Statement on Evidence-Based Practice in Psychology. (2005). American Psychological Association. Available: www.apa.org/practice/guidelines/evidence-based-statement.aspx

Poole, H., White, S., Blake, C., Murphy, P., and Bramwell, R. (2009). Depression in chronic pain patients: Prevalence and measurement. *Pain Practice*, 9(3), 173–180.

Practice Guidelines for Chronic Pain Management. (2010). American Society of Anesthesiologists Task Force on Chronic Pain Management & American Society of Regional Anesthesia and Pain Medicine. Available: http://anesthesiology.pubs.asahq.org/article.aspx?articleid=1932775

Recognition of Psychotherapy Effectiveness. (2012). American Psychological Association. Available: www.apa.org/about/policy/resolution-psychotherapy.aspx

Riedel, B.W., Lichstein, K.L., Peterson, B.A., Epperson, M.T., Means, M.K., and Aguillard, R.N. (1998). A comparison of the efficacy of stimulus control for medicated and nonmedicated insomniacs. *Behavior Modification*, 22(1), 3–28.

Roy-Byrne, P.P., Sherbourne, C.D., Craske, M.G., Stein, M.B., Katon, W., Sullivan, G., Means-Christensen, A., and Bystritsky, A. (2003). Moving treatment research from clinical trials to the real world. *Psychiatric Services*, 54, 327–332. DOI: 10.1176/appi.ps.54.3.327

Ryu, S.H., Katona, C., Rive, B., and Livingston, G. (2005). Persistence of and changes in neuropsychiatric symptoms in Alzheimer disease over 6 months: The LASER–AD study. *The American Journal of Geriatric Psychiatry*, 13(11), 976–983.

Sackett, D.L., Rosenberg, W.M., Gray, J.M., Haynes, R.B., and Richardson, W.S. (1996). Evidence based medicine: What it is and what it isn't. *British Medical Journal*, 312(7023), 71–72.

Salkovskis, P.M. (Ed.). (1996). *Frontiers of cognitive therapy*. New York: Guilford Press.

Savva, G.M., Zaccai, J., Matthews, F.E., Davidson, J.E., McKeith, I., and Brayne, C. (2009). Prevalence, correlates and course of behavioural and psychological symptoms of dementia in the population. *The British Journal of Psychiatry*, 194(3), 212–219.

Segal, Z.V., Whitney, D.K., and Lam, R.W. (2001). CANMAT Depression Work Group. *Clinical Guidelines for the Treatment of Depressive Disorders*, 298–378.

Seminowicz, D.A., Shpaner, M., Keaser, M.L., Krauthamer, G.M., Mantegna, J., Dumas, J.A., Newhouse, P.A., Filippi, C.G., Keefe, F.J. and Naylor, M.R., 2013. Cognitive-behavioral therapy increases prefrontal cortex gray matter in patients with *chronic pain*. *The Journal of Pain*, 14(12), pp.1573–1584.

Shapiro, A.K., and Shapiro, E. (1997). *The powerful placebo: From ancient priest to modern physician*. Baltimore, MD: Johns Hopkins University Press.

Shapiro, D.A., Barkham, M., Rees, A., Hardy, G.E., Reynolds, S., and Startup, M. (1994). Effects of treatment duration and severity of depression on the effectiveness of cognitive-behavioral and psychodynamic-interpersonal psychotherapy. *Journal of Consulting and Clinical Psychology*, 62(3), 522–534.

Sharma, M.P., and Andrade, C. (2012). Behavioral interventions for insomnia: Theory and practice. *Indian Journal of Psychiatry*, 54(4), 359–366.

Shedler, J. (2010). The efficacy of psychodynamic psychotherapy. *American Psychologist*, 65, 98–109. DOI: 10.1037/a0018378

Siev, J., and Chambless, D.L. (2007). Specificity of treatment effects: Cognitive therapy and relaxation for generalized anxiety and panic disorders. *Journal of Consulting and Clinical Psychology*, 75(4), 513–522.

Sloan, T., and Telch, M.J. (2002). The effects of safety-seeking behavior and guided threat reappraisal on fear reduction during exposure: An experimental investigation. *Behaviour Research and Therapy*, 40(3), 235–251.

Smith, M.L., Glass, G.V., and Miller, T.I. (1980). *The benefits of psychotherapy*. Baltimore, MD: Johns Hopkins University Press.

Smith, M.T., Perlis, M.L., Park, A., Smith, M.S., Pennington, J., Giles, D.E., and Buysse, D.J. (2002). Comparative meta-analysis of pharmacotherapy and behavior therapy for persistent insomnia. *American Journal of Psychiatry*, 159(1), 5–11.

Spector, A., Orrell, M., Lattimer, M., Hoe, J., King, M., Harwood, K., Qazi, A., and Charlesworth, G. (2012). Cognitive behavioural therapy (CBT) for anxiety in people with dementia: Study protocol for a randomised controlled trial. *Trials*, 13(1), 197–206.

Stanley, M.A., Diefenbach, G.J., and Hopko, D.R. (2004). Cognitive behavioral treatment for older adults with generalized anxiety disorder: A therapist manual for primary care settings. *Behavior Modification*, 28(1), 73–117.

Stepanski, E.J., and Rybarczyk, B. (2006). Emerging research on the treatment and etiology of secondary or comorbid insomnia. *Sleep Medicine Reviews*, 10(1), 7–18.

Stiles, W.B., Barkham, M., Connell, J., and Mellor-Clark, J. (2008). Responsive regulation of treatment duration in routine practice in United Kingdom primary care settings: Replication in a larger sample. *Journal of Consulting and Clinical Psychology*, 76, 298–305. DOI: 10.1037/0022–006X.76.2.298

Swineford, L.B., Thurm, A., Baird, G., Wetherby, A.M., and Swedo, S. (2014). Social (pragmatic) communication disorder: A research review of this new DSM-5 diagnostic category. *Journal of Neurodevelopmental Disorders*, 6(1), 41–48.

Szymanski, J., & O'Donohue, W. (1995). Fear of spiders questionnaire. *Journal of Behavior Therapy and Experimental Psychiatry*, 26(1), 31–34.

Tang, M. (2001). Clinical outcome and client satisfaction of an anger management group. *Canadian Journal of Occupational Therapy*, 68, 226–228.

Tang, N.K., Wright, K.J., and Salkovskis, P.M. (2007). Prevalence and correlates of clinical insomnia co-occurring with chronic back pain. *Journal of Sleep Research*, 16(1), 85–95.

Task Force on Promotion and Dissemination of Psychological Procedures. (1995). American Psychological Association. Report of Division 12 Board. Available: www.div12.org/sites/default/files/InitialReportOfTheChamblessTaskForce.pdf

Taylor, D. J., Mallory, L.J., Lichstein, K.L., Durrence, H.H., Riedel, B.W., and Bush, A.J. (2007). Comorbidity of chronic insomnia with medical problems. *Sleep*, 30(2), 213–218.

Thase, M.E., Greenhouse, J.B., Frank, E., Reynolds, C.F., Pilkonis, P.A., Hurley, K., Grochocinski, V. and Kupfer, D.J. (1997). Treatment of major depression with psychotherapy or psychotherapy-pharmacotherapy combinations. *Archives of General Psychiatry*, 54(11), 1009–1015.

Thomas, R., and Zimmer-Gembeck, M.J. (2007). Behavioural outcomes of Parent-Child Interaction Therapy and trip P-Positive Parenting Program: A review and meta-analysis. *Journal of Abnormal Child Psychology*, 35, 475–495. DOI: 10.1007/s10802-007-9104-9

Thorpe, S.J., and Salkovskis, P.M. (1995). Phobic beliefs: Do cognitive factors play a role in specific phobias? *Behaviour Research and Therapy*, 33(7), 805–816.

Tobin, D.L., Banker, J.D., Weisberg, L., and Bowers, W. (2007). I know what you did last summer (and it was not CBT): A factor analytic model of international psychotherapeutic practice in the eating disorders. *International Journal of Eating Disorders*, 40(8), 754–757.

Turk, D.C., Meichenbaum, D., and Genest, M. (1983). *Pain and behavioral medicine: A cognitive-behavioral perspective* (Vol. 1). New York: Guilford.

Verheul, R., and Herbrink, M. (2007). The efficacy of various modalities of psychotherapy for personality disorders: A systematic review of the evidence and clinical recommendations. *International Review of Psychiatry*, 19, 25–38. DOI: 10.1080/09540260601095399

Von Ranson, K.M., Wallace, L.M., and Stevenson, A. (2013). Psychotherapies provided for eating disorders by community clinicians: Infrequent use of evidence-based treatment. *Psychotherapy Research*, 23(3), 333–343.

Wampold, B.E. (2001). *The great psychotherapy debate: Model, methods, and findings*. Mahwah, NJ: Lawrence Erlbaum Associates.

Wampold, B.E., and Bhati, K.S. (2004). Attending to the omissions: A historical examination of evidence-based practice movements. *Professional Psychology: Research and Practice*, 35(6), 563–570.

Wampold, B.E., and Brown, G.S. (2005). Estimating therapist variability: A naturalistic study of outcomes in managed care. *Journal of Consulting and Clinical Psychology*, 73, 914–923.

Wampold, B.E., Imel, Z.E., Laska, K.M., Benish, S., Miller, S.D., Flückiger, C., Del Re, A.C., Baardseth, T.P., and Budge, S. (2010). Determining what works in the treatment of PTSD. *Clinical Psychology Review*, 30, 923–933.

Wampold, B.E., Lichtenberg, J.W., and Waehler, C.A. (2002). Principles of empirically supported interventions in counseling psychology. *The Counseling Psychologist*, 30(2), 197–217.

Wampold, B.E., Minami, T., Baskin, T.W., and Tierney, S.C. (2002). A meta-(re)analysis of the effects of cognitive therapy versus "other therapies" for depression. *Journal of Affective Disorders*, 68, 159–165.

Wennberg, J.E., Fisher, E.S., Stukel, T.A., Skinner, J.S., Sharp, S.M., and Bronner, K.K. (2004). Use of hospitals, physician visits, and hospice care during last six months of life among cohorts loyal to highly respected hospitals in the United States. *British Medical Journal*, 328(7440), 607.

Wennberg, J.E., and Gittelsohn, A.M. (1973, December). *Small area variations in health care delivery*. Washington, D.C.: American Association for the Advancement of Science.

Westen, D., Novotny, C.M., and Thompson-Brenner, H. (2004). The empirical status of empirically supported psychotherapies: Assumptions, findings, and reporting in controlled clinical trials. *Psychological Bulletin*, 130(4), 631–663.

Wetzels, R.B., Zuidema, S.U., de Jonghe, J.F.M., Verhey, F.R.J., and Koopmans, R.T.C.M. (2010). Determinants of quality of life in nursing home residents with dementia. *Dementia and Geriatric Cognitive Disorders*, 29, 189–197.

Wilson, J.L., Armoutliev, E., Yakunina, E., and Werth, L.L., Jr. (2009). Practicing psychologists' reflections on evidence-based practice in psychology. *Professional Psychology: Research and Practice*, 40(4), 403–409.

Wolitzky-Taylor, K.B., Horowitz, J.D., Powers, M.B., and Telch, M.J. (2008). Psychological approaches in the treatment of specific phobias: A meta-analysis. *Clinical Psychology Review*, 28(6), 1021–1037.

Part II

Treatment Interventions for Symptoms

Section One
Physical Symptoms

Chapter 4

Pain Protocol

Cognitive behavioral intervention for chronic pain is focused on pain adaptation. That is, successful treatment will reduce pain distress, improve coping, and increase daily functional ability. This process is done through a combination of pain education, movement exposure, and cognitive reframing.

It is important for the clinician to emphasize that treatment will not cure the patient's pain. Most often, pain patients have tried many solutions to eliminate pain prior to their arrival in the consulting room; consequently, this therapy should not be another treatment chapter dedicated to pain eradication. Pain patients have often had far too many failures when this has been the goal. Instead, treatment is grounded on the assumption that the patient's pain will remain present the entire time. The patient will learn skills to turn down the pain, so that the pain will bother them less and they can do more of the things that matter to them.

The treatment program is composed of ten sessions. The first segment of treatment focuses on the patient's pain narrative, collaborative goal setting, and pain education. The second segment initiates core movement exposure. The third segment addresses cognitive distortions in pain and fear. The final sessions focus on sleep behaviors associated with pain, and skill inoculation for future flare ups of pain.

Session One: The Pain Story

Agenda

1. Discuss pain adjustment goal.
2. Complete interview.
3. Administer psychometric baseline/tracking measures.
4. Establish SMART goals.

Materials

Psychometric assessment is included in the first session, as it is in all sessions. The purpose of ongoing evaluation of pain is to provide the clinician with information about a client's level of pain distress, quality of life, and pain fluctuation. It is important for the clinician to explain to the patient that the brief assessment will be done weekly so that both the patient and the clinician can see how well the treatment is (or is not) working. The assessment information is used as a compliment to what the patient reports. The baseline assessment should include the following:

- *Subjective Units of Distress Scale (SUDS)*: This is a scale for measuring the subjective intensity of distress currently being experienced by the patient. This scale can be found on the Internet, for instance at: http://at-ease. dva.gov.au/professionals/files/2012/12/SUDS.pdf
- *Pain Interference Scale*: A short self-report instrument. A version is available at: https://cde.drugabuse.gov/sites/nida_cde/files/PROMIS%20Adult %20ShortForm%20v1.0%20Pain%20Interference%206b.pdf
- *Pain Catastrophizing Scale*: A brief self-report measure. It can be found at: www.worksafe.vic.gov.au/__data/assets/pdf_file/0018/10953/pain_ catastrophizing_scale.pdf

Weekly assessment after that should focus on just the SUDS and Pain Catastrophizing Scale (PCS), or Thomas-Kilmann Conflict Mode Instrument (TKI).

Protocol

Initial Comments to the Patient

The session can be started by identifying to the patient that they have been referred for pain treatment, not because they "are crazy," or that the "pain is in their head," but rather because they have been dealing with pain for a long time. The pain has taken a toll on them, their lives, and perhaps even robbed them of things they used to love to do. It is hard to figure out how to adjust to this kind of pain! Therapy is focused on helping them understand their pain differently and teaching them techniques to manage it better, so that it interferes with their lives much less. It is important for the therapist to state, "The pain isn't going anywhere. It's been here for years, and many things have been tried to eliminate it. This therapy isn't miraculous and won't eliminate your pain, but it can help you to do more in your life and be bothered less by it."

The Patient's Pain Narrative

A key portion of the initial session is directed at hearing the patient's pain narrative. It is important that the clinician pay careful attention to this history, as elements of the patient's unique narrative will be used in later sessions to illustrate key pain concepts.

Key Questions to Ask in the Assessment

The following are key questions to ask in the assessment:

- Where is the pain?
- When did the pain start?
- How would you describe the pain (sharp, tingling, burning, dull, etc.)?
- What things have you tried to treat it? Have any been effective?
- Has the pain gotten better or worse with time?
- What medications do you take?
- What kind of daily pattern do you notice with your pain (is it better/worse in morning, day, or night)?
- What things make the pain worse?
- What things make the pain better?
- What is a typical day like for you? What do you do?
- How many hours of sleep do you get a night? Does the pain interfere with sleep?
- Are you receiving any kind of disability payment related to your pain, or do you have litigation pending related to it?
- How much alcohol do you drink per day during the week? And on the weekends?
- Do you take anything else to help manage the pain (i.e. cannabis or other drugs)?
- What activities can you no longer do because of your pain?

SMART Goals

The last portion of the first session is devoted to discussing SMART goals. These are Specific, Measurable, Achievable, Relevant, and Time-limited.

It is essential that these goals be meaningful and relevant to the patient. Therapists will need to identify core activities the patient is no longer able to do because of the pain. This can be done by asking the following questions:

- What would you be doing in your life now if you did not have pain?
- What things has the pain made you give up? What do you miss the most?

- How would your life be different without pain?
- What would you like to be able to do in 10 weeks that you are not doing now?

Patients can often identify several things that have changed or are missing because of pain. Patients need to understand that the timeframe is 10 weeks; therefore, the treatment goal needs to be realistic. In order to measure progress, it needs to have clearly identifiable numbers associated with it. Often times, these numbers are things like time or minutes (of an activity), distance (feet), frequency (number of times it is done), and so on.

Homework Assignment

Practice or homework for this session will be devising the short-term goals for the next 10 weeks (Table 4.1, see Resource Pack, p. 332). These short-term goals will be reviewed with the therapist at the beginning of the next session and revised as necessary then, or in future sessions.

Table 4.1 Example: Short-Term Goals: 10 Weeks

1.	
2.	
3.	

Session Two: Feedback and Education about Pain and Cognitive Behavioral Therapy

Agenda

1. Check-in and review homework (smart goals).
2. Administer treatment trackers: SUDS/PCS.
3. Review assessment results.
4. Discuss specificity theory.
5. Discuss gate control theory.
6. Explain CBT model of pain.

Protocol

This session starts with a "check-in" or review of the patient's status and weekly administration of treatment trackers. "Checking in" is the first step in every subsequent session. It provides both the clinician and the patient with the opportunity to assess treatment progress weekly.

Check-in should also include homework review. Did the patient complete assigned practice? Does it need revising? If they did not, what were the obstacles? How can the obstacles be overcome (because they will happen again)? Incomplete homework needs to be finished together at the session, or the clinician will risk reinforcing avoidance and poor adherence.

The next portion of the session will review the assessment results and what they say about the patient's pain. This can be a discussion of the activities or areas of their life that pain interfered with, the way they think about their pain, the feelings/anxiety they have about their pain, and the amount of distress it causes (this discussion can be related to what is reported on the SUDS). The clinician will remind the patient that this is a baseline, and that some of these instruments will be completed weekly.

Teaching about Pain

The core content, or goal, of this session is a teaching one. It is designed to help the patient begin to make sense of their pain in a very different way. It is focused on having the patient move from a very medicalized understanding of their pain to a more integrated biopsychosocial viewpoint. The clinician will use elements of the patient's own history to exemplify key concepts, thereby anchoring them to the patient's experience in a meaningful way.

Often an easy way to introduce this is to state something like, "Now I'd like to talk with you about pain, so that you can understand your pain better." The clinician will need to explain that understanding pain can help manage it better.

The clinician will briefly review three models of pain: (1) Specificity, (2) Gate Control, and (3) Cognitive Behavioral models. Although this may seem like a lot of material, it is not as much as one might think, because the concepts are interconnected and build upon one another.

Specificity Model of Pain

The specificity theory is introduced first, as this is often the conceptualization that many patients and medical providers have of pain. It is the "traditional" medical model of pain. Specificity theory is simple as it states that "pain is caused by tissue damage." There is a one-to-one correspondence between the amount of tissue damage and the amount of pain: "Big damage causes big pain; small damage causes small pain." This theory is ascribed to by many medical providers—because it seems to make sense. However, there are several problems with the explanation.

The first and most obvious is the issue of pain fluctuation. Many pain patients often have the experience of "random shots" of pain when doing passive activities like watching television. If this theory is correct, then in order to have pain, there has to be a new injury (since pain equals tissue damage). The patient would have had to cause injury to themselves by watching television! Has that really happened? Most patients are quickly able to identify that this is not the case.

The relationship between pain magnitude and damage amount is also suspect. A simple example is the "headline" about the person who lifts up the car or injures themselves in a situation to save a child, and they report no knowledge or feeling of the pain they have incurred. Another example is the soldier who during war sustains grievous injuries rescuing others, yet does not "feel it." There are also news reports about people going to the emergency room with objects sticking out of their skulls and felt nothing. If the Specificity Theory were correct, these people should have excruciating pain (remember: big damage equals big pain); yet they do not. Conversely, there are several examples of when a very small injury can cause a great amount of pain—a paper cut or hitting your "funny bone."

The pain patient will have information in the history they have provided to you that can be anchored to illustrate the idea that the experience of chronic pain is disconnected from tissue damage. For example, they have pain that fluctuates during the day. Does this mean that they are healing and re-injuring themselves at multiple points in the same day? What happens when they take pain meds and the pain goes away, and then it comes back when the meds wear off? Does the pain go away because the medication has "healed the tissue" and comes back because "the tissues got re-injured again?"

It is clear that "specificity" is not correct. The patient has likely run up against this theory in other medical treatments for their pain. For example, they may have had a flare and then gone into their doctor who ended up ordering imaging to search for damage (because, remember, pain equals damage). However, the imaging result shows no change from the chronic condition or no physical finding—yet the patient still has pain. Sometimes patients are told that their pain was "all in their head." Yet, it is not something they are "making up" because their pain is real!

HOW CAN THIS HAPPEN?

It is important for the clinician to explain to the patient that the patient's pain is viewed as "real" by the clinician, and that at no point will their pain be viewed as "fabricated" or "made up."

Gate Control Model of Pain

The clinician will then move to the next model of pain. Gate Control was built on the idea that "specificity" really did not accurately explain the variations in pain experienced by people. Gate Control says very simply that pain is a "message"—a message that is sent from sensory receptors in a part of the body directly to the brain (Melzack and Wall, 1967). The message is transmitted via the spinal cord, and there is a "gate" that controls the transmission in it (this gate is called the dorsal root ganglion, and will come up later as well). When the gate is "open," the pain message is transmitted in clear, high definition to the brain, and the brain says very clearly: "Pain!" When the gate is "closed," the message is weakened, or blocked (Melzack and Wall, 1967). The brain does not receive the signal in the same way.

The clinician can then link the idea of gate opening and closing to the patient's pain story. When the pain feels "better," the gate is closed. When the pain is worse, the gate is open. This model of pain is relevant to researchers who understand that the "pain gate" they discovered responds to other factors that open and close the pain gate. Several things have been found to open the pain gate, thereby influencing the experience of pain:

- *Emotions*: stress, anxiety, depression, anger, or feeling afraid of the pain.
- *Behaviors*: not moving at all leads to deconditioning and weakness; pushing through pain and overdoing it may lead to giving up activities.
- *Thinking*: catastrophic thinking about the pain and feeling like it is hopeless and will only get worse.
- *Physical/medical factors*: not enough sleep, substance and narcotic abuse.
- *Social*: being isolated, not feeling supported, having people tell you your pain is not real (Otis, 2007).

Conversely, many things also close the gate or turn down the volume on the pain:

- *Emotions*: feeling relaxed, contented, peaceful, and happy.
- *Behaviors*: doing things you value and enjoy, striking a balance with activity (not too much or too little), exercise, and not dropping activities because of pain.
- *Thoughts*: not thinking catastrophically about the pain, believing there are things you can do to manage and control it, not attending to the pain.
- *Physical*: getting enough sleep, appropriate exercise and movement, medications.
- *Social factors*: feeling supported and connected to people around you, spending time with friends and family you enjoy, feeling understood (Otis, 2007).

Cognitive Behavioral Model of Pain

The Cognitive Behavioral model of pain is introduced to clients next as the third pain model. Patients are directed to observe that thoughts, feelings, and behaviors are all identified as things that open and close the gate and influence pain. Thoughts, feelings, and behaviors are like rivers that run into the pool of pain. CBT focuses on each of these elements to reduce the flow into the pain lake.

Homework Assignment

Assigned practice for this session is identifying the things that open and close the pain gate (Table 4.2 and 4.3, see Resource Pack, p. 332). The clinician can partially complete some of it with the patient in session.

Table 4.2 Example: Things that Open My Pain Gate/Increase Pain

Thoughts:
Feelings:
Behaviors: Things I do or don't do:
Physical:

Table 4.3 Example: Things that Close My Pain Gate/Decrease Pain

Thoughts:
Feelings:
Behaviors: Things I do or don't do:
Physical:

(Adapted from McKellar, Murphy & Darchuk, 2012)

Session Three: Graded Movement Exposure

Agenda

1. Check-in—review practice.
2. Administer trackers and review changes.
3. Ask patient to relate pain changes to the gate.
4. Explain the fear of movement cycle.
5. Discuss "hurt does not equal harm."
6. Explain walking program and assign walking homework.

Protocol

This session starts with a check-in and review of practice from the prior week and administration of treatment trackers.

Ongoing treatment feedback and information regarding progress (or lack thereof) are important components of CBT. From this point forward, when the patient reports an increase or decrease in pain, it is essential to "validate and get to the gate." This means that if pain is increased, the clinician needs to query, "What do you think opened the pain gate this week?" (which feelings, thoughts, or behaviors opened the gate) and conversely, if it is decreased, "What do you think closed the gate?"

Discussing Increasing Movement

Fear of movement is highly associated with chronic pain. Effective treatment is predicated on addressing and disproving this fear. The reason for this is simple—when someone has pain, and they move, it hurts. Pain is a "wonderful teacher" and one of the things that it teaches people is "not to move." People with pain become afraid to move, fearing that they will experience pain, and also, that doing so will cause further "damage."

Fear of movement causes people to move less (Figure 4.1). In doing so, they become more deconditioned (creating risk for more pain and debility). They give up activities they once loved, which contributes to depression, anger, social withdrawal, and so on. Anger, depression, and anxiety in turn open the pain gate, increasing pain, which makes them want to move less. They have negative thoughts connected to this experience (i.e., "I'll never be OK again," etc.), which escalates the pain. Patients then move even less, and the vicious cycle continues and worsens.

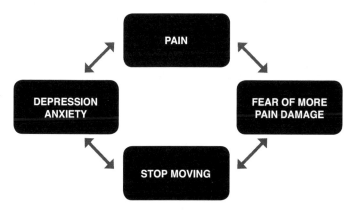

Figure 4.1 Pain Results in Reduced Movement

The goal of this session is to break the cycle, via increase in movement. This movement increase will be gradual, and is based on where the patient is currently.

One of the key cognitive distortions that occurs in pain has to do with movement. Pain patients have usually ascribed to the specificity theory for such a long time (remember, this is the idea that anytime there is pain, it means that there is damage), that they fear that when they move they are causing damage. They tend to say to themselves: "Every time I hurt means that I have done harm or damage to myself." In actuality, this is not the case. When it comes to chronic pain, *hurt does not equal harm.* An example of this is the random shot of pain that can occur during sleep or sometimes when you are just sitting. Did the pain happen because you actually injured yourself? No. When there is chronic pain, pain can be initiated by a great many factors, but there is no new damage.

The clinician needs to explain that when they begin moving again, they should expect to be sore and that they will feel the same pain they have had for a long time. Because of their pain and because they were not moving, they have been deconditioned. Therefore, when they start moving, there will be some soreness. It is important for the clinician to establish that "sore" is different from the feeling of "flare." Pain patients know what a flare is—a very sharp increase in pain, often followed by days of discomfort. The goal here is not a flare, but rather to move again and recognizing that it will not be pain-free.

Homework Assignment

Walking is a central component of moving again, and the clinician will need to assign homework with the expectation that the patient will walk daily. This is non-negotiable. Walking is a core component of almost all activity (provided that the patient has allowance to walk from their physician).

Setting the initial walking and movement goals follows a simple formula. The clinician must ask the patient how long they can do a particular activity (such as walking, standing, etc.) before they have to stop. This is an indication of the "flare point" and the signal that the movement has gone on too long. Once the flare or "stop" point is clear, the clinician will need to subtract "20 percent" from that figure, to establish the start point. For example, if someone can walk for 10 minutes before they have to stop, the new movement goal is starting at 8 minutes (10 less 20 percent or 2 minutes equals 8).

Each week, walking and movement will be increased gradually by a minute or two. The formula to increase is simple: If the patient is able to walk a certain number of minutes for 2 days in a row, without any flare, then on the third day, they can increase by 1 minute. Each increase follows this same pattern— doing the movement 2 or 3 days/times, and establishing that they are not flared. The homework for this session is to start the walking program (Table 4.4, see Resource Pack, p. 333).

Table 4.4 Example: Walking Program

	Week									
	1	*2*	*3*	*4*	*5*	*6*	*7*	*8*	*9*	*10*
Day 1										
Day 2										
Day 3										
Day 4										
Day 5										
Day 6										
Day 7										

(Adapted from McKellar, Murphy & Darchuk, 2012)

Session Four: Movement Exposure and Movement Patterns

Agenda

1. Check-in and review practice, including walking.
2. Administer trackers and review them.
3. Explain push–crash–burn.
4. Explain pacing.
5. Set three activity/movement goals—derived from SMART goals.

Protocol

This session starts with a review of walking with reinforcement provided for progress and increased movement! The patient is reminded again that "hurt does not equal harm." If pain escalated following walking, the clinician will need to reduce the walking number by 20 percent, and start at a lower point.

This session delves further into movement and directly links movement now with the patient's SMART goals, or their own valued activities.

Patient education focuses on the key movement pattern: Inactivity or not moving from the prior session will actually substantially increase pain. This pattern is called "Push–Crash–Burn." Push–Crash–Burn can be illustrated by this graphic (Figure 4.2).

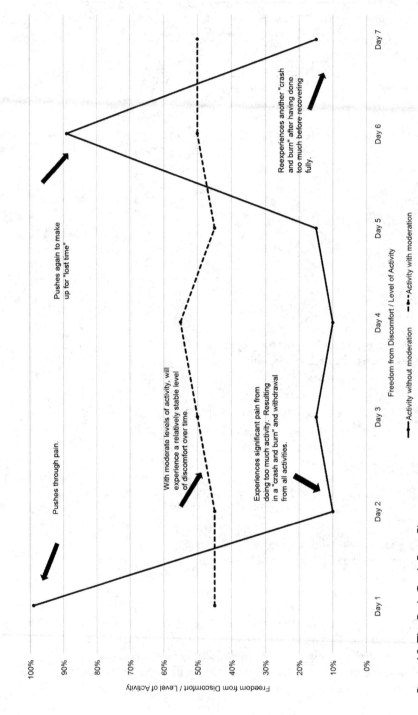

Figure 4.2 The Push-Crash-Burn Phenomenon
(Adapted from Otis, 2007)

The graphic is then explained. Every pain patient has days when they wake up and feel "good." Because they feel good, they plan their day and do as much as they can when they have less pain than usual. What happens, though, is that when they overdo it or are overactive, they "push" through the pain, wanting to get as much done as possible because they do not know when their next good day will happen.

The next day (Day 2) is a "Crash." Pain patients who say "Every time I'm active, I pay for it the next day" know exactly what this feels like. This is a flare, and a huge increase in pain. The flare is such that they cannot move for 3 days—some even end up in bed!

And then, after several days of rest following the flare, they wake up on Day 6, feeling better. Because they feel better, they attempt to make up for lost time—and, again, do everything they missed when they were inactive from the flare. This results in overactivity and more pushing through behavior. But the next day, they awaken again in flare—and the cycle repeats itself.

The problem is that the more the cycle repeats, the more disabled they become. Many pain patients will recognize themselves in this pattern. It is important to point out that this is a "disability" pattern. When someone is only able to be active 1 or 2 days a week, this is a *disability*. This pattern increases fear of movement because every time something is done, it ends in flair.

Pacing Rather than Pushing Activity

There is an alternative to Push–Crash–Burn. It is called pacing (Otis, 2007). Pacing is the new movement style and behavioral alternative to pushing that the therapist will introduce. The idea of it is simple: Doing a small amount every day, prior to the point of flare allows one to be consistent in activity, engaged in their life, and able to build gradually and increase what they can do.

Many patients who have been "pushers" will be opposed to this new way of moving. More specifically, they will object to doing less because their impulse is to push. The clinician can address this by pointing out the following mathematically: If you push and do "90 percent" one day, and "80 percent" on the other day, in a week this adds up to total of "170 percent" (80 + 90 percent). Contrast this to doing "50 percent" seven days of the week: this ends up being more (350 percent), because $7 \times 50 = 350$ percent.

Homework Assignment

The next step is to take the SMART goals and operationalize them to fit the movement formula. This means taking what the patient can do now, and reducing it by 20 percent. The patient does the movement for 2 to 3 days, and if there is no flare, they increase it by a small amount. Every 2 to 3 days, they can increase the movement without flare. Activity can also be cycled. Movement can also be scheduled in cycles with a pause or break in between. Initially it is performed once a day, and if there are no flares, it can be done two or three times a day (with pauses in between). The goal is ultimately to move them to the "SMART" goal end point, or close to it, by the end of treatment.

An example of movement pacing can be made of yard maintenance. If the smart goal is 20 minutes, and the person can only do 7 minutes before they flare, the movement start point is set at 5 minutes of, say, raking, and plant-ing flowers. They can start with one cycle of 5 minutes and do this for 2 days, seeing if they flare. If they do not, they can add in another cycle every day, making it two cycles of 5 minutes (with a break in between). Again, they must monitor for flair. Alternately, they can increase the interval time if they would like, from 5 to 6 minutes, again monitoring for pain escalation.

A final consideration to movement is that activity needs to be spread out during the course of the week. Remember, the patient will still be walking daily, and hopefully, increasing their distance. They need to be reminded of this! Patients should be prompted to spread their activities out during the week, so that they are not all clustered on one day (if they cluster it all, they are likely back in the Push–Crash–Burn pattern).

The clinician may feel as though they are assigning too much homework or activity. It is important to note that most activities are only a few minutes, and in actuality, a very small part of a 24-hour day. Every day is generally filled with multiple activities. It is important for the patient to learn how to schedule and pace things appropriately with pain.

The homework for this session is continued walking, and starting three activities derived from the SMART goals, via pacing, and starting movement at an appropriate level (Table 4.5, see Resource Pack, p. 333).

Table 4.5 Example: Activity Program

Activity	Time Plan	Day 1	Day 2	Day 3	Day 4	Day 5	Day 6	Day 7

Session Five: Pain, Stress, Danger, and the Brain

Agenda

1. Check-in to review practice including walking and behavioral activation.
2. Administer trackers and review changes.
3. Ask patient to relate pain changes to the gate.
4. Review practice and increase movement goals, or decrease if flare.
5. Explain pain and stress relationship.
6. Review endocrine and immune impact of chronic stress
7. Discuss how chronic stress changes the pain brain.

Materials

Two useful apps that can be recommended to patients are Breath2relax and Virtual Hope Box. They can be found online by searching for Breath2relax app and virtual Hope Box app.

Protocol

Begin this session by reviewing practice including walking and behavioral activation.

The Stress–Pain Relationship

For many pain patients, there is a direct relationship between pain and stress, and it is important for them to understand why this happens.

This session can start with a simple question: "When you are under a lot of stress, does your pain increase? Or does it go away?" Patients are readily able to identify that pain is increased by stress. The reverse is also true; when they are in pain, their pain increases their stress. Because pain and stress are so closely connected, reducing stress can reduce pain.

The reason for this has to do with the neurobiology of pain—really the way the brain interprets pain. Simply put, pain is a warning signal that alerts the brain to danger. For instance, when you burn your hand, pain tells you to stay away from the flame. This is an amazing survival mechanism. It is effective for pain related to imminent danger and new injury situations. But what about when you have continuous pain and there is no new "injury"? Does the brain still interpret this chronic pain as a threat and as a life-threatening danger? The answer is yes. The brain reads *all pain* as a threat and as danger. It does not matter if it is a pain that is 15 years old; it still gets interpreted as a threat.

When the brain interprets pain as danger, it activates the fight/flight, or stress response. This causes a number of things to happen. First, there is the immediate feeling of stress that results in muscle tension, an increased heart rate, nausea, and increased breathing. Next, the brain causes the adrenal gland to release cortisol, which in the short term reduces inflammation. Over the long term, however, cortisol not only stops working against inflammation, it actually increases inflammation. Over time, inflammation is bad, as it activates our pain sensors. Those sensors start sending more and more pain messages to the brain (up the gate in the spinal cord). And with more pain messages from the tissues, the brain gets more pain signals. More pain only increases the stress response. The brain goes into even higher alert. And the cycle repeats. The brain becomes so concerned about the threat of ever increasing pain that it actually makes the sensors more sensitive and actually creates more pain. The brain does this so that it will always be warned about pain. This is why chronic pain becomes worse over time. It can be said that pain is in the brain! This is illustrated in Figure 4.3.

The brain and the nervous system learn all this from chronic stress. And just as we know that pain can cause the brain and its sensors to change, we know that this learning can be changed. The sensors that have been upregulated by chronic pain and increased stress can also be downregulated. Pain receptor sensitivity and quantity can be changed by reducing the stress response (so the brain calms down); less cortisol is released; and the tissues and receptors down regulate and reduce (Figure 4.4).

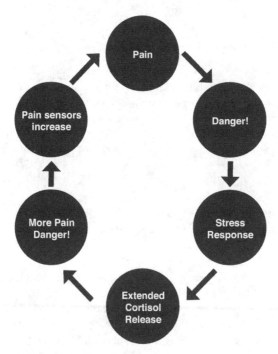

Figure 4.3 How Pain Leads to More Pain

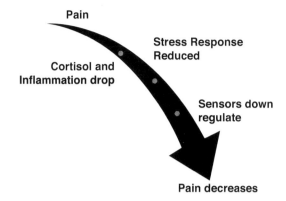

Figure 4.4 Reducing Stress Decreases Pain

There are several ways to reduce the physiological stress response. Diaphragmatic breathing, progressive muscle relaxation, and visualization are all effective.

It is important when teaching breathing to make sure the client is doing it correctly (shallow breathing or hyperventilation will only increase the stress response). A very helpful and instructive app for both patients and clinicians to learn proper technique is "Breathe2relax."

It is important for the clinician to note that the first several times a client does relaxation, it will not really work. This is because, like everything else, relaxation takes practice. And eventually, like riding a bike, the body develops "muscle memory" to learn the technique. Once it is learned, the more the patient does it, the more effective it becomes.

There are several other relaxation techniques available, including visualization and progressive muscle relaxation. A useful app with guided instructions for visualization techniques and progressive muscle relaxation is "virtual hope." Alternately, the clinician may wish to teach visualization by having the client think about a peaceful place for them. And then guide them down a path to their peaceful place, remain in the place for a while, and then guide them down the path out. The therapist will ask them to notice the sights, sounds, smells, light, temperature, and touch of the place in order to assist with visualization. The therapist can also teach progressive muscle relaxation by instructing the client to clench and then release muscle groups, starting with the toes and working up through the body to the head.

Homework Assignment

The assignment for the client is to continue walking and continue working on movement goals. In addition, the client should practice relaxation one time per day for 10 minutes.

Session Six: Thinking about Pain and the Pain Ignition Switch

Agenda

1. Check-in and review practice.
2. Administer trackers and review changes including walking and behavioral activation.
3. Ask patient to relate pain changes to the gate.
4. Discuss automatic thoughts and how they relate to pain.
5. Identify common pain distortions.
6. Complete one example in session and assign homework.

Protocol

How Thoughts and Pain Interact

Pain is complicated. Patients have learned at this point that pain impacts behavior, movement, mood, and the stress response. The brain itself changes the way it processes pain based on whether or not it perceives pain as a threat or a serious danger, and that can lead to changes in sensory receptors (reviewed in the prior session). It is important now to look at thoughts and how they are related to pain, and how thoughts contribute to the danger signal that sets off the pain alarm, which leads to an increasing fear of pain or decreasing movement. Thoughts are intimately connected to emotion and memory. A thought can be like a fishing line that pulls out of the water of our mind many related thoughts. When you experience pain, you typically think about other painful experiences.

You may think about how badly you felt in the past as you think about times you were hurt or suffering—and you may even remember feeling very helpless. Often the pain thoughts are highly inaccurate and irrational. What happens, though, is that these thoughts often open the in gate.

The powerful impact of thoughts on pain is evidenced in a simple experiment. Ask your patient to think about their pain and to really focus on it. Do they feel it more? Just thinking about pain can actually cause the brain and central nervous system to light the pain ignition switch.

Pain thoughts have several characteristics. For instance, they are often automatic, they happen frequently, they are negative and irrational, they are catastrophic, and they are sometimes very frightening. It is like they are whispering all of these things to us. In this session, the client will be asked to start listening.

The easiest way to educate the pain patient is to show them a list of common distortions (Table 4.6):

Table 4.6 Common Distorted Thoughts

All or Nothing Thinking Should Statements	An unrealistic and perfectionistic standard of how you 'must' 'should' or 'ought' to be doing	I should be able to do this_____. I must be able to _____ like a normal person my age
Personalization	Believing that you are the cause of the negative situation or have done something to bring it about	I have pain because I did X My pain is punishment for X
Fortune Telling	Making a future prediction that you will fail or things will go badly.	I just know that if I go play golf I will end up in bed for days
Good 'Ole Days Bias	Using rose colored glasses to describe how you used to be	I never had pain before I never had any real problems before the pain
Disqualifying the Positive	Telling yourself that positive steps and small accomplishments 'don't count'.	Yes, I walked yesterday for 15 minutes, but this is nothing like how I used to be. I'm still a mess.
Emotional Reasoning	Directly translating how you feel into reality.	I feel like I am falling apart. I am actually falling apart! I need to see the doctor.
Labeling	Describing yourself in a broadly negative way	I'm a mess. I'm a failure.
Catastrophizing	Very strong negative thinking	My life is over! I'll never be OK. I can't take this pain!
Mental Filter	Tunnel vision. Only seeing one negative detail and missing everything else.	When I have pain my whole life is just shot
Overgeneralization	Using a one time event to predict the future in a negative way	Last time I cleaned my house I ended in bed for 4 days. I cannot ever clean without ending up in bed again.

(Adapted from Thorn, 2017)

The patient should be asked "Which ones resonate most with you?" Often, the patient will see themselves quite easily in the distortions.

After prototypical distortions are reviewed, it is important for the clinician to identify key words that can help indicate that a thought is irrational. Two very common key words are "must" and "should." The clinician then needs to turn to a pain example from the patient's own unique experience to illustrate

Table 4.7 Example: Thought Record

Event	Thought/Image	Feeling	Behavior
Ex: pain increase	Ex: thinking about myself ending up in a wheelchair Think I hurt myself more	Ex: sad, stressed	Ex: decide to go bed

the impact of the negative thoughts. There have been 6 weeks of pain examples, so the clinician needs to pick one and fill out the form as shown in Table 4.7.

Homework Assignment

Complete a Thought Record (see Resource Pack, p. 333) for a pain-related incident in the week; preferably more than one. The patient should be asked to circle the "hottest" thought, or the one that distresses them the most. This will help in the next session to arrive at the core distortion.

Session Seven: Changing Pain Thinking

Agenda

1. Check-in—review practice including walking and behavioral activation.
2. Administer trackers and review changes.
3. Ask patient to relate pain changes to the gate.
4. Identify core distortions based on homework/or patient experience.
5. Challenge and complete balanced thought example.
6. Create coping card.

Protocol

Reviewing Core Thought Distortions

The focus of this session is on identifying the core distortions that the patient tells themselves. This often means thoughts about the future, the present, self-appraisals, and thoughts about "damage" and illness projection.

If the patient did not complete the pain example from the prior session, the clinician will have them fill it out at the beginning of this one. Once the clinician has identified the hottest or most distressing thought, the clinician needs to teach the client how to challenge it.

Several questions can be helpful, namely:

- Is this thought true 100 percent of the time?
- What is the actual evidence for this thought?
- What does this event say or mean about me?
- Who would I be without this thought?
- What would I tell my best friend if this happened to them?

These questions allow the patient to get distance from the thoughts. For instance, the patient may say about his or her pain: "Here we go again; this will never get better." This "fortune telling" prediction can be challenged by asking the patient, "If your best friend said that to you, what would you say?"

Sometimes clients will respond by saying, "I would tell them it is just a flare and it will pass." The clinician can point out that the thought applied to someone else is more rational than the one the patient applied to themselves.

Teaching Coping

To arrive at a balanced thought, the therapist will take the irrational thought and blend it with the counterargument thought. This acknowledges the thought, and at the same time disputes it. For example, the therapist can say as if they were the patient: "Even though I feel that the pain will never get better (irrational thought), I have had this pain before and it always passes (counterargument)."

This statement should then be written on a coping card. The patient should be given a list of coping statements and asked to select ones that make the most sense to them. They can circle the ones that seem to be best suited to themselves and these can be added to the coping card.

Coping Statements

- I have been through this before and it always ends.
- This is just a wave of pain and I know how to ride it out.
- I have skills to deal with this and know what to do.
- I am safe and this will pass, I will just let it ride through my body.
- It will be over soon.
- Pain is like volume, I know what turns it up and I know how to turn it down.
- I have survived this before.
- I am not falling apart (adapted from McKellar, Murphy & Darchuk, 2012).

The coping card is then to be used in situations when they feel the pain and they need to challenge their pain thinking (which is generally connected to so many other thoughts, perceptions, feelings, and sensations).

Homework Assignment

Direct the patient to identify specific events, write down the negative thoughts associated with those events, and write evidence supporting and refuting those thoughts on a chart as shown in Table 4.8, see Resource Pack, p. 334.

Table 4.8 Example: Thought Record

Event	Thought	Evidence For Thought	Evidence Against Thought	Blended Thought
Ex:	Ex:	Ex:	Ex:	Ex:

Session Eight: Doing What Matters the Most— Long-Term Goals

Agenda

1. Check-in—review practice including walking and behavioral activation.
2. Administer trackers and review changes.
3. Ask patient to relate pain changes to the gate.
4. Explain values and complete values exercises.
5. Create activity plan based on values.
6. Assign practice.

Protocol

After the review of the homework assignment and a discussion of negative thoughts associated with events, go on to a discussion of long-term goals.

Long-Term Goals

This session focuses on the patient's long-term goals, with particular emphasis on ones that reflect their personal values and the things that matter most to them in their life.

By now, the patient has changed movement patterns, developed skills to manage the pain-related stress response, and learned to refute the thoughts that ignite the pain switch. This session strives to integrate this learning into the bigger life picture by having them consider doing the things they treasure the most.

Values are the ideals or standards that matter to someone. They are like directions that inform us which way to go in our lives. Like directions, you never arrive at them. For instance, you can always keep driving north. In a like manner, you never stop driving in the direction of your value. Goals are stops along the way, but not final destinations.

It is important for the patient to stop and take the time to think about the things they would like to do in their life—despite their pain. The purpose is simple: to have them engage in the things they would do anyway, irrespective of pain. This is a part of final movement exposure and teaching the patient that they are not sidelining themselves from the game because of the pain. Rather, they are learning to play the game differently.

Identify Values and the Steps to Achieve Those Values

The primary step in this session is to assist the patient in identifying the things that matter.

This can be done in two steps. The first is an exercise:

- *Eulogy exercise*: Imagine you are an observer at your own eulogy and the celebration of your life. Everyone that you love and who has mattered to you is there. What would you like them to say about you?

   The patient can even be asked to write it down. This exercise can help crystallize the things that are really important, while identifying core values.

The second step is to have the patient peruse the following list and identify or circle the things that appeal to them:

VALUES

- *Parenting*: Spending time with children, going to activities;
- *Leisure*: Hobbies, passions, outdoor pursuits, artistic pursuits, cooking, theater, movies, vacations;
- *Spirituality*: Church, studying religious texts, learning about other religions, prayer, mediation;
- *Personal Growth*: Reading about self-improvement, listening to radio or watching TV shows;
- *Health*: Nutrition, exercise, learning about wellness;
- *Work*: Career, achievement, learning about profession, education;

- *Community/Environment*: Taking care of own home, yard, local community groups, learning about environmental issues;
- *Social Justice*: Helping others with challenges, advocacy organizations;
- *Caring for Animals*: Spending time with dog/cat/bird, researching a pet;
- *Family relationships*: Getting together with family, planning holidays, talking on the phone;
- *Intimate Relationships*: Spending time with partner, doing something for them;
- *Social Relationships*: Spending time with friends, meeting new friends;
- *Nature*: Gardening, time outside, bird watching, hunting, camping;
- *Travel*: Learning about new places/cultures, languages, planning trips (adapted from McKellar, Murphy & Darchuk, 2012).

Homework Assignment

The values associated with the client's desires need to be translated into activities. Some activity suggestions are given above. It is important to ask the patient to start one or two activities that matter to them. Planning needs to specify the amount of time they will do it, the frequency, the place, etc. (Table 4.9, see Resource Pack, p. 334). The rules of pacing and distributing activity evenly throughout a week need to be observed.

Table 4.9 Example: Activity Plan

Value	Activity (What You Will Do)	Plan (Time, Frequency)
1.		
2.		
3.		

Session Nine: Sleep and Pain

Agenda

1. Check-in—review practice including walking and behavioral activation.
2. Administer trackers and review changes.
3. Ask patient to relate pain changes to the gate.
4. Explain relationship between sleep and pain.
5. Do sleep assessment.
6. Review sleep hygiene.
7. Assign practice.

Materials

1. Insomnia Severity Index: This is a brief, seven-question index which can be found at: http://deploymentpsych.org/system/files/member_resource/Insomnia%20Severity%20Index%20-ISI.pdf
2. National Sleep Foundation Diary: This diary can be downloaded at: https://sleepfoundation.org/content/nsf-official-sleep-diary

Protocol

Role of Sleep in Pain Management

Thus far, treatment has focused on the things that are happening during the day. But pain does not just happen during the day, it also happens at night. It negatively impacts sleep and our sleep habits or behaviors.

There is a reciprocal relationship between sleep and pain. Pain often interferes with an individual's ability to fall asleep and stay asleep. When pain is worse, sleep is worse. Many pain patients sleep fitfully or only a few hours a night.

Reduced sleep, in and of itself, also feeds pain or opens the pain gate. Sleep is a time that the body and mind use to restore and recover from the day. Lost sleep causes inflammation in the tissues and weakens the immune system. Inflammation is particularly bad for the pain. Lost sleep also causes changes in mood and is associated with an increase in negative emotions (for instance, anger, sadness, anxiety). Negative emotions in turn open the pain gate and increase pain.

An important physical mechanism for closing the pain gate then is management of sleep and increasing the amount and quality of sleep.

The clinician will be asked to administer the Insomnia Severity Index in order to quantify the amount of sleep dysfunction that exists.

Pain patients often have many sleep interfering behaviors, which is why stimulus control education is essential. These include lying awake in bed during pain exacerbations, resting in bed during the day, watching television, engaging in activity during the day, and changing their sleep schedule based on pain.

It is important for patients to be aware of other sleep interfering behaviors, including increased caffeine during the day, physical exercise or activity too close to bed, television or electronics in the bedroom that emit light during the night.

Stimulus control can be explained to the patient as "body learning." The body and brain often learn things even when we are not aware of it. One kind of learning is called conditioning, which happens out of our awareness. For example, if you have ever gotten sick on a food, you develop an aversion because your body has come to associate getting sick with that food. You learned it and did not realize it until you got near the food again. The same thing happens with the bed and pain. When you lay in the bed, awake, resting, or in flare, your body comes to equate bed with pain. This means that when you get into bed, the brain goes into high alert, the pain ignition switch is hit, the gate opens, and pain escalates. The brain has learned a simple equation, bed equals pain.

The same thing happens if you lie in bed while awake. The body learns that bed equals being awake. The body is confused when you go to bed. It does not know if it should stay up (which it does sometimes) or go to sleep (which it does sometimes). If you watch TV in bed, read in bed, use your smart phone in bed, the body associates bedtime not with winding down, but winding up. The body learns that bed sometimes equals stimulation.

In order to break these patterns, the brain and body must be given new sleep patterns to learn. This means that bed should only be used for two activities: sleep and sex.

To learn new sleep patterns, inform your patient that if he or she is in bed for more than 20 minutes awake, they need to get out bed. They need to find a less stimulating activity to do, such as listening to calming music, drinking herbal tea, reading something rather dull. They are only to return to bed when they feel sleepy. If they are unable to sleep again in 20 minutes, they need to repeat the cycle. They may need to repeat this several times.

The pain and sleep association can be unlearned as well. First, if they are sleeping in a chair or couch, or someplace not their bed on a regular basis, this needs to stop. They are to sleep only in bed. The bed is not to be used for resting or for riding out a flare. The bed should not be associated with flare pain. Changing position in bed can sometimes help (i.e., switching the side of the bed you are sleeping on, or starting to sleep at the foot of the bed).

A final sleep interfering behavior involves changing the sleep schedule and napping, both of which interfere with sleep drive. It is important to get out of bed at the same time every day, no matter how tired one may be. For each hour that one gets up later, it is 1 hour later at night they will go to bed. Sleeping in for 2 hours means bed time is now 2 hours later. It can take several days to regulate sleep like this.

Finally, it is important to have a wind down routine at night. A wind down routine is when you do relaxing, nonstimulating activities prior to bed. This can be a bath, warm tea, music, reading, prayer; in other words, any activity that signals to the brain that it is time to slow down.

Homework Assignment

The patient will be asked to identify two sleep behaviors they are engaging in. Homework for the week will be changing those behaviors. The patient should be asked to complete the national sleep diary and record their sleep behaviors during the week, including those that will be changed.

Session Ten: Termination, Flare Inoculation, and the Flare Kit

Agenda

1. Check-in—review practice including walking and behavioral activation.
2. Administer trackers and review changes.
3. Ask patient to relate pain changes to the gate.
4. Identify treatment gains (changes in behavior, pain, treatment trackers, etc.).
5. Discuss flare expectancy.
6. Outline skills that have worked for patient; create a "flare kit."

Materials

Ten index cards and plastic sandwich bag will be required for this final session.

Protocol

It is important at the beginning of this session to review the treatment trackers (PCS and SUDS). The clinician will need to outline changes and progress, hopefully, by pointing out decreases in some of the trackers. However, if there is no change, the clinician needs to point to some of the other gains the patient has evidenced (more activation, less pain fear, less negative and catastrophic thinking, more behavioral activation that reflects the patients' values, and so on). How far has the patient gotten toward achieving SMART goals?

Introducing the Flare Kit

The patient should be asked, "What are the things that you have learned that close your pain gate?" The clinician can work with the patient to help them identify several factors. While this is happening, the clinician should write each skill on an index card (i.e., "using coping statements," "breathing," "doing something I like," "reading," etc.). The goal is to have ten index cards, or more. These should be placed in the baggy.

The index cards form the basis of the flare kit. It is important to explain to the patient, that as they know from experience pain ebbs and flows. The nature of chronic pain is that they WILL flare. It is not a matter of if, but when. It is important that when flare happens, that they are prepared and use the strategies they have learned. This is what the flare kit is for.

They need to understand that it does not mean they have regressed back to the beginning. Instead, it means that something has caused the pain gate to open, but they have the tools to close it. The tools are the things they have learned in treatment along with the flare kit.

Patients are instructed to use the flare kit by pulling a card from the deck. Each card represents a skill and they should do it, or pull another card from the deck.

The final portion of this session will be spent setting up a booster session in 12 weeks to monitor progress.

Booster Session

Agenda

1.   Check-in—administer trackers and review changes.
2.   Review ongoing behavioral activation.
3.   Ask patient to relate pain change (up or down) related to the gate.
4.   Refresh skills for things that have opened the gate.
5.   Reinforce and/or modify/add mechanisms that close the gate.

Protocol

The goal of this session is simple: to monitor progress, reinforce prior learning, and refresh areas in need of tuning. If the patient has demonstrated continued gain, this should be strongly reinforced. If there has been a decline, the patient needs to be queried as to what has opened the gate? If it is activity patterns, then pushing needs to be reviewed. If it is sleep, that needs to be reviewed. No matter what the reason for the increase in pain, it must be reviewed.

Tips for Clinicians

Pain patients present with particular obstacles and roadblocks. These challenges include perseveration on the pain, answer-seeking behaviors, medication and escape behaviors, and negative prior medical experiences.

Pain perseveration, or discussion of pain and its consequences, is the behavior that many therapists are familiar with and find a deterrent. It is important for the therapist to empathize with the pain, but at the same time to ask the patient to apply their pain experience to the pain model (in other words, to validate and get to the gate).

Many pain patients have histories of doctor shopping and medication-seeking. These behaviors stem from two erroneous beliefs or distortions. The first is the superstitious belief that if they find the exact location or cause of their pain, then their pain will be cured. Finding this answer represents the "magic key" to pain elimination. It is important to identify to the patient that this belief is a variation of specificity theory. There is not a one-to-one correspondence between pain severity, location, and injury. For instance, research related to back pain demonstrates little relationship between radiographic findings and pain severity (many persons with no pain have positive finding in neuroimaging).

It is important for the clinician to ask the following questions: "What would it mean if you got a result that showed you the exact location and reason for pain? What would you be doing differently?" Those questions can be followed up with others, such as: Do they imagine that there will be a procedure that is a magic bullet? What is the evidence for that, after so many years of pain and so many attempts?

It may be necessary to point out to the client that having been in pain for a long time, and after trying many doctors, medications, and treatments, their pain has not been eliminated. By constantly searching for answers, it may be avoidance of accepting the pain as a part of their lives. It keeps them from moving forward and it may keep them stuck and always looking for the magic cure. Instead, it is important for them to think about the pain differently; instead of pursuing the dead end of cure, they should focus on learning to self-manage it—without more medications and doctors.

Medication-seeking behaviors are another "escape/avoidance" mechanism that reinforces pain anxiety and avoidance. This is driven by the desire to be 100 percent pain free. Often, patients have been taking and changing medications for years. What is the evidence that medication has fixed their pain? For most patients, the answer is that there is very little evidence. Further questioning can reveal additional distortions. Does the patient believe the "right medication" will heal the underlying cause of pain? If so, then it is essential to identify that this kind of healing occurs with acute injuries, but it does not occur with problems that are several years old.

Finally, many patients can present as angry, irritable, and pessimistic about any intervention for their pain. This can represent a particular challenge for the clinician. It is vital for the clinician to understand that this is a product of the patient's learning history. They may have had many solutions offered to them, many with the promise—directly or indirectly—that they will be pain free when they are done. And none of them have worked. They have reason to be skeptical. The therapist should empathically validate the patient's skepticism. This is where CBT pain management can be differentiated from their prior learning experiences. Instead of curing the pain, the goal is different; to understand their own pain so that they can manage it better, and do the things in their lives that matter to them—even with the pain. Treatment is directed at turning down the volume on the pain and not turning it off.

References

Murphy, J.L., McKellar, J.D., Raffa, S.D., Clark, M.E., Kerns, R.D., & Karlin, B.E. (2012). *Cognitive behavioral therapy for chronic pain among veterans: Therapist manual.* Washington, DC: U.S. Department of Veterans Affairs.

Melzack, R., & Wall, P.D. (1967). Pain mechanisms: a new theory. *Survey of Anesthesiology*, *11*(2), 89-90.

Otis, J. (2007). *Managing chronic pain: A cognitive-behavioral therapy approach.* New York: Oxford University Press.

Thorn, B.E. (2017). *Cognitive therapy for chronic pain: a step-by-step guide.* New York: Guilford Publications.

Chapter 5

Sleep Protocol

Sleep is a basic biological need, just like eating, drinking, or sex. It is something the body requires in order to be able to function.

Sleep is produced by two biological systems that work together. The first system is known as the "sleep drive" or the "homeostatic sleep system." The sleep drive or homeostatic sleep system can be most easily compared to a fuel tank. During the night when we sleep, we fill up our sleep tank. As our sleep tank fills, the level of a brain chemical called adenosine drops. Adenosine controls our wakefulness; when it is low we wake up. When it is high, we are easily lulled into sleep. When our sleep tank reaches full, adenosine is at its lowest level. This makes us awaken. As we go through the day, for each hour we are awake, we burn fuel in the "sleep tank." Adenosine is a byproduct of our energy burn and builds during the day (like the exhaust from an engine). When we have burned all of our sleep fuel, we end up running on empty and it can be said that the adenosine "exhaust" is at its highest level after a day of activity, and we are ready to sleep. We sleep in order to replenish the tank. This can be viewed as the "drive" to sleep.

The second biological system related to sleep is the circadian alerting system, or the "sleep clock." It regulates the timing of wakefulness and sleepiness during our day. You may know this as your biological day/night rhythm. It is controlled by the relationship between structures in the brain and light, and our energy use during the day. The structure that is responsible for this is called the suprachiasmatic nucleus in the hypothalamus. The circadian alerting system sends "alerting signals" during the day and turns those signals down at night. In this way, it runs on a 24-hour cycle.

The interaction between these two systems is illustrated in the graph shown in Figure 5.1.

There are, however, other important elements that influence sleep, including conditioned arousal factors, environmental/stimulus control factors, and lifestyle factors.

Conditioned arousal factors are based on "classical conditioning." This is the natural pairing that happens when two things occur together in time, and

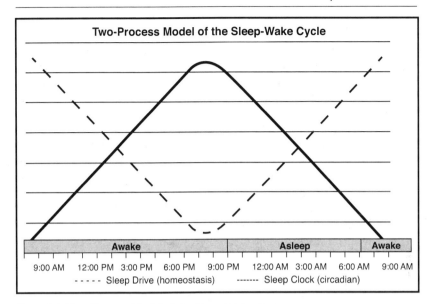

Figure 5.1 Two-Process Model of the Sleep-Wake Cycle
(Adapted from Edgar, Dement and Fuller, 1993)

end up producing the exact same response. When someone has insomnia, conditioned learning impacts the bed itself. Arousal (or being awake) becomes connected to the bed. If you spend night after night in bed awake, the bed becomes "paired" with being "awake" (and not sleep!). This means that when you go to bed, your body has learned to "stay awake" and not fall sleep. The same thing can happen with someone who worries in bed or gets frustrated about their inability to sleep soundly. Sometimes people even worry about not sleeping! Bed becomes "paired" with "worry time" or feeling frustrated. Various states, such as waking, anxiety, and frustration, can come to represent arousal; if these states occur while in bed, this will directly interfere with sleep.

Stimulus control impacts sleep. There may be bed activities and aspects of the bedroom environment that interfere with sleep. Such factors could include light stimulation, electronic devices (phones, television, tablets), working or studying in bed, or eating in bed. All of these are examples of activity and stimulation parings that interfere with the learned sleep response.

But lifestyle factors also influence sleep. Lifestyle factors refer to daily habits and choices, and include dietary selections and meal timing. For instance, caffeine increases alertness and arousal, while alcohol consumption can change sleep structure. Also, eating a heavy meal shortly before sleep revs up the metabolism—which increases alertness. Exercise is another revving up factor and if carried out too soon before bedtime keeps arousal levels high.

How Insomnia Develops

Insomnia does not occur in every person who has lifestyle issues, worries, or bad habits. And it does not happen suddenly in one or two nights. Instead, insomnia develops over time in persons with a vulnerability to it. Spielman's "3P model" of insomnia explains how this occurs (Spielman, Caruso & Glovinky, 1987). The first P is "predisposition." Predisposition has to do with the heritable traits that create the "diathesis" or vulnerability to insomnia. Some of these traits that predispose people to insomnia include being a "high arousal" individual, having anxiety, or being female. Of course, not everyone with these traits develop insomnia. The activating ingredient is the second P—a precipitating event or stressor. A precipitating event or stressor can be a medical event (i.e., pregnancy, pain, etc.) or a life event that causes a person to begin losing sleep. If you are not predisposed to insomnia, when a stressful event ends your sleep quickly normalizes. However, in the individual who is prone to insomnia, sleep does not return. Instead, insomnia perpetuates—this is the final P. Perpetuating factors include those that have already been referred to in this chapter—stimulus control, hygiene, anxiety, sleep beliefs, napping, and resting in bed.

Cognitive behavioral therapy (CBT) for sleep addresses insomnia by dealing with both the precipitating and the perpetuating factors. CBT begins with sleep education so the client understands why they have insomnia and the rationale for treatment. This is followed by sleep restriction treatment, which pairs rapid sleep onset and real sleep time with the actual time in bed. CBT addresses and eliminates sleep interfering factors, such as frustration, anxiety, and alertness in bed. This therapeutic approach modifies stimulus control techniques and lifestyle factors to prevent sleep spoiling.

Session One: The Sleep Assessment

Agenda

1. Administer the Pittsburgh Sleep Quality Index, the Morning–Eveningness questionnaire, the Dysfunctional Beliefs and Attitudes Scale (DBAS), the STOP scale, and the Insomnia Severity Index.
2. Complete sleep interview/history taking.
3. Assign the sleep diary.

Materials Needed

1. Pittsburgh Sleep Quality Index: A brief questionnaire which is available at www.sleep.pitt.edu/research/ewExternalFiles/PSQI%20Article.pdf
2. Morningness–Eveningness Questionnaire: A nineteen-item questionnaire available at www.ubcmood.ca/sad/MEQ.pdf

3. DBAS: This brief scale, along with many others, is available in the book *STOP, THAT, and One Hundred Other Sleep Scales* by Shahid, Wilkinson, Marcu, and Shapiro (Springer, 2012).
4. STOP-Bang Sleep Scale: Available in Shahid et al. (2012).
5. Insomnia Severity Index: A brief, seven-question index available at http:// deploymentpsych.org/system/files/member_resource/Insomnia%20 Severity%20Index%20-ISI.pdf
6. Semi-structured interview to assess sleep disorders: See Clinical Practice Guidelines for the Management of Patients with Insomnia in Primary Care. Available: www.guiasalud.es/egpc/traduccion/ingles/insomnio/ completa/apartado06/diagnostico.html
7. *Or*, a more structured interview is the Sleep Disorders Interview at http:// deploymentpsych.org/content/insomnia-tools
8. The Rush Sleep Diary: This can be found at the American Psychological Association website: www.apa.org/pubs/videos/4310583-diary.pdf or, at CBT-I Coach there is a diary. Available: http://t2health.dcoe.mil/apps/ CBT-i

Protocol

The sleep assessment is integral for the treatment of sleep-related disorders. The clinician needs to learn about the factors that are contributing to insomnia, so that the interventions based on each factor can be developed.

Conditions that Need to Be Treated Prior to Starting CBT-Sleep

The clinician's first job is to identify medical and psychiatric issues which may be interfering with sleep. These will need to be addressed prior to initiating any kind of behavioral sleep intervention. Sleep impairment can be linked to a number of underlying medical and psychological disorders. But, if the under- lying conditions are not addressed, behavioral sleep treatment may have limited or no efficacy. Examples of medical conditions that impact sleep include thyroid disorders, congestive heart failure, breathing/lung conditions, and allergies. Medical conditions directly related to sleep that will need to be addressed prior to CBT are obstructive sleep apnea, restless leg syndrome, and periodic limb movement disorder. Psychological conditions that impact sleep are myriad, and include depression, trauma-related disorder/posttraumatic stress disorder, mood cycling disorders, psychosis, and anxiety. The clinician will need to make a careful evaluation regarding whether or not any of these conditions exist, and if so, refer the client to an appropriate medical provider.

For psychological conditions, each such condition will need to be treated initially. Sleep treatment is a brief intervention, and being so, can easily be "tacked on" to the end of a CBT protocol for other disorders (pain, depression, anxiety), as the final leg of treatment.

Sleep Assessment Instruments

There are several structured interviews that exist for sleep, which allow the clinician to obtain a retrospective history of sleep issues and the client's overall psychological and medical health. It is important, regardless of the instrument used, for the clinician to assess when the insomnia happens (before sleep, during sleep, or waking too early), how long it has existed, and how much it is impairing daily functioning. Factors that impact sleep (stress, whether the client is an owl or a lark, diet/caffeine, sleep associated behaviors) should be queried, as this will impact the formulation. Use of sleep medications, herbal supplements, and alcohol and other substances to force sleep will need to be assessed. Medical history (major conditions), apnea symptoms, and psychological disorders (mood, anxiety, trauma) should be explored.

One suggested structured interview is the Sleep Disorders Interview at http://deploymentpsych.org/content/insomnia-tools

The clinician will need to assess four areas important to behavioral intervention for sleep: the client's daily sleepiness, which is an indicator of how sleep deprivation is impacting functioning; the morning and evening routines, in order to establish their circadian rhythm; their degree of insomnia, to quantify severity and track progress in later sessions; and their obstructive sleep apnea to determine a high base rate co-occurring sleep condition.

Homework Assignment

The sleep diary is important to assign to complete over the next week. It is essential to get an idea of how much time the client is in bed, how much sleep is actually produced, how many times they awaken, how much they nap, and what kinds of behaviors they are engaging in. This is a core weekly assignment and it will allow both the clinician and the client to objectively view what is happening with sleep and improvement over time.

There are several variations of sleep diaries. It is important that the diary track the factors above. Two suggested ones are the 2-week sleep diary available at the National Sleep Foundation and the Rush Sleep Diary, which can be found at the American Psychological Association (www.apa.org/pubs/videos/4310 583-diary.pdf). Alternately, a convenient free patient smart phone app can be obtained through CBT-I Coach.

Session Two: Insomnia Conceptualization and Client Education

Agenda

1. Review assessment measures and conceptualization of sleep issues.
2. Teach the two-factor model of sleep (sleep drive and sleep clock).
3. Discuss arousal and stimulus control.
4. Review sleep diary and calculate sleep produced.
5. Assign sleep RX (restriction therapy).

Materials

The assessment measures administered in the prior week: Morningness–Eveningness questionnaire, DBAS, the STOP scale, and the Insomnia Severity Index.

In addition, the client will need to provide their sleep diary information (CBT I app or Rush Sleep Diary). And the CBT I calculator or Sleep Calculator 1 (which will allow the client to determine the amount of sleep produced, time in bed, and match bed time to sleep time) will be required (It is available at http://deploymentpsych.org/content/insomnia-tools). Also, the Sleep Calculator 2 will be needed; again, see http://deploymentpsych.org/content/insomnia-tools.

Protocol

Interpretation of Sleep Assessment Results and Conceptualization

The clinician should review the sleep diary quickly at the beginning of the session. This will provide an idea of when the client is going to bed, how long they are in bed, when they get up, and if they are napping during the day. It will tell you about other sleep-interfering behaviors like late eating, drinking, exercising or taking medications.

Reviewing the Insomnia Severity Index will render a numerical score that quantifies the subjective severity of the insomnia reported by the client. The items in the Insomnia Severity Index assess the following: (1) difficulty falling asleep, (2) difficulty maintaining sleep, (3) early morning awakenings, (4) satisfaction/dissatisfaction with sleep pattern, (5) interference of sleep problems with daily functioning, (6) sleep problems being noticeable by others, and (7) levels of distress/worry caused by the sleep problems. Scores on this index range from 0 to 28; 0–7: No clinically significant insomnia; 8–14: Subthreshold insomnia; 15–21: Clinical insomnia (moderate severity); and 22–28: Clinical insomnia (severe). Your client should have a score of at least 15 to be considered appropriate for treatment.

The Morningness–Eveningness Questionnaire will establish whether your client is an owl or a lark. It can be compared to the sleep diary to determine if there is a mismatch between the client's individual circadian rhythm or sleep clock and their actual bed time. If there is a mismatch, then the treatment will work on shifting the client's sleep clock to their necessary work/sleep schedule.

The DBAS will establish if there is a strong cognitive or anxious component to insomnia. Negative and catastrophic thoughts about sleep increase arousal and interfere with sleep. These are often extreme beliefs (i.e., If I do not go to sleep now, there is no way I will be able to function tomorrow).

Finally, the STOP Scale will give you and your client clues as to whether he or she has clinically significant apnea. A score greater than two positively answered questions (out of four possible questions) will necessitate medical evaluation for apnea.

Explanation of Sleep Systems

It is important to explain to the client the idea of the sleep drive and the sleep clock, as well as the arousal factors that interfere with sleep.

Clients will better understand the idea of the biological sleep drive if a car analogy is used. The clinician can explain that when we sleep, we "fill" our sleep tank. As we go through the day, we "drive" and our tank empties. At night, when the tank is on "E," we are compelled to sleep in order to refill the sleep tank. If we nap during the day, we "fill" the tank and this means that we need to drive longer or stay awake longer to empty it—just like a car needs to drive farther in order to be on "E" if a few more gallons of gas are added.

No matter what time we get up, we need to "drive" the same amount of time before we are on "'E." For example, if you are normally awake 16 hours a day before arriving at "E," and your day starts at 6 am, you will arrive at "E" at 10 pm (and then you go to sleep). If you decide to sleep in the next day and get up at 8 am, you will still need to drive for 16 hours. Bed time will be pushed back to 12. It is important to regulate wake times with this in mind! This is why a standard wake time is so essential, because that is when our "drive time" starts.

The circadian rhythm should be described as the "sleep clock" that controls our alertness. It responds to light (to keep us awake) and calls us to sleep at night. It runs on a 24-hour cycle. Some people are "morning people" or larks; others are "night people" or owls. Individual circadian patterns can be a problem when the demands of society conflict with it (i.e., if you are an "owl" and you have a job that starts at 7 am). The circadian rhythm can be altered somewhat by timing the light exposure, getting up at the same time every day, and managing activities.

Arousal is the final factor that needs to be discussed. High arousal can over-ride the clock and the sleep drive and keep you "wired but tired." Arousal includes states such as stress, anxiety, and anger, as well as any activity during which we are awake and alert. However, arousal disrupts sleep onset.

It is very important that the body and the brain do not connect the bed to "arousal" behaviors. This includes behaviors like lying awake in bed. For this reason, stimulus control (or making the bed a sleep zone) will need to be discussed initially, so that arousal factors do not override the sleep drive and the clock reset you will be planning.

Stimulus control intervention should include the following instructions to the client.

Stimulus Control Instructions

1. The bed is only to be used for two activities: sleep and sex. This means no to watching TV and reading, eating, drinking, conversing, or worrying in the bed.
2. Do not watch the clock. In fact, you may wish to turn it away from you.
3. If you are unable to fall asleep within 15 to 20 minutes, get out of the bed. Do not watch the clock, but estimate roughly how long you think you have been in bed. Go to another room. Do nonstimulating activity, have warm tea or milk, listen to music, read, watch TV, etc. Make sure what you watch is not too exciting. Only go back to bed when you feel very sleepy.
4. Return to bed.
5. If you are not asleep within 15 to 20 minutes, repeat Step 3. You may need to do this several times a night.

(Adapted from Bootzin and Perlis, 2011)

The Sleep Prescription

The next intervention for this session will match the amount of sleep produced to the actual time in bed. The goal is to create rapid sleep onset. For most people, the easiest way to do this is to restrict the time in bed to match the actual amount of sleep produced.

In order to estimate the match of bed time to sleep, an index called sleep efficiency will be calculated.

Sleep efficiency = total amount of sleep produced for 7 days/total amount of time spent in bed for 7 days.

High sleep efficiency means that the bed is used efficiently for sleep. This means that you are sleeping most of the time you are in bed. High sleep efficiency ratings are numbers greater than 85 percent. On the other hand, low sleep efficiency is a score less than 85 percent. By definition, people with insomnia have low sleep efficiency. If a score is less than 85 percent, then time in bed needs to be reduced to match the amount of sleep produced. This is called the "sleep prescription."

Calculating Sleep Effiency

The client's sleep efficiency is calculated by inputting the information from the sleep diary over the past week into one of many sleep efficiency calculators available online. This can be done most easily with an excel spreadsheet in the Sleep Calculator *2* or the CBT I calculator.

Homework Assignment

The "sleep prescription" will be developed based on information from the sleep diary. It is the exact time that you are instructing the client to go to bed, based on the actual amount of sleep they produce. Guidelines to create the Sleep RX are reviewed below.

Decreasing Time in Bed/Sleep Restriction RX

1. Criterion: Sleep efficiency greater than 85 percent.
2. PRESCRIBED TIME IN BED (TIB): Total sleep time produced (how much they are actually sleeping BASED on sleep calculator) plus 15 minutes added on.
3. BED TIME is set based on subtracting prescribed TIB from desired wake time.
4. The client is not allowed to sleep outside of the sleep window at all. This includes naps.

(Adapted from Spielman et al., 2011)

The minimum time in bed should be no less than 5 hours.
The client will be given a formal sleep prescription:

Sleep RX

1. Your bed time is _____.
2. Set your alarm at _____ and get up this same time EVERY morning, regardless of how much sleep you got the night before.
3. DO NOT nap during the day.

The client's sleep diary will be reviewed in every session and sleep efficiency will be calculated weekly. Time in bed will be adjusted based on the following rules across every remaining session:

Titration Rules

1. Sleep efficiency greater than 90 percent. Increase TIB by 15 minutes. Increase until Insomnia Sleep Index (ISI) is less than 10.
2. Sleep efficiency between 85 percent and 90 percent; Stay at same TIB.
3. Sleep efficiency less than 85 percent; decrease TIB in by 15 to 30 minutes.

(Adapted from Spielman et al., 2011)

Session Three: Arousal and Worry

Agenda

1. Assess sleep quality ISI.
2. Review and adjust sleep RX per titration rules (increase or decrease TIB).
3. Review adherence with stimulus control instructions.
4. Discuss sleep hygiene.
5. Prescribe worry time.
6. Teach one relaxation technique.

Materials

1. Insomnia Severity Index.
2. The CBT I calculator or Sleep Calculator 1: these allow you to determine the amount of sleep produced, time in bed, and match of bed time to sleep time.
3. Planned worry worksheet (see the Anxiety Reduction Exercise Chart below).
4. Sleep hygiene instructions.

The client will need to provide their sleep diary information, which they obtained through the CBT I app or the Rush Sleep Diary.

Protocol

The beginning of the session will start with review of the client's sleep diary and calculation of sleep efficiency. Time in bed will either be increased or decreased based on titration rules outlined in Session Two. Persisting insomnia severity will be assessed to determine the degree of sleep-related impairment the client continues to report.

Arousal and Sleep

The relationship between arousal and sleep will need to be discussed with regard to anxiety factors, lifestyle, and environmental issues. Clinicians may wish to use the two-stage model diagram outlined earlier in the chapter. The simple idea is that in order to sleep, arousal must be low. Arousal is high when we are awake and alert during the day (our circadian cycle) and need to get things done. It is low at night when we sleep. If arousal is too high, it prevents sleep.

There are environmental and behavioral factors that increase arousal. These include lifestyle factors (for instance, alcohol use, caffeine use, and cigarette use) before bed and dietary factors (heavy meals late before sleep). Light is also a factor that increases arousal. Structures deep in the brain that control arousal are turned on and off by light. Television and electronics are a form of light; even closed eyes sense light and send that information to the brain. It is important that TV not be on at night and electronics switched off during sleep for this reason.

Sleep Hygiene Instructions

1. No caffeine 4 to 6 hours before bed.
2. No heavy meal within 3 hours of bed.
3. No smoking before bed.
4. Lights low or off in bedroom.
5. No TV in room; TV not on at night.
6. Comfortable room temperature.
7. Room dark.
8. Do not exercise 2 hours before bed.
9. Do not use bed as a "worry place"; if worried, get out of bed.

Anxiety and worry also impact arousal. Anxiety has physical manifestations that reflect increased arousal. For instance, muscle tension, increased respiration, increased heart rate, body temperature changes, alertness, and attention changes all suggest physical factors related to increased arousal.

Relaxation training is a way to decrease this physiological arousal. Clients should be instructed initially in diaphragmatic breathing, utilizing the methods outlined in Chapter 4. Clients should be instructed to practice for 5 minutes at a time three times per day.

Thoughts and worries also increase arousal. For many people with insomnia, worry becomes an activity that happens in bed at night, when they cannot sleep. This actually increases arousal and blocks sleep. These can be the worries of the day, big concerns, small ones, or even worry about sleep (Note: sleep worry will be addressed in the coming sessions). Often, thinking about worries is not constructive or solution oriented, but instead ruminative and repetitive.

It is important to cut the link between "worry time" and "bed." The easiest way to do this is to assign specific worry time. This means that the client will be instructed to "worry" at set times every day in a specific format with a worry work sheet. Worry time will need to be scheduled at least 4 hours before bed and should be confined to no more than 15 minutes. It is important to provide structure to this time, and the worksheet below can be helpful for clients in determining the things that they have the ability to change from those that they do not.

Homework Assignment

The clinician will instruct the client to complete the worksheet daily. It is advisable to do this for the first time in session (Table 5.1, see Resource Pack, p. 335). Clients should list their problems and worries first. They need to look at this list and assign each "worry" to one of two categories: things they can completely control and things that they cannot. The client will then be instructed to fold the paper between the "Things I have control over" and "Things I do not have control over." The clinician will then take the sheet and tear down the folded line and hand the client the column with "Things I do not have control over." The client should be instructed to tear this list up and throw it away as it is non-productive thinking and something which they cannot influence—no matter how much they think about. The client's focus should then be directed to the "problems I can control" and begin to think about a solution for each problem. Solutions are to be written in the "solutions" column (Table 5.2, see Resource Pack, p. 335).

Table 5.1 Example: Worry Worksheet

Anxiety Reduction Exercise

Make a list of problems, worries, concerns, tasks, fears, or other issues that cause feelings of being overwhelmed, racing thoughts, and feelings of anxiety:

1. _____

2. _____

3. _____

Separate the list in the Anxiety Reduction Exercise into the two categories listed below. Remember, something the client has control over is something that they have complete control over.

At night, before sleep, clients are to take the problem/solutions list with them and set it next to the bed. Clients will then be instructed that when worry comes in bed, they are to respond to these worries by acknowledging the list next to them and saying to themselves, "I have already addressed these problems today." They can then intentionally turn their thoughts to something else. One technique for thought-shifting can be to think of a favorite movie or novel and imagine the life of a favorite character or plot past the original ending.

Table 5.2 Example: Things I Can Control

Things That I Have Control Over	Things That I Do Not Have Control Over
1.	1.
2.	2.
3.	3.
Solutions	

Session Four: Irrational Sleep Beliefs

Agenda

1. Assess sleep quality with the Insomnia Severity Index.
2. Review and adjust sleep RX per titration rules.
3. Discuss ABC model of cognitive distortion related to sleep.
4. Review target distortions (refer to DBAS).
5. Ask client to complete one sleep example in the coming week; the example might be something they know they have thought about when not able to sleep, or imagine they were not sleeping and the "hottest thought" they had.
6. Teach another relaxation technique.

Materials

1. The Insomnia Severity Index.
2. The CBT I calculator or Sleep Calculator 1.

3. The Sleep Calculator 2.
4. The DBAS.

The client will need to provide their own sleep diary information (from the CBT I app or from the Rush Sleep Diary).

Protocol

The session will begin with the Insomnia Severity Index assessment to review current insomnia status.

Sleep will need to be titrated according to the rules (TIB to increase, decrease, or stay the same). Sleep RX will be written for the coming week.

The clinician will then introduce the ABC model as it applies to sleep:

A: ACTIVATING EVENT: Circumstance (i.e., feeling tired during the day, insomnia for years).

B: BELIEF: The thoughts that are pulled forward when thinking about the event (i.e., "I will never be able to function like a normal person without sleep"; I will make a terrible mistake at work because I am tired"; "My sleep problem has been going on for so long, I will never be able to sleep normally again").

C: CONSEQUENCE: The feeling that results from the thought. In one of the examples from B, thinking that one will lose one's job because of a sleep-related mistake can lead to feelings of anxiety and hopelessness. Similarly, thinking that sleep will never improve can lead to feelings of helplessness.

The thoughts that come at us at night about our sleep have a catastrophic, global and irrational quality. They are not reassuring. These actually cause sleep-related anxiety and, in turn, arousal. The thoughts people have about not sleeping and the consequences related to those thoughts actually create insomnia. Such thoughts are pernicious, in that many times people are not even aware they are thinking them.

It is important for the clinician and client to begin to examine these beliefs together. Time spent in therapy will focus on identifying the thoughts, and then really looking at them together.

The DBAS can be quite helpful in identifying common sleep-related distortions. Anything with a score greater than 5 is an indicator of core irrational thought or distortion. The clinician can get a flavor of the content of client thinking from this instrument.

Some questions that can be asked to elicit and, ultimately, identify core distortions are as follows:

- What is the worst outcome if insomnia continues?
- What scares you the most about your insomnia?
- What frustrates you the most about your insomnia?
- What thoughts run through your head when you notice fatigue (or concentration issues or other insomnia symptoms)?
- At what point have you decided to take sleep medications in the past? Tell me about that process.
- What do you worry would happen if you could never use sleep medication?

The client and therapist will then complete an example related to sleep in session. The client will be instructed to "Tell me about a recent night when you have struggled with insomnia. What do you imagine you were thinking in bed?"

Homework Assignment

For homework, the client will be asked to complete an example during the week. There may be a variety of thoughts associated with each event. The client should be instructed to circle the most distressing or "hottest" thought (Table 5.3, see Resource Pack, p. 336).

Relaxation can include visualization or progressive muscle relaxation, both of which were explained in the pain protocol.

Table 5.3 Example: Beliefs, Feelings, and Behavior

Event	Belief/Thought/Image	Feeling	Behavior
Ex: Bad sleep 4 days in a row.	Ex: I have no ability to manage my sleep problem. It is out of control	Ex: Anxious Hopeless	Ex: Wide awake, unable to relax. No pull to sleep Stressed

Session Five: Challenging Irrational Sleep Beliefs and Dismantling Safety Behaviors

Agenda

1. Assess sleep quality.
2. Review and adjust sleep RX per titration rules (increase TIB).
3. Discuss ABC–D model of sleep.
4. Review client example and common distortions.
5. Challenge questions. Probability and possibility.
6. Coping Statements.
7. Safety behaviors.

Materials Needed

1. Insomnia Severity Index.
2. The CBT I calculator or Sleep Calculator 1 (which will allow you to determine the amount of sleep produced, time in bed, and match of bed time to sleep time).
3. Sleep Calculator 2.
4. DBAS.
5. ABCD worksheet.
6. Index card for coping statements.

Protocol

This session will start with sleep titration and the Insomnia Severity Index to address sleep efficiency and persisting insomnia.

The client's thought record from the prior week will need to be reviewed. This will allow the clinician and client to see the most anxiety-provoking thought (the "hottest" thought), in addition to the information gleaned from the DBAS.

It is now time to work on examining and reframing the hot thoughts. The clinician will explain the "D" and "E" of the ABC-D-E model.

A: ACTIVATING EVENT: Circumstance (i.e., feeling tired during the day, insomnia for years).

B: BELIEF: The thoughts that are pulled forward when thinking about the event (i.e., "I will never be able to function like a normal person" or "I will make a terrible mistake at work because I am tired"; "My sleep problem has been going on for so long, I will never be able to sleep normally again").

C: CONSEQUENCE: The feeling that results from the thought. In our example, thinking that one will lose one's job because of a sleep-related mistake can lead to feelings of anxiety and hopelessness. Or, thinking that sleep will never improve can lead to feelings of depression or helplessness.

D: DISPUTING: Challenging the distorted or irrational belief. For example, reviewing the actual number of times the client has been fired because they were tired and made a mistake (probably 0) to develop an actual probability (0 percent probability based on history). Revised thought: "I cannot sleep, I feel tired, I might even make a mistake, but I can still function effectively at my job overall. Not sleeping does not equal getting fired."

E. EFFECT: Cognitive or emotional effect of revised beliefs. Often this means a more realistic appraisal, leading to less anxiety and arousal.

Interventions to Challenge Irrational Thoughts

There are several techniques and questions that can be used to challenge irrational insomnia thoughts (Table 5.4, see Resource Pack, p. 336). For instance:

* Probability vs. Possibility is a technique that can be used to challenge catastrophic thoughts quite easily. It starts with identifying what the catastrophic outcome that the client imagines will happen from not sleeping. An example could be, "If I don't sleep, I won't be alert when I'm driving and I will total my car." The client will then be asked about the *real* probability of this by identifying the number of times this has actually happened. For many clients, this will be a very low number, close to 0. Then the client will need to be asked about the number of times they have driven in their lives where they did not get the perfect night's sleep before. This number will typically be high.

  The real probability equals the number of times an event has really happened divided by the number of times in their lives they have done the behavior.

It is important to point out to the client the error of overestimation that occurs when we are thinking irrationally. We have to learn how to "fact check" our own sleep-related thoughts. Possibility means that in the whole realm of things it could happen. As, for example, getting struck by lightning. Getting struck by lightning is certainly possible; however, possible does not mean that it is probable that you will get struck by lightning. Possible *does not* equal probable.

Table 5.4 Example: The Thought Chart

Event	Thought	Evidence For Thought	Evidence Against Thought	Blended Thought and New Feeling
Ex:	Ex:	Ex:	Ex:	Ex:

Additional challenge questions that can provide evidence against an irrational thought include:

- Is this thought true 100 percent of the time?
- What is the actual evidence for this thought?
- What does this event say or mean about me? Is that true?
- Who would I be without this thought?
- What would I tell my best friend if this happened to them?

The Coping Card

It is important to provide the client with a coping card. This is a tool that they can use to remind themselves of their more realistic thoughts when the anxiety-provoking, sleep-related sleep thoughts come at them. This card should be an index card that they can read when they need, and can even keep beside their bed.

The first statements on the card should be the new rational thoughts that you have developed in this session to address their core fears. Other thoughts that can be included can come from the list below. The client should be asked to circle the ones that they find most reassuring.

Coping Statement

- I have survived this before and nothing catastrophic happened.
- I know that what I am worried about is not probable and have calculated it.
- Just because I did not sleep last night does not mean that I cannot sleep tonight.
- I can overcome my sleepiness at work and function. I have many times before!
- Many people function without enough sleep, and I am no different than most.

- One bad night of sleep does not mean that my day cannot still be a good day.
- I am not falling apart.
- I am going to have good and bad days and this is normal.
- I do not have to like my insomnia in order to still be able to function Okay.
- A few nights of not sleeping does not equal a lifetime of not sleeping.
- It is impossible for me to go the rest of my life without any sleep at all. This will end.
- I have learned skills to deal with this and I understand sleep now.

Safety Behaviors

Finally, the clinician will need to assess for safety behaviors. They are the things the client does to prevent themselves from having to confront the feared consequences of insomnia. Every time they avoid confronting these feared consequences, the "insomnia fear" increases.

The client will need to be advised to stop doing them (and use the coping cards to assist them). Safety behaviors can even include avoiding internal thoughts (the more you try to avoid a thought, the more afraid you become of it). Examples of safety behaviors are the following:

- not doing an activity that is important because you have not had enough sleep;
- using a sleeping pill when you think you might have insomnia;
- avoiding a certain thought or image because you think it will impact your sleep.

The clinician will need to review and challenge the thoughts associated with them to identify the core distortion. Any distortions should be challenged in the same manner as has been recommended in this session already.

Homework Assignment

The homework assignment is to continue to fill out the Sleep Diary and to record in the Thought Chart. The Thought Chart should be used daily.

Session Six: Termination, Relapse Planning, and Prevention

Agenda

1. Final assessment using the Insomnia Severity Index and the DBAS.
2. Outline progress.
3. Discuss expectation of future sleep difficulties.

4. Create a "relapse" plan (when to start restriction therapy again). Discuss trigger situations for relapse and the "danger signs" that indicate issues need to be addressed right now.
5. Strategies for stopping a slip from becoming a relapse.

Protocol

The clinician will need to review the progress the client has made in treatment. This will include improved overall sleep level and how much more efficiently they are falling asleep. The Sleep Diary and the Thought Chart should be reviewed and discussed. Clients will likely need to be reminded of the skills that they have developed and what they have found to be effective in addressing their sleep issues.

Insomnia Inoculation

It is important for the client to understand that just because they are doing better, it does not mean that they will not have episodes of sleeplessness in the future. This is part of the normal variation in sleep, and it is essential for them not to engage in "all or nothing thinking" and to not view a "spurt" of bad sleep as an indication of "treatment failure." A bad night of sleep does not mean that they have relapsed. For clients with insomnia, starting to worry about whether or not insomnia has come back creates a self-perpetuating cycle. It increases their arousal, which then contributes to insomnia. It is, therefore, important to create the expectancy that there will be some times when they have a hard time sleeping—and to remember that this is normal.

The most critical aspect of this is how they respond to it. A specific plan can help them to deal with sleep difficulties and reduce their anxiety. Reviewing in advance the triggers, skills, and restriction skills maintains sleep self-efficacy beliefs. Clients need to be reminded that they themselves have already developed highly effective skills to manage their sleep issues and that they have enough knowledge to continue to do so. They already know what to do. The therapist will need to start off initially by reviewing what they and the client know about what the particular triggers are that set off the insomnia cycle in the past for the client.

My Insomnia Triggers

1. _____

2. _____

3. _____

Skills that I Can Use to Manage My Insomnia

1. _____

2. _____

3. _____

The clinician needs to then identify the specific skills that can help the client address their insomnia. This may be things such as using the coping cards, using relaxation techniques, engaging in planned worry, avoiding caffeine, regular and nutritious meals, and regular exercise.

Finally, it will be important to review the indicators that the client will need to start sleep restriction therapy again. These indicators are included in the box below.

"Sleep Red Alert": Time to Start Sleep Restriction Again

1. Being fatigued during the day or evening consistently.
2. Feeling drowsy during the day for several days in a row.
3. Feeling the need to take naps during the day or evening.
4. Feeling like you are not getting enough sleep in general.

The client knows how to track their sleep, how to calculate their efficiency, and how to set their bed time. If they have difficulty remembering how to do so, they can re-initiate contact with the clinician for "booster" sessions. They need to be reminded that this intervention has worked for them in the past, which significantly increases the probability it will be effective for them in the future.

References

Bootzin, R.R., and Perlis, M. L. (2011). Stimulus control therapy. In Perlis, M., Aloia, M. and Kuhn, B. (eds.). *Behavioral Treatments for Sleep Disorders* (pp. 21-30). Elsevier. DOI: 10.1016/B978-0-12-381522-4.00002-X

Edgar D.M., Dement W.C., & Fuller C.A. (1993). Effect of SCN lesions on sleep in squirrel monkeys: Evidence for opponent processes in sleep-wake regulation. *Journal of Neuroscience*, 13: 1065–1079

Spielman, A. J., Caruso, L. S., & Glovinsky, P. B. (1987). A behavioral perspective on insomnia treatment. *Psychiatric Clinics of North America.*

Spielman, A.J., Yang, C.M., and Glovinsky, P.B. (2011). *Sleep restriction therapy*. In M. Perlis, M. Aloia and B. Kuhn. (Eds.). Behavioral Treatments for Sleep Disorders, (pp. 9–20). Oxford: Elsevier.

Section Two
Mood Symptoms

Chapter 6

Depression Protocol

As indicated in Chapter 1, one of the most effective treatments for depression is cognitive behavioral therapy (CBT). As explained in that chapter, CBT helps people with depression to restructure negative thought patterns so that they are better able to interpret their environment as well as their interactions with others in a positive and realistic way. One of the objectives of CBT when dealing with depression is to help people recognize things that may be contributing to their depression and to also help them change behaviors that may be making the depression worse. An important behavioral aspect of CBT is to get clients to engage in activity they value or enjoy. This key ingredient in the success of CBT for depression will be reflected in the seven-session treatment protocol given in this chapter.

Session One: Getting Started

Agenda

1. Orientation.
2. Assessing client concerns.
3. Setting initial treatment goals.
4. Assigning homework.

Materials Needed

The Patient Health Questionnaire (PHQ-9). Available at www.cqaimh.org/pdf/tool_phq9.pdf or the Beck Depression Inventory–Second Edition (BDI-II). The BDI-II is available from the PsychCorp or other test companies.

Protocol

Initially, the Beck Depression Inventory (2nd ed.) or the PHQ-9 should be administered. The results are discussed with the client while eliciting the client's concerns about their mood. The therapist helps the client talk about their concerns which leads to a listing of some initial treatment goals.

Next, the therapist should discuss CBT as the treatment approach. Among the points that should be included in this discussion are the following:

- CBT is a skills-based, present-focused, and goal-oriented treatment approach.
- CBT targets the thinking styles and behavioral patterns that cause and maintain depression.
- Depression in adults is commonly associated with thinking styles that are unrealistically negative, self-focused and critical, and often tending toward hopelessness.
- In CBT, cognitive skills are used to identify the typical "thinking traps" (cognitive distortions) that clients commit and challenge them to consider the evidence more fairly.
- Since depressed adults tend to demonstrate increased isolation, withdrawal, simultaneous rejection of others, and decreased activity and enjoyment in activities, treatment will encourage more activity.
- Other behavioral interventions include problem solving.
- Treatment is generally time-limited and will be done in seven sessions.

Return to the initial goals and begin to spell out some mutually agreed upon goals. One of these goals is likely to be increased activity levels. The clinician should be mindful that in depressed persons this goal setting is a cognitive task and cognition can be impacted in depression. Thus, some clients may find it challenging and the clinician may need to provide more structure and prompting to assist the client in formulating and retrieving goals. This goal setting will lead to the homework assignment for this session.

Homework Assignment

Ask the client to work on a short list of goals during the coming week. What areas of their life and their functioning have been most troublesome to them

Table 6.1 Example: Goals List

Specific Life Areas I Want to Improve	Check Which Three Are Most Important
1.	
2.	
3.	

(e.g. work, family, social, recreational, financial, health, sleep, etc.)? What have they stopped doing since they have been depressed that they did earlier? What would they like to address and improve? Request that they think about which goal in the list would be most important (Table 6.1, see Resource Pack, p. 337).

Session Two: Learning More about CBT

Agenda

1. Assess weekly mood with the PHQ-9.
2. Setting initial goals.
3. Goal setting.
4. Thoughts and feelings.
5. Increasing activities.
6. Homework assignment.

Protocol

Review homework and review both the client's concerns and treatment goals listed in the homework. Which three are most important? Would the patient like to change these goals or add to them?

Establish a treatment plan based on the agreed-upon goals. Point out that goals must be observable, measurable, and achievable, and must relate to cognitive or behavioral changes relevant to the patient's presenting problems. Goals are tied to specific skills to be addressed in treatment. Discuss how goals increase the continuity of sessions; allow for directed, focused treatment; and enable the patient and therapist to assess the progress of therapy and identify change in an objective manner. Indicate that these goals may change during the course of treatment and that one reason may be that together you may discover new information leading to the modification of goals.

As you discuss goals and the patient's problems, do so in cognitive and behavioral terms. Then, begin to talk about the difference between thoughts and feelings and how certain thoughts contribute to depression. Help the patient become aware of how their thoughts influence feelings in ways that are not helpful. Ask them to list some of their thoughts that are related to their depression.

Encourage more behavioral activation. For instance, ask the client to make special efforts to increase their activity level and to record their activity. Note that activities such as walking help improve mood and reduce behaviors associated with negative mood.

Homework Assignment

Instruct the client to use the Thoughts Record chart below to begin to pay attention to unrealistic and counterproductive thoughts associated with negative emotion. This means thoughts that happen when they feel sad, anxious, depressed, discouraged, or angry. Ask them to rate on the SUDS scale of 0 (no distress) to 100 (extremely upset or distressed) how much the thought bothered them. It should be filled out during the week and brought to the next session (Table 6.2, see Resource Pack, p. 337).

Table 6.2 Example: Thoughts Record

Thoughts/Image	Situation	SUDS Rating (0–100)
1.		
2.		
3.		

Encourage more activity. For the depressed client, this can be difficult in the beginning. The clinician will need to start with a physical activity that is accessible, easy and low cost. They will need to be certain to minimize barriers to activity. It is essential that an activity is identified that they can complete successfully as this will build behavioral momentum. Depressed clients may list an activity they feel they "should do" (i.e. lifting weights or jogging every day). The clinician will need to be watchful for this as this is a trap in that it is not something that they likely enjoy nor will it be immediately reinforcing. Walking is an excellent suggested start for many clients. It is free, easy, can be done with a companion or alone, and generalizes to other activity.

The clinician will need to establish a realistic activity level with the depressed client. Again, depressed clients may give an unrealistic appraisal of how active they think they "should be." Clinical failure with behavioral activation can be avoided by setting a low goal, one that the clinician is sure the client will be able to achieve with a high degree of success. Our suggested formula for this is to ask the client how long they can do activity X (like walking) before they stop for any reason. The clinician should then take the client's time-based activity estimate and reduce it by 20 percent. This number will represent an achievable goal. If the client is able to do it consistently, they can increase the activity level by 10 percent. If they are unable to do it, they should be advised to reduce the activity by 10 percent.

Ask the client to keep a record of their physical activity during the week, using the Activities Record Chart (Table 6.3, see Resource Pack, p. 338).

Table 6.3 Example: Activities Record

Physical Activities (For Instance, Walking, Biking, Bowling, Climbing Stairs, Etc.)	How Many Days?	How Many Minutes Each Day?

Session Three: Identifying Automatic Negative Thoughts

Agenda

1. Assess weekly mood with PHQ-9.
2. Review homework.
3. Review daily physical activity/walking.
4. Introduce automatic thoughts and distortions.
5. Identifying Automatic negative thoughts.
6. Homework assignment.

Materials needed

Tables 6.2, 6.4 and 6.5.

Protocol

Review the homework assignment and go over the unrealistic and/or unproductive thoughts the client was aware of. Indicate that in this session, there will be more discussion of thoughts that contribute to depression. Also, review the activity record and reinforce the client's efforts to become more active.

Follow up on the discussion of the Thought Record by indicating that CBT patients learn to improve their own mood and change their behavior by modifying the way they think about situations. Emphasize that a key tool in identifying and examining the associations between thoughts, feelings, and situations is the Thought Record, which they will be asked to fill out each week.

Discuss the cognitive behavioral model (as depicted in Figure 6.1), which suggests that three layers of cognitive dysfunction exist in individuals struggling with depression.

Discuss automatic thoughts and images and how they relate to specific situations and/or events and occur quickly throughout the day as we appraise ourselves, our environment, and our future. Although we may be unaware of these

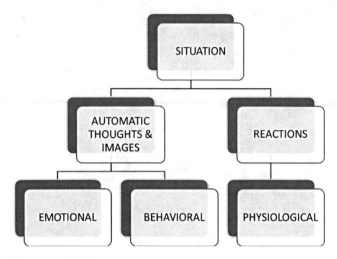

Figure 6.1 Cognitive Model

thoughts and images, we are generally very familiar with the emotions that they create within us.

Point out that maladaptive automatic thoughts are distorted reflections of a situation, which are often accepted by us as true. These automatic thoughts tend to be dysfunctional beliefs about oneself, the world, and the future that are triggered by situations or exaggerated by psychiatric states, such as anxiety or depression. An example of an automatic thought is "Nothing ever goes right for me."

Note that various beliefs grow up around the automatic thoughts and that when depressed people may tend to store up information consistent with negative beliefs but ignore evidence that contradicts them. Use the chart shown in Table 6.4 to further discuss automatic negative thoughts.

Homework Assignment

Complete one example in the chart below in session, using an example provided by the client. Instruct the client to continue to use the Thoughts Record Chart to pay attention to automatic negative thoughts that contribute to depression. It should be filled out during the week and brought to the next session (Table 6.2, see Resource Pack, p. 337).

Continue to encourage increasing physical activity. Ask the client to keep a record of their physical activity during the week, using the Activities Record Chart (Table 6.5, see Resource Pack, p. 338).

Table 6.4 Automatic Negative Thoughts Chart

Category	Definition	Example
All-or-nothing thinking	Seeing things as either all good or all bad and allowing no middle ground.	"I'm a failure" or "I'm a total success and perfect"
Fortune telling	Predicting that things will turn out negatively, without considering other possible outcomes.	"Things never work out for me." "Everything I touch goes rotten."
Disqualifying the positive	Telling yourself that positive experiences don't count	"Just because I succeeded at something, doesn't mean I really have ability. That was a fluke."
Emotional reasoning	Believing that what you feel must be true.	"I feel like a loser. I am a loser"
Labeling	Attaching a global, extreme, negative label to yourself or others.	"I am stupid." "I'm a wreck" "I'm unlovable"
Catastrophizing	Expecting extremely negative consequences; exaggerating situations to be the worst possible outcome.	"I can't stand it anymore!" "My life is ruined."
Mental filter	Focusing on a single negative detail instead of seeing the whole picture.	"I had a disagreement with my spouse about the dishwasher, they never support me" (even though spouse completed 15 other household tasks that week)
Mind reading	Believing that you know what others are thinking, especially how they feel about you.	"They think I'm weird, crazy, incompetent, etc."
"Should" statements	Having fixed ideas about how you or others "should," "ought to," or "must" be. Leads to feeling guilt, anger, and resentment.	"I really should have been able to prevent this." "Things should always be fair." "I must be able do this." "I should have known this was coming."
Personalization	Seeing yourself as the cause of negative events for which you are not responsible.	"I'm not a likeable person" (friend doesn't answer the phone)
Just World	Believing that good things only happen to good people, and bad things happen to bad people.	"My life is hard and I'm depressed because I am a bad person. I did X. I deserve this."

(Adapted from Thorn, 2017)

Table 6.5 Example: Thoughts Record

Thought/Image	Specific Automatic Thought	Stuation	SUDS Rating (0–100)
1.			
2.			
3.			

Session Four: Challenging Automatic Thoughts

Agenda

1. Assess weekly mood with PHQ-9.
2. Review homework assignment, including daily physical activity/walking.
3. Introduce evaluating the validity of automatic thoughts and assumptions.
4. Discuss interrupting and intervening with automatic negative thoughts.
5. Activity.
6. Homework assignment.

Materials Needed

Four Questions List

Protocol

Begin by reviewing the homework recorded in the Automatic Negative Thoughts Record and the Activities Record. Discuss the types of automatic thoughts the client has noted.

In going over the Thoughts Record, discuss the maladaptive automatic thoughts and point out that this is the first step in the cognitive component of therapy. The focus of treatment from this stage on is to intervene with dysfunctional automatic thoughts. Indicate that the patient must master identifying and challenging thoughts to be able to deal effectively with their depression.

It is important for the patient to understand the rationale for identifying automatic thoughts before acquiring the skill of addressing his/her own thoughts. Using the cognitive model introduced in Session Three can be helpful in continuing to help the individual better understand automatic thoughts. Applying the patient's recent automatic thoughts to the cognitive model can facilitate his or her awareness of thoughts that contribute to their depression.

Discuss hot thoughts during this session. Hot thoughts are automatic thoughts that occur in combination with a change in emotion or mood. Hot thoughts may be very important or very strong thoughts that are often associated with dysfunctional core beliefs, and should be targeted in therapy. To identify which automatic thoughts are "hot," the client should be asked to circle the "thought that bothers them the most" from the Automatic Negative Thoughts chart provided in the previous session's homework. The therapist can also look for the thought with the highest SUDS rating. Alternately, the therapist can also listen for verbal cues, such as the language used as the client expresses the thought. You can watch for nonverbal cues, such as increased volume of speech or fidgeting. Changes in facial expression, shifts in position, or hand movements can be helpful in determining whether a patient is experiencing an automatic hot thought. Listening to tone, pitch, volume, and the pace of a patient's speech is also beneficial. When you notice these actions, this is a good time to bring it to the client's attention and help them in identifying an automatic thought associated with the shift in emotions.

Next, begin discussing the techniques for challenging maladaptive thoughts, pointing out their importance for CBT. Indicate that once they have learned to become aware of their negative thoughts, the next stage is to try and answer the thoughts back and find more realistic and helpful alternatives. The clinician can give them a list of four questions they can use to help them respond to their negative thoughts.

Four Questions to Respond to Negative Thoughts

1. What is the evidence for your thought? Are there facts to back up your thought?
2. What alternative reasons could there be for what has happened? Think of as many alternative explanations as you can.
3. What is the effect of thinking in the way you do?
4. What are the thinking errors you are making? Identify the type of distorted thinking.

Homework Assignment

As the homework assignment, instruct the client to continue their Thoughts Record, which will be revised to allow them to identify aspects of their automatic negative thoughts. In the revised Thoughts Record, they are to classify the type of negative thought (see Resource Pack, p. 339) and then ask four questions in challenging the negative thoughts. Also, request that they continue to build on their activities and increase the amount of activity in which they engage on a daily basis (Activity Record, see Table 6.3 Resource Pack, p. 338).

Table 6.6 Example: Negative Thoughts Record

Thought/Image	Specific Automatic Thought	Is There Evidence to Support this Thought?
1.		
2.		
3.		

Session Five: Behavioral Activation—Pleasant Events and Values

Agenda

1. Assess weekly mood with PHQ-9.
2. Review homework assignment, including daily physical activity/walking.
3. Introduce behavioral activation.
4. Identify pleasant events based on values.
5. Homework assignment.

Protocol

To begin this session, go over the homework assignment. Review the Negative Thoughts Record and check to see if the client was able to correctly classify the kinds of distortion. And did he or she ask questions to challenge the accuracy of negative thoughts?

Also, in going over the homework, you should discuss the Activity Record. Indicate to the client the Activity Record is related to what is called behavioral activation in CBT. Behavioral activation is based on the theory that one of the reasons that people become depressed is because they are no longer enjoying what they are doing. A simple equation, then, is if they change the things they are doing in their life, this will equal more opportunities for reinforcement or pleasure. Changing the kinds of pleasant events based on values will help to change their mood. The clinician must assist the client in identifying activities that have been reinforcing in the past, that the client will enjoy based on past experiences, and the things that they value. Values are the ideals or standards that matter to someone. They are like directions that inform us which way to go in our lives. Like directions, you never arrive at them. For instance, you can always keep driving north. In a like manner, you never stop driving in the direction of your value. Goals are stops along the way, but not final destinations.

Identify values and behavioral steps to achieve those values

The primary step in this session is to assist the patient in identifying the things that matter. This can be done in three steps. The first is an exercise:

- *Eulogy exercise*: Imagine you are an observer at your own eulogy and the celebration of your life. Everyone that you love and who has mattered to you is there. What would you like them to say about you?

    The patient can even be asked to write it down. This exercise can help crystallize the things that are really important, while identifying core values.

The second step can be to look at the client's initial treatment goals, as they are often based on values.

The third step is to have the patient peruse the following list and identify or circle the things that appeal to them:

VALUES

- *Parenting*: Spending time with children, going to activities;
- *Leisure*: Hobbies, passions, outdoor pursuits, artistic pursuits, cooking, theater, movies, vacations;
- *Spirituality*: Church, studying religious texts, learning about other religions, prayer, mediation;
- *Personal Growth*: Reading about self-improvement, listening to radio or watching TV shows;
- *Health*: Nutrition, exercise, learning about wellness;
- *Work*: Career, achievement, learning about profession, education;
- *Community/Environment*: Taking care of own home, yard, local community groups, learning about environmental issues;
- *Social Justice*: Helping others with challenges, advocacy organizations;
- *Caring for Animals*: Spending time with dog/cat/bird, researching a pet;
- *Family relationships*: Getting together with family, planning holidays, talking on the phone;
- *Intimate Relationships*: Spending time with partner, doing something for them;
- *Social Relationships*: Spending time with friends, meeting new friends;
- *Nature*: Gardening, time outside, bird watching, hunting, camping;
- *Travel*: Learning about new places/cultures, languages, planning trips.

The client should be asked to select activities. Treatment momentum might be also accelerated by anchoring the client's activities to the initial goals—based on values—that they created at the beginning of treatment.

Behavioral activation, then, not only involves monitoring daily and weekly activities, but also learning how their activities affect their mood. Point out that they have already been monitoring their activity with the Activity Record. This has involved writing down which activities he or she completes each day or week. Now, this effort to increase activities will be stepped up with the idea of doing fewer avoiding behaviors and more engagement behaviors—all with the idea of bringing about improvements in their mood. As a result of this stepped up effort at behavioral activation, there will be greater emphasis on activity assignments and any other needed strategies to help the client to remember to complete assignments.

Homework Assignment

Encourage continued use of the Negative Thoughts Record (see Resource Pack, p. 339) to have them not only identify automatic negative thoughts but to intervene in these thoughts too. They should continue to classify the type of negative thoughts they have, but also to ask four questions in challenging the negative thoughts.

Also, request that they continue to build on their baseline physical activities, including walking (see Activity Record in Resource Pack, p. 338).

Based on discussion during this session, there should be a list of activities the client needs to return to, assignments related to these activities, and thoughts that interfere with these activities. The Behavioral Activation Chart (shown in Table 6.7 (see Resource Pack, p. 339) is for this purpose. During the session, you and the client should choose a few activities and a date for completion should be given to a few.

Table 6.7 Example: Behavioral Activation Chart

Value Based Activity	Planned Day/Date	Done?	Mood After (0–10)
1.			
2.			
3.			

Session Six: Problem Solving

Agenda

1. Assess weekly mood with PHQ-9.
2. Review homework.
3. Introduce problem-solving skills.
4. Homework assignment.

Protocol

Review the homework assignment, offering positive feedback and reinforcement for the client's efforts. Encourage the individual to continue their work at identifying and interrupting negative thoughts and increasing their activities.

The main part of this session will be an introduction and discussion of problem solving. Begin by stating that problem-solving techniques involve a process by which an individual attempts to identify effective means of coping with problems of everyday living. This often involves a set of steps for analyzing a problem, identifying options for coping, evaluating the options, deciding upon a plan, and developing strategies for implementing the plan. Emphasize that problem-solving strategies are used in CBT with a wide range of problems, including anxiety and depression.

Point out that problem-solving techniques teach skills that will help them in feeling increased control over various issues in their life that might in the past have felt overwhelming.

Indicate that they have learned to challenge their negative and unrealistic thoughts and beliefs, now they can use problem solving to deal with a situation that can be addressed and dealt with. There may be depressing situations in the patient's life (such as loneliness, estrangement from a family member, or financial concerns) for which solutions are available.

Present the client with the problem-solving approach called "The SOLVED Technique" and discuss how it can be used.

The SOLVED Technique

S: Select a problem you would like to solve.

O: Open your mind to all possible solutions.

L: List the potential pros and cons of each potential solution.

V: Verify the best solution.

E: Enact the best solution or plan.

D: Decide if the solution or plan worked.

Address during the discussion of the SOLVED technique that frequently this technique should be combined with techniques to intervene in distorted or unrealistic thoughts.

As the last aspect of this discussion, explain to the client how they can construct more realistic and accurate statements to counter their negative thoughts. When the patient becomes aware of having a distorted thought, they can come up with a more logical and accurate thought to replace the distorted thought.

Homework Assignment

Instruct the patient to continue to use the Negative Thoughts Record (Table 6.8, see Resource Pack, p. 340) to not only identify automatic negative thoughts but also to intervene in these thoughts. They should continue to classify the type of negative thought they have, but also ask themselves the four questions in challenging the negative thoughts. In addition, they should now come up with more accurate and realistic thoughts to replace their distorted thoughts.

Also, request that they continue to build on the efforts to increase their activities by adding more behaviors and events to their daily and weekly schedules in their Activities Record, see Resource Pack, p. 338.

Table 6.8 Example: Negative Thoughts Record

Thought/Image	Specific Automatic Thought	Is There Evidence To Support This Thought?	Construct A More Realistic Statement
1.			
2.			
3.			

There should be an ongoing list of activities for the client during the coming week. These should be recorded in the Behavioral Activation Chart. During the session, you and the client should have selected some activities along with projected completion dates for activities (use Table 6.7, see Resource Pack, p. 339).

Session Seven: Treatment Planning and Ending Treatment

Agenda

1. Assess weekly mood with PHQ-9.
2. Review homework.
3. Discuss ending treatment.
4. Discuss a plan for self-management in the future.
5. How the client will maintain changes.

Protocol

Review the homework assignment and give positive feedback for the client's positive efforts at bringing about behavior and thinking changes.

After administering the PHQ-9 (or the BDI-II), as was done in the initial session, go over the results, pointing out the substantial progress the client has made since the first session. Review the goals the client set at the beginning of treatment. Reinforce those what were achieved and talk about continuing to move forward with each of them.

The rest of this session will be devoted to preparing the patient for ending treatment, which will include addressing techniques for preventing relapse. Let the client know that end-of-treatment planning is a collaborative process of preparing the patient and assessing his or her readiness for ending treatment. Point out that an important aspect of treatment is that the client is able to move beyond reliance on the therapist to apply the skills learned throughout the program on their own.

It is important to be aware that end-of-treatment planning actually begins at the first session when you give the patient some indication of the frequency and duration of treatment, but that the planning for the end of treatment is an ongoing process, culminating in the final session. In this final session, there should be a review of treatment and an introduction to relapse-prevention skills. The termination of treatment should be discussed in an empowering and thoughtful way by recognizing and normalizing the patient's typical fears ("Can I function on my own without my weekly sessions?"), assuring them that there are safeguards in place (for instance, that you can be reached in an emergency and that booster sessions will be available), and offering encouragement that CBT is, ultimately, a self-management program.

In this session, a considerable block of time should be devoted to reviewing what was learned, which includes the different cognitive and behavioral skills the patient was taught. You might start this discussion by asking them to enumerate what they have learned. It is frequently instructive to ask what was particularly meaningful to them about their time in therapy. You may give a handout that reflects the skills taught so that the client can take this with them. They should also be encouraged to keep the other handouts and homework completed during treatment as a reminder of their skills.

End the session by discussing relapse prevention. Many patients are concerned that they will not be able to cope with stress, psychological problems, or depression in the future without regular therapy sessions. It is, therefore, important to go over with the client potential stressors and symptoms they may encounter in the future. Go over a plan with the patient in which you discuss the tools the patient has learned that he or she can apply in particular situations in the future. Also, discuss how and when they might need to contact you (or another mental health professional) for the booster sessions.

Chapter 7

Anger Dysregulation Protocol

Anger is a normal, healthy emotion when it is expressed appropriately. Expressed inappropriately, it can become a destructive force. Combine anger with blame, hostility, and aggression, it can lead to negative—sometimes even legal—consequences for the individual.

It is when anger has become destructive and with serious consequences that patients are referred to doctors, medical clinics, and emergency departments for anger management or, as it is sometimes called, anger dysregulation therapy.

What follows is a seven-session treatment program for clients with anger dysregulation.

Session One: Anger-Management Orientation and Assessment

Agenda

1. Curriculum and expectations for clients.
2. Questionnaires and surveys.
3. Goals.
4. First social skill: making good choices.
5. Homework assignment.

Materials Needed

1. The State-Trait Anger Expression Inventory-2 (STAXI-2): The STAXI-2 is a 57-item inventory which measures the intensity of anger as an emotional state (State Anger) and the disposition to experience angry feelings as a personality trait (Trait Anger). The instrument consists of six scales measuring the intensity of anger and the disposition to experience angry feelings. Items consist of 4-point scales that assess intensity of anger at a particular moment and the frequency of anger experience, expression, and control. It is available from Sigma Assessment Systems, Inc.
2. Anger Log (see Resource Pack, p. 340).

Protocol

After having the client complete the assessment instrument, the rest of the session is used to establish rapport and begin to help the client better understand anger. Rapport is very important in anger-management treatment so that in later sessions, when the client is discussing his or her anger issues in more details, they will feel that you are trustworthy and that you are willing to work with them—rather than judging them.

You may start out by asking questions about their life and their background. You can ask about their history of anger problems and how their anger may have created difficulties in the past. You can also ask specific questions such as "What do you hope to get out of this course of treatment?" and "How do you expect to be different when treatment ends?"

Begin to educate the client about anger by saying that in the most general sense, anger is a feeling or emotion that ranges from mild irritation to intense fury and rage. Many people often confuse anger with aggression. Aggression is a behavior that is intended to cause harm or injury to another person or damage to property. Hostility, on the other hand, refers to a set of attitudes and judgments that motivate aggressive behaviors.

To initiate discussion, ask the client if he or she ever confused anger with aggression. If so, ask them to elaborate on this.

Point out that anger becomes a problem for people when it is felt too intensely, is felt too frequently, or is expressed inappropriately. Feeling anger too intensely or frequently places extreme physical strain on the body. Ask the client to talk about some ways anger may have been affecting them physically.

Indicate that often the inappropriate expression of anger initially has apparent payoffs (e.g., releasing tension, controlling people). In the long term, however, these payoffs lead to negative consequences. That is why they are called "apparent" payoffs; the long-term negative consequences far outweigh the short-term gains. Encourage the patient to list some payoffs to using anger that they are familiar with. And follow up by asking them to talk about the negative consequences that they have experienced as a result of expressing their anger inappropriately.

Next, talk about common myths about anger (U.S. Health & Human Services, 2016):

- *Myth 1: Anger is inherited.* One misconception or myth about anger is that the way people express anger is inherited and cannot be changed. Evidence from research studies, however, indicates that people are *not* born with set and specific ways of expressing anger. Rather, these studies show that the expression of anger is learned behavior and that more appropriate ways of expressing anger can also be learned.

- *Myth 2: Anger automatically leads to aggression.* A related myth involves the misconception that the only effective way to express anger is through aggression. There are other more constructive and assertive ways, however, to express anger. Effective anger management involves controlling the escalation of anger by learning assertiveness skills, changing negative and hostile "self-talk," challenging automatic beliefs, and using a variety of behavioral strategies. These skills, techniques, and strategies will be discussed in later sessions.

- *Myth 3: You must be aggressive to get what you want.* Many people confuse assertiveness with aggression. The goal of aggression is to dominate, intimidate, harm, or injure another person—to win at any cost. Conversely, the goal of assertiveness is to express feelings of anger in a way that is respectful of other people. Expressing yourself in an assertive manner does not blame or threaten other people and minimizes the chance of emotional harm. Assertive skills will be discussed in more detail in future sessions.

- *Myth 4: Venting anger is always desirable.* For many years, there was a popular belief that the aggressive expression of anger, such as screaming or beating on pillows, was therapeutic and healthy. Research studies have found, however, that people who vent their anger aggressively simply get better at being angry. In other words, venting anger in an aggressive manner reinforces aggressive behavior.

Ask the client if prior to the discussion of these myths if they ever believed any of these myths about anger to be true. Request they talk about their prior beliefs about anger.

Then, introduce ten important points about anger:

Ten Important Points About Anger

1. Anger is a normal human feeling.
2. Anger serves as a natural adaptive response to threats, allowing you to fight and defend yourself when attacked.
3. Anger is a powerful emotion.
4. An anger trigger is what makes you mad.
5. You can feel anger in your body.
6. Anger can be productive, especially when you express your angry feelings in an assertive—not aggressive—way.
7. Your anger log can help you understand your anger.
8. Good anger management means:
   - You can see that you are angry;
   - You can know why you are angry;
   - You can do something about it.

9. You can calm yourself and monitor yourself through the process.
10. Simple relaxation tools, such as deep breathing and relaxing imagery, can help you calm down your anger.

While using the ten important points about anger as reference, indicate in this session that although most people experience anger in response to certain situations, chronic anger and aggressive response styles are learned. Once learned, anger then becomes a routine, familiar, and predictable response to a variety of situations. There are multiple ways that people learn this response style. Some people learn to be angry by observing or copying the behavior of others; some learn to be angry and behave aggressively by being reinforced or rewarded for it. However, extensive psychological research confirms that events that happen during heightened states of emotion, such as anger, fear, and joy, are more memorable than less dramatic occurrences. This may be particularly relevant to military veterans.

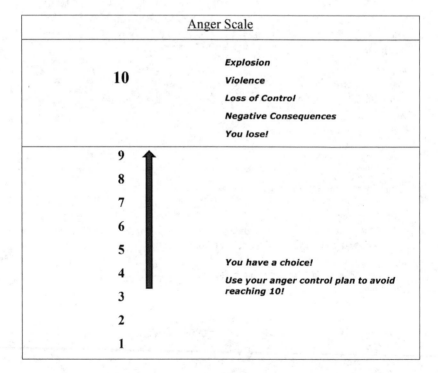

Figure 7.1 Anger Scale
(Adapted from U.S. Health & Human Services, 2016)

Emphasize that when anger is displayed frequently and aggressively, it often results in negative consequences. Then ask, "How have you learned to respond with anger in situations?" Follow this up with the question, "In what ways has this learned response been maladaptive?"

While indicating that they can learn new ways of responding by becoming aware of the events and circumstances that trigger their anger and the negative consequences that result from it, also let them know that they will need to develop a set of strategies to effectively manage their anger. These treatment sessions will help them learn more about strategies to manage anger. To set the stage for later sessions, ask them about some anger control strategies that they are aware of or have used in the past.

Finally, point out that a simple way to monitor their anger is to use a 1 to 10 scale called the Anger Scale (Figure 7.1). A score of 1 on the Anger Scale represents a complete lack of anger or a total state of calm, whereas 10 represents an angry and explosive loss of control that leads to negative consequences.

Table 7.1 Example: Anger Log (Week 1)

Day One:	
Incident:	**Incident:**
What made me mad? What was my Anger Scale score? How did I act? What was the outcome?	What made me mad? What was my Anger Scale score? How did I act? What was the outcome?
Day Two: . . .	. . .
Day Three: . . .	. . .
Day Four: . . .	. . .
Day Five: . . .	. . .
Day Six: . . .	. . .
Day Seven: . . .	. . .

Homework Assignment

Provide the client with an Anger Log and instruct them to fill out this log each day to help both of you track their anger. For each day of the upcoming week, they should monitor and record the highest number they reach on the anger scale. The Anger Log should be brought into each session filled out so that you can both discuss it.

Anger Log

Anger has a way of sneaking up and taking control of our thoughts and actions before we realize what is happening. However, with practice, you can get better at catching your anger before it takes over. Filling out an Anger Log (Table 7.1, see Resource Pack, p. 340) will help you achieve your goal to handle your anger in a more productive way.

Instructions: Either at the end of the day or after your anger has passed, take a moment to reflect on the situation in which you felt angry—or even just a bit frustrated. By completing this every day, you will be able to remember the times you got angry for the next session.

Session Two: Understanding Anger and Using Immediate Anger-Management Strategies

Agenda

1.   Homework review.
2.   Introduce anger basics.
3.   Immediate anger management strategies.
4.   Homework assignment.

Materials Needed

Anger Log Week (see Resource Pack, p. 341).

Protocol

To begin Session Two, there should be a review of the Anger Log. Have the client discuss each of the incidents recorded in the Anger Log so that he or she becomes more comfortable talking about their anger and so both clinician and client begin to better understand the typical anger episodes that take place.

It is important to start discussing anger-management strategies early in the treatment. The client can be asked what strategies, if any, they have already tried to use to stop themselves from getting so angry. In addition, they can be asked how successful these management strategies have been.

Most often, while many clients with anger problems have tried various ways of controlling or delaying their anger, they have typically not worked very well. Generally, this is because their anger arousal is so high that thinking about using a previously decided on solution is completely forgotten or just cannot be used as they intended. Therefore, it is useful to begin introducing some anger-management strategies that they can use immediately.

These strategies are called "immediate" strategies and are designed to be used when anger is rapidly escalating and intense. A good rule of thumb is that these are to be used when the anger meter reaches a 7 of 10. The client can be encouraged to implement these immediately. For example, they can be told about thought-stopping approaches, time out, and using a mantra.

The first immediate strategy to discuss is timeout.

- *Timeout:* The timeout is a basic anger management strategy that should be in everyone's anger control plan. This can also be called "breaking contact." It means leaving the situation that is causing the escalation or simply stopping the discussion that is provoking your anger. They should be advised to return to the anger-producing situation again only when they have calmed sufficiently.

The formal use of a timeout can also involve our relationships with other people. These relationships may involve family members, friends, and coworkers. The formal use of a timeout involves having an agreement, or a prearranged plan, by which any of the parties involved can call a timeout and to which all parties have agreed in advance. If necessary, the person calling the timeout can leave the situation. It is agreed, however, that he or she will return to either finish the discussion or postpone it, depending on whether the parties involved feel they can successfully resolve the issue.

A timeout is important because it can be used effectively in the heat of the moment. Even if a person's anger is escalating quickly as measured on the Anger Scale, he or she can prevent reaching 10 by taking a timeout and leaving the situation.

Ask the client to try to think of situations where they could use the timeout strategy. Request that they describe how they would use timeout in each situation. In discussing this strategy, review any possible challenges or difficulties they might anticipate in using timeout.

The second immediate strategy to discuss is thought stopping.

- *Thought stopping.* Another approach to controlling our anger is called "thought stopping," which is an immediate anger control strategy. In this approach, you simply tell yourself through a series of self-commands to stop thinking anger-fueling thoughts that are escalating anger. The Rubber Band technique is one of the simplest and most concrete ways to do this. The client wears a rubber band or rubber bracelet around their wrist at all times. Every time they find themselves having a thought that would lead to anger, they snap the rubber band. The physical sensation switches attentional focus away from the negative thought and provides an opportunity to get distance from the thought. This can also be combined with taking a timeout immediately, taking a few deep breaths, or use of a mantra.

Encourage the patient to think of specific examples of thought-stopping statements they could use when they become angry. Discuss the situations in which they would use thought-stopping statements.

- *Develop a mantra.* The client can come up with a mantra or short saying that they can tell themselves when their anger is escalating that they think might be helpful. It could be as simple as "Stop, breathe, and leave" or "It's not that important." They should be instructed to use such a mantra until they are calm.
- *Breathing:* This will be introduced formally in sessions that address anger-related physical arousal and diaphragmatic breathing instruction. Many clients may already be familiar with breathing techniques through yoga, meditation, or prior intervention. Even if they are not, they can be instructed to take two or three "cleansing" breathes while inhaling deeply and exhaling slowly. It can be described as "exhaling" the stress.

Homework Assignment

The homework assignment for the next week is to continue to fill out the Anger Log and to try one or more anger-management strategies introduced in this session. They should be instructed that the new anger-management strategies might not seem to have an instant effect, but they should be tried many times in order for them to begin to have a beneficial effect.

Anger Log

Instructions: Either at the end of the day or after your anger has passed, take a moment to reflect on the situation in which you felt angry—or even just a bit frustrated. By completing the Anger Log (Table 7.2, see Resource Pack, p. 341) every day, you will be able to remember the times you got angry for the next session.

Table 7.2 Example: Anger Log (Week 2)

Day One:	
Incident:	**Incident:**
What made me mad? How did I act or behave? Did I use a strategy? What was the outcome?	What made me mad? How did I act or behave? Did I use a strategy? What was the outcome?
Day Two: . . .	. . .
Day Three: . . .	. . .
Day Four: . . .	. . .
Day Five: . . .	. . .
Day Six: . . .	. . .
Day Seven: . . .	. . .

Session Three: Your Anger Triggers and Learning Your Cues

Agenda

1. Review homework assignment.
2. Introduce anger triggers.
3. Discussion of anger triggers.
4. Pros and cons of anger expressions.
5. Direct and indirect expressions of anger.
6. Assign homework.

Materials Needed

Anger Log Week 3 (see Resource Pack, p. 341).

Protocol

As in the previous session, the first part of this session is devoted to a review and discussion of the homework. The anger incidents reported in the Anger Log should be reviewed. Also, have the client describe their attempts to use new anger-management strategies.

Now that the individual is more aware of what anger is, they need to understand what makes them angry. That, too, has been a question in the Anger Log. Now, they can see this as learning to recognize their anger triggers. Explain that an anger trigger is something that provokes or causes your anger. It can be almost anything, but typically adults' anger is triggered by things such as stress, financial concerns, abuse, an insult or slight by another person, or overwhelming requirements on your time and energy. You can review the Anger Logs for the first 2 weeks to pick out some of the client's usual triggers. Point out that though they might have certain triggers, their family members or friends may have completely different triggers. Things that bother or annoy one person will not be upsetting to another.

To put it another way, indicate that when you get angry, it is because you have encountered an event in your life that has provoked your anger. Many times, specific events touch on sensitive areas. These sensitive areas or "red flags" usually refer to long-standing issues that can easily lead to anger. In addition to events that you experience here and now, you may also recall an event from your past that made you angry. Just thinking about these past events may make you angry now.

Ask the client to think about some of the general events and situations that trigger anger for them, and ask them to talk about these. Then, inquire about some of the red-flag events and situations that trigger anger for them.

Indicate that a second important way to monitor anger is to identify the cues that occur in response to the anger-provoking event. These cues serve as warning signs that you have become angry and that your anger is escalating. Cues can be broken down into four cue categories: physical, behavioral, emotional, and cognitive (or thought) cues (U.S. Health & Human Services, 2016). As you describe each category, ask the patient to recall the cues that they have noticed when they get angry.

- *Physical cues*: These cues have to do with the body response. For instance, they could include an increased heart rate, tightness in the chest, feeling hot, or being flushed.
- *Behavioral cues*: These cues have to do with what you do. For example, behavioral cues include things such as clenching your fists, raising your voice, or staring at others.
- *Emotional cues*: These cues relate to feelings that often go along with anger. For instance, emotional cues could be fear, hurt, jealousy, or disrespect.

- *Cognitive cues*: Cognitive cues are what you think about in response to the event. They include hostile self-talk or images of aggression and revenge.

After discussing the cues that they are aware of, go on to a discussion of how anger gets expressed. This discussion will have relevance for helping the client further understand not only why they need to change how they react to their anger triggers but how other people may be responding to them. You might start with the question, "What are the cons or disadvantages of expressing your anger?" Encourage the client to list various things that might go wrong when they are expressing their anger. For instance, some of the items on this list might include the following:

- people might be frightened of me;
- they might avoid me;
- I might feel stupid or embarrassed at times;
- I might lose friends;
- I might do things that cause me trouble;
- people might see me as aggressive;
- I may act (or actually be) out of control.

Once this list has been completed and discussed, pose another question: "What are pros or advantages of expressing your anger?" Help the client make a list of all the positive aspects of expressing their anger. Items that could be on this list would include:

- people may trust me;
- others might like it when they know how I feel;
- I never have to keep my anger hidden inside;
- I could feel better about myself because I express my anger;
- I might use my anger constructively;
- I might feel less stress or anxiety.

Again, after compiling this list and talking about each point, go on to a third question for this session. That question is, "How do you know when you're angry?" The client may indicate that it is obvious, to himself and others, when he is angry. However, have them state various ways that they (and others) recognize when he or she is ticked off. Often, clients will indicate that they know they behave mad when they are shouting or swearing, they are red in the face, or their fists are clenched. Let them know that there are differences between direct and indirect signs of anger. The signs they may have mentioned are more likely to be direct signs of anger, signals such as a raised voice, yelling, cursing, clenched fists, threatening others, pushing, shoving, hitting, and hostility or rage.

Explain that despite these outward signs that they are angry, there are usually indirect signals that others may not see or recognize. These might include excessive sleeping, chronic fatigue, anxiety, numbness, depression, sulking, overeating, loss of appetite, crying, constant criticizing, mean or hostile joking, and abuse of alcohol or drugs. These are signs of anger that are not quite so obvious, but they are also anger signs that the individual may not recognize as being related to their anger either. Discuss which one of these signs are part of their reactions to anger triggers in their life.

Homework Assignment

The homework assignment is to once again instruct the client to continue to fill out the Anger Log tracking their anger. New items are included to incorporate what the client is learning in each session.

Table 7.3 Example: Anger Log (Week 3)

Day One:	
Incident:	**Incident:**
What made me mad? What was my Anger scale score? What were my physical cues? My thinking cues? My behavior cues? How did I act or behave? Did I use a strategy? What was the outcome?	What made me mad? What was my Anger scale score? What were my physical cues? My thinking cues? My behavior cues? How did I act or behave? Did I use a strategy? What was the outcome?
Day Two: . . .	. . .
Day Three: . . .	. . .
Day Four: . . .	. . .
Day Five: . . .	. . .
Day Six: . . .	. . .
Day Seven: . . .	. . .

Anger Log (Week 3)

Instructions: Either at the end of the day or after your anger has passed, take a moment to reflect on the situation in which you felt angry—or even just a bit frustrated. By completing the Anger Log (Table 7.3, see Resource Pack, p. 341) every day, you will be able to remember the times you got angry for the next session.

Session Four: Anger's Early Warning Signs and a Breathing Strategy

Agenda

1. Review homework.
2. Discussion of bodily reactions to anger triggers.
3. Discuss the relationship between physical arousal and anger escalation
4. Identifying physiological reactions to anger triggers
5. Teach diaphragmatic breathing to manage anger facilitating physical arousal
6. Homework assignment

Materials Needed

Anger Log (see Resource Pack, p. 341).

Protocol

Start Session Four with a review of the homework. By this point, the client should be more open about their anger and more skilled at identifying their anger triggers. In addition, they should be thinking more about some of the cues and signs of anger, and have begun to identify strategies they find helpful and/or behaviors that they use when their anger is maladaptive.

Next, discuss an overview of anger triggers. You may say that by now he or she realizes that anger is a feeling that comes after they believe someone has been disrespectful, hurt their feelings, been rude, or betrayed their trust. In addition, they might get frustrated or angry when things don't go their way or they can't control others. In other words, our anger triggers lets us know that we are unhappy with something happening around us. Point out that as you have already talked about, people express their anger in many different ways. Ask the client this question: "What are appropriate or constructive ways to express your anger?" Review the anger log for examples of situations, cues, and adaptive/maladaptive responses with the client.

Before learning other approaches to dealing with their anger, they must be aware of the early warning signs of anger. These are not the triggers necessarily.

Instead, they are the physical ways the body responds to triggers. Our mind "reads" certain physical responses that happen in our body as "anger." This physical response feeds the anger. This session will focus on how to become increasingly aware of the physical response to anger . It will teach the client to address the physical component of their anger, reduce the physiological arousal, and de-escalate their anger.

Discuss how anger affects our bodies. Point out that research shows that there are physical reactions in our bodies when we are angry. For instance, examples of physiological reactions to anger triggers include shallow breathing, tight muscles, and a rapid heartbeat. Discuss how our emotions are directly related to feelings and thoughts, yet there is also a connection between the physical reactions and the emotions we experience. If the client seems doubtful about this, ask them to think about times when their pulse raced on hearing some news or feeling something emotional. Or how their mouth went dry when they were standing in front of an audience. These – and other physical changes – occur while people are experiencing a strong emotion, such as anxiety, fear, or anger.

There are definite physical responses caused by anger because our nervous system automatically reacts to strong emotions such as anger. Since the body's reaction to anger sets off an emergency signal to the body, in order to meet this emergency, the nervous system activates and prepares the body to deal with the emergency. Typically, the body's first response to anger is an increased breathing rate. This is the body's way of taking in more oxygen. When you breathe faster, your heart pumps faster. This increases the pressure on your arteries. When you are angry, you might break into a sweat. This helps cool your body. Also, your face is likely to either turn pale or flushed. When you are angry, your hands can also turn cold. You might find yourself shaking or experience pains in the chest.

Although the client has already been instructed to use a few breaths for immediate anger management, the clinician will now take the opportunity to more formally teach breathing and practice it with the client.

Diaphragmatic breathing is a simple technique that can be used to short circuit the anger response. Changing breathing patterns from rapid and shallow to slow and deep can de-activate the stress/anger or sympathetic nervous system. When this happens, the brain no longer reads "anger."

It is important when teaching breathing to make sure the client is doing it correctly (shallow breathing or hyperventilation will only increase the stress response). A very helpful and instructive app for both patients and clinicians to learn proper technique is "Breathe2relax." We recommend that the clinician breathe with the client in session for several minutes. Some clients feel self-conscious, and if this is the case, the clinician can tell them they can both close their eyes and focus on the physical breathing experience.

It is important again for the clinician to note that the first several times a client does relaxation it will not really work. This is because, like everything else, relaxation takes practice. And eventually, like riding a bike, the body develops "muscle memory" to learn the technique. Once it is learned, the more the patient does it, the more effective it becomes.

The client should be instructed to begin using breathing as soon as they notice their early physical anger response. This is part of the reason that they have been focusing in the last several weeks on physical anger cues – so that they can begin to implement this breathing strategy at their earliest awareness.

Inform the client that if they practice this technique regularly, they can become good at it and it will be effective in helping them relax when their anger is escalating. They can practice this at home, at work, on the bus, while waiting for an appointment, or even while walking. The key to using deep-breathing as an effective relaxation technique is to practice it frequently and to apply it in a variety of situations. This can become an effective immediate strategy if practiced often. It is important to emphasize that initially they will not be successful in mastering breathing. It is a skill, like riding a bike, which relies on "body learning." If they expect immediate relaxation, they are just setting the stage for failure with this skill.

All of this is why they must be aware of physical reactions caused by anger triggers and recognize the effects anger can have on their health. By becoming more aware of how anger affects their body, they can make changes in their reactions to prevent damage to their health.

Homework Assignment

The homework assignment is to continue to track their anger with the Anger Log, but to become more aware of their physiological reactions to their anger triggers. They should also be instructed to practice the breathing technique at least once a day for 10 minutes.

Anger Log (Week 4)

Instructions: Either at the end of the day or after your anger has passed, take a moment to reflect on the situation in which you felt angry—or even just a bit frustrated. By completing the Anger Log (see Resource Pack, p. 341) every day, you will be able to remember the times you got angry for the next session.

Session Five: Developing an Anger Control Plan

Agenda

1. Review homework
2. Review Immediate Strategies
3. Introduce Preventative Strategies

4.   Create Client Specific Anger Control Plan
5.   Homework assignment

Materials Needed

Anger Log (see Resource Pack, p. 341).

Protocol

The homework should be reviewed with positive reinforcement for compliance. It is important that the client become more aware of anger triggers and physiological responses. Point out that by being able to identify physiological responses, then appropriate anger management responses will be possible. Reinforce their practicing breathing as a response to anger cues.

After review and discussion of homework, then talk to the client about responding appropriately to the early warning signs of anger. Indicate that by learning to keep calm and stay in control in the face of anger triggers and physiological responses, then it is possible to learn—and use—essential tools to manage the body's responses to anger. With practice, then he or she can manage their responses when they are getting angry.

In this session, you can tell the patient, that they will begin learning about specific strategies to manage their anger. The first strategy they will learn is to develop an anger control plan. An anger control plan refers to the list of strategies they will identify to manage and control their anger. Their plan will consist of both immediate and preventative strategies.

You may first sum up what the client has learned so far. They have learned how to monitor and rate their anger by using the Anger Scale. Then, they learned how to identify the events that trigger their anger, as well as the physical, behavioral, emotional, and cognitive cues associated with each event. In this session, they will begin to develop their own anger control plan Some people refer to their anger control plans as their toolbox and the specific strategies they use to control their anger as the tools.

An effective set of strategies for controlling anger should include both immediate and preventive strategies. The client has already learned immediate strategies. Immediate strategies are intended for use when anger is high or rapidly escalating, when the client knows they are on the upper end of the anger meter (anger that is greater than 7/10 on the anger scale). These include time-outs, deep-breathing exercises, and thought stopping. It can be helpful to review with the client the major immediate strategies they have learned thus far, and assess with them, which they have found most effective.

Preventative strategies are strategies that are used when clients observe initial anger cues. They are used 'early' to inhibit or prevent anger escalation. These are strategies to use when they know they are in situation that is one which they have learned can trigger them or when they notice the initial anger cues that they have been learning comprise their anger response. They are best implemented when the anger scale is less than 7. These can involve things like alternate behaviors, exercise, seeking social support, etc. Additional strategies that are preventative will be reviewed in upcoming sessions. These include using assertive communication techniques and challenging automatic thoughts. The clinician may wish to ask the client what kinds of activities in the past have helped to distract effectively or calm them when they were upset? What kinds of things made them feel less agitated? Behaviors and activities that have been effective in the past will likely be effective in the future, and the clinician should use this history to inform potential preventative strategies.

Introduce the idea of developing an Anger Control Plan. An Anger Control Plan is a written list of what immediate and preventative strategies the individual will use to respond to their anger cues and their anger triggers.

Table 7.4 Sample of an Anger Control Plan

Anger Control Plan	
Immediate Strategies	Preventative Strategies
1. Take a timeout (formal or informal).	1. Talk to a friend (someone you trust).
2. Thought stopping.	2. Tear up a newspaper.
3. Deep breathing.	3. Use assertive communication.
4. Rubber Band Technique.	4. Exercise (take a walk, go to the gym, etc.).
	5. Listen to music.
	6. Play video games.
	7. Pray or meditate.

To finish the session, emphasize that in order for any of the various strategies to work they must be practiced daily. It is especially important when their anger is triggered to interrupt any possible angry response before they respond inappropriately. To do that, they must remember their Anger Control Plan and use an immediate or preventative strategy. The more they practice these strategies, the better able they will be to use them automatically and effectively.

Homework Assignment

The homework assignment will focus on practicing the five immediate strategies and developing an anger control plan. They will continue to fill out the Anger Log, but they should try to respond to any anger trigger by using their Anger Control Plan (Table 7.5, see Resource Pack, p. 342).

The client should fill out the following Anger Control Plan:

Table 7.5 Example: Anger Control Plan

Anger Control Plan	
Immediate Strategies	Preventative Strategies
1.	1.
2.	2.
3.	3.

Anger Log (Week 5)

Instructions: Either at the end of the day or after your anger has passed, take a moment to reflect on the situation in which you felt angry – or even just a bit frustrated. By completing this every day, you will be able to remember the times you got angry for the next session (see Resource Pack, p. 341).

Session Six: The Aggression Cycle

Agenda

1. Review homework assignment.
2. Learning about the aggression cycle.
3. Learning progressive muscle relaxation as a preventative technique.
4. Homework assignment.

Materials Needed

Anger Log (see Resource Pack, p. 341).

Protocol

Review the homework assignment and discuss the Anger Log as well as the development of the Anger Control Plan. Also discuss the use of immediate strategies and how they would rate their anger after implementing immediate strategies or immediate strategies combined with preventive strategies.

After discussing the homework and the progress the client has made in the past week, introduce the aggression cycle. The aggression cycle serves as an integrative framework that incorporates the concepts of the Anger Scale, cues to anger, and the Anger Control Plan.

In explaining the aggression cycle, point out to the client that an episode of anger can be viewed as consisting of three phases: *escalation, explosion,* and *post-explosion* (U.S. Health & Human Services, 2016). Together, these three phases make up the aggression cycle. The *escalation phase* is characterized by cues that indicate anger is building. As they should recall, cues are warning signs, or responses, to anger-provoking events. If the escalation phase is allowed to continue, the explosion phase will follow. The *explosion phase* is marked by an uncontrollable discharge of anger that is displayed as verbal or physical aggression. The *post-explosion phase* is characterized by the negative consequences that result from the verbal or physical aggression displayed during the explosion phase. These consequences may include going to jail; making restitution; being terminated from a job; losing family and loved ones; or feelings of guilt, shame, and regret.

Ask the patient to notice that the escalation and explosion phases of the aggression cycle correspond to levels or points on the Anger Scale. The points on the Anger Scale below 10 represent the escalation phase—the building up of anger. The explosion phase, on the other hand, corresponds to a 10 on the Anger Scale. A 10 on the Anger Scale represents those times when they have lost control and express anger through verbal or physical aggression that leads to negative consequences.

Remind them that one of the primary objectives of anger-management treatment is to prevent them from reaching the explosion phase. This is accomplished by using the Anger Scale to monitor changing levels of anger, attend to the cues or warning signs that indicate anger is building, and use the appropriate strategies from your anger control plans to stop the escalation of anger. If the explosion phase is prevented, the post-explosion phase will not occur and the aggression cycle will be broken.

Ask the client to indicate what phase of the aggression cycle they are in if they reach a 7 on the Anger Scale? The aggression cycle starts with a period of mounting or escalating anger; this proceeds to an explosion of anger; then there is a cooling down or post-explosion period. Then, ask what phase they would be in if they reach 10 on the Anger Scale?

In discussing the aggression cycle, discuss in detail the following features of the phases of the aggression cycle (Figure 7.2):

1. Escalation phase:
    (a) denial and minimization of incidents
    (b) increase in hostile self-talk

     (c) intimidating body language
     (d) more frequent and intense anger;

2.   Explosion phase:

     (a) violence
     (b) verbal aggression
     (c) uncontrollable discharge of tension
     (d) major destructiveness;

3.   Post-explosion phase:

     (a) jail
     (b) termination from program or service
     (c) financial cost
     (d) loss of family or loved ones
     (e) guilt, shame, etc. (U.S. Health & Human Services, 2016)

At the panic level of stress (Figure 7.3), the perceptual field almost disappears and we can focus only on ourselves. We can no longer process any outside information. At this point, we are at high risk for violent behavior and becoming a threat to ourselves or others. Feelings of anger may come out explosively in a "fight or flight" response. This is what people refer to as a "blind rage." Often people will not be able to remember what they said or did during this level of stress.

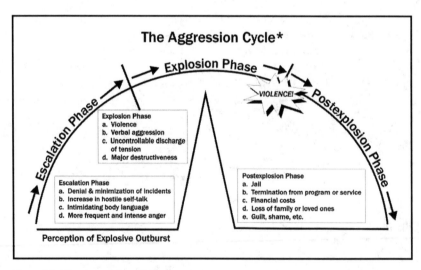

Figure 7.2 The Aggression Cycle

(Reilly, Shopshire, et al., 2012; Adapted from Walker, 1979)

Panic Stress Level

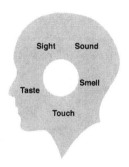 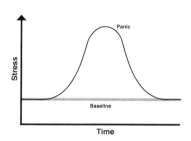

Figure 7.3 The Panic Level of Stress

At this point, after the client has indicated they understand the aggression cycle, introduce progressive muscle relaxation. Remind them that one of the immediate and preventative strategies learned in the last session was deep-breathing as a relaxation technique. This week they are learning a new relaxation procedure: progressive muscle relaxation. Remind them that as with other strategies learned in this anger-management program, the strategies learned in this session must be practiced as often as possible. The simplest way to do progressive muscle relaxation is to have the client tense specific muscles for 15 seconds and then have them release the tension. To keep it simple, they can be instructed to do it in order from their feet to the top of their heads. Muscles can be tensed and relaxed in the following order: toes, feet, calves, thighs, buttocks, abdomen, chest, hands, arms, biceps, neck, face.

Homework Assignment

The homework assignment is to continue working on the Anger Control Plan (see Resource Pack, Anger Control Plan, pp. 341–342), practice using immediate strategies, and to daily practice deep muscle relaxation. Also, continue to record in the Anger Log (see Resource Pack, Anger Log (weeks 3–8), p. 341).

Anger Log (Week 6)

Instructions: Either at the end of the day or after your anger has passed, take a moment to reflect on the situation in which you felt angry—or even just a bit frustrated. By completing the Anger Log every day, you will be able to remember the times you got angry for the next session.

Session Seven: Cognitive Restructuring and Visualization

Agenda

1. Review homework assignment.
2. Review cognitive restructuring.
3. Practice.
4. Teach visualization as an additional preventative strategy,
5. New homework assignment.

Material Needed

Anger Log (see Resource Pack, p. 341).

Protocol

Review the homework assignment. Give positive feedback for practicing deep muscle relaxation and using immediate strategies. Emphasize the need to practice every day.

In this session, you will review the A-B-C-D Model as a form of cognitive restructuring. Cognitive restructuring should now be cited as an example of a preventative anger control strategy.

A-B-C-D Model
A = *Activating Situation or Event*
1. Ask yourself, "What happened?" 2. Example: Somebody cuts you off on the freeway as they suddenly change lanes to exit.
B = *Belief System* *(your beliefs and expectations of others)*
1. What you tell yourself about what happened that influenced your action? 2. Examples: Drivers should pay more attention. No one should put another driver at risk. This person should be taught a lesson.
C = *Consequence* *(emotional consequence)*
1. How did you react (feelings and behavior)? 2. Examples: Anger and frustration. Yell, curse, and show finger. Engage in road rage.
D = *Dispute the belief*
1. Examine your beliefs and expectations. 2. Are they unrealistic or irrational? 3. Alternative thoughts that would help you in a healthier manner?

The A-B-C-D Model is consistent with the way some people conceptualize anger-management treatment. In this model, "*A*" stands for an activating event. The activating event is the "event" or red-flag event. "*B*" represents our beliefs about the activating event. It is not the events themselves that produce feelings such as anger; it is our interpretations and beliefs about the events. "*C*" stands for the emotional consequences. These are the feelings experienced as a result of interpretations and beliefs concerning the event. "*D*" stands for dispute.

At this point, introduce Automatic Negative Thoughts (or ANTs). These are also known as irrational beliefs. Indicate that our thinking and our thoughts are often automatic, and they can happen outside of our awareness. That includes thoughts that cause anger; thoughts, too, can be fast and automatic. As anger increases, thoughts may become more negative. Here, for example, are some common ANTs:

Table 7.6 Automatic Negative Thoughts Chart

Category	Definition	Example
All-or-nothing thinking	Seeing things as either all good or all bad and allowing no middle ground.	"It was all their fault." "I am either on top or not." "All drivers are reckless."
Fortune telling	Predicting that things will turn out negatively, without considering other possible outcomes.	"I am going to be pissed if things don't go as planned."
Disqualifying the positive	Telling yourself that positive experiences don't count	"I got pissed last week, which means I still have no control of my anger."
Emotional reasoning	Believing that what you feel must be true.	"I am pissed because someone did something, and that means they intended to cause harm."
Labeling	Attaching a global, extreme, negative label to yourself or others.	"All cops are jerks." "My family is selfish."
Catastrophizing	Expecting extremely negative consequences; exaggerating situations to be the worst possible outcome.	"I can't stand it anymore!" "My life is ruined."
Mental filter	Focusing on a single negatve detail instead of seeing the whole picture	"My wife is horrible because she forgot X [disregard that she has really helped out in the last couple of weeks]."

Continued

Table 7.6 Continued

Category	Definition	Example
Mind reading	Believing that you know what others are thinking, especially how they feel about you.	"They did that on purpose."
Overgeneralization	Making a general conclusion based on a single incident. Assuming that things will turn out a certain way because they did so before.	"Everyone disrespects me." "I never get the credit I deserve."
"Should" statements	Having fixed ideas about how you or others "should," "ought to," or "must" be. Leads to feeling guilt, anger, and resentment.	"I must be respected." "I should be treated fairly." "Everyone should follow the rules."
Personalization	Seeing yourself as the cause of negative events for which you are not responsible.	[Walk in the door and wife is short. This means she is pissed at you for something.]

(Adapted from Thorn, 2007)

After reviewing and discussing these examples of ANTs, ask the patient to identify some of their own Automatic Negative Thoughts. Discuss these in terms of how they contribute to their anger. Complete on example using the ABC framework in session, with emphasis on identifying the specific automatic thought from the chart above. Have the client complete the chart below as part of their homework for the week. (Table 7.7, see Resource Pack, p. 342)

Ask the patient to recall that in the last session progressive muscle relaxation as a relaxation technique was introduced and practiced. In this session, you will be introducing visualization. This, like the other tools discussed so far, once learned, needs to be practiced as often as possible. Ask the client to get comfortable, relax through taking some deep breaths, and close their eyes. The client

Table 7.7 ANT Chart

Activating EVENT/ SITUATION	Belief THOUGHT	Belief (ANT) EXACT THOUGHT (from category above)	Consequence FEELING BEHAVIOUR

should be instructed to imagine a favorite safe and peaceful place. They should start the exercise by imagining the path that they take to get there. Take them down the path. Ask them to notice all the sensory cues of this path – the temperature of the air, the feel of the place on their skin, feet, hands, the scent of the place, the sounds, the light and visual appearance. Eventually they will arrive at their special place. Tell them they will remain here for several minutes. Ask them once again to notice all the sensory elements of this place. When they are ready to leave, ask them to go back using the same path they used to enter. Begin a backward countdown from 5, and indicate that when you reach one, they will open their eyes, alert, refreshed, and relaxed

Homework Assignment

The homework assignment is to continue to track their anger and how they handle it (or prevent it) through the Anger Log. They should be reminded that it is essential that they practice both immediate and preventive strategies in order to make them work more effectively.

Anger Log (Week 7)

Instructions: Either at the end of the day or after your anger has passed, take a moment to reflect on the situation in which you felt angry—or even just a bit frustrated. By completing the Anger Log (see Resource Pack, p. 341) every day, you will be able to remember the times you got angry for the next session.

Session Eight: Cognitive Restructuring II

Agenda

1. Review homework assignment
2. Challenging thoughts as preventative strategy
3. Coping statements as a preventative strategy
4. Assign homework

Materials Needed

1. Anger Log (see Resource Pack, p. 342).
2. Index card for coping statements.

Protocol

Review the homework assignment. Make sure that the client is adding strategies to their Anger Control Plan. Also, go over and discuss the ANTs they recorded in their Identifying Automatic Negative Thoughts Chart.

Begin discussing how to challenge their ANTs. This involves a continuation of the conversation related "*D*" in the A-B-C-D model. Remind the client that you have already stated that it is essential to not only identify any automatic thoughts or beliefs, but also to dispute them with more balanced ways of looking at the activating event.

This then leads to talking about challenging negative thoughts and beliefs. In order for the client to dispute or challenge ANTs, they must first identify them. Once they are identified, then these thoughts must be disputed with a balanced alternative. What this leads to is replacing ANTs with ideas that allow them to have a more realistic and accurate interpretation of the event, which will, in turn, prevent the explosion phase of the aggression cycle.

Show the patient a copy of The Challenging Thought Chart. This table provides a framework for considering more realistic and balanced interpretations of the events that trigger their anger. Have the individual note that the table calls for looking at the evidence that undermines the automatic negative thought or belief. Suggest that when they are filling out this table and *examining the evidence that goes against the automatic thought or belief*, they might ask themselves the following questions:

- What would I tell my best friend in this situation?
- Is this thought true 100% of the time?
- Do I know for certain that _____?
- Is there another explanation?
- Is there another point of view?

An essential feature of the A-B-C-D model is changing ANTs to more balanced thinking. This 'blended thought' represents a combination of the original thought and the evidence against it. For example, an irrational or

Table 7.8 Example: The Challenging Thought Chart

Event	Thought	Evidence For Thought	Evidence Against Thought	Blended Thought & New Feeling
Ex:	Ex:	Ex:	Ex:	Ex:

illogical automatic thought might be, "This is unfair. Things should always be fair." The evidence against that thought might be, "In reality life is not fair 100% percent of the time. If I expect that, I will be always be angry and disappointed. There are things in this situation that I do have control over and I need to focus on those." The blended thought might be, "Even though I think things should be fair 100% of the time. I also know that this thought is unrealistic and not supported by the evidence. There are things I have control over in this situation however, that I can focus on change."

Other more balanced ways of thinking are included in the list of coping statements below. The list below includes sample statements that could be used when the client is thinking of a balanced way to see the automatic thought. Have them take a look at this list to get ideas of statements that may be meaningful to them. They can go on to make their own list of statements that they might find helpful and meaningful during difficult times and place them on their personal coping cards.

Sample Coping Statements

1. I don't have to escalate this. I have anger-management skills that I can use.
2. Ride it out. There will be an end.
3. I have anger now, but the anger does not have me. I am not my anger.
4. I have other ways to make the situation better than to seek revenge.
5. I'm having a rough time now, but I can handle it. I have handled much worse.
6. I have planned for this. I have skills for dealing with this anger.
7. Nothing is falling apart; I just need to focus on something else.
8. What would I tell a friend if this happened to them?
9. I have other ways to protect myself than by using aggressive words and actions that end up hurting me more in the end.

Homework Assignment

The homework assignment is for the client to continue working on their Anger Control Plan (see Resource Pack, pp. 341–342) to prevent reaching the explosion phase of the aggression cycle. They should also practice using the A-B-C-D Model or thought stopping as a part of their Anger Control Plan. They should be instructed to complete *The Challenging Thought Chart* (see Resource Pack, p. 343) in the coming week.

And as part of the assignment, they should track their anger on the Anger Log for Week Eight.

Anger Log (Week 8)

Instructions: Either at the end of the day or after your anger has passed, take a moment to reflect on the situation in which you felt angry—or even just a bit frustrated. By completing the Anger Log (see Resource Pack, p. 342) every day, you will be able to remember the times you got angry for the next session.

Session Nine: Assertive Communication I

Agenda

1. Review homework assignment
2. Introduce assertiveness training
3. Discuss three communication styles
4. Introduce LADDER
5. Assign homework

Materials Needed

Anger Log (see Resource Pack, p. 343).

Protocol

Begin by reviewing the homework assignment and the client's use of challenging thoughts statements. Emphasize the importance of being aware of ANTs and challenging and replacing those whenever they appear.

Introduce assertive communication in this session. Explain the definition of assertiveness and explain the differences between three communication styles: assertive, aggressive, and passive. Indicate that assertive communication can be used as a preventative anger control strategy for their Anger Control Plan.

Talk about how people's interact with others can be a source of stress in their life. Assertiveness training (or using assertive communication) can reduce stress by teaching people to stand up for their legitimate rights without violating the rights of others or letting others violate your rights.

You are assertive when you stand up for your rights in such a way that the rights of others are not violated. Beyond just demanding your rights, you can express your personal likes and interests spontaneously, you can talk about yourself without being self-conscious, you can accept compliments comfortably, you can disagree with someone openly, you can ask for clarification, and you can say no. In short, when you are an assertive person, you can be more relaxed in interpersonal situations. Some people think that assertiveness training turns nice people into complainers or calculating manipulators. Not so. It's your right to protect yourself when something seems unfair. You are the one who best knows your discomfort and your needs.

Assertive communication is most effective when used with people you know well. If you find yourself becoming angry when interacting with strangers or individuals you do not interact with regularly, an immediate, or different preventative, anger control strategy may be more helpful.

Point out that assertiveness is a skill that can be learned, and it is not a personality trait that some are born with and others are not. The first step in assertiveness training is to identify the three basic styles of communication. Demonstrate by sharing the Three Communication Styles Chart below.

Table 7.9 Three Communication Styles

Aggressive Communication	Passive Communication	Assertive Communication
1. Opinions, feelings, and wants are honestly stated, but at the expense of someone else's feelings.	1. Opinions, feelings, and wants are withheld.	1. State rights and feelings clearly without violating someone else's rights.
2. Emphasize your rights over others.	2. Typically characterized by avoidance of difficult topics. Avoid responsibility and consequences.	2. Ideal communication style.
3. The underlying message is, "I'm right and you're wrong."	3. The underlying message is, "My opinions and needs don't matter."	3. The underlying message is, "You and I may have our differences, but we are equally entitled to express our opinions to one another."

(Davis, Eshelman & McKay, 2008)

In reviewing the three communications style chart, go over the situations and responses below and have the client decide which communication style is represented by each response:

Situation 1:   Plans to vacation together are abruptly changed by a friend. They call and tell you.
Response 1:   "Wow, that is a surprise. Let me think about it and call you back."

Situation 2:   Your child habitually leaves his/her room a mess.
Response 2:   "You're a mess and this place is a mess!"

Situation 3:   Your spouse or partner gets silent instead of saying what is on his/her mind.

Response 3:   "Here it comes! The big silent treatment. Would it kill you to actually clue me in just once?"

Situation 4:   A relative or friend frequently borrows small amounts of money and never pays it back. S/he asks again for a small loan which you'd rather not give.

Response 4:   "I'm sorry. I don't have money to lend. When you can, I would appreciate it if you could pay me back the money I let you borrow before."

Situation 5:   Your partner or spouse criticizes you in front of other people.

Response 5:   "I feel hurt when you criticize me in front of other people. If you have something to say, please bring it up when it is just the two of us."

Situation 6:   You have a day off from work and you want to go out with friends you haven't seen in a while. Your spouse or partner wants you to do something else.

Response 6:   "Oh, alright. I guess I can see my friends another time."
                            (Adapted from Davis, Eschelman & McKay, 2008)

The acronym LADDER is a series of six steps you can tell your client about which may assist them in order to deal with problems assertively (Davis, Eschelman & McKay, 2008):

L—*Look* at your rights, what you want, what you need, and your feelings about the situation.

A—*Arrange* a time and place to discuss your problem that is convenient for you and the other person.

D—*Define* the problem situation as specifically as possible. Begin your statement with the phrase, "When you do . . ."

D—*Describe* your feelings so that the other person has a better understanding of how important an issue is to you. Use "I" statements that express your feelings without evaluating or blaming others. Begin your statement with the phrase, "I feel . . ."

E—*Express* your request in one or two easy to understand sentences. Instead of expecting others to read your mind, clearly state your wishes and needs. Begin your statement with the phrase, "I would prefer if you . . ."

R—*Reinforce* the other person for compromising

Inform the patient of the short-form assertiveness technique, which is designed for situations where they lack the time or energy to utilize the entire

LADDER plan. Assertiveness can be condensed to four basic statements: "*When you . . .*", "*I feel . . .*", "*Because I think . . .*", and "*I would prefer if . . .*" Table 7.10 shows how to construct a statement based on the short-form assertiveness technique, along with some do's and don'ts for assertiveness

Emphasize with the client that while some individuals master assertiveness skills with just a few weeks of practice and notice a significant reduction in their anger, others may require several months of practice in order to recognize changes in their anger.

Table 7.10 Constructing a Statement

Do	Don't
1. "When you . . ."	
• Describe the other person's undesirable or offensive behavior objectively.	• Describe your emotional reaction to the behavior.
• Use concrete terms.	• Use abstract or vague terms.
• Be specific. State the time and place of behavior.	• Generalize to "all the time."
• Describe the action, not the motive behind it.	• Guess at the other person's motives or goals.
2. "I feel . . ." or "I think . . ."	
• Express your feelings.	• Deny your feelings.
• Express your feelings calmly.	• Unleash emotional outbursts.
• State your feelings in a positive manner.	• State feelings negatively.
• Direct yourself to the specific undesirable behavior, not the whole person.	• Attack the entire character of the person.
3. "I would prefer if you . . ."	
• Ask explicitly for change in the other person's behavior.	• Merely imply that you would like change.
• Request a small change.	• Ask for too large of a change.
• Request only one or two changes at one time.	• Ask for too many changes.
• Specify the concrete actions you want to see stopped, and those you want performed.	• Ask for changes in traits or qualities that are vague or difficult to define.

Homework Assignment

Indicate that assertive communication can be added to the Anger Control Plan as a preventive strategy. Encourage them to continue to add strategies to their Anger Control Plan (see Resource Pack, p. 342).

As part of the homework assignment, indicate that they are to use the modified Anger Log to track their anger and their use of anger-management strategies (see Resource Pack, p. 343). Instruct them to use assertive communications at least once a day during the coming week.

Session Ten: Assertive Communication II

Agenda

1. Review homework assignment.
2. More information on assertiveness.
3. Assign homework.

Protocol

Start Session Ten with a review of the homework. Ask about their use of assertive communication and discuss in what situations they were able to use assertiveness.

In this session, you will teach them more about assertive communication. The focus in this session will be on learning to listen, compromising, and consequences. Start off this section by reminding them that assertive communication can be used as a preventative anger control strategy.

Continue to discuss communication and indicate to the client that as they practice the LADDER technique in real life situations, they will find that sometimes they need to deal with an issue that is important to the other person before he or she will be able to focus on what they have to say. When listening assertively, it is important for the individual to focus their attention on the other person so that they can accurately hear the speaker's opinions, feelings, and wishes. Point out that assertive listening involves three steps:

1. *Prepare*: Do not try to listen assertively when you are angry!
2. *Listen* (bite your tongue) and *clarify* (ask clarifying questions if you do not fully understand what is being said).
3. *Acknowledge*: Use the following phrase: "I hear you saying _____. Is that right?"

(Davies, Eschelman & McKay, 2008)

Being willing to compromise is also an element of assertiveness train-ing. When interests are in conflict, a fair solution that totally satisfies both parties is often difficult, if not impossible, to achieve. Instead, look for a workable compromise you both can live with. Although a compromise may naturally emerge in your discussion, sometimes you might need a list of alternative solutions.

Typical compromise situations include:

1. My way this time, your way next time.
2. If you'll do _____ for me, I'll do _____ for you.
3. We'll do this one my way, but we'll do _____ your way.
4. We'll try my way this time, and if you don't like it you can veto it next time.

(Davies, Eschelman & McKay, 2008)

A second route to compromise is to ask this question, "What would you need from me to feel okay doing this my way?"

Assertive communication will not work when speaking to every individual. If you find yourself in a situation where you have attempted to use assertive communication techniques and the other person has not responded well, you can try to make the consequences of not responding to your request explicit. This is not to be used as a form of manipulation or as a threat. Instead, you are clearly stating what will happen if your needs are not met. This approach should only be used with persons who do not respond to any of the techniques discussed above. This approach should not be used when you are angry or upset. For example, you could make the following two-part statement:

1. "If you _____, then I am going to (or not going to) _____."
2. Ask the client to think of situations in their life when assertive listening and compromise are often needed. Discuss these situations and together construct some statements that could be used.

Homework Assignment

Instruct the client to continue to add strategies to their Anger Control Plan (see Resource Pack, p. 342). Plan to review the Plan at the next session to see how many strategies are on the Plan.

Furthermore, ask the client to continue to track their anger and responses with the short Anger Log (see Resource Pack, p. 343). Emphasize the import-ance of using cognitive restructuring, assertive communication, including assertive listening and compromise.

Session Eleven: Wrapping it All Up

Agenda

1. Review homework assignment.
2. Review and revise Anger Control Plan.
3. Assess problems and difficulties.
4. Closing exercise.
5. Discuss booster sessions.

Protocol

In this final session, review the homework and make sure the client has been using the techniques that were learnt in the treatment. If they have been using them, give positive reinforcement and discuss the results of their use of the techniques. Use the first part of the session for troubleshooting and encouragement to continue to practice the techniques they have learned.

Also, go over the Anger Control Plan and do any needed revision so that it works best for them.

As part of closing, ask the client what they have learned about anger management. Discuss this to learn what they consider the most important aspects of anger management for them. Encourage them to continue to improve their anger-management skills and ask that they pinpoint some ways of doing that. Ask: "Are there specific areas that you feel need improvement?" And as a final question, ask how they can use the strategies in their Anger Control Plan to better manage their anger (see Resource Pack, p. 342).

To complete the final session, indicate that while no further formal treatment sessions are scheduled, you will be available for follow up or booster sessions in the future. If they find they are not dealing with their anger appropriately or are forgetting to use the tools and techniques learned in the treatment, they can return for practice or encouragement.

References

Davis, M., Eshelman, E.R., and McKay, M. (2008). *The relaxation and stress reduction handbook*. New York: New Harbinger Publications.

Thorn, B. E. (2017). *Cognitive therapy for chronic pain: a step-by-step guide*. New York: Guilford Publications.

U.S. Department of Health & Human Services (2016). *Anger Management for Substance Abuse and Mental Health Client's: Participant's Workbook*. Substance Abuse and Mental Health Services Administration. Available: http://store.samhsa.gov/product/Anger-Management-for-Substance-Abuse-and-Mental-Health-Clients-Participant-Workbook/SMA14-4210

Walker, L. (1979). *The battered woman*. New York: Harper & Row.

Section Three
Anxiety Symptoms

Chapter 8

Anxiety about the Medical Setting and Treatment

Clients often express fear of the medical setting. This is usually referred to as white coat hypertension and, sometimes specifically, as needle phobia or as blood injection injury phobia.

Blood injection injury phobia can lead to several important consequences. It can cause people to avoid important medical tests (i.e., blood work) and treatments. Or it can cause people to avoid the doctor's office or hospital. People with this difficulty will often avoid visiting loved ones or friends in the hospital. It can extend to fear of the dentist and dental procedures that use needles.

Essentially, white coat hypertension is fear of the medical setting. It is anxiety that occurs when people visit the doctor—or even anticipate an appointment with a doctor. The fear response is triggered—causing an increase in heart rate—and that leads to elevation in blood pressure or in office "hypertension." This fear response can lead to behavioral avoidance of the doctor's office, or more succinctly, medical setting phobia.

In many cases, people with blood injection injury phobia will have an associated fear of the medical setting and the associated rise in blood pressure related to this fear.

Session One: Assessment and Education

Agenda

1. Clinical history of complaint.
2. Classification of phobic response.
3. Education about how phobia develops and is maintained.
4. Introduction of cognitive behavioral therapy (CBT) model.

Materials Needed

1. Blood Injection Injury Questionnaire.
2. Blood Injection Injury Symptom Scale.
3. Severity Measure for Specific Phobia.

Protocol

An important component of blood injection injury assessment, as well as fear of the medical setting (white coat hypertension), is to evaluate the client's prior learning experiences related to doctors, hospitals, illness/disease, blood, needles, and dentists.

The clinician should begin the session with administration of the instruments mentioned above to assist with classification of the client's phobia (blood injection injury, fear of the medical setting, or both).

A review of the learning history should include an inquiry into sources of past learning. Past learning falls into three categories. These categories are direct experience, informational learning, and modeling. Direct experience is the traumatic experience the client may have had in the past with the particular object or situation. Informational learning is what they have learned from the media, reading, or hearing stories from others. Observational learning or modeling is what they have learned from being in direct contact with other persons who may have modeled behaviors for them.

For individuals with blood injection injury, it is important to understand that this disorder frequently starts in childhood and clinicians should be sure to assess this childhood learning. The client should be asked if they had direct traumatic experience with blood, injections, or doctor's offices. The clinician should ask if there is anyone who they have known directly who has had difficulty with illness, or negative experiences in medical settings, or was afraid of illness. Alternately, they should be asked about things that they have read or heard about illness, hospitals, including stories of persons who were sick and fictionalized programs.

It will also be important to understand avoidance behaviors in these phobias. These include things like:

- not scheduling or cancelling doctor's appointments;
- avoiding hospitals or visiting loved ones in hospitals;
- avoiding programs on TV or news reports having to do with disease or blood;
- not going to the doctor or dentist;
- failing to follow up with blood tests;
- looking away when blood is drawn;
- attempting to distract themselves when blood pressure is taken.

Once the clinician has established the presence of either blood injection injury phobia or fear of the medical setting, the next step is education.

Education will serve three functions. First, it will normalize or reassure the client regarding their experience, and counteract inaccurate attributions they have made about being mentally unfit. Second, it will help them understand why and how this has occurred. Finally, it will lay the framework for the introduction of the cognitive behavioral model of phobia treatment.

Figure 8.1 Anxiety May Have a Genetic Component

Medically related phobias like blood injection injury phobia often have a genetic component. This may mean that the client's family tree contains examples of other relatives who have had medical anxiety, needle, or blood fears; some may even have stories of relatives who have passed out in medical environments. For individuals who are genetically susceptible to this kind of disorder, it can begin with a difficult or traumatic medical experience, through modeling (observational learning of family members or other significant individuals) or informationally (experience with media, TV, or reading). Often, there may be a combination of these three factors (Rachman, 1976, 1977).

The anxiety response develops through simple classical conditioning: a difficult or traumatic event or experience creates a strong feeling of fear. This fear response is strong enough to become welded to that situation or object, and in short order, all things associated with it provoke the same strong fear response.

Fear of medical situations, blood, and injection injury is maintained by escape and avoidance behaviors. These behaviors have short-term payoff because they temporarily reduce anxiety, but in the long run, they are counterproductive because they actually magnify it.

The diagram below can be helpful in explaining to clients how the short-term payoff works (Figure 8.2). It can be helpful to use an example of the client's specific anxiety or phobia when discussing this.

It is important for the clinician to emphasize that the client's anxiety is attached to a specific thought(s) or fears about the situation. These thoughts amplify anxiety, to the point that the fear becomes so strong that the client will do anything to "escape" or leave the situation or to avoid it in the future. Avoidance only works in the short term. When they leave, or avoid, they feel better; a sense of relief. This relief makes the urge to repeat this escape and avoidance behavior even stronger.

Figure 8.2 Short-Term Avoidance Outcome/Payoff

The cost of avoidance and escape is that it increases long-term anxiety. This is because it does not allow the client opportunity to actually ever disprove the catastrophic thought they have about the situation. Instead the thought goes unchallenged, seeming more and more "accurate." The client comes to believe that the feared medical situation will have the worst possible outcome if they stay in it, and fear continues to escalate. The diagram shown in Figure 8.3 illustrates this.

Figure 8.3 Long-Term Avoidance Outcome/Cost

CBT works in part by changing this behavioral pattern. It facilitates approach of the situation, or having the client confront the situation or event they are afraid of. It is done in a gradual or controlled manner. Approaching the situation allows the client the opportunity to systematically test whether or not their belief is actually accurate.

Figure 8.4 Thoughts Often Feed the Anxiety

CBT for blood injection injury and medical anxiety is focused on behavior (approach and avoidance) as discussed above, but also on thoughts that feed the anxiety, the emotions that occur and learning to tolerate them, and the physical response (Figure 8.4). Treatment will address each of these elements, as shown in Figure 8.5.

A final piece of education related to blood injection injury and the fainting response is important. This is specifically for those who have passed out at the sight of blood or during a medical procedure, or who report potential fainting symptoms. Although many phobic clients often fear that they will pass out, this fear is unfounded for all phobias, except for blood injection injury. Blood injection injury phobia can lead to fainting response called the vasovagal response. Techniques to manage this will be introduced later in this protocol.

The vasovagal response in blood injury injection phobia is caused by the activation of two parts of the autonomic nervous system—the sympathetic and

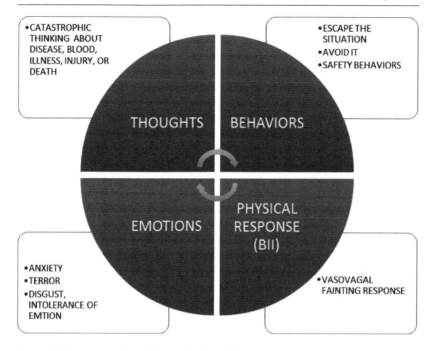

Figure 8.5 Treatment Can Address the Main Elements of Anxiety

parasympathetic response. The initial fear or disgust response is controlled by the sympathetic nervous system. It causes familiar anxiety physical symptoms like increased heart rate. For people who are sensitive to the vasovagal response, a part of the brain stem is "switched on" when this happens. This is called the vagal branch nerve and it causes a rapid "correction" in the sympathetic response. It triggers a rapid drop in blood pressure, leading to fainting or passing out.

People with the vasovagal response report several symptoms prior to losing consciousness, including nausea, feeling lightheaded, hot or cold, sweating, feeling confused, inability to speak/form words, weakness, visual disturbance, and feeling nervousness.

Recovery occurs rapidly by having the individual lay down, which allows blood pressure to return to its normal level.

Homework Assignment

The client should be encouraged to read about blood injection injury phobia and/or fear of the medical setting/phobia. The clinician may wish to point the client to a website which they feel provides accurate information.

Session Two: Developing a Hierarchy and Managing the Vasovagal Response

Agenda

1. Check-in and homework review.
2. Review of assessment findings from the prior week.
3. Identify feared situations.
4. Rank order feared situations to create a hierarchy.
5. Identify catastrophic prediction related to hierarchy.
6. Identify safety behaviors for response prevention.
7. Teach applied pressure technique for blood injection injury.
8. Assign homework.

Materials Needed

Severity Measure for Specific Phobia.

Protocol

While reviewing the homework assignment, the clinician can answer any questions the patient may have. The clinician may find it helpful to review the measures from the previous week and make a note of the particular items that the client has endorsed as anxiety-provoking.

This session will focus on developing an exposure plan to approach the client's fears. The person with blood injection injury phobia and fear of the medical setting phobia is often afraid of several of the situations reviewed in Tables 8.1 and 8.2, respectively. It may be quite helpful to have the client review this list and circle the things that make them anxious or that disgust them. Both anxiety and disgust are components of blood injection injury phobia.

Next, it is important for the client to rate the feared situations with regard to the magnitude of anxiety that they produce. Ask the client to list situations and rate them using the Symptom Units of Distress Scale (SUDS) (1–100) (Table 8.3, see Resource Pack, p. 344).

Next, the clinician will assist the client in ordering their feared situations from lowest to highest on the basis of the SUDS rating; this is the hierarchy rating (Table 8.4, see Resource Pack, p. 344).

The clinician will explain that they are going to ask the client to start doing the things they have been afraid of with the assistance of the therapist. This will start with the lowest level activity. The clinician will ask the client to stay in the situation until their SUDS drops by 50 percent. The important thing is NOT how perfectly they behave in the situation, but that they STAY in the situation until they have finished "riding the anxiety wave." The clinician will explain

Table 8.1 Blood Injection Injury

Medical injections of any kind

Open cut or wound with bleeding

Seeing my own blood

Seeing someone else's blood

Seeing something mutilated

Going to the doctor's office

Going to the dentist

Going to a laboratory for a draw

Going to a hospital

Seeing someone else give blood

Giving blood

Watching a TV program with blood or surgery

Looking at a needle or syringe

Touching a needle or syringe

Watching someone else get an IV

Getting an IV

Reading about blood, injury, or needles

Looking at pictures of blood, injury or needles

Tying a rubber band around my arm to tourniquet it for an injection & touch my vein

Touch or hold a piece of blood red meat

Table 8.2 Medical Setting Phobia/Fear

Going to the doctor

Having a physical exam

Talking to the doctor about my symptoms

Having any kind of medical test

Having my blood pressure taken by a nurse

Taking my blood pressure by myself

Making a doctor's appointment

Making an appointment for a medical test

Going to the hospital

Visiting someone in the hospital

Listening to a news story about disease or prevention

Reading an article or story about someone with a serious disease

Talking to someone who is really sick with a serious disease

Talking about a disease with someone

Table 8.3 Example: List of Symptoms and Rating Based on SUDS

Situation	SUDS Rating

Table 8.4 Example: Hierarchy of Exposure

1. (most distressing)
2.
3.
4.
5.
6.
7.
8.
9. (least distressing)

that the client will move up the hierarchy once a particular situation is mastered (SUDS = 50 percent drop).

Then, go on to discuss safety behaviors. Indicate that sometimes, in order to reduce the discomfort, we have from our symptoms, we use tricks to help us cope. Safety behaviors are "tricks" or actions used with the intent of preventing something that is feared. Just like avoidance, safety behaviors give short-term relief (they make us feel better) at the cost of long-term increased anxiety and symptom fear. Safety behaviors prevent us from challenging the beliefs that maintain anxiety.

Here are a few common safety behaviors:

- having someone with you at all times (not really feeling safe by myself);
- sitting near a door or exit (escape dangerous panic);

- planning an escape route (to escape an "unsafe" situation);
- things we do in our mind (distraction, counting);
- breathing (to control the anxiety and avoid it more);
- carrying a beverage with you or snack (distraction);
- having a "lucky" object with you (superstition);
- praying to distract yourself.

It is important to identify the client's safety behaviors. The client should be asked to list them, with the intent of not using them later during exposure (Table 8.5, see Resource Pack, p. 345).

Table 8.5 Example: List of Safety Behaviors

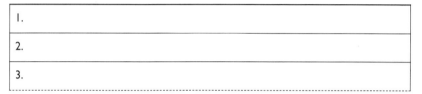

| 1. |
| 2. |
| 3. |

The client with a history of fainting or risk of fainting will next need to be instructed in applied pressure prior to starting exposure for blood injection injury. They will need to practice it and become familiar with it, as it will later be used during exposure for blood injection injury. This technique works by counteracting the fainting response, by increasing and maintain blood pressure, through the contracture and release of large muscle groups (Öst, 1987).

The client should be instructed to:

- find someplace to sit;
- simultaneously squeeze and then release the muscles in the legs, arms, and torso;
- tense for 10 to 15 seconds;
- release for 30 seconds;
- repeat five times.

Homework Assignment

The client should be instructed to perform applied pressure (five repetitions of large muscle tensing) on five separate occasions daily. The client may wish to monitor blood pressure before they do the exercise and then after, to document the desired increase in blood pressure (if the client has access to a blood pressure cuff).

Session Three: Starting Exposure

Agenda

1. Check-in and review practice.
2. Review exposure principles with the client.
3. Review response prevention (safety behaviors).
4. Select lowest item and hierarchy and identify specific catastrophic prediction.
5. Complete at least one exposure in session, using applied pressure if appropriate.
6. Homework assignment.

Materials Needed

The clinician will need to have items available to begin exposure. This may include materials like pictures of feared objects or blood, the objects themselves, like needles (capped), unused capped syringes, medical videos of injections or bleeding, rubber tourniquets, blood pressure cuffs, etc. Or it may involve exposure to an aspect of the medical setting (waiting room), or having blood pressure taken by a medical professional (which will need to be arranged prior to the session). Also, needed is the Severity Measure for Specific Phobia.

Protocol

To begin this session, the clinician should review the patient's daily practice with performed applied pressure. Did they practice five times daily? Did they monitor their blood pressure during each exercise?

Following a review of the homework, indicate that the focus of this session will be on in vivo exposure. Explain that exposure will begin with lowest item on the hierarchy (see Table 8.6, Resource Pack, p. 344). This may consist of looking at photos, watching videos, or looking at props (like pressure cuffs or needles or syringes).

The clinician will explain that they will approach the client's fear by having them complete items on the hierarchy starting with the least anxiety-provoking. It will be done in session with the support and guidance of the clinician. The clinician should explain that the process will consist of completing one exposure task multiple times, in rapid succession, taking time between trials only to record responses in Table 8.7, see Resource Pack, p. 345. The clinician should indicate that rapid repeat exposure will allow the client to learn to ride the anxiety wave, and allow them the chance to test whether or not their feared predictions are true. Done repeatedly, it will cause the anxiety to drop. The goal might be explained in another way as doing each step on the hierarchy repeatedly until the client gets "bored" with it, or, in clinical terms, habituates to it.

Table 8.6 Example: Hierarchy of Exposure

I. (most distressing)
2.
3.
4.
5.
6.
7.
8.
9. (least distressing)

Table 8.7 Example: Catastrophic Prediction Chart

Situation	Prediction/Fear

Before actual exposure is started in session, the clinician will need to help the client elucidate the thought attached to their fear. This thought is the catastrophic prediction about what might happen when the client is in the situation they fear. This will allow the therapist and client to test whether or not the prediction actually comes true during exposure, or in other words, if it is accurate. For people with blood injection injury, the catastrophic prediction may be something like a fear of "bleeding out" uncontrollably, fainting or passing out, losing control of themselves or feeling agitated. For people with medical setting anxiety, catastrophic prediction may mean their finding out that they have a disease or illness or being told they have high blood pressure, for instance.

A brief review of safety behaviors from the prior session should be conducted with the intent of not having the client use these avoidance techniques during exposure (see List of Safety Behaviors, p. 221 or Resource Pack p. 345, Table 8.5 "List of Safety Behaviors"). The clinician should explain that client needs to allow themselves to experience anxiety fully within the framework of the therapeutic setting. If the client is not "in it" or allowing themselves to ride the anxiety wave, they will not learn how to surf the crest and come out the other side.

Next in the session, exposure will be conducted. The client will be asked to record the results of their practice, including the exposure activity they did; the sensations they had; the thoughts; and SUDS before, during, and after on the Exposure and SUDS Chart shown in Table 8.8 (see Resource Pack, p. 346). They will be asked to repeat exposure until their SUDS drops by at least 50 percent.

It is important for clients who experience the vasovagal or fainting response, or have symptoms related to it, to use applied pressure during exposure to counteract blood pressure drop.

Table 8.8 Exposure and SUDS Chart

Exposure Task	SUDS Before	Sensations	SUDS During	Thoughts	SUDS After

The client will be instructed to record the results of their practice, including the exposure activity they did; the sensations they had: the thoughts; SUDS before, during, and after. They will be asked to repeat exposure until their SUDS drops by at least 50 percent.

Homework Assignment

The practice for the week will consist of having the client complete exposure steps on the hierarchy using the process and filling in the Exposure and SUDS Chart. The clinician may wish to select one or two steps on the hierarchy for the client to work on (for chart forms see Resource Pack, pp. 344–346).

Session Four: Continuing Exposure

Agenda

1. Check-in and review of homework practice.
2. Discuss obstacles.
3. Perform exposure tasks in sessions.
4. Assign further practice/exposure.
5. Assign homework.

Materials Needed

As in the previous session, the clinician will need to have items available to begin exposure. This may include materials like pictures of feared objects or blood, the objects themselves, like needles (capped), unused capped syringes, medical videos of injections or bleeding, rubber tourniquets, blood pressure cuffs, etc. Or it may involve exposure to an aspect of the medical setting (waiting room), or having blood pressure taken by a medical professional (which will need to be arranged prior to the session).

Special consideration should be taken to arranging situational exposure scenarios beforehand, if they involve other medical professionals or aspects of the medical setting. This may be observational scenarios like watching a blood draw or injection or IV start. It may also involve having blood pressure taken in the medical setting repeatedly. Or it may be the actual experience of a blood draw or needle stick.

If situational exposure is completed in this session, the clinician should be aware that their presence or the therapist themselves may function as a safety behavior. The client may think that the only reason that they do not have anxiety is because the clinician is there keeping them safe. This can be challenged by conducting exposure without the clinician present, and having the client practice exposure outside the confines of the therapy setting

Protocol

While a review of the homework and practice is always important, in these sessions, it is especially important to review the practice from the prior week. If the client did not complete exposure on their own, the clinician should query about the obstacles to exposure and reasons underlying avoidance. What did the client fear might happen if they did the exercise? If the client did not complete assigned practice, then that exposure will need to be done first in session.

The content of these sessions will focus on completing the exposure hierarchy. The process is the same as that used in Session Three. The specific fear thought related to the situation or stimulus will be identified and then tested via repeated rapid exposure. Exposure will be completed until the SUDS drops by 50 percent.

As before, for clients who experience the vasovagal or fainting response, or have symptoms related to it, they should be asked to use applied pressure during exposure to counteract blood pressure drop.

Also, as previously, the client and clinician together can fill out the Catastrophic Prediction Chart and the Exposure and SUDS Chart (for charts see Resource Pack, pp. 344–346).

Homework Assignment

The practice for the week will be the same as for Session Three. The client should complete exposure steps on the hierarchy using the process and fill in the Exposure and SUDS Chart as they practice exposure on their own. The clinician may wish to select one or two steps on the hierarchy for the client to work on (for chart forms see Resource Pack, pp. 344–346).

Session Five: Continuing Exposure

Agenda

1. Check-in and review of homework practice.
2. Discuss obstacles.
3. Perform exposure tasks in sessions.
4. Assign further practice and exposure.

Materials Needed

As in the previous session, the clinician will need to have items available to begin exposure. This may include materials like pictures of feared objects or blood, the objects themselves, like needles (capped), unused capped syringes, medical videos of injections or bleeding, rubber tourniquets, blood pressure cuffs, etc. Or it may involve exposure to an aspect of the medical setting (waiting room), or having blood pressure taken by a medical professional (which will need to be arranged prior to the session).

Protocol

While a review of the homework and practice is always important, in these sessions, it is especially important to review the practice from the prior week. If the client did not complete exposure on their own, the clinician should discuss the obstacles to practicing exposure and try to determine the reasons underlying avoidance. What did the client fear might happen if they did the exercise? If the client did not complete assigned practice, then that exposure will need to be done first in session.

Session Five will be identical to Session Four. The goal is exposure and completing the exposure hierarchy. The process is the same as that used in both Session Three and Session Four. The specific fear thought related to the situation or stimulus will be identified and then tested via repeated rapid exposure. Exposure will be completed until the SUDS drops by 50 percent.

Also, as previously, the client and clinician together can fill out the Catastrophic Prediction Chart and the Exposure and SUDS Chart (for charts see Resource Pack, pp. 345–346).

Homework Assignment

The practice for the week will be the same as for Session Four. The client should complete exposure steps on the hierarchy using the process that has been practiced in the sessions. They should fill in the Exposure and SUDS Chart as they practice exposure on their own. The clinician may wish to select one or two steps on the hierarchy for the client to work on.

Session Six: Review of Progress and Future Planning

Agenda

1. Review homework and practice.
2. Review treatment progress including psychometric tracking and the hierarchy.
3. Discuss techniques the client has found effective.
4. Discuss future challenges and coping techniques.

Materials Needed

Severity Measure for Specific Phobia.

Protocol

The clinician will begin this session by reviewing the client's practice during the past week. In addition, the clinician should discuss the client's progression through the hierarchy. This should include discussion of the catastrophic predictions the client had and which ones the client was able to allow themselves to disprove. It should also reinforce the client's capacity to ride the anxiety wave until completion, repeatedly, until the anxiety became a much less distressing ripple.

It is important next to identify the techniques the client has found effective, so that a coping plan can be created for future challenges. The clinician will need to question the patient regarding the things that the client has found most helpful. The client and clinician will create a list that can be written in the chart shown in Table 8.9 (see Resource Pack, p. 346).

Table 8.9 List of Skills to Reduce Fear

Skills That Have Worked To Help Me Reduce My Fear

The clinician should emphasize that behaviorally, if these skills have worked in the past, then they will also work for the client in the future if any similar anxiety-provoking situations occur. It is important for the clinician to remind the client that anxiety related to their feared stimulus may surface in the future, although likely with less intensity. This does not mean that treatment has failed, but it is a normal phenomenon that can occur when a fear has been deconditioned. It is called spontaneous recovery (like the smoker who has the urge for a cigarette after 20 years). It is easily addressed by using the techniques the client has acquired—namely, staying in the situation, riding it out, and continuing to approach things that make them anxious.

Finally, the patient can be informed that any time they feel the need for booster sessions, they can return in order to continue to make progress.

References

Öst, L.G. (1987). Applied relaxation: description of a coping technique and review of controlled studies. *Behaviour research and therapy*, 25(5), 397–409.

Rachman, S. (1976) The passing of the two stage theory of fear and avoidance: Fresh possibilities. *Behavior Research and Therapy*, 14, 125–131.

Rachman, S. (1977). The conditioning theory of fear of acquisition: A critical examination. *Behavior Research and Therapy*, 15, 375–387.

Chapter 9

Illness Anxiety

Hypochondriasis can be defined as worry about illness that persists, despite medical reassurance and negative examination findings. It can have many consequences, such as frequent "checking" for symptoms; repeat doctor visits and medical tests; or, alternately, avoidance of medical settings and tests.

It is important for the clinician to understand prior to starting treatment that initial disputation of the reality of the client's symptoms is likely to be ineffective. It is more than likely that they have had multiple discussions with health care providers about their symptoms and interpretation of them before they have arrived at your door. They have also very likely tried to force themselves "not to think" about their symptoms with the unfortunate result that they could not stop thinking about their symptoms.

The focus of this treatment of illness anxiety is on habituation to the ambiguous medical meaning of symptoms and sensations, reducing the fear of catastrophic illness thoughts, and increasing tolerance (or reducing anxiety) associated with physical sensations and the medical setting. Treatment is, ultimately, a combination of cognitive and exposure therapy.

Session One: Illness Anxiety

Agenda

1. Baseline assessment.
2. History of medical concerns, symptoms, safety behaviors.
3. Treatment goals.
4. Cognitive behavioral model (CBT) illness anxiety.
5. Homework and practice assignment.

Materials Needed

1. Health Anxiety Inventory.
2. Illness Attitude Scale.

Protocol

Treatment, as in most protocols in this book, will start with a baseline evaluation of illness anxiety. The Illness Attitude Scale is a measure that can be used weekly to assess changes in disease anxiety and fear of negative or catastrophic disease outcomes as it is sensitive to changes in treatment. The Health Anxiety Inventory is of assistance for initial evaluation because it allows for identification of several specific components of health anxiety, including key cognitive distortions (thoughts of disease, death, pain), fears (of disease or death), and behaviors (such as safety).

It is important for the clinician to begin the initial session by validating the client's experience that they have symptoms that have caused them a lot of concern, and even interfered with their quality of life. The focus of much of this session will be on obtaining the client's illness and symptom story. The clinician should ask the client about the kinds of physical symptoms they experience or notice. They should ask about symptoms and concerns that have brought them to the doctor's office. The clinician should make a note of the symptoms, as they will be specifically addressed in later sessions.

Equally important is to ascertain the experience the client has with both the medical setting and the disease or illness itself. The clinician will need to inquire about what the medical provider has specifically told the client with regard to the illness at hand. What was the client's experience of this? Did they feel dismissed? Did they feel they were being told they were "crazy"? That their symptoms were not taken seriously enough? Or that their provider simply did not have the ability to detect their disease?

The clinician should also find out about the client's past experiences with illness and/or disease, including personal knowledge of anyone who has had the illness in question. Prior learning and social modeling can all influence illness anxiety.

Safety behaviors are an area that the clinician will need to evaluate as well. Safety behaviors are the actions that the client engages in to protect themselves from the feared disease. These include things like going to the doctor, seeking reassurance from friends or family, researching the disease on the Internet, reading about the disease, "checking" their body for symptoms, adopting diet or lifestyle modifications to prevent disease, or simply avoiding the doctor or medical settings. Some of these will show up as items on both the Illness Attitude Scale and the Health Anxiety Inventory.

Additionally, it is helpful to establish the cost of the client's symptoms on their daily functioning or social environment. Are there things that their symptoms have prevented them from doing that they used to do? Do they find it hard to complete things they need to without worrying about the symptoms? Do they spend a lot of time researching their illness? Have their symptoms created any strain on their relationships?

The clinician will need to emphasize that the goal of treatment is not to eradicate the symptoms that the client has been dealing with. The clinician will be working on the basis that the client's experience of their symptoms is real. The symptoms are not "made up." Nor are the symptoms "all in their head." The client should never be instructed to "just not to worry" or "not think" about their symptoms. This kind of advice has not worked in the past for clients experiencing illness anxiety.

Instead of offering platitudes, treatment is directed at giving them tools to manage their symptoms. The goal for the client is to learn skills so that their symptoms bother them less and therefore improve the quality of their life.

The clinician will need to explain the CBT of illness anxiety treatment. The idea is simple: Symptoms do not happen in isolation. At any one moment in time, they are connected to thoughts about their symptom, the feelings that occur in reaction to the symptom, and actions that respond to it (behaviors). The easiest way to illustrate the multidimensional nature of symptoms is to ask the client to describe a time when they last had the symptom:

- What were they thinking or picturing when they had the symptom?
- How did they feel when they had the symptom (i.e. worried, peaceful)?
- Did they do anything in response to it (seek reassurance, look it up)?

Research shows that specific kinds of thoughts, feelings, and behaviors can increase or decrease physical symptoms (Figure 9.1). Thoughts, feelings, and behaviors are like rivers that run into the symptom pool.

They can either increase the volume on the symptom—making it harder to cope with it—or they can turn down the volume—making it less bothersome or quiet.

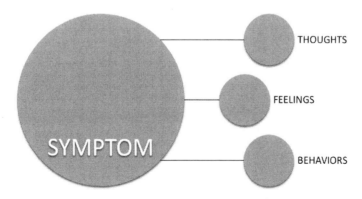

Figure 9.1 Thoughts, Feelings, and Behaviors Lead to Symptoms

What Factors Influence Symptom Intensity?

Research shows that there are many different things that impact symptom intensity for symptoms that persist without easy explanation. These intensity impactors fall into several categories. The client can be asked to consider some of the factors shown in Table 9.1, using the following questions:

- When you have been stressed, have your symptoms gotten better? Or worse?
- When you have not slept like you should, have your symptoms been worse?
- When your symptoms made you do less in your life, did the symptoms get cured? Or did they keep getting worse?
- When other people commented on your difficulties or that they thought something was wrong with you, did the symptoms get better? Or did you and the symptoms feel worse—and not better?
- If someone told you your symptoms were "all in your head," how did it make you feel? Did your symptoms disappear? Or feel even more upsetting?
- When you have pain, what happens to your symptoms? Are they exacerbated?
- Does thinking about the symptoms reduce them? Or make them feel worse?
- Describe the last time you felt happy or experienced joy. In that moment, were your symptoms at their strongest? Or were they less bothersome?

Conversely, there are several things that can make the symptoms less upsetting, and can actually turn down the volume on symptoms, as shown in the chart in Table 9.2.

The clinician should explain that CBT works by teaching the client skills that give them the ability to turn down symptom volume so that symptoms are less distressing and impact their lives less negatively. They will also learn tools to manage the things that make symptoms feel worse.

The clinician should then take time in this first session to help the client identify, from the charts above, the factors that are associated with the ebb and flow in their symptoms. Alternately, they have had times when their symptoms were less bothersome.

Homework Assignment

This week for practice, the client will identify the things that based on their own experience with their symptoms make them worse or make them better. They should add those things to the charts shown in Tables 9.3 to 9.5 (see Resource Pack, p. 347).

Table 9.1 List of Factors that Increase Symptom Volume

Behaviors	Decreasing or stopping things you used to be able to do, doing too much (or nothing), avoiding anything the reminds you of illness, researching illness frequently, "body scanning", avoiding the doctor or hospital or spending too much time at the doctor's office
Feelings	Stress, Anxiety, Depression, PTSD, hopelessness, helplessness
Thoughts	Thinking about the symptoms, expecting the worst, focusing on how you "used to be." Picturing terrible disease outcomes in your life.
Physical Factors	Pain, poor sleep, substance use, sedentary life style, bad nutrition
Medications	Narcotics, tranquilizers, sedating medications
Social	Lack of support, isolation, others doing too much or too little for you, others who disregard your symptom

Table 9.2 List of Factors that Decrease Symptom Volume

Behaviors	Doing something you like to do or that makes you feel good, being physically active, exercise, doing things you did before
Feelings	Relaxation, contentment, hopeful, not feeling scared about symptom
Thoughts	Not focusing on the symptoms, being in the present moment, not expecting the worst, knowing you can do something (even with the symptoms), knowing you can survive the worst
Physical Factors	Good sleep, good nutrition, stress management, exercise
Social	Feeling close to someone in your life, support, knowing others are there for you

Table 9.3 Example: List of Symptoms

My Symptoms
1.
2.
3.

Table 9.4 Example: List of Factors that Increase Symptom Intensity

Physical	
Behaviors	
Feelings	
Social	
Thoughts	

Table 9.5 Example: List of Factors that Decrease Symptom Intensity

Physical	
Behaviors	
Feelings	
Social	
Thoughts	

Session Two: Treatment Goals and Behavioral Activation

Agenda

1. Review practice and homework.
2. Provide feedback about baseline assessment trackers/individual symptoms.
3. Identification of life areas negatively impacted by illness anxiety.
4. SMART goals based on values/disrupted functional areas.
5. Start walking program.
6. Assign practice: short- and long-term goals.

Materials Needed

1. Health Anxiety Inventory and Illness Attitude Scale.
2. Homework charts: Copies will be needed for every session to hand out to the client.

Protocol

The second session should start with a review of the practice assignment. The clinician should ask the client to look at their symptoms over the past week and to see whether they identified things that increased or decreased the intensity of their symptoms. If the practice charts are not completed, the clinician and client can do them together at the beginning of the session.

Having then discussed factors that have an impact on their symptoms, the clinician will need to explain how important it will be in this treatment to address those factors that not only increase or decrease symptom intensity, but also the things in their life that have been most impacted by their symptoms. This could be their ability to work, to be a parent, or to be a spouse. It could be the things that they used to do every day around the house, as well as engaging in hobbies or sports. It could even be the things that they used to do to take care of themselves that they do not do anymore.

It can be pointed out to them that they are in treatment because their symptoms have been challenging and they have not found solutions or answers to them. It is often after many weeks or months of treatments and after many trips to doctor's offices. In addition, it can be stated that many times when people have been dealing with symptoms for a long time, their symptoms really do interfere with their life. Sometimes people stop doing things that they used to do because the symptoms prevent them from feeling effective and competent or they feel embarrassed. Furthermore, symptoms sometimes interfere with their ability to simply enjoy an activity that they used to love. It can be said quite directly that it is very likely that there are things that they are no longer doing that they used to do before their symptoms and problems started.

The clinician should explain the goal of therapy, which is to have them start doing the things that really matter to them again—despite their symptoms. However, this may mean doing things differently than they did before. But, it all starts by figuring out the areas in their life that have been most impacted by their symptoms. It is important to identify exactly what their symptoms have taken from their life and what work has to be done over the next several weeks to help the client fill those gaps.

Suggest to the client that these are some questions they should ask themselves:

- What would I be doing in my life now if I had not had the problems that caused my symptoms?
- What specific things have the symptoms made me give up?
- What do I miss the most?
- How would my life be different without my symptoms?
- What would I like to be able to do in 12 weeks that I am not doing now?

The chart shown in Table 9.6 helps them record their answers to these questions (see Resource Pack, p. 348).

Having discussed some of the activities that they would like to do more often, it is time to begin work on setting up goals based on the activities they identified

Table 9.6 Example: List of Activities to Do Again

Activities that I'm not doing anymore and would like to do again
1.
2.
3.

above. Indicate that together they will set up goals in a very specific way and construct a plan to get them to where you want to be. The procedure used will have to do with SMART goals. SMART goals will provide them with the structure and targets that will help them reach their goals. You can point out to the client that SMART is an acronym that stands for the following:

Specific: The more specific the goal, the easier it is to attain. For example, if their goal is to be more social, the specific goal of having coffee with one friend each week is easier to check off as an accomplished goal.

Measureable: If a goal is measureable, it means it can be tracked over time. The goal of reading for 20 minutes three times a week is measureable; "reading more" is not.

Achievable: A goal of being able to sit in a noisy, crowded room for 20 minutes twice a week is more achievable than "Learn to tolerate all noise."

Relevant: The goal has to matter to them personally. Losing 25 pounds is a worthwhile goal for many people, but it would be irrelevant if their major issue was to cope with attention and memory difficulties from their discussion.

Time-limited: The goal must be structured such that it has an end point or expiration date. When do they plan to achieve this goal? How much time do they give themselves?

Indicate that it can be started with developing three short-term goals for them to work on in these sessions (Table 9.7, see Resource Pack, p. 348).

Table 9.7 Example: Short-Term SMART Goals: 12 weeks

1.	
2.	
3.	

Short-term goals can lead to long-term goals. Long-term goals are things they aspire to be doing or to have them happen 1 year from now. The idea is to use their short-term goals now to springboard into where they would like to be in the longer term (Table 9.8, see Resource Pack, p. 349).

Table 9.8 Example: Long-Term SMART Goals: 12 Weeks from Now

1.	
2.	
3.	

The clinician will next look at the client's SMART goals and help them develop an activity plan based on those goals (Table 9.9, see Resource Pack, p. 349). Realistic activity planning is essential as it is important that the client is able to actually complete the goals they have set. Being able to meet their goals is reinforcing and creates behavioral momentum. This may mean starting with a very modest and low level of activity and gradually increasing the activity time every few days as they successfully complete activities.

Table 9.9 Example: Activity Plan Chart

Activity (Time in minutes)	M	T	W	TH	F	S	SUN

The last thing to discuss in this session is how symptoms tend to impact clients in various ways, often by stopping them from taking care of themselves the way that they know they should. It can be pointed out that good self-care leads to better health and that treatment is aimed at them as a whole person and not just at their symptoms. In other words, they are just their symptoms. That usually means that taking care of themselves involves being physically active.

For instance, walking is a wonderful activity to start with for several reasons. The more they can walk and the better their endurance, the better able they will be to do activities that are meaningful to them. Walking is the core of many

activities. It is free and easy to do anywhere; it can be done alone or with someone else (even a beloved pet).

In summary, exercise has an important, non-negotiable role in their symptom
and health management. It can be helpful to review the beneficial impact of
exercise on their health. The benefits of exercise include increased muscle
strength, endurance, improved metabolism and blood sugar regulation,
improved sleep, and improved mood. We also know that exercise actually
improves brain functioning. Some studies have demonstrated that regular
exercise causes the brain to release and use BDNF (a protein like "miracle grow"
for the brain). BDNF actually causes cells in important areas of the brain having
to do with memory (hippocampus) and attention, problem solving, and
judgment (frontal lobes) to regenerate and grow. Thus, we can think of exercise
like "medication" for the body and brain—only better. This is because it is cost
free, has no negative side effects, and makes you physically and mentally stronger
in the long run.

Therefore, a walking program is highly recommended. The clinician can
explain that they will be having the client start a walking program. This means
that the client will walk every day. It is important to have the client start
physically at a level they can tolerate without having their symptoms flare. This
means that if they can walk 20 minutes without headache or dizziness, they
should start there. However, if they can only walk for 5 minutes, they can start
there. The clinician will then indicate that each week the client will increase
their walking time by 1 to 2 minutes.

Homework Assignment

The practice and homework assignment will include the client filling out the
Activity Plan Chart and starting the walking plan. In terms of the walking plan,
they should start by recording their walking starting point as below:

MY WALKING START POINT: _____ MINUTES

Once they have started walking, they should increase their walking by 2 or
3 minutes every day.

The charts shown in Tables 9.10 and 9.11 should be given to the client and
they should be asked to record in these charts every day. The Symptom Meter
will be reviewed weekly as will be the planned activity and walking. The
clinician, in assigning homework, should keep in mind that the whole goal of
treatment is to get the client engaged back in life and this needs to be strongly
reinforced every week. Therefore, the charts shown in these tables will be given
at the end of each session to the client as part of the homework assignment.

The first chart is the Symptom Meter. Every day they should record the
highest number (between 1 and 100) that they reach on the Symptom Meter.

Symptom Meter

For each day of the upcoming week, write the highest number you reach on the Symptom Meter. Schedule a reminder each day for you to remember to monitor your symptoms.

_____ M _____ T _____ W _____ Th _____ F _____ Sat _____ Sun

And every day they should write on the Things That Made My Symptoms Chart (Table 9.10, see Resource Pack, p. 350) what made their symptoms better or worse.

And for their walking program, they should record the number of minutes they walked (Table 9.11, see Resource Pack, p. 350)

Table 9.10 Example: List of Things that Made the Symptoms

	Things That Made My Symptoms	
	Better	Worse
Physical		
Behaviors		
Feelings		
Social		
Thoughts		

Table 9.11 Example: The Walking Chart

	Week									
	1	2	3	4	5	6	7	8	9	10
Day 1										
Day 2										
Day 3										
Day 4										
Day 5										
Day 6										
Day 7										

Session Three: Identifying Negative Thinking Styles

Agenda

1. Review homework and practice.
2. Negative thinking and symptom amplification.
3. Automatic negative thoughts and examples.
4. Homework and practice: Catching Automatic Negative Thoughts (ANTs).

Materials Needed

Charts for homework.

Protocol

The clinician begins Session Three by reviewing practice and homework. Has the client recorded their symptom ratings on the Symptom Meter? Have they kept track of what things make their symptoms better or worse? Have they been walking and recording how many minutes per day they are walking? In general, in the past week have their symptoms been better or worse?

Treatment in this session will focus on how thinking can impact symptoms. The clinician and client will work on identifying helpful thoughts that can turn down symptom volume and negative thoughts that increase symptom volume. It is important that the client realize that learning to listen to their thinking is an important skill in symptom management.

The clinician next introduces ANTs. Point out that thinking is often automatic and it can happen outside of our awareness. Thoughts attached to symptoms occur every time they notice their symptoms. As they become more "tuned in" to their symptoms, these thoughts come more rapidly. The content of these thoughts is often negative, catastrophic, and anxiety-provoking. The thoughts can be frightening, and sometimes they are highly inaccurate.

ANTs impact symptoms specifically because they increase anxiety and the stress response. Stress does not help symptoms to abate, but rather turns up the symptom volume. This can be easily established by asking the client if their symptoms go away when they are under a lot of stress. Or do they get worse and do they interfere more with the things they are trying to handle? The following box illustrates how symptoms lead, ultimately, to more intense symptoms:

Illness Symptoms → Negative/Catastrophic Thoughts (including illness images) → Stress/Anxiety → Increased Symptom Volume

---

It is important for the clinician to explain that ANTs often take many different forms. Errors in thinking or distortions often fall into specific kinds of categories. Knowing the kinds of negative thinking that happen can help the client to identify their own thinking patterns.

Examples of ANTs are provided in Table 9.12. The clinician may wish to have the client read the list and circle the ones which seem most applicable to them.

Table 9.12 Examples of ANTs

Distortion	Definition	Example
All or Nothing Thinking	Seeing things as either all good or all bad. No middle ground!	"If I don't get rid of these symptoms I won't be able to do anything!" "I'm nothing like I was before"
Fortune Telling	Predicting that things will turn out negatively without considering other possible outcomes.	"It doesn't matter what I do, my symptoms will just keep getting worse" "I know I won't be able to do this"
Disqualifying the positive	Telling yourself that positive experiences don't count	"Yes, my symptom bothered me less last week, but that means nothing"
Emotional Reasoning	Believing what you feel must be true	"I *feel* like a wreck. This means that I am a wreck"
Catastrophizing	Expecting extremely negative consequences; exaggerating situations to be the worst possible outcome	"I can't take this anymore" "My life is ruined"
Mental Filter	Focusing on a single negative detail instead of seeing the whole picture	"I'm not able to do this activity as well as I would like to. My whole life is a mess' "I have a symptom of dizziness. This means I have MS"
Mind Reading	Believing that you know what others are thinking, especially how they feel about you	"They think I am nuts" "They think I'm incapable of handling things" "They think I'm stupid"

Continued

Table 9.12 Continued

Distortion	Definition	Example
Overgeneralization	Making a general conclusion based on a single incident. Assuming things will turn out a certain way because they did so before	"The last time I did this I felt so much worse. This means that this will keep getting worse every time I do it"
Should or Must Statements	Having fixed ideas about how you or others "should," "ought to," or "must" be. Leads to feeling nervous, sad, and worried	"I should be able to do this" "I must feel exactly the same as I did before in order to be OK"

(Adapted from Thorn, 2017)

Homework Assignment

For each day of the upcoming week, write the highest number you reach on the Symptom Meter. Schedule a reminder each day for you to remember to monitor your symptoms.

_____ M _____ T _____ W _____ Th _____ F _____ Sat _____ Sun

And every day they should write on the Things That Made My Symptoms Chart what made their symptoms better or worse (see Resource Pack, p. 350).

And for their walking program, they should record the number of minutes they walked (see Resource Pack, p. 333).

Finally, keep track of ANTs in the Thoughts Record Chart shown in Table 9.13, see Resource Pack, p. 351.

Table 9.13 Example: Thoughts Record Chart

Automatic Thoughts I Had Which Relate To My Illness Symptoms	Circumstances When I Had This Thought	How Many Times I Had This Thought
1.		
2.		
3.		

Session Four: Challenging Negative Thinking

Agenda

1. Review homework.
2. Disputing negative thoughts.
3. Reframing symptom thoughts and body noise.
4. Coping statements.
5. Practice and homework assignment.

Materials Needed

ANT examples from the prior week.

Protocol

The clinician will need to begin this session by reviewing practice from the previous week. Careful attention should be paid to the catastrophic thoughts associated with symptoms. If the client has difficulty identifying them outside of the treatment sessions, this can be done at the beginning of the session by reviewing various situations, activities, or events, and querying the client about specific thoughts. Behavioral activation will need to be monitored and the clinician will need to determine if the client is continuing to increase activity and walking levels identified as smart goals.

The clinician will next explain that the focus of this session will be learning ways to look at their automatic thoughts differently. Learning a different perspective on automatic thoughts can make them less frightening. Fear feeds symptom volume. Challenging thoughts reduces this fear. During this session and the next several sessions, there will be work on ways to reduce this symptom fear.

This process can be most easily started by reviewing the thought record from the prior week. There may be multiple thoughts or images listed. The clinician should ask the client to identify the most upsetting or " hottest" thought. This thought may be one of the client's core illness fears.

The clinician should next complete the first four columns of the chart, as shown in Table 9.14 (see Resource Pack, p. 351), with the client (situation, feeling, distressing thought, and ANT category). This specific thought should be identified with the client using Table 9.12, Examples of ANTs.

It is important for the clinician to explain that challenging thoughts one has had for a very long time can initially be quite difficult. This has nothing to do with the client, but rather with the way our brains process information automatically. Research has demonstrated that when people are feeling a difficult emotion like sadness, fear, or anger, that the brain automatically retrieves examples of

Table 9.14 Example: Situations, Feelings and Rating Your Emotions Chart

Situation Symptom (who, what, where, when)	Feeling (List emotion and rate intensity 0–100)	Thought (What are exact thoughts. Circle most upsetting thought)	Specific ANT (What category of ANT does this fall into?)	Alternate Thought (In response to challenge questions)	Re-rate Feeling (emotion, 1–100)

other times when they felt the same way. This is called state-dependent retrieval. When we are depressed, we think about other times we were in the dumps. When we are scared about something, we think about other times this happened. The mind does not automatically access information that might challenge how we are thinking or feeling.

The clinician can illustrate this with a simple example in session. They can ask the client if the last time they were depressed, was their mind filled with happy memories? The last time they felt anxious or scared, was their mind filled with recollections of feeling secure, safe, and content?

The clinician will follow this by providing the client with tools to challenge this thinking bias. The clinician should point to the distressing thought and ask the following:

- What would I tell my best friend if they told me this thought?
- Has this thought been true 100 percent of the time?
- Is there another explanation for this thought?
- What is the actual evidence for this thought?

The remaining column in the chart "alternate thought" should be completed next. The client should be asked to re-rate their emotions.

A final technique for reframing can be helpful to review with the client. This is the concept of body noise. Body noise is the sensation our bodies produce every day: muscle tension, itching, aches, gut sensations, lightheadedness when hungry, heart beat increases and decreases, sweating. These are indicators that the body is working.

When someone has illness anxiety, this normal body noise is often interpreted differently. Body noise becomes filtered through the lens of anxiety. Thoughts and memories linked to this fear come rushing forward. State-dependent retrieval occurs. Evidence that might point to normal body noise does not surface to contradict the negative thoughts and memories in the mind.

This concept can be explained in terms of a house analogy. Houses make lots of noise. Normal house sounds are creaking of floors, settling noise, wind noise, furnace noise, appliance noise, and pipe noise. These noises occur daily. Someone who has a lot of fear of intruders and break-ins would naturally be attentive to these noises. They would likely interpret every sound as a potential threat and need to be investigated. They would feel anxious and think about all the crime stories they have heard. They will continue to be on high alert for the sound. This can be contrasted with the person who is not anxious about crime. They will hear the same sound and think that it is just a normal house sound. They will tune it out and go about their day.

Body noise is like house noise. Learning to challenge thinking can help the client think about the house noise in a way that is less threatening. The clinician may wish at this point to point to some of the symptoms the client reports and associated catastrophic thoughts. They may wish to point to evidence against this thought.

- How common is this specific symptom in the population?
- If symptom equals disease 100 percent of the time, how many people then would have the disease? Is this accurate? Or does symptom not equal disease 100 percent of the time?
- Is there an alternate explanation for this symptom? What might that be?
- Is it possible that house noise is being automatically interpreted through the anxiety lens?

The clinician may wish to complete an additional row in the chart during this exercise, to demonstrate the impact of the reframing on the feeling the client experiences.

Homework Assignment

Homework and practice for the next week will consist of continuing to challenge negative thoughts. The client will also need to continue the walking program and activity program started in Session One and Session Two, filling in the charts that were initially provided in the first session.

The Situations, Feelings and Rating Your Emotions Chart will be helpful (Table 9.14, see Resouce Pack, p. 356).

Session Five: Exposure to Illness-Related Thoughts

Agenda

1. Homework review.
2. Avoidance behaviors.
3. Safety behaviors and response prevention.
4. Imaginal exposure to illness thoughts.
5. Homework assignment.

Materials Needed

Client cell phone, blank paper for writing.

Protocol

At the beginning of this session, the clinician should review the homework assignment for the past week. The most important aspect of the assignment was to challenge negative thoughts. Go over the Situations, Feelings, and Rating Your Emotions Chart and continue to fill it in during the session if necessary. Behavioral activation will need to be monitored and the clinician will need to determine if the client is continuing to increase activity and walking levels identified as smart goals.

The clinician should then discuss the role of avoidance in illness anxiety. People with illness anxiety tend to avoid many things: thoughts, physical sensations, and situations. The last session focused on being aware of and challenging negative thoughts.

In this session, also, imaginal and thought exposure will be introduced and discussed. The goal is to help the patient stop avoiding and become more comfortable in talking about their fears and their symptoms.

But, first, it helps to begin by discussing negative thinking, anxiety, their symptoms, and loss of quality of life. In doing so, the clinician will need to remind the client that they have learned how ANTs, or negative thinking, turns up the volume on their symptoms and physical sensations. The illustration below demonstrates where behavior and activity fit into our symptom/emotion/thought cycle:

Physical Symptom → Negative/Catastrophic Thoughts → Stress/Anxiety → Increased Physical Symptom → Behavioral Response

---

It is helpful to explain that the "behavioral response" is how the client responds to the symptoms that upset them.

What are the typical behavioral responses to physical symptoms that are frightening? Most people with illness anxiety have negative automatic thoughts that tell them that their physical sensations mean that they have some awful or dreaded disease. For instance, many patients who worry about their health are frightened that physical pains mean that they have some form of cancer. They may avoid going to the doctor so that they do not hear the bad news they are telling themselves is true. Alternately, they may keep going to the doctor in order to be reassured in some way that the symptom is not dangerous.

They may also try to control their symptoms or avoid thinking about them. But that does not work very well and they end up ruminating about their symptoms and the disease or illness they fear they have. This is because every time you tell yourself not to think about something, it actually binds the thought to you more. This can be demonstrated with a simple example. Tell the client NOT to think about a red apple. What do they think about? Trying to control thoughts actually makes them stronger.

Frightening symptom thoughts can stop people from doing their normal activities. They may begin acting in ways in order to control their symptoms, such as leave or avoid situations that remind them of illness, avoid other people, or search the Internet for signs of the disease they fear. As a result, life becomes much more limited as activities and situations are restricted or cut off completely. Thus, the person's quality of life suffers.

The things that clients experiencing illness anxiety do to avoid their symptoms and protect themselves are typical avoidance and protective measures. Because they are so typical, it is important for the clinician to address these responses and normalize what the client does to avoid and protect. By providing education to the client regarding usual escape and avoidance responses and teaching the person that these are attempts to try to function normally, it will normalize these responses in a noncritical way.

The clinician should explain that while escape and avoidance can be normal coping mechanisms that can assist people when there are eminent dangers, like a fire, they are actually counterproductive in chronic anxiety conditions. In the short term, leaving or avoiding a situation or trying not to think about it may seem helpful, because they may feel less worried or less anxious. But in the long term, avoidance behaviors hurt. They harm people because they stop them from learning to cope with their symptoms. And because ANTs exacerbate fears and anxiety, escape and avoidance, in the long run, do not teach people how to challenge and change their negative thought patterns. Also, anxieties get stronger and fear of the symptoms returning increases.

Patients with illness anxiety also develop what are called "safety behaviors." These are behaviors that are intended to reduce the discomfort they have from their symptoms. Like escape and avoidance, safety behaviors provide short-term benefits, but over the long run, they serve to increase anxiety and symptom fear. And, they too prevent people from challenging the beliefs that maintain anxiety.

Given below are some typical safety behaviors:

- going to the doctor repeatedly for symptoms ("just in case" there is actual disease).
- seeking reassurance from people about symptoms (because symptoms "equal" disease).
- seeking reassurance about disease on the internet or through reading (because, again, symptoms "equal" disease).
- body checking or scanning (to prevent disease).
- breathing (to control the anxiety and avoid it more).
- always having your cell phone with you ("just in case").
- carrying medication with you at all times.
- carrying a beverage with you or snack.
- having someone with you at all times (not really safe by myself).
- avoiding anything that reminds one of disease (TV programs, hospitals, doctor).
- lifestyle changes to "prevent" the disease.

The clinician will need to ask the client to list their safety behaviors (Table 9.15, see Resource Pack, p. 352). This is essential prior to starting exposure, as the clinician will need to instruct the client to *not* use them during exposure.

Table 9.15 Example: List of Safety Behaviors

My Safety Behaviors

The clinician next needs to explain that the way to break the protection/avoidance trap is do its opposite. This means having the client approach or do the things that they have been avoiding, but doing them gradually, and without safety behaviors. The following should be explained:

- When we do something that we are afraid of, we give ourselves an opportunity to learn that what we fear actually does not happen (i.e., that the symptoms will cause overwhelming fear or anxiety).
- When we allow ourselves to experience or think about something that frightens us, and do it repeatedly, we get used to it (habituate) and become less afraid of it.

- Each time we do the thing that makes our symptoms worse, the fear gets smaller and smaller (the fear iceberg melts). Eventually, we do not even notice the stress and fear associated with our symptom.

The clinician can next turn to imaginal exposure practice. This can begin with an explanation that people with illness anxiety avoid three different kinds of things:

1. thoughts about the disease;
2. physical symptoms associated with the disease;
3. situations or places that trigger disease fears.

The clinician and client will begin addressing avoidance behavior by having the client approach their thoughts about the specific disease they are afraid of. They will be asked to do this first in the therapeutic environment. Although people with illness anxiety fear disease, what they fear most are the consequences of it—imagined suffering, treatment, disability, life, and relationship changes. This exercise will allow these fears to be articulated and, through repetitive retelling, the client will habituate to them. The goal of this exercise is to habituate the client to fears and thoughts they have about illness, without using their safety behaviors (i.e., researching disease, reassurance, distraction).

Prior to starting this, the client or clinician will need to make sure to have recording device (i.e., cell phone) of some kind or a pad of paper to write on. The client may have a preference to write or speak. The client will be asked to imagine having the disease and to describe what this would feel like and how it would impact them. The client will be asked to repeat this scenario several times in session and outside of session. The more this is done, the more they will reduce the anxiety associated with their thoughts. The goal is simple: to have the client become so used to the thoughts, that it "bores them" to keep talking about it.

Prior to starting this, safety behaviors will need to be reviewed. The client will need to be instructed not to engage in them during exposure. The ideal is for the client to be 100 percent present during exposure so that they can learn to approach their scary thoughts. And before this is started, the client should rate their Subjective Units of Distress Scale (SUDS); then during and after the exercise, the SUDS should also be rated. The goal of this exercise is to have the SUDS drop by at least 50 percent from the initial rating (Table 9.16, see Resource Pack, p. 352).

The client should be asked to imagine actually having the disease. This exercise involves them telling the full disease story—from the time of diagnosis onward. They should be instructed to describe how it impacts them and the treatments; how it affects their lives and the lives of their loved ones. Finally, they need to describe how it ends. Below is a list of what should be included:

- Describe their symptom;
- describe the disease they are afraid they have;
- describe how they imagine they would be diagnosed;
- describe the treatment;
- describe the disability that might be associated it;
- describe the suffering they fear they might have;
- describe the impact of the disease on their loved ones;
- describe the course of the disease.

Table 9.16 Example: The Exposure and SUDS Rating Chart

Exposure Task	SUDS Before	Sensations	SUDS During	Thoughts	SUDS After

Homework Assignment

As the assignment for the week, the client will need to repeat this exposure exercise by either listening to their recording or reading their written story daily, preferably multiple times each day. They should be asked to record their SUDS before, during, and after. Safety behaviors should not be used during exposure for this week.

The client will also need to continue the walking program and activity program started in Session One and Session Two, filling in the charts that were initially provided in the first session.

Session Six: Physical Symptom Exposure

Agenda

1. Review homework.
2. Physical symptom hierarchy.
3. Review of safety behaviors and response prevention.
4. Recreating physical sensations and exposure.
5. Homework and practice assignment.

Protocol

Thought exposure from the prior week's assignment will need to be reviewed. If the client did not complete it, the obstacles to doing so will need to be clarified, as these are likely related to anxiety. If it was not done, the clinician will need to complete this exposure with the client before moving on to this session. Behavioral activation will need to be monitored and the clinician will need to determine if the client is continuing to increase activity and walking levels identified as smart goals.

At the beginning of this session, the clinician needs to explain that in the case of illness anxiety, a plan to approach distressing physical disease-related symptoms gradually will be developed. The intent of this is to allow the client, with the support of therapy, to learn to move through their symptoms. The purpose of this is to allow them a chance to challenge catastrophic thoughts and decrease the fear and stress associated with their symptoms.

The overarching goal is to learn to "ride the anxiety wave" long enough to come out the other side and challenge their dire predictions. Anxiety can be imagined as a wave; sometimes waves are slow building and sometimes they are fast. But waves always "peak" and the "peak" is always followed by a crash. Like a wave, anxiety does not last forever. So, treatment may be described to the patient as teaching them to "surf the anxiety wave."

An "organization plan" can help. To begin to construct an organization plan, it is helpful to know which symptoms bother the patient the most and which ones bother them the least. Therapy will start by working with the least bothersome symptoms. The first thing to do is to ask the client to identify their symptoms and rate them using the SUDS, which rates symptoms from 1 to 100. The chart shown in Table 9.17, see Resource Pack, p. 353 should be explained to the patient.

Table 9.17 Example: Identifying and Rating Physical Symptoms

Symptoms	SUDS Rating

After listing and rating symptoms, the clinician will help the client build the "symptom tolerance hierarchy." It can be explained that treatment will now focus on beginning to approach their symptoms starting with the least anxiety-provoking symptoms (Table 9.18, see Resource Pack, p. 353).

Table 9.18 Symptom Hierarchy Rating Chart

My Symptom Hierarchy Based On SUDS Rating
1. (most distressing)
2.
3.
4.
5.
6.
7.
8.
9. (least distressing)

A rank order of low anxiety symptoms to high anxiety symptoms will need to be constructed.

But, having rated the symptoms in the Symptoms Hierarchy Chart, the clinician can go on to plan greater exposure to their physical symptoms and the symptoms associated with them. Initially in these sessions, there should be discussion of the symptoms that are least bothersome and anxiety-provoking. This kind of discussion helps the client to ride through the anxiety with support from the clinician.

However, also in this session, exposure will consist of recreating the symptoms. Clients with illness anxiety will experience physical symptoms in different ways. Below are some suggestions for ways to recreate the physical symptoms the individual may experience:

- *Feeling light-headed*: breathe as quickly as you can out loud for 1 minute/controlled hyperventilation. Or shake head from shoulder to shoulder rapidly for 30 seconds.
- *Head rush*: head between legs for half a minute.
- *Breathlessness*: go up a flight of stairs for 1 minute, repeat.
- *Feeling dizzy*: spin in a chair for 1 minute.
- *Loss of control/insanity/derealizaiton*: stare at self in mirror, stare at fluorescent lights.
- *Head/muscle tension*: squeeze your face and head muscles for 1 minute.
- *Inattention*: read something for 20 minutes and let your mind wander.

- *Derealization/depersonalization*: spin in chair for 1 minute.
- *Embarrassment*: create symptoms in front of others intentionally (sweating, hyperventilation); explain that you are having an anxiety attack;
- *Heart pounding/attack*: go up one or two flights of stairs; exercise vigorously for 1 minute;
- *Noise sensitivity*: listen to sound in restaurant or atrium.

The goal in this method is to repeat exposure to the symptoms over multiple trials until the SUDS rating has dropped by at least half. Trials should be conducted in relatively rapid succession, with time allotted for the client to write down their SUDS, sensations, and thoughts. The clinician should identify the client's core catastrophic prediction *prior* to exposure. Following exposure trials, challenge the client to identify whether or not their catastrophic prediction was accurate (Table 9.19, see Resource Pack, p. 354). Did what they feared would happen, actually happen?

In this practice under the supervision of the therapist, ask the client to record the results of their practice, including the exposure activity they did; the sensations they had; the thoughts they had; and the SUDS rate before, during, and after (The Exposure and SUDS Rating Chart, see Resource Pack, p. 352). Point out that instead of them talking to someone, going to the doctor, or searching frantically on the Internet for information about their symptoms, they are learning to tolerate their physical symptoms.

Table 9.19 Example: Symptoms Predictions Chart

Recreated Symptoms	Prediction/Fear	Prediction Correct (Y/N)?

Homework Assignment

The homework assignment for this next week will consist of repeating exposure for the symptoms on the hierarchy. The client will need to be instructed to do it in the same massed manner done in session repeatedly until SUDS drops by 50 percent. They need to be instructed not to use safety behaviors. When they have successfully completed one level on the hierarchy, they should be instructed to move onto the next one. Results and predictions should be recorded in the charts shown in these. As in previous homework assignments, they should be reminded to continue the walking program and activity program.

Session Seven: Situational Exposure

Agenda

1. Homework and practice review.
2. Situational exposure and moving up the hierarchy.
3. Situational exposure with structured therapist support.
4. Interrupted exposure or premature escape responding.
5. Situational plus interoceptive exposure.
6. Homework and practice.

Protocol

Review the homework and practice to begin Session Seven. It is important to find out what obstacles the client may have encountered in the past week in challenging their ANTs and in learning to ride through the anxiety and tolerating their anxiety. If for some reason the client did not complete any part of the homework and practice, the therapist will need to closely query the reason for avoidance. What was the client afraid of? What were they telling themselves about the situation? Catastrophic predictions related to this will need to be challenged using the questions identified below:

- What were the client's core catastrophic predictions prior to exposure?
- Following exposure trials, were their catastrophic predictions accurate?
- Did what they feared would happen, actually happen?

If physical symptom exposure was not done in the previous week, this exposure will need to be completed prior to moving on to situational exposure.

In addition, the clinician should still be monitoring behavioral activation and determining if the client is continuing to increase activity and walking levels.

After the homework review, the clinician will begin by explaining that people with illness anxiety often avoid places or situations that remind them of illness. This session will focus on learning to approach these situations.

The clinician may also wish to address assisting in a particularly difficult situational exposure by accompanying the client during the initial trials. Ideally, however, this should be limited to initial exposure, as the clinician does not want to become a "safety" behavior that the client uses to avoid being "100 percent" in the situation (i.e., with the clinician repeatedly present, the client can tell themselves, "I could only do this with the therapist there").

Some clients may struggle with remaining in a situation for the duration or "riding the anxiety wave" until its natural end. The clinician can review with the client how to handle it if they have left a situation prematurely, so as to continue to approach it. Given that scenario (premature escape), the client should be asked to reapproach the scenario as quickly as possible and enter it again, tracking ANTs, noting their anxiety, and using coping cards. This can be called "paused" exposure.

For clients who have had a difficult time with physical symptoms, the clinician may wish to add a recreation of physical symptoms to situational exposure. For example, the client with a fear of driving alone can be asked to drive alone until the SUDS drops. If watching pharmaceutical ads on TV produces anxiety, they should be asked to watch such ads while being fully aware of their anxiety without attempting to find a way of escaping or turning to safety mechanisms. They should ask themselves whether their feared worst outcome actually happened.

Homework Assignment

The client will be asked to continue to record the results of their practice, including the exposure activity they did; the sensations they had; the thoughts; and the SUDS before, during, and after (Table 9.20, see Resource Pack, p. 354). All of the practice assignments of the previous session should be continued here. Again, they should be encouraged to repeat their exposure to situations, thoughts, and symptoms until their SUDS drops by at least 50 percent (Table 9.21, see Resource Pack, p. 355).

They should be encouraged to carry their coping statements cards with them and refer to them frequently. And, finally, they should be reminded to continue to be active and to walk daily.

Table 9.20 Example: Situations Exposure Predictions Chart

Situation	Prediction/Fear	Prediction Correct (Y/N)?

Table 9.21 Example: Situational Exposure Practice Results Chart

Exposure Situation	SUDS Before	Sensations	SUDS During	Thoughts	SUDS After

Session Eight: Sleep and Symptoms

Agenda

1. Review practice including walking and behavioral activation.
2. Explain relationship between sleep and illness anxiety.
3. Do sleep assessment.
4. Review sleep hygiene.
5. Assign homework and practice.

Materials

1. Insomnia Severity Index: this is a brief, seven-question index which can be found at: www.ons.org/sites/default/files/InsomniaSeverityIndex_ISI.pdf
2. National Sleep Foundation Diary: this diary can be downloaded at: https://sleepfoundation.org/content/nsf-official-sleep-diary

Protocol

Start this eighth session with a review of homework and practice. Is the client continuing to record the results of their practice, including the exposure activity they did; the sensations they had: the thoughts: and the SUDS before, during, and after? Are they continuing to walk and be active? Are they still exposing themselves to situations, thoughts, and symptoms until their SUDS drops by at least 50 percent?

The clinician should still monitor behavioral activation and make sure the client is continuing to increase activity and walking levels.

The main focus of this session is on sleep and anxiety. The client should be reminded of the factors that influence symptom volume, one of which is sleep.

One way to begin is by administering the Insomnia Severity Index. That can then lead to a discussion of the relationship between illness anxiety and sleep.

Begin a discussion by pointing out that studies suggest that innate worriers —those individuals who seem by nature more anxious and nervous—are much more vulnerable to the impact of sleep loss. That is, if you are a worrier, whether about illnesses or other things, you are likely to suffer more than other people from sleep difficulties. On the other hand, if you are given to anxiety and worry, you are most likely to benefit from sleep therapy. If quality sleep can be restored, then it may have a positive effect by reducing worry and fears.

So, it may be important to look at sleep and anxiety in two ways. One, if you are anxious and worried, that may cause you to disturbed sleep and maybe insomnia. Second, if you experience sleep deprivation, you are inclined to be more worried and more anxious. When symptoms are worse, sleep is worse. Many anxious patients sleep fitfully or only a few hours a night.

Reduced sleep may increase certain symptoms, such as pain symptoms. Sleep is the time that the body and mind use to restore and recover from the day. Lost sleep causes inflammation in the tissues and weakens the immune system. Inflammation is particularly bad for the pain. Lost sleep also causes changes in mood and is associated with an increase in negative emotions, such as anxiety. An important way to reduce symptoms is to manage sleep and increase the amount and quality of sleep.

Anxious individuals often engage in many behaviors which interfere with sleep. These include lying awake in bed when feeling anxious or being aware of pain sensations, resting in bed during the day, watching television near bedtime, and changing their sleep schedule based on negative thoughts or symptoms. In addition, some patients will disrupt their sleep through having too much caffeine during the day, engaging in physical exercise or activity too close to bedtime, having a television or other electronics in the bedroom—these may emit light during the night.

Stimulus control can be explained to the patient as "body learning." When you lay in bed, awake, and worrying, your body comes to equate bed with anxiety. This can mean that when you get into bed, your brain thinks it is time to be anxious and you start worrying. The same process happens if you lie in bed while awake. If you are anxious and cannot fall asleep, your body learns that being in bed equals being awake. In order to break these patterns, the brain and body must be given new sleep patterns to learn. This means that bed should only be used for two activities: sleep and sex.

To learn new sleep patterns, inform your patient that if he or she is in bed for more than 20 minutes awake, they need to get out of the bed. They need to find a less stimulating activity to do, such as listening to calming music, drinking herbal tea, reading something rather dull. They should return to bed when they feel sleepy. If they are unable to sleep again in 20 minutes, they need to repeat the cycle. They may need to repeat this several times.

If the patient's body and brain have learned an anxiety and sleep association, then that association can be unlearned, too. They should go to bed only when sleepy and make sure they do all of the things mentioned above that can reduce interference with sleep. No matter what poor sleep habits the client has been doing, those should be stopped. The bed and bedtime should not be associated with stimulation and anxiety—only with sleep.

Finally, it is important to have a wind down routine at night. A wind down routine is when you do relaxing, nonstimulating activities prior to bed. This can be a bath, warm tea, music, reading, prayer; in other words, any activity that signals to the brain that it is time to slow down.

Homework Assignment

The patient should be asked to identify two sleep behaviors they are engaging in. Homework for the week will be changing those behaviors. The patient should be asked to complete the national sleep diary and record their sleep behaviors during the week, including those that will be changed. As in previous homework assignments, they should be reminded to continue the walking program and activity program.

Session Nine: Stress Management and Symptoms

Agenda

1. Review of practice and homework.
2. Review the relationship between stress and illness anxiety.
3. Teach breathing techniques and visual imagery.
4. Relaxation instruction.
5. Homework and practice assignment.

Materials Needed

Breath to relax app.

Protocol

Begin this session, as in previous sessions, with a review of the homework and practice during the past week. Is the client continuing to record the results of their practice, including the sleep behaviors? Are they continuing to walk and be active? Are they still exposing themselves to situations, thoughts, and symptoms?

A focus of this session will be to discuss the impact of stress on illness anxiety. Stress is one of the factors that turns up illness anxiety symptom volume. Various stressors can be a cause, or at least a risk factor, for illness anxiety. Thus, if the patient is experiencing major life stresses, or simply feeling overburdened by the stress associated with daily life, the result can be an exacerbation of the feeling that they have a serious physical illness.

If it is apparent that stress is contributing to the worry or preoccupation with having a significant illness, then it is important to deal with the stress. That means learning a relaxation technique, which can be an asset in the long-term management of stress. Patients experiencing illness anxiety generally have a heightened reaction to physical sensations, but they are also more likely to become stressed.

Relaxation training is one way that clients can learn to sooth their nervous system. However, first the clinician can instruct the client in slow breathing, a method of relaxation that reduces the stress response. The clinician can show the client a slow breathing technique by using the "belly breathing" method identified in the app Breathe2relax (a helpful app which can help clients learn to breathe in a relaxed manner). In this instruction, the clinician will place one hand on their own diaphragm and one on their breastbone. When they breathe deeply and inhale, the hand on the diaphragm will rise, while the one on the breastbone will remain still. It is important that the exhale be extended as long as possible, so that the rate of breathing is slowed; this could be referred to as stretching out the exhale. This will prevent the hyperventilation response that is so closely aligned with panic symptoms. The clinician will ask the client to focus on the feeling of "the breath," clearing the mind of thoughts and worries. They will give the client permission to have their thoughts "drift" while instructing the client to "return to the breath" as soon as they notice that they have strayed from it.

The clinician will ask the patient to practice this breathing method once a day, for 10 minutes. It will *not* be effective for the first several days that the client does it because effectiveness comes with practice as the body learns to master this kind of breathing; note that this is body learning—like riding a bike. The clinician will need to emphasize that learning to do this kind of breathing or "retraining" the breathing response will take several days.

A second strategy to bring to the client's attention is visualization. This also is a strategy that can easily be taught. The clinician can ask the client to think about a relaxing, comfortable, and peaceful favorite place. They should imagine taking a path to this place, paying special attention to the sights, sounds, smells, and touch of the path. When they arrive at their special place, they should be encouraged to notice all of the sensory details. They can stay there as long as they would like. When they are ready to leave, they should be encouraged to return along the same path, counting down 3–2–1 to be aware that they are feeling alert, refreshed, and relaxed.

Finally, the clinician can instruct the client in progressive muscle relaxation (PMR), a third strategy. The technique for PMR is simple: The client should be asked to tense and then relax specific muscles, one at a time. One of the easiest ways to do this is by going from the "tip of the toes to the top of the head." The clinician starts by having the client to tense their toes then relax, followed by ankles, calves, thighs, buttocks, abdomen, fists, forearms, biceps, shoulders, and face. The order does not matter as long as all large muscle groups are involved.

Homework Assignment

The clinician will ask the client to practice the three strategies learned in this session: slow breathing, visualization, and PMR. Each method should be practiced at least once a day. Before and after practicing these strategies, they should rate their stress in Table 9.22, see Resource Pack, p. 355.

Finally, continue to encourage more activity, especially walking.

Table 9.22 Example: Rating My Stress Chart

Stress Rating Before (1–10)	Relaxation Practice Time	Stress Rating After (1–10)

Session Ten: Wrapping up

Agenda

1. Homework and practice review.
2. Review treatment progress.
3. Discuss spontaneous recovery.
4. Implement spontaneous recovery coping kit.

Materials Needed

1. Health Anxiety Inventory.
2. Illness Attitude Scale.

Protocol

Begin the final session with a review of the practice assignment. Specifically, check on the client's practice with the three strategies learned in Session Eight: slow breathing, visualization, and PMR. Did the client practice each at least once a day? Review their stress levels before and after each practice. Because this is the last session, review how well they are doing with challenging ANTs, learning to rise through anxiety, and being active.

After review, the initial part of this last session will focus on the gains that the client has made in treatment in the past several weeks. The clinician can review for the client the regular decrease in anxiety. And by administering the Health Anxiety Inventory and the Illinois Attitude Scale, the clinician can point out objectively the progress made by the patient.

Also, the clinician can point out that the client has learned to allow themselves to experience the symptoms and situations that made them anxious, and that they have learned to challenge and disprove the negative, fearful thoughts they had about themselves and illness.

Next, the clinician will need to address the future, and any fearful expectation that their illness anxiety may surface again in a muted form. This does not mean treatment has failed, but is normal when something has been extinguished. The important thing in this situation is for the client to use the tools that worked in the past to address it. This can generate a discussion of all the tools the client now has at his or her disposal to deal with stress and anxiety. The patient may be reassured that like all anxiety they have learned to deal with throughout these sessions, they can also deal with any thoughts or worries in regards to the return of previous symptoms, thoughts, or fears. Specifically, the client can be told that they can now successfully ride out any anxious thoughts or worries.

Finally, the patient can be reminded that should they feel like they are not dealing with anxiety in an effective manner, they can return for one or more booster sessions.

References

Thorn, B.E. (2017). *Cognitive therapy for chronic pain: a step-by-step guide*. New York: Guilford Publications.

Chapter 10

"Anxiety Attacks"—Panic

Session One: Assessment and Panic Education

Agenda

1. Baseline assessment: Panic Attack Questionnaire (PAQ).
2. Obstacles to panic treatment.
3. Normalization of panic disorder.
4. Causes of panic.
5. Explanation of CBT panic.
6. Practice assignment: panic tracking–Panic Severity Measure.

Materials Needed

1. PAQ.
2. Panic Severity Measure.

Protocol

The first part of panic disorder treatment is assessment. The clinician should explain that this step is integral so that the client understands the severity and frequency of the panic. The clinician also needs to understand the client's constellation of panic symptoms and panic-producing situations for treatment to proceed. Safety behaviors, physical symptoms, avoidance patterns, prototypical situations, and panic-related fears will all need to be evaluated prior to initiating intervention.

An excellent assessment instrument is the PAQ.

Following assessment, with the PAQ, the focus of the rest of this session rests upon normalizing panic as an anxiety disorder and explaining what causes it.

Panic is a very common anxiety disorder, and 80 percent of the population has had at least one (Kroenke et al., 2007). Many panic patients have the erroneous core belief that they are going "crazy." They believe that panic "shouldn't happen" to a sane person (a thought highly associated with panic disorder). Yet, studies estimate that at least one in twenty people will have at least one panic attack in their lifetime (Kessler et al., 2005). In any given year, more than 5 percent of the population will have had a panic attack. Does this mean many people are crazy? Or does it mean that anxiety, and even strong anxiety, happens to sane people every day?

For a certain number of people, that single panic attack can become a panic disorder. The reason for this is a combination of many factors: genetics, lower arousal threshold, bodily sensitivity, catastrophic thinking style, and the "fight/ flight" response (Figure 10.1).

Figure 10.1 A Combination of Factors Leads to Panic Disorder

For people with a genetic susceptibility to panic (family histories of panic, depression, and anxiety), a single panic attack can flip the switch into panic disorder.

Typically, people with panic disorder have several characteristics that work together to create panic. Chief among them is an exquisitely sensitive awareness to any kind of bodily change or symptom. This means that they are likely to notice a change in heart rate, temperature, or visual or auditory sensation more than the typical person. On the one hand, this is a benefit, as it allows them to respond to concerning symptoms very early. However, on the other hand, it makes it difficult for them to ignore feelings and sensations that are perfectly normal, and do not necessarily need attention. Importantly, individuals with a panic disorder also have a unique interpretative style, one which tends to be not only focused on the body, but also which is catastrophic. Thinking is extreme, strong, and negative about their physical sensation. The thinking style itself sets off an "alarm" which escalates the anxiety response.

In addition to sensitive "body radar," people with panic disorder have a very sensitive sympathetic nervous system—one that triggers the fight/flight response easily as illustrated in Figure 10.2. The fight/flight response is the instinctive response to threat (it tells us to "get out" or use aggression to survive a life-threatening situation). The sympathetic nervous system causes our heart to beat faster, increases muscle tension, body temperature, sweat, respiration—all to prepare us to mobilize (Figure 10.3). For people with panic disorder, this "fight and flight" alarm is triggered at a lower point than for the average person. This means that anxiety and the symptoms associated with it start at a "lower set point."

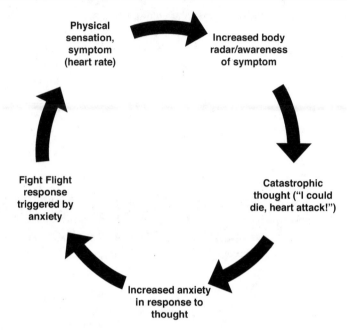

Figure 10.2 A Sensitive Sympathetic Nervous System May Be Related to Panic Disorder

It is important to inform the client that the fight/flight response also explains how panic disorder gets worse and is maintained. When a panic attack starts, the instinctive response is to "flee." When someone leaves a situation at the height of panic, that situation automatically becomes connected with "high fear and high threat" in the brain. This means that every time they go back into that situation, the brain trips the "fight/flight" alarm in response to the "situation threat factor"—and panic ensues.

Leaving a situation (escape) and avoiding it does not ever allow someone to ride the panic wave until it ends (which it always does). Simply put, escape and avoidance does not allow the individual to challenge the negative predictions that they have about their panic. Many people with panic fear catastrophic outcomes (the panic assessment/PAQ will identify several). Panic attacks, although they feel awful and even fatal, are NOT actually fatal.

Figure 10.3 Avoidance Increases Panic Disorder

Figure 10.4 Avoidance Does not Allow Challenging of Catastrophic Thoughts

In contrast, when someone with panic remains in a situation and allows themselves to experience their symptom, it gives them the chance to find out that what they fear actually does not happen. They have the chance to challenge the "catastrophic" and frightening thoughts that come at them. In other words, they ride the panic wave until it ends (Figure 10.4).

The clinician may point out to the client that cognitive behavioral therapy works by addressing the catastrophic thinking that people have about panic, changing avoidant behavioral patterns, and facilitating a gradual approach to difficult symptoms and situations. Thoughts, feelings, and behaviors that drive panic are each addressed separately and individually.

In this initial session, it is often valuable to point out some of the treatment obstacles frequently encountered with clients with a panic disorder. To start with, panic disorder is unique in that the very discussion of it is something that is feared by most who have it. People with panic are afraid to talk about panic, because they have had the experience that when they feel anxious, panic will often ensue. They are afraid of the physical symptoms of arousal itself (i.e., an increased heart rate), for it is those symptoms which cue the beginning of the panic experience. Put simply, panic patients are afraid of their own fear response.

It is essential for the clinician to acknowledge this fear during the first session. Since they fear that discussion may cause a full-blown panic attack, the clinician will need to compassionately acknowledge the client's anxiety about this. The next step will be to reassure and educate the client by letting them know that even though it is difficult to discuss their panic, talking about it in treatment actually diminishes the panic in the long run. This is because talking is a form of exposure, and this is something that will be discussed in a later session.

It may help the client to make the analogy to sunlight and ice. Talking about panic is like shining warm sunlight on the iceberg of panic. Each time the client talks about it, it melts away more of the fear, and the panic gets weaker.

Some clients fear that they will have a major panic attack in session, consequently the clinician will also need to address this. They will need to reassure the client that contrary to their fear, experiencing panic and anxiety in session is not a catastrophic outcome, but actually a therapeutic one. If it should happen, it provides the clinician and the client opportunity to better understand their panic and implement intervention in the moment. Experiencing fear or panic in session is not an intrusion, but actually the mechanism by which improvement happens (i.e., it is exposure). Should the client experience a panic attack in session, it is essential for the clinician to have the client remain with them until the panic has abated. This is important for the simple reason that if the client leaves while in a state of panic, the relief of escaping will likely reinforce future therapeutic avoidance.

Homework Assignment

The homework for the first week is to track any panic attacks or to record instances when they were fearful they would experience a panic attack. The clinician should emphasize that by documenting when panic happens, the symptoms that they have, and the things they do in response to panic, that this information will later be used to create specific interventions for them. It is a learning tool for both the client and the clinician. It is therefore very important to track panic, even if doing so makes them uncomfortable. Remember, writing about it and talking about are forms of exposure. They can use the chart shown in Table 10.1 (see Resource Pack, p. 356) to record their experiences.

Table 10.1 Example: Panic Attacks and Panic Attack Fears Chart

Panic Situation (who, what, where, when?)	Rate Panic Severity (0–100)	Duration of Panic Attack (minutes)	Physical Feelings (body sensations during panic)	Behaviors (What did I do when I had my panic attack)

Session Two: Cognitive Distortions and the A-B-C-D of Somatic Symptoms

Agenda

1. Review of homework assignment.
2. Assessment with the Panic Severity Measure.
3. Catastrophic thinking and the panic cycle.
4. Thinking about physical sensations differently/Co2 cycle.
5. Practice.
6. Homework assignment.

Materials Needed

1. Panic Severity Measure.
2. PAQ (for review).
3. Automatic Negative Thoughts (ANTs) Worksheet.

Protocol

As the first item in this second session, go over the chart that the client filled out during the week. Discuss each entry in the chart so you both have a better understanding of what happened.

Prior to session, the clinician should review the PAQ filled out the first week. It is important to pay special attention to items related to catastrophic thinking (i.e., fears of going crazy, dying, suffocating, passing out, permanent disconnection from reality, fear of being out of control). Items that the client has positively endorsed will be used as examples in this session to illustrate the impact of catastrophic thinking on symptoms and the panic cycle.

Next, administer the Panic Severity Measure.

Then, start introducing new learning by explaining the panic cycle and thoughts. Figure 10.5 will help in the explanation.

Figure 10.5 (The Panic Cycle) demonstrates the panic cycle and the role that thoughts have in panic disorder. As the figure illustrates, people who have panic disorder start by noticing a physical sensation. They have a catastrophic

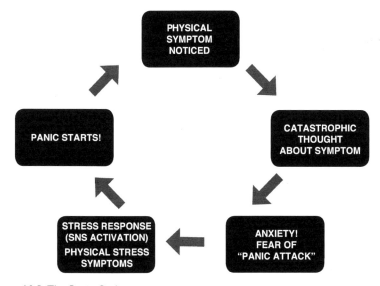

Figure 10.5 The Panic Cycle

thinking style about this sensation and the outcome associated with it. Common fear-producing thoughts include:

- fear of passing out during a panic attack;
- fear of having a heart attack and dying;
- fear of going crazy;
- fear of losing control of themselves;
- fear of permanently being disconnected from reality;
- fear of rejection from others;
- fear of being seen as "crazy" or "weak";
- fear of suffocating to death;
- fear of getting violent and/or causing harm to others.

It is important to ask the client to identify the physical symptoms that they notice at the start of panic (i.e., feeling dizzy, light-headed, heart rate increasing). These symptoms can be linked to specific catastrophic thoughts (or images) that will be addressed in this session.

Next, introduce The Hyperventilation Response.

Most of the physical symptoms of panic are caused by hyperventilation. Education about the hyperventilation response is essential because it allows the client to reattribute their symptoms to the actual physiologic cause. It provides a fact-based, realistic counterpoint to the catastrophic explanations they have developed themselves. For example, when a client experiences feelings of derealization (feeling as though they are "looking outside themselves"), the catastrophic thought is "I am going crazy and/or I am going to be permanently disconnected from reality." Following Co2 education, the alternate rational appraisal is, "This is a temporary feeling that is caused by over breathing and will pass."

Education should start by explaining that the physical symptoms of panic are not imaginary. They are caused by hyperventilation. Hyperventilation occurs because the fear response, once activated, increases the rate of breathing. Hyperventilation causes chemical changes in the blood itself. Normal blood content reflects a careful balance of oxygen and carbon dioxide. Overbreathing creates an influx of oxygen into the blood stream. In response to this, carbon dioxide levels in the blood drop. The drop in carbon dioxide in the blood stream causes the following physical symptoms:

- weakness
- fainting
- dizziness
- confusion
- agitation
- derealization (feeling outside of yourself)

- seeing images that are not there
- suffocation feeling.

Overbreathing also causes calcium levels in the blood to drop. This causes feelings of

- numbness and tingling (in hands and feet)
- spasms or cramps
- muscle twitching.

The client will undoubtedly have some of the physical symptoms listed above. It is important for the clinician then to specifically identify the normal physiologic response that the client is having in response to overbreathing.

Following the explanation of the Hyperventilation Response, introduce the A-B-C-D Model. The A-B-C-D Model can be used to explain and challenge

---

A-B-C-D Model

A = Activating Situation or Sensation

1. Ask yourself, "What happened?"
2. Example: Mark feels light-headed.

B = Belief System (your beliefs and expectations of others)

1. What you tell yourself about what happened that influenced your action?
2. Examples: "I am really not OK. I don't know why this happening to me. I'm either losing my mind or going crazy. I could be schizo!

C = Consequence (emotional, phyiscal, behavioral consequence)

1. How did you react (feelings and behavior)?
2. Examples:
   - Feeling: Anxiety, Despair.
   - Physical: Increased hyperventilation. Light-headed, weaker.
   - Behavior: Escape/Avoidance. Leaves whatever situation he is in and goes home to lay down.

D = Dispute the belief

1. Examine your beliefs and expectations.
2. Are they unrealistic or irrational?
   What is the actual evidence that you will have a heart attack or that you are going crazy?
3. Re-appraisal, alternative thoughts
   "This is a temporary feeling that occurs in response to hyperventilation. It will pass when my breathing returns to normal."

panic. Sometimes thoughts are helpful and rational, but at other times, our thoughts are inaccurate and not helpful. We all have a mix of these kinds of thoughts. Thoughts become a problem when they are catastrophic, irrational, judgmental, self-critical, and rigid. These kinds of thoughts are often not based on a realistic appraisal of the situation.

In the A-B-C-D Model, "*A*" stands for an activating event. The activating event is the "event" or physical symptom/situation. "*B*" represents our beliefs about the activating event or situation. It is not the events themselves that produce feelings like stress or anxiety; it is our interpretations and beliefs about the events. "*C*" stands for the emotional consequences. These are the feelings experienced that result from our interpretation. "*D*" stands for dispute. This is when the irrational thoughts are examined, challenged, and ultimately modified to reflect a more realistic appraisal of the situation.

Catastrophic and frightening panic thoughts often fall into very specific error categories.

It can be helpful for the clinician to review the kinds of thinking errors that occur in panic, so the client becomes aware of them and learns to challenge them. Reviewing common thinking errors can also serve "to normalize" the client's experience—so that they feel "less crazy."

The clinician can explain that thinking is often automatic, and happens outside of awareness. Thoughts attached to our symptoms are often fast. However, as we become more "tuned in" to our symptoms, thoughts come even more rapidly, get more extreme, and more negative. The more we connect with them, the more powerful they become. The catastrophic thoughts we refer to as ANTs.

Shown in Table 10.2 is a worksheet with examples of common ANTs. The client can be asked to read from this worksheet and circle the thinking errors that resonate the most with them. At the end of the worksheet, there is a space to list the automatic thoughts and space to start identifying ways to dispute them.

- List some of your ANTs.

_____

_____

_____

- How might you dispute these beliefs?

_____

_____

_____

Table 10.2 ANTs Worksheet

Category	Definition	Example
All-or-nothing thinking	Seeing things as either all good or all bad and allowing no middle ground.	"I am a wreck and cannot be fixed." "I am mentally flawed and my brain is not right."
Fortune telling	Predicting that things will turn out negatively, without considering other possible outcomes.	"If I have a panic attack at the kid's school all of the other parents will talk behind my back and it will shame my child."
Disqualifying the positive	Telling yourself that positive experiences don't count	"I felt anxious last week when I went to the store. This means that nothing I do works to reduce my anxiety" [even though panic didn't occur in several other situations].
Emotional reasoning	Believing that what you feel must be true.	"I am having a hard time with focus and feel a bit confused right now. My brain must be damaged."
Catastrophizing	Expecting extremely consequences; exaggerating situations to be the worst possible outcome.	"I can't stand it anymore!" "I will never be OK." "My life is ruined by panic."
Mental filter	Focusing on a single negative detail instead of seeing the whole picture.	"I still feel nervous when I drive. I am a failure and therapy is not working" [disregard that you haven't had a panic attack in a week].
Mind reading	Believing that you know what others are thinking, especially how they feel about you.	"They think that I am crazy." "Everyone here KNOWS I am having a panic attack."
Over-generalization	Making a general conclusion based on a single incident. Assuming that things will turn out a certain way because they did so before.	"I forgot my car in the parking lot. This means that I am losing my mind. I must have dementia."
"Should" statements	Having fixed ideas about how you or others "should," "ought to," or "must" be. Leads to feeling nervous, sad, and worried.	"If I were really OK and a strong person, I should never have these symptoms." "I must be able to never have a panic attack in order to do this job."

Homework Assignment

The major homework assignment this week is to practice capturing ANTs. Once the client has identified some of his or her ANTs, they can begin to focus on disputing catastrophic thinking.

The following box provides a framework for identifying situations, emotions, and ANTs that are relevant to the client's panic. First, they must identify the situation and symptoms attached to the ANTs. Next, they should identify the ANTs and record them. Then, they should dispute or challenge the ANTs and re-rate their emotions. The following section of the A-B-C-D Model chart can be helpful to the client:

Disputing Your Beliefs

Below is a list of questions that can be asked to dispute thoughts:

D = Dispute the belief

1. Examine your beliefs and expectations.
2. Are they unrealistic or irrational?
3. Alternative thoughts that would help you in a healthier manner?

Questions to ask:

1. What would I tell my best friend in this situation?
2. Is this thought true 100 percent of the time?
3. Do I know for certain that _____?
4. Is there another explanation?
5. Is there another point of view?
6. What is the evidence for _____?

Each day this week when they notice a physical sensation, feel anxious, pulled to avoid something or panic, they should write that down on a chart shown in Table 10.3, see Resource Pack, p. 356. The client should also be instructed to document instances of panic by using the Panic Situations, Feelings, and Behaviors chart (Table 10.1)

Table 10.3 Example: Situations, Feelings, and Rating Your Emotions

Situation Symptom (who, what, where, when)	Feeling (List emotion and rate intensity 0–100)	Thought (What are exact thoughts. Circle most upsetting thought)	Specific ANT (What category above does this fall into?)	Alternate Thought (In response to challenge questions)	Re-rate Feeling (emotion, 1–100)
Examples: Jan finishes exercising and notices her heart is beating fast and she feels lightheaded	Nervous Anxious (70)	"My heart doesn't feel right" "I'm having another panic attack" "This is out of control. I'm out of control"	Over-general-ization Emotional reasoning	"My heart is beating faster because of exercise" "Light-headness is temporary and from hyper-ventilation" "There is no actual evidence that I am an out of control wreck in ALL areas of my life"	Hopeful, calmer Anxiety (30)

Session Three: Cognitive Distortions, A-B-C-D, and Social Anxiety

Agenda

1. Review homework.
2. Assessment with the Panic Severity Measure.
3. Disputing negative thoughts.
4. Imaginal situational/social exposure.

5. Coping statements.
6. Practice and homework assignment.

Materials Needed

Panic Severity Measure and PAQ (for review).

Protocol

The clinician will need to begin this session by reviewing practice from the following week. Careful attention should be paid to the catastrophic thoughts associated with symptoms. If the client has difficulty identifying them outside of the treatment sessions, this can be done at the beginning of the session by reviewing various situations (activating events) and querying the client about specific thoughts.

It is once again important for the clinician to remind the client that every time they talk about the panic, as anxiety-provoking and stressful as it may be, they are approaching it. With each approach, panic becomes slightly weaker.

After the homework review and initial remarks, this session will focus on the social components of panic. Many persons with panic disorder have several inaccurate fears related to panic and the social environment. These fears can often drive the avoidance of situations where there are other people or crowds (agoraphobia).

What are the prototypical social cognitive distortions in panic?

Here are a few of the typical social cognitive distortions:

- Everyone can see that I am having a panic attack.
- I am making a fool of myself.
- People think that I am crazy.
- Everyone knows I am out of control.
- I am a nervous wreck and everyone knows it.
- If people find out about my panic, something awful will happen.

The clinician can assist the client in starting to identify social cognitive distortions by reviewing situations from the PAQ where panic has happened to the client in the past. To be most effective in doing this, it helps to ask the client specific details about any identified social situation. Here are some questions to ask:

- What do you think will happen if other people notice you are having a panic attack?
- Has this actually happened before?
- How do you know that everyone around you knew (that you were having a panic attack)?

- Did anyone actually tell you that?
- Did other people tell you that were crazy?
- If you saw someone who looked nervous, what would you think about them? Does this differ from what you say to yourself?
- Do you know anyone who became permanently disconnected from reality by panic attacks?

It can be helpful for the clinician to briefly discuss what is called the "impression and thought control distortion." Panic patients often think that the things they do directly influence the content of perceptions and thoughts that other people have. For example, panic patients often think that if they appear panicky, then other people say they are "crazy" and will have a negative impression of them. Conversely, they believe that if they are calm, they will create a positive social impression. And it is important to point out that it is impossible to plant thoughts in another person's head through your behavior or actually control another's impression of you. The clinician can illustrate this in the session by telling the client that they are at this very moment trying to plant a specific thought in the patient's head by speaking calmly. Did the client read the thought? Most will admit that they *could not* read the thought.

The worst-case scenario exercise (which is also imaginal exposure) can be of utility to further challenge social distortions. In the *Worst-Case Scenario Exercise*, the clinician should explain that often when we have avoided something for a long time, many irrational negative thoughts are attached to avoidance. One of the quickest ways to learn to challenge these thoughts is to do what we call the "worst-case scenario exercise." To think through what you *imagine* would be the most negative thing that could happen in a particular situation, address each thought, and develop a plan for "management." In this way, the client will feel prepared to address the worst-case scenario.

Here are some questions to challenge the worst-case scenario thoughts:

- Will this situation or symptom cause me to die?
- Will it cause me severe physical damage?
- Can I survive an uncomfortable feeling?
- Do I know anyone who has actually died of embarrassment or panic?
- Will I lose my job or my livelihood if I feel upset or embarrassed in this situation?
- Will my loved ones stop loving me?
- Will I be able to still be an independent person?
- What is the evidence that I will lose everything?

In thinking through the worst-case scenario and the questions, it is also important to think about solutions. Ask the client to think about and list things they can do in this situation, things they can say to others, or things they can say to themselves. It is important to emphasize that these things allow them to stay in the situation, and are not based on distracting themselves from the anxiety:

1. _____

2. _____

3. _____

Next, discuss coping statements with the client. These are rational thoughts that they can say to themselves in order to challenge the catastrophic thoughts. The technique is simple. Ask the client to look at the list below and select statements which they find the most reassuring:

Coping Statements

- I am not my symptom. Just because I feel nervous does not mean I am a wreck.
- Every person has been anxious and can understand what it feels like to be nervous. I label myself differently than they label me.
- My problem is a typical human problem. Many people have had a panic attack!
- Even though I feel this way, panic disorder has never actually caused insanity.
- This physical symptom is caused by hyperventilation and will pass when my breathing stabilizes. It is only temporary.
- I have skills to deal with my symptom and I know what to do.
- I set the tone with other people. If I am calm and in control about my symptom, then they will follow my example.
- I am safe and this will pass. I am not in any life-threatening danger.
- This symptom has a volume control. I know what turns it up and what turns it down.
- I have survived this symptom before and it has not killed me.
- I am not falling apart.

Ask the client to write the thoughts that resonate most with them on an Index Card to carry with them.

Homework Assignment

Homework and practice for the next week will consist of continuing to challenge negative thoughts. The chart shown in the Resource Pack, p. 356, the Situations, Feelings, and Rating Your Emotions Chart, will be helpful. The client should also be instructed to document instances of panic by using the Panic Situations, Feelings, and Behaviors chart (Table 10.1).

Session Four: Interoceptive Exposure I

Agenda

1. Homework and practice review.
2. Assessment with Panic Severity Measure.
3. Review of avoidance and panic maintenance.
4. Riding the symptom wave.
5. Activity hierarchy based on Symptom Units of Distress Scale (SUDS).
6. Starting exposure.
7. Homework and practice assignment.

Materials Needed

Panic Severity Measure and PAQ (for review).

Protocol

The clinician will need to begin this session by reviewing practice from the following week. Going over the Situations, Feelings, and Rating Your Emotions Chart will be important to monitor the client's ability to recognize ANTs and substitute thoughts.

Prior to this session, the PAQ should have been reviewed by the clinician with careful attention to physical symptoms of panic and safety behaviors in the PAQ. Since these symptoms will be the focus of this session, the clinician will need to know what they are in order to create an exposure hierarchy, initiate response prevention, and identify catastrophic thoughts associated with panic.

At the beginning of this session, the clinician should briefly review the role of avoidance in panic maintenance. People with panic disorder avoid many things: thoughts, physical sensations, and situations. The last session focused on approaching thoughts, and this session will focus on teaching the client how to approach the physical sensations that cue panic.

Also, in this session, interoceptive exposure will be introduced. Interoceptive exposure usually takes at least two sessions because while most panic disorder clients will have several symptoms that require exposure, they cannot all be replicated in one session.

It helps to start by discussing negative thinking, anxiety, panic symptoms, and loss of quality of life. In doing so, the clinician will need to remind the client that they have learned how ANTs, or negative thinking, turns up the volume on physical sensations. The illustration below demonstrates where behavior and activity fit into our symptom/emotion/thought cycle:

Panic Symptom → Negative/Catastrophic Thoughts → Stress/Anxiety → Increased Physical Symptom → Behavioral Response

It is helpful to explain that the "behavioral response" is how we respond to the symptoms that upset us.

What are the typical responses to scary physical symptoms? Most people with panic disorder.

- stay **VIGILANT** to the symptom;
- try to **CONTROL** the symptom;
- try to **AVOID** having the symptom;
- try **NOT TO WORSEN** the symptom.

Panic patients often do the following in order to control, avoid, and not worsen the symptom:

- limit the things they do (to not have the symptom or not make it worse);
- stop doing things completely (to avoid experiencing it at all);
- leave a situation once they notice the symptom (not make it worse);
- start using safety behaviors to feel less anxious (an attempt to "control" it).

As a result, life becomes much more limited as activities and situations are restricted or cut off completely. With this, the person's quality of life suffers.

The things that clients with panic disorders do to avoid their symptoms and protect themselves are typical avoidance and protective responses. Because they are so typical, it is important for the clinician to address these responses and normalize what the client does to avoid and protect. By providing education to the client regarding usual escape and avoidance responses and teaching the person that these are attempts to try to function normally, it can assist the client to unnecessarily label themselves in a negative way.

The clinician should explain the following:

- Escape and avoidance are a NORMAL coping response that our brain uses.
- We have a protective instinct, which is an exquisite survival mechanism. It senses "danger" and has us "stop" whatever we are doing when the "danger alarm rings."
- This protective mechanism works well for dangerous situations (like fire) or even serious injuries (like broken legs, cuts, burns). In these dangerous situations, leaving a situation or stopping activity keeps us safe and allows us to heal.
- But this mechanism becomes a problem in chronic conditions like panic because it "protects" us so much that it stops us from doing the activities we should be doing.
- The protective/avoidance mechanism actually helps in the short term. That is, when we stop doing something because our symptom is noticeable and it makes us anxious or uncomfortable, we feel better right away.

- Stopping an activity equals feeling better in the short term.
- But, stopping does not teach us to cope with our symptoms, nor does stopping challenge the inaccurate catastrophic thoughts that we have about it. Instead, our fear and stress about our symptoms gets stronger.
- Stopping activity actually causes us to fear our symptoms even more. This stress response in turn increases symptom volume. And when our symptoms get worse, we stop doing more and more.

Stopping Activity = Long-Term Increase in Panic/Anxiety and Symptom Worsening

---

Go on to discuss safety behaviors. Indicate that sometimes, in order to reduce the discomfort we have from our symptoms, we use tricks to help us cope. Safety behaviors are "tricks" or actions used with the intent of preventing something that is feared. Just like avoidance, safety behaviors give short-term relief (they make us feel better) at the cost of long-term increased anxiety and symptom fear. Safety behaviors prevent us from challenging the beliefs that maintain anxiety.

Here are a few common safety behaviors:

- having someone with you at all times (not really safe by myself);
- sitting near a door or exit (escape dangerous panic);
- planning an escape route (to escape an "unsafe" situation);
- not driving on freeways (the fear is that it is unsafe/dangerous to drive in heavy traffic);
- always driving your own car (so that you can leave if you need to);
- not traveling far from home (longer distance is unsafe and it is easier to go home to stop panic);
- having a conversation with only one person at a time (so there is less chance to feel overwhelmed and embarrassed);
- things we do in our mind (distraction, counting);
- breathing (to control the anxiety and avoid it more);
- always having your cell phone with you ("just in case");
- carrying medication with you at all times (to avoid "dangerous" panic);
- carrying a beverage with you or snack (to avoid a choking feeling or dry mouth).

The clinician next needs to explain that the way to break the protection/avoidance trap is do its opposite. This means having the client approach or do the things that they have been avoiding, but doing them gradually. The following should be explained:

- When we do something that we are scared of, we give ourselves opportunity to learn that what we fear actually does not happen (i.e., that you are not going to suffocate to death from a panic attack).

- When we allow ourselves to experience a symptom that frightens us, and do it repeatedly, we get used to it (habituate) and less afraid of it.
- Each time we do the thing that makes our symptoms worse, the fear gets smaller and smaller (the fear iceberg melts). Eventually, we do not even notice the stress and fear associated with our symptom.

Introduce planned approaches. The clinician needs to explain that in the case of panic symptoms, a plan to approach the symptoms gradually will be developed. The intent of this is to allow the client, with the support of therapy, to learn to move through their symptoms. The purpose of this is to allow the client a chance to challenge catastrophic thoughts and decrease the fear and stress associated with their symptoms.

The goal is to learn to "ride the anxiety wave" long enough to come out the other side and challenge their predictions. Anxiety is indeed like a wave; sometimes it is slow building and sometimes it is fast. It always "peaks" and the "peak" is always followed by a crash. Like a wave, it does not last forever (no panic attack has ever lasted forever!). Treatment is actually teaching the client to "surf the anxiety wave."

It is time to discuss the "organization plan." To start, the clinician will explain that it is helpful to know which symptoms bother the client the most and which ones bother the client the least. Therapy will start by working with the least bothersome symptoms. The first thing to do is to ask the client to identify their symptoms and rate them using the SUDS (1–100) (Table 10.4, see Resource Pack, p. 357).

Table 10.4 Identifying Situations and Rating Symptoms

Symptom/Situation	SUDS Rating

After listing and rating symptoms, the clinician will help the client build the "symptom tolerance hierarchy." Explain that treatment will now focus on beginning to approach their symptoms starting with the least anxiety-provoking symptoms (see Resource Pack, p. 359).

A rank order of low-anxiety symptom to high-anxiety symptoms will need to be constructed.

Having rated the symptoms in the Symptoms Hierarchy Chart, go on to use exposure. Exposure will start with recreating the symptoms in the therapist's office. Several suggestions for this are identified below:

Recreating Physical Symptoms

*   *Feeling light-headed*: breathe as quickly as you can out loud for 1 minute/ controlled hyperventilation. Or shake head from shoulder to shoulder rapidly for 30 seconds.
*   *Head rush*: head between legs for half a minute.
*   *Breathlessness*: go up a flight of stairs for 1 minute, repeat.
*   *Feeling dizzy*: spin in a chair for 1 minute.
*   *Suffocation*: breathe through a straw for 1 minute.
*   *Dizziness*: spin in place for several seconds.
*   *Loss of control/insanity/derealizaiton*: stare at self in mirror, stare at fluorescent lights.
*   *Heat*: sit in a car with windows up, dressed warmly, heat on.
*   *Head/muscle tension*: squeeze your face and head muscles for 1 minute.
*   *Heart attack*: go up one or two flights of stairs; exercise vigorously for 1 minute.
*   *Noise*: listen to sound in restaurant or atrium.
*   *Choking*: swallow in rapid succession several times.
*   *Attention*: read something for 20 minutes and let your mind wander.
*   *Derealization/depersonalization*: spin in chair for 1 minute.
*   *Choking/breathlessness*: breathe through a straw with nose pinched for 1 minute.
*   *Embarrassment*: create symptoms in front of others intentionally (sweating, hyperventilation); explain that you are having an anxiety attack.

The goal in this method is to repeat exposure to the symptoms over multiple trials until the SUDS rating has dropped by at least half. Trials should be conducted in relatively rapid succession, with time allotted for the client to write down their SUDS, sensations, and thoughts.

The clinician should identify the client's core catastrophic prediction *prior* to exposure (Table 10.5, see Resource Pack, p. 358). Following exposure trials, challenge the client to identify whether or not their catastrophic prediction was accurate. Did what they feared would happen, actually happen?

In this practice under the supervision of the therapist, ask the client to record the results of their practice, including the exposure activity they did; the sensations they had; the thoughts they had; and the SUDS before, during, and after by filling out Table 10.6, see Resource Pack, p. 358.

Table 10.5 Example: Symptoms Predictions Chart

Recreated Symptoms	Prediction/Fear	Prediction Correct (Y/N)?

Table 10.6 Situational Exposure Practice Results Chart

Exposure Task	SUDS Before	Sensations	SUDS During	Thoughts	SUDS After

Homework Assignment

The homework assignment for the next week will consist of continuing to document instances of panic by using the Panic Situations, Feelings, and Behaviors chart (Table 10.1).

Also, the client should continue to practice exposure and use the Exposure Practice Results Chart. They should use the hierarchy that was created to practice reducing their SUDS.

Session Five: Interoceptive Exposure II

Agenda

1. Review of homework assignment.
2. Assessment with Panic Severity Measure.
3. Activity hierarchy based on SUDS.
4. Exposure practice.
5. Homework assignment.

Materials Needed

The Panic Severity Measure.

Protocol

Session five will begin with a review of the homework. The homework was to continue filling out the Situations, Feelings, and Rating Your Emotions Chart. In addition, the client was to continue to practice what was begun in this session by continuing to fill in the Exposure Practice Results Chart. As part of the review, the therapist can also review obstacles the client may have encountered in the past week to symptom exposure exercises. Those that were not completed will need to be conducted in this session.

Session Five will focus on the remaining symptoms on the hierarchy, with exposure in session. The process is exactly the same as described in Session Four where the client was instructed to recreate the symptom, pause to document their reactions, and then repeat. The process is conducted until the SUDS drops by 50 percent. The client is asked to identify whether their most feared prediction was proven or disproven.

Ultimately, the therapist may wish to combine exposure scenarios for symptoms to mimic actual panic attack (i.e., feeling dizzy and sweating—using hyperventilation in a heated parked car).

Homework Assignment

The homework for Session Five will be the same as for Session Four, using the same charts and procedures.

Session Six: Situational Exposure

Agenda

1. Check-in and review of homework and practice.
2. Panic: quality of life/activity cost.
3. Situational exposure.
4. Situational hierarchy.
5. Coping cards and statements.
6. Practice/homework.

Materials Needed

Panic Severity Measure and PAQ (for review).

Protocol

The clinician may find it beneficial to review the PAQ prior to the session, paying special attention to situations and locations that the client has endorsed

as being particularly difficult for them. This will allow the clinician to prepare for discussion of approach, with specific examples related to the client.

The homework and practice review should reinforce the client's continual
practice of exposure and using the Exposure Practice Results Chart. They
should be utilizing the hierarchy that was created to practice reducing their
SUDS.

In this, the main focus is on situational exposure. The clinician should be
cautioned that situational exposure should *not* be started before the client has
completed interoceptive exposure, which was the primary topic of discussion
and practice in Session Four and Session Five. If the client needs one more
week to work on interoceptive exposure, then they should be accommodated
and this session could be delayed by a week (or longer, if need be). This is
important because the client needs to use the skills they have developed for
interoceptive symptom management as they approach situations.

The clinician will start talking about situational exposure by explaining that
the techniques that the client has mastered to diminish panic associated with
physical symptoms will be used to address the situations that the client has
been forced to avoid. Also, the therapist should reinforce to the client how
they have learned to "ride the symptom wave." This will be no different for
situational exposure as the client, at this point, has learned firsthand the value
of allowing themselves to experience the symptom in order to lessen how
much it bothers them.

Below is a list of several prototypical situations that persons with panic disorder tend to avoid:

- traveling far from home;
- traveling alone;
- situations where they are the focus of attention;
- driving;
- driving on freeways;
- standing in line;
- going to stores;
- dining in restaurants;
- going to a movie theater or auditorium;
- going to a mall;
- attending sporting events;
- eating or drinking in public;
- riding in an elevator;
- walking alone on the street;
- talking to someone in authority;
- being in enclosed spaces;
- visiting the doctor.

Table 10.7 Panic Attack Avoidance Chart

Activities and Location that Fear of Having a Panic Attach Have Made Me Avoid

1. _____

2. _____

3. _____

The clinician will ask the client to read the above list and indicate which situations have been difficult for them, or ask the client to spontaneously identify activities that they are no longer doing. Table 10.7 is a chart for recording these situations (see Resource Pack, p. 359).

Table 10.8 Situation Hierarchy Rating Chart

My Symptom Hierarchy Based On SUDS Rating
1. (most scary)
2.
3.
4.
5.
6.
7.
8.
9. (least scary)

After the list is completed, the clinician will explain that the client is now going to approach these activities in the same systematic and controlled way they used to manage physical symptoms. This will start by rating each activity they listed previously using the SUDS (1–100) in the Identifying Situations and Rating Symptoms Chart previously introduced (see Resource Pack, p. 357).

Having made this list of situations, they should be transferred to the following chart so that they can be placed in rank order—from least to most scary (Table 10.8, see Resource Pack, p. 359):

The clinician should next explain that the client is going to be asked to start doing some of the activities that they have not been able to do for a while. The client should be told that it will start by having the client do the activity that is the least scary. The clinician will ask the client to stay in the situation until their SUDS drops by 50 percent. The important thing is *not* how perfectly they behave in the situation, but that they *stay* in the situation until they have finished "riding the anxiety wave."

Starting with the least scary situation in the Situation Hierarchy Chart, the client will move up the hierarchy once a particular situation is mastered (i.e., the SUDS drops by at least 50 percent).

While engaging in situational exposure practice, the client should keep track of their catastrophic predictions prior to exposure (see Resource Pack, p. 360). And with the clinician in the next session, they can assess whether their catastrophic prediction was accurate.

Homework Assignment

The client will be asked to record the results of their practice, including the exposure activity they did; the sensations they had; the thoughts; and SUDS before, during, and after (Situational Exposure Practice Results Chart, see Resource Pack, p. 358). They should be instructed to repeat exposure until their SUDS drops by at least 50 percent.

Session Seven: Situational Exposure II

Agenda

1. Homework and practice review.
2. Situational exposure and moving up the hierarchy.
3. Situational exposure with structured therapist support.
4. Interrupted exposure or premature escape responding.
5. Situational plus interoceptive exposure.
6. Coping statements.
7. Homework and practice.

Materials Needed

Coping statement cards.

Protocol

Review the homework and practice to begin Session Seven. It is important to find out what obstacles the client may have encountered in the past week in doing situational exposure exercises. If for some reason the client did not complete a planned exposure exercise, the therapist will need to closely query the reason for avoidance. What was the client afraid of? What were they telling themselves about the situation? Catastrophic predictions related to this will need to be challenged using the questions identified below:

• What were the client's core catastrophic predictions prior to exposure?
• Following exposure trials, were their catastrophic predictions accurate?
• Did what they feared would happen, actually happen?

The clinician may also wish to address assisting in a particularly difficulty situational exposure by accompanying the client during the initial trials. Ideally, however, this should be limited to initial exposure, as the clinician does not want to become a "safety" behavior that the client uses to avoid being "100 percent" in the situation (i.e., with the clinician repeatedly present, the client can tell themselves, "I could only do this with the therapist there").

Some clients may struggle with remaining in a situation for the duration or "riding the anxiety wave" until its natural end. The clinician can review with the client how to handle it if they have left a situation prematurely, so as to continue to approach it. Given that scenario (premature escape), the client should be asked to re-approach the scenario as quickly as possible and enter it again, tracking ANTs, noting their anxiety, and using coping cards. This can be called "paused" exposure.

For clients who have had a difficult time with physical symptoms or inter-oceptive features of panic, the clinician may wish to add a recreation of interoceptive symptoms to situational exposure. For example, the client with a fear of driving on freeways can be asked initially to drive on the freeway until the SUDS drops. If sweating is a panic trigger for them, they can be asked to drive on the freeway next with the heat on full blast, windows closed, and wearing a winter coat in order to recreate this symptom (and demonstrate that their feared worst outcome will not happen).

Ultimately, the therapist may wish to combine exposure scenarios for symptoms to mimic actual panic attack (i.e., feeling dizzy and sweating—using hyperventilation in a heated parked car).

The clinician may also wish to use imaginal exposure here in the session. This can be implemented by asking the client to imagine the worst outcome for the situation they are approaching on the hierarchy. A list of skills can be developed to address the worst-case fears.

These solutions can then be added to Table 10.9 (see Resource Pack, p. 361).

Table 10.9 Coping Card Statements

Solutions to Address the Worst-Case Fears

What are things I can do, that I can say to others, or that I can say to myself in this situation?

1. _____

2. _____

3. _____

Coping Statements

The clinician may hand the client coping statement cards, and then the client can be assisted in further refining the coping cards by adding additional statements for situational exposure. Below are typical coping statements that may be included on the cards:

- Even though this feels uncomfortable, this feeling will not destroy my job, family, or relationships.
- No one has ever died of shame or embarrassment.
- Just because I feel crazy right now does not mean I am crazy.
- I do not have the ability to control other people's thinking, only my own.
- This uncomfortable feeling is temporary. It is impossible for it to last forever.
- I have survived worse before.
- I have skills to deal with this.
- Anxiety is a wave and I know how to ride it out.
- This will end, it always does.
- There is no such thing as a permanent lifelong panic attack.
- Even though I have the thought that I am weak, the fact that I am doing this at all disproves that.

Homework Assignment

The client will be asked to continue to keep track of their exposure predictions (Situational Exposure Prediction Chart, see Resource Pack, p. 360) and to record the results of their practice, including the exposure activity they did; the sensations they had; the thoughts; and the SUDS before, during, and after (Situational Exposure Practice Results Chart, see Resource Pack, p. 358). Again, they should be encouraged to repeat their exposure to these situations until their SUDS drops by at least 50 percent.

They should also be encouraged to carry their coping statements cards with them and refer to them frequently. If there is a need for the therapist to assist in staying in a situation, plans can be made for carrying that out.

Session Eight: Stress Management

Agenda

1. Check-in and review of practice.
2. Review impact of stress on panic arousal and fight/flight.
3. Discuss soothing and stress nervous systems.
4. Description of relaxation and disabling of stress response.
5. Relaxation instruction.
6. Homework and practice assignment.

Materials Needed

1. Panic Severity Measure
2. Breathe to relax app.

Protocol

Begin this session, as in previous sessions, with a review of the homework and practice during the past week. It is important to review their situational exposure practice and the challenges and barriers they encountered.

A focus of this session will be to discuss the impact of stress on panic arousal. And relaxation is taught at the end of this protocol—for two primary reasons. The first is that if relaxation techniques are taught earlier then the client can use relaxation to avoid being 100 percent *in* a situation. In our experience, clients sometimes use breathing techniques as a distraction, or safety mechanism, to prevent them from remaining in feared situations or states and from testing their catastrophic predictions.

This does not minimize the importance of relaxation training for long-term management of stress. Panic patients, as discussed in earlier sessions, have a sensitive fight/flight response and lower arousal thresholds generally. This means that they evidence heightened reactivity to stressors and are more likely to become stressed and with greater frequency than those without panic disorder.

The clinician should offer education on the nervous system at this point. It can be explained that we have two kinds of nervous systems—the stress nervous system (sympathetic) and the soothing nervous system (parasympathetic). We are a balance of both. We use our stress system to keep us focused and alert when we need it (like driving in rush hour), but we can also use the soothing nervous system when we have to be relaxed to have certain biological functions (falling asleep, going to the bathroom, or having sex, for instance).

When someone is in panic, these symptoms are often out of balance. The stress nervous system is "switched on" and often gets stuck. The fight/flight response and physical stress symptoms get amplified. However, it becomes important to learn how to "switch off" the stress nervous system and "switch on" the soothing nervous system in an intentional way.

Relaxation training is one way that clients can learn to "switch on" the soothing nervous system. The clinician should instruct the client in one of several relaxation techniques over the next two sessions. But, introducing breathing first builds on the teaching that was previously done in regard to hyperventilation. Thus, the client has already learned that breathing is a core component of the stress response because they have learned about hyperventilation. It should be pointed out to the client that hyperventilation actually "switches on" the stress response and panic symptoms.

Conversely, slow breathing "switches off" the stress response, and it turns on the relaxation nervous system (parasympathetic).

It is recommended that the clinician model diaphragmatic breathing with the patient in the session by using the "belly breathing" method identified in the app Breathe2relax (this is a very helpful app which can help clients learn to breathe in a relaxed manner). In this method, the clinician will place one hand on their own diaphragm and one on their breastbone. When they breathe deeply and inhale, the hand on the diaphragm will rise, while the one on the breastbone will remain still. It is important that the exhale be extended as long as possible, so that the rate of breathing is slowed; this could be referred to as stretching out the exhale. This will prevent the hyperventilation response that is so closely aligned with panic symptoms. The clinician will ask the client to focus on the feeling of "the breath," clearing the mind of thoughts and worries. They will give the client permission to have their thoughts "drift" while instructing the client to "return to the breath" as soon as they notice that they have strayed from it.

The clinician will ask the client to practice this breathing method once a day, for 10 minutes. It will *not* be effective for the first several days that the client does it because effectiveness comes with practice as the body learns to master this kind of breathing; note that this is body learning—like riding a bike. The clinician will need emphasize that learning to do this kind of breathing or "retraining" the breathing response will take several days.

A second strategy to bring to the client's attention is visualization. This also is a strategy that can easily be taught. The clinician can ask the client to think about a relaxing, comfortable, and peaceful favorite place. They should imagine taking a path to this place, paying special attention to the sights, sounds, smells, and touch of the path. When they arrive at their special place, they should be encouraged to notice all of the sensory details. They can stay there as long as they would like. When they are ready to leave, they should be encouraged to return along the same path, counting down 3–2–1 to be aware that they are feeling alert, refreshed, and relaxed.

Finally, the clinician can instruct the client in progressive muscle relaxation (PMR), a third strategy. The technique for PMR is simple: The client should be asked to tense and then relax specific muscles, one at a time. One of the easiest ways to do this is by going from the "tip of the toes to the top of the head." The clinician starts by having the client to tense their toes then relax, followed by ankles, calves, thighs, buttocks, abdomen, fists, forearms, biceps, shoulders, and face. The order does not matter as long as all large muscle groups are involved.

Homework Assignment

The clinician will ask the client to practice the three strategies learnt in this session: slow breathing, visualization, and PMR. Each method should be practiced at least once a day. Before and after practicing these strategies, they should rate their stress in the chart below (see Resource Pack, p. 360).

Table 10.10 Example: Rating My Stress Chart

Stress Rating Before (1—10)	Relaxation Practice Time	Stress Rating After (1—10)

Session Nine: Wrapping up and Planning For the Future

Agenda

1. Practice review.
2. Administer final symptom tracker and review changes.
3. Review treatment progress.
4. Symptom understanding and solution implementation.
5. Discuss spontaneous recovery.
6. Implement spontaneous recovery coping kit.

Materials Needed

1. Panic Severity Measure
2. Ten Index Cards and a plastic sandwich bag will be required for this final session.

Protocol

Begin the final session with a review of the practice assignment. Specifically, check on the client's practice of the three strategies learned in Session Eight: Slow breathing, visualization, and PMR. Did the client practice each at least once a day? Review their stress levels before and after each practice.

After review, the initial part of this last session will focus on the gains that the client has made in treatment in the past several weeks. The clinician can review for the client the cumulative week-by-week drop in the Panic Severity Measure, which can help the client see their own progress.

Also, point out that the client has learned to allow themselves to experience the symptoms and situations that made them panic, and they have learned to challenge and disprove the catastrophic thoughts they had about themselves.

Next, the clinician will need to address the future, and the expectation that panic may resurface in a muted form. This can lead to helping the client develop a plan or have some tools at the ready to deal with future anxiety and any potential recurrence.

Education regarding spontaneous recovery is important because panic patients can have all-or-nothing thinking about panic. This means that to them either the "panic is gone" or "the panic is rampant." To them, there may not be an in-between. However, it should be indicated to them that this is a false dichotomy. While many patients at the end of the panic protocol, frequently experience little recurrence of symptoms, others can have times where the symptoms make themselves apparent again, although in a more muted way. This is not treatment failure; it is a normal behavioral phenomenon following response extinction.

Spontaneous recovery is when a previously extinguished behavior resurfaces briefly. For example, if someone has quit smoking several years earlier, they may suddenly have the urge to smoke again out of the blue. Or someone who has been "cured" of a dog phobia may feel a twinge of fear after many years when they see a dog.

The same expectation may apply to panic. If it recurs briefly, it is normal. Typically such a recurrence is muted and damped down relative to prior panic. It is not to be feared, but understood as a product of our behavioral animal learning. And most importantly, the client has skills to handle it (which they did not have before).

The clinician will ask the client to identify the things that they have learned that have helped them to deal with the panic. For each skill or thought identified, the clinician will write it down on an Index Card or in the chart shown below (Table 10.11, see Resource Pack, p. 361).

For each skill identified by the client, the clinician should note it on an Index Card or on the chart. By the end of this exercise, the clinician should have

Table 10.11 Example: Skills I have Learned to Deal with My Panic

Skills That I Have Learned That Make My Symptoms Better	
Thoughts	
Behaviors	
Situation	
Social	

several cards or several skills written on the chart. This will be placed in the plastic baggy and labeled *Panic Skill Kit*.

The client should be instructed that if the anxiety and panic feelings reappear, they need to remind themselves of all the things that they have learned that they used to manage it effectively in the past. The key is that if certain skills worked in the past, they will work in the present. The best predictor of future behavior is past behavior. One way of doing this is by pulling a card from the kit (or noting a skill written in the chart) and doing it.

The clinician should then state clearly to the patient that just because a symptom is there and upsets them it in no way means that they are "back to the beginning." It is a normal recovery experience. Most importantly, now the person has skills to deal with any reappearing symptoms.

Booster Session

Finally, we recommend that the clinician schedule a booster session to take place in 8 to 10 weeks to assess progress and troubleshoot any difficulties. They may want to use the PAQ or the Panic Severity Measure to provide a numerical assessment of progress.

References

Kessler, R.C., Berglund, P.A., Demler, O., Jin, R., and Walters, E.E. (2005). Lifetime prevalence and age-of-onset distributions of DSM-IV disorders in the National Comorbidity Survey Replication (NCS-R). *Archives of General Psychiatry*, 62(6): 593–602.

Kroenke, K., Spitzer, R.L., Williams, J.B., Monahan, P.O., and Löwe, B. (2007). Anxiety disorders in primary care: Prevalence, impairment, comorbidity, and detection. Anxiety disorders in primary care. *Annals of Internal Medicine*, 146(5): 317–325.

Section Four
Interpersonally Disruptive Symptoms

Behavioral Management of Agitation and Disruptive Behaviors in the Confused or Demented Patient

Both verbal and physical agitation are behaviors that alarm families and caregivers. This protocol is designed to help both caregivers and loved ones to better cope with the disruptive behaviors related to agitation. The protocol will help bring attention to both internal and external factors that maintain agitation and teach interventions that can bring about changes in the client's behavior.

There are two basic categories of behavioral disturbance with which the clinician will have to contend: (1) excesses—aggressive, perseverative, and sometimes primitive behavior and (2) deficits and failures to participate in self-care or in initiating normal behaviors. Dealing with these behavioral disturbances with behavioral management has several advantages. Behavioral management involves few side effects, is low cost, is effective in the long term (relative to medication which only works when it is consumed), and when medications are used they are only modestly effective for behavioral management.

The assessment in respect to these behaviors is different from other assessments in this book. Here, assessment is based on observation of the behavior by the care provider. Also, assessment is based on the timeline of behavior (i.e., when did it start?). It is important that assessment include classification of the kind of behavior(s), as well as documentation of the degree/severity of the behaviors, and the outcome of behavior (or the possible function of the behavior).

The interventions, then, are based on functional assessment. That is, the interventions and management approaches have to do with addressing the identified cause or function of behavior. Interventions can take the form of medical management (when there is delirium, for instance), environmental management, caregiver approach management, and contingency management.

Session One: Etiology and Observation

Agenda

1. Assessment and observation.
2. Etiology and reversibility.

3. Types of behavioral disturbance.
4. Next session.

Materials Needed

1. The Overt Behavior Scale (OBS).
2. The Agitated Behavioural Scale (ABS). Available: www.tbims.org/combi/ abs/abs.pdf

Protocol

The first session is devoted to assessment and observation, as well as to determining the etiology and reversibility of the behavioral symptoms displayed by the patient. However, because patients who display agitation and other behavioral disturbance are often cognitively impaired or confused, using a CBT approach directly with the patient is not usually feasible. The reason for this is that CBT is reliant upon the patient's insight and awareness of the problem, their ability to think abstractly, and to remember session content to facilitate change. For the confused, memory-impaired, cognitively compromised or demented patient this is simply not possible, nor a realistic expectation. The caregiver or the care provider can participate in the behavioral management training and learn how to best improve care of the patient.

Assessment, thus, will be based on observations of the behavior by a care provider. Using the OBS provides for classification along several domains, along with intensity and likely outcomes. The ABS is also based on observations of the caregiver and helps track frequency and occurrence of disturbing behaviors at various time points.

Determining the timeline of agitated and disturbed behavior is a primary consideration in assessing if there is a medical or reversible etiology. Any new or sudden changes in behavior should be considered in the context of what may be happening medically with the patient. Delirium is often common in dementia and older adults and it can be ruled out with a blood test in many instances. A hallmark or warning feature of dementia is that it is often associated with a sharp drop in the patient's mental status or an alteration in their orientation and their ability to sustain attention. Use of the Mini Mental State Examination can be helpful, with particular attention to items like the serial 7's and orientation. Collateral informant reports may be of additional utility in establishing if there has been an abrupt change from the patient's known baseline.

It is also important for the clinician to review the medications the patient is taking. Some medications, such as steroids, dopamine agonists, and anticholinergics, may increase confusion (which can trigger agitation) or otherwise contribute to agitation. Benzodiazepines and hypnotics can additionally contribute to confusion, particularly if taken for longer periods of time or longer acting agents are used.

It is important to note that the causes of behavioral disturbance can relate to pain, constipation or other reasons for physical discomfort, or sensory deficits, including hearing loss and changes in vision.

These causes, in addition to delirium, are important to identify because many are reversible. This means that when the underlying issue is addressed (i.e., delirium, or constipation), the behavioral disturbance associated with it will likely remediate.

Through assessment with the caregiver, the type of behavioral disturbance can often be identified. The common types of behavioral disturbances are:

- *Agitated behaviors*: disruptive verbalizations, wandering, sexually inappropriate behaviors, noncompliance with care, disrobing.
- *Aggressive behaviors*: inappropriate or aggressive verbalization and physical aggression.
- *Perseverative behaviors*: repetitive behaviors (vocalizations, including moaning, noises), actions (i.e., constantly unwrapping the same roll of toilet paper) or self-stimulating behaviors (rocking, rubbing, etc.).

Behavioral disturbances can also be viewed as deficits, which means that there is a failure to initiate elements of self-care (i.e., getting dressed, brushing teeth), use the toilet (if capable), or to bathe. Certain changes in social behavior can also be a deficit. At times, caregivers may overlook deficits, for instance, if the patient suddenly becomes quiet or nonreactive. The reason for such behavioral deficits being ignored is that they usually do not present a care problem for the care provider. Nonetheless, deficits may reflect an underlying medical condition. If they are not addressed, or cannot be remediated, they can also accelerate functional decline in the impaired or demented patient. The reason for this is that once a skill is lost from the behavioral repertoire (i.e., getting dressed), it is very difficult to reacquire or relearn for the demented patient, because their cognitive impairments interfere with new explicit learning.

Session Two: Specific Intervention Derived from Functional Assessment

Agenda

1. Review of session one.
2. Functional analysis.
3. Specific functions of behavior.
4. Considerations for implementation.
5. Specific interventions.

Protocol

Begin this second session with a brief review of Session One. For instance, the clinician can review the previous discussion of etiology and reversibility of the agitation and confused behaviors as well as types of behavioral disturbance.

In this session, the first thing to discuss with the caregiver is functional analysis. Functional analysis has to do with determining the function of the patient's behavior. One of the reasons for figuring out the purpose of the behavior is to better understand if there are contingencies that are maintaining the behavior. It is well to point out that agitated behavior can have many consequences, some of which may reinforce the behavior. But it is important to note that a single behavior can have multiple functions.

What are some of the specific functions of behavior?

Here is a listing of six kinds of functions of disruptive behaviors:

- *Attention seeking*: In certain care environments, disruptive behavior creates an opportunity for attention or even social connection with another person. This includes "negative attention."
- *Stimulation*: Disruptive behavior can be a means of increasing stimulation (in a boring or low arousal environment) or decreasing stimulation (in a loud, active, or confusing environment). Often disruptive verbalizations have to do with lowering stimulation, while verbal and physical agitation may be related to stimulation-reduction strategies.
- *Calming/neuroleptic*: Some behaviors can reduce feelings of anxiety and reduce heightened arousal. Wandering behaviors may fall in this category.
- *Escape/avoidance*: Behavior can be a means of stopping an interaction that the client does not want to continue, finds anxiety-provoking or makes him or her feel uncomfortable (i.e., to stop getting dressed or to prevent someone from bathing them).
- *Autonomy/control or power struggle*: Disruptive behaviors in this category may be a way for the client to assert themselves when they are feeling powerless, confused, minimized, or treated like a child (an example would be a client shouting, "No! I won't do this!"). Such behaviors may arise when the patient is feeling less in control of their daily lives or their care.
- *Confused behaviors*: Behaviors such as walking into someone else's room or urinating in a trash can, or being mixed up about whether it is day or night, may be signaling their confusion.

The purpose of learning more about the purposes of behaviors is to be better informed before implementing behavioral strategies. In order to be most effective in putting behavioral interventions in action, it is best to consider three things:

- When trying to change a behavioral contingency, often the target disruptive behavior may at first increase. This does not necessarily mean the intervention is not working. In fact, it may mean just the opposite: it is starting to work and will soon have its desired effect.
- When an intervention is tried, it is essential that it be done consistently. If there are more than one care provider, communication among all care providers is necessary so that the same approaches and consequences are used by all who provide care to the patient.
- Using contingencies on a variable (inconsistent) schedule makes the reinforcement stronger.

Having done a functional assessment of the patient and reviewed three important things to consider prior to implementation, the next step is to review a list of specific interventions to see which ones should be tried. Below are several possible interventions for behaviors that might be described as attention-seeking behaviors:

- *Planned time out*: Brief removal from the environment (if possible) when the patient exhibits behavior, or as an alternative, reduce the patient's participation in an activity or an environment. This approach must be utilized consistently in order to be effective. Case example: A patient who hits other patients during mealtimes could be removed immediately from the dining environment and allowed to return when calm.
- *Planned ignoring*: If the caregiver is comfortable with this strategy, ignore the behavior or pretend it is not happening. In effect, the care provider withdraws reinforcement to decrease the target behavior.
- *Differential reinforcement*: The caregiver may reinforce only socially appropriate or nonaggressive behavior. Case example: If a patient is often yelling, screaming, hitting other patients, or being physically aggressive, the caregiver will choose to target physical abusiveness and verbally abusive behaviors. To reinforce socially appropriate behaviors, the patient is given the opportunity to earn small rewards in three 1-hour periods daily. When he or she exhibits the appropriate behavior, then there will be reinforcement (for instance, reinforcement could consist of a cup of coffee, a snack, or a hand massage). If the patient earns sufficient rewards over 1 week, then they can be rewarded with a bigger reinforcer (e.g., a trip outside).
- *Changing the response contingency*: When the care provider tolerates abuse or, on the other hand, they become visibly upset, this may serve as a reinforcement that provides no particular penalty for the patient. But, if the caregiver sets a boundary and modifies their behavior, the reinforcement is changed. Case example: The care provider might say, "When you say those things, it makes me and others uncomfortable. I will not stay here and listen, when you say those things." The caregiver then leaves for a

period of time. This pattern should be consistently maintained when the behavior returns.

- *Alternative differential reinforcement*: This is a strategy that could be used with a patient who is cognitively intact and are verbal and capable of comprehending. The care provider would say, "When you use those words, they make me and others uncomfortable. What is another word you can use instead?" Then, ask the patient to come up with an alternative word that is appropriate. Once they have done that, ask them to use that word in the original substituting the new, socially appropriate word for the previous inappropriate word. When they have done that, then the caregiver reinforces the improved verbalization.

Next, here are several interventions for managing behaviors that are assessed as stimulation-based behaviors or to calm anxious or distressed patients:

- *Boredom reduction*: These strategies could be utilized when it appears that arousal is too low or boredom has set in. The caregiver can work on ways to reduce boredom or create another source of stimulation. For example, the care provider might encourage engagement in activities that depend on one of the patient's abilities, such as music, coloring, or folding clothes. Sometimes, providing the patient with a simple tactile object to hold, such as a stuffed animal or doll, may satisfy the need for stimulation. Or stimulation that can be helpful may involve providing auditory stimulation by way of playing the patient's favorite type of music, setting up opportunities for having conversations with others, or increasing visual stimulation through providing coloring books or art materials, or making photo albums available.
- *Behavioral substitutes*: Substituting a new behavior for an old one can be a useful strategy at times. For instance, certain perseverative behaviors could be disruptive or disturbing, but perhaps the caregiver can find a substitute behavior. For instance, if the inappropriate behavior involves rubbing or touching, substitute an object it is appropriate to touch or rub. If the patient is disturbing others by obsessively making noise, the care provider could substitute another source of auditory stimulation (such as head phones with calming music or nature sounds). If the patient tears up the wrong things, then the caregiver should substitute a more appropriate behavior, such as folding towels or coloring.
- *Setting substitution*: This approach may be useful for a behavior such as self-stimulation or masturbation. The caregiver can state to the client that the behavior is not appropriate in this setting because it makes others uncomfortable. But the care provider could substitute a private location, explaining that the behavior may not be the problem, but the setting is the problem.

- *Exercise*: Exercise is one kind of strategy that can be used to decrease stimulation. For example, wandering can fall in this category. Physical agitation can be reduced with regular, scheduled physical exercise. Walking is one kind of physical exercise that may change the need to deal with stimulation.
- *Monitor safety*: Wandering may not be a problem as long as the patient is safe. Therefore, the major caregiver strategy is to make sure the individual is safe while wandering. This could mean that the care provider ensures that there are simple barriers to entry in unsafe areas (for instance, a nursing station, a stairway, or a kitchen). Other safety interventions could capitalize on perceptual disturbance of some dementia patients. Some such safety interventions could involve painting the door knob the same color as the door, taping or painting a floor black to look like a "cliff," or taping a grid on the floor may decrease a patient's exploration.

The following strategies can be useful when the disturbing behavior is intended to stop an interaction the patient perceives as unpleasant.

- *Contingency change*: Instead of stopping care giving altogether, the care provider may use "behavioral pauses." The provider might say, "I'm leaving now but will return in __ minutes to continue." This works best if the caregiver returns at the designated time and continues care; if the provider uses the same response when the disturbing behavior occurs again; and if the same pattern of responses by the caregiver is repeated several times. Cautions are that the provider should not discontinue care as this is likely to reinforce the behavior, should provide care on a regular schedule to reduce confusion and uncertainty, should reinforce all cooperation no matter how small.
- *Distraction*: Distraction is a useful technique for managing agitation once it has begun. Case example: When a patient was refusing to take her medications, the care provider drew her attention to a family picture on the wall, which they then talked about. After a few minutes, the patient's anger passed, and she was cooperative in taking her medication.

The following interventions may prove useful when there is a power struggle going on:

- *Choices*: The caregiver can offer the patient choices. It is not helpful to ask a yes-no question such as: "Would you like to take your bath now?" This only creates greater opportunity for refusal and a continued power struggle. Instead, offer acceptable choices: "Would you like to take your bath now or after you've had your walk?" Allowing legitimate choices increases the patient's sense of control and increases their autonomy.

- *Break tasks into smaller ones*: By breaking tasks into smaller ones (i.e., when the patient is getting dressed, just ask them to put on their socks), and by reinforcing each step, it is more likely that the larger task can be completed. This intervention is based on "foot in the door" studies in which it has been found that someone will do a big task for you if they have already agreed to do a small one.

Next are interventions that may be useful when the caregiver is dealing with confusion:

- *Reducing confused behaviors*: If the patient is going into the wrong room or they are mistaking or failing to recognize certain rooms or objects (i.e., toilet), then the confusion may be reduced if their own photo is placed on their door or color coding is used to identify objects that belong to them. Further, a calendar could be placed where they could see it often. It is preferred that the calendar be digital with only the date and time; this aids in orientation. If they are able to read, label rooms and objects with signs (i.e., "Bathroom" or "Toilet"). Remove objects they are mistaking (i.e., trash cans). Case example: A red bracelet was placed on a patient and a square of red paper was placed on all of his possessions, helping him to remember what belonged to him.
- *Reducing "sun downing" or day/night confusion*: The strategy is to reset their day/night rhythm using the natural light cycle. This means opening curtains and shades on windows with first morning light and getting the patient out of bed. Also, restrict napping during the day. Try to get them outside in the natural light to reset circadian rhythm. This should be done by combining physical exercise with being outside. Set bed time when the sun goes down. Arrange a pre-bedtime calming routine and allow no light or excessive stimulation in the bedroom after sundown. This may take several days to "reset" the body clock.

Homework Assignment

Ask that the care provider try to implement some of the interventions learned in this session based on a functional behavioral analysis.

Session Three: Approach Consideration

Agenda

1. Review of Session Two.
2. Introducing approach considerations.
3. Homework assignment.

Protocol

Briefly review what was learned in Session Two with the caregiver. Ask if some interventions were used and review how those were implemented and allow the caregiver to ask questions about the interventions.

Then, point out to the caregiver that while confused or demented patients have areas of their cognitive functioning that are impaired, there are also islands of preservation. For instance, social perception is one area of functioning that may remain intact for many behaviorally disruptive patients. That is, they are still able to perceive the moods of other people and or they are capable of responding to nonverbal cues—even when they may not respond verbally. For the caregiver, this necessitates that the provider be aware of their own non-verbal approach behaviors with the patient. It is well to point out that the nonverbal behavior of a care provider can actually set the "tone" for a patient and for the provider–patient interaction.

Stability in caregiving is also highly important. Environmental changes increase the risk of agitation and confusion, and this will include provider changes, especially if there is a change in caregivers. It is usually highly disruptive for the confused patient who has "learned" one caregiver to have to abruptly learn to adapt to a new provider.

Instruct the caregiver on these *nonverbal approach considerations*:

- *Establish a clear nonverbal identification of the caregiver's role*: If the caregiver is a professional caregiver, this needs to be clear. That is best communicated through the care provider wearing a uniform or wearing a name tag. If the provider is wearing "street clothes," this can be confusing for a patient.
- *Always identify yourself*: When approaching the patient, always identify yourself. Furthermore, state purpose of your visit and tell the patient exactly what you are doing prior to all interactions.
- *Use nonthreatening body language*: The caregiver should utilize a nonthreatening stance and nonthreatening gestures. For instance, they should move slowly with their arms at their side (not behind their back). Their palms should be at the side or exposed.
- *Utilize a soft speaking voice*: Always speak softly, slowly, and simply. Pause often and use easily understood words.
- *Employ visual modeling of desired behavior*: If the care provider can offer cueing for behavior in multiple modalities, compliance can be increased. For example, in helping a patient get dressed, the caregiver can visually model certain behavior, such as showing how to hold a pair of pants and how to insert one leg in the pants. The care provider should keep in mind that the capacity to understand nonverbal cues and to imitate is generally preserved longer than verbal comprehension.
- *Demographic considerations*: It is important to consider cultural and social factors in working with disruptive patients. Based on their own past learning

experiences, some agitated patients may have difficulty with persons of a specific gender, race, or ethnicity. If a pattern is detected, efforts should be made to use care providers that do not have this negative stimulus value for the client. Additionally, the caregiver may note for some agitation patients they may respond better to a deeper male voice, which may sound more authoritative. Alternately, other patients may feel safer and less threatened by female care providers.

Following the discussion of nonverbal approach considerations, the clinician should discuss *verbal approach considerations*:

- *The three Rs of immediate agitation management*:
  - Reorientation: Identify yourself and your role to reduce confusion.
  - Reassure: Let the patient know that everything is okay; use a calm voice.
  - Redirect: Use redirection and distraction to capitalize on memory loss in dementia. Often, given enough time, the patient will forget the source of their agitation.
- *Fixed choice options*: Caregivers should give patients choices, but those choices should be those the providers decide on. Open-ended questions, such as "Would you like to get dressed?", should not be used as they tend to invite a negative response.
- *Patient-driven signaling*: Use signaling to allow patients increased control in care. For instance, the caregiver can ask the patient to signal with a finger, eye blink, or verbalization, when they are ready to do the next step in care. Case example: "I'm going to change your dressing. Raise your finger to let me know when you are ready for me to start to change the dressing." This approach can reduce surprise and uncertainty in care.
- *Use a non-confrontational verbal style*: Many behavioral problems can be triggered when patients are confronted with their own deficits and inability to no longer do things for themselves. Problems can often be avoided by simply *not* making an issue of them and allowing patients to preserve their sense of autonomy. Case example: Instead of telling a woman that she can no longer cook, the caregiver had the gas to the range turned off. In another instance, the care provider avoided a confrontation over the patient's desire to continue to drive by disabling the car.

Homework Assignment

The caregiver should be encouraged to use both nonverbal and verbal approach considerations. They should be asked to report back in the next session as to which approaches they used and how they turned out.

Session Four: Environmental Analysis

Agenda

1.   Review homework assignment.
2.   The effect of the environment.
3.   Homework assignment.

Protocol

To begin Session Four, review the homework assignment with the care provider. Were both verbal and nonverbal approaches utilized in the last week? What was the success of these approaches? What questions does the caregiver have about the strategies taught in Session Three?

The major goal of this session is to help the caregiver get a better sense of how the environment might be affecting the patient.

Discuss the effect of factors in the environment that could be having an impact on the patient. Environmental factors may include stimulation, the imitation of the behavior of other people, and the negative interactions that might come about with certain individuals.

As indicated in previous sessions, stimulation may be a significant factor for many patients displaying disruptive behaviors. There may be too much stimulation in the environment because of excessive noise, too much activity or movement, or too much light. On the other hand, some patients react to an absence or paucity of stimulation. This might be the case in an environment in which there is too little activity, too little sound or noise, too few people, or too little opportunity for enjoyable entertainment.

Modeling by other people with whom the patient comes into daily contact could present a problem as well. If there are other patients, including those with disruptive or agitated behaviors, then there could be a modeling effect. That is, a patient may tend to imitate the behavior of others who are in his or her daily environment.

Also, certain people with whom the patient comes into contact could trigger negative behaviors. This could be related to the way a particular individual approaches the patient. Or it could relate to other characteristics of that person.

To help the patient handle environmental factors, the first key is for the caregiver to do an assessment of environmental factors. The caregiver can determine which situations, events, or people trigger off disruptive, agitated, or confused behaviors. When a pattern is recognized, the next step is to intervene with a strategy to modify or alter the environment.

One strategy is simplification. Simplification involves making the environmental demands on the patient easier and simpler. That may mean reducing the stimulation if there is too much stimulation or introducing tasks as a sequential pattern of steps rather than the patient being presented at one time with a set of contingent instructions. One instruction at a time, for instance, would reduce the stress on the patient.

Structuring is also a useful strategy. Disruptive, agitated, and confused patients are dependent on their caregivers for structure. By providing routines and regularly followed procedures, the patient's tension will be reduced and he or she is more likely to respond favorably to the predictability in a structured environment. Most patients have a reduced capacity to respond adaptively to new and/or ever-changing situations. They are likely to do much better with consistency. Consistency in this context means:

• regular time and procedure for bedtime and waking;
• regular meal times;
• getting dressed and doing hygiene at the same time daily;
• going for walks and doing activities at the same times every day;
• having the same caregivers as much as possible.

Homework Assignment

Have the caregiver analyze the patient's environment to determine which environmental patterns cause problems for the patient and then to find a way to modify the environment to reduce the stress and tension for the patient. That would include deciding how to institute more structure and predictability into the patient's daily schedule.

Session Five: Behavioral Deficits; Excess Dependency and Decreased Social Interaction

Agenda

1. Review of homework assignment.
2. Excess dependency.
3. Decreased social interaction.
4. Depression and adjustment issues.
5. Pleasant Activities Checklist.
6. Homework assignment.

Materials Needed

Pleasant Activities Checklist. Available: www.oxfordclinicalpsych.com/view/ 10.1093/med:psych/9780199334513.001.0001/med-9780199334513-appendix-15

Protocol

This session starts with a review of how the caregiver may have analyzed the patient's environment to determine which environmental patterns cause problems for the patient. Once they did an analysis, the clinician will want to know if the care provider found new ways to modify the environment to reduce the stress and tension for the patient. It is especially important to determine if the provider was able to add more structure and predictability into the patient's daily schedule.

The concept of excess dependency is introduced in this session. Excess dependency has to do with patients exhibiting symptoms of greater functional incapacity than is organically warranted. That is, is the patient engaging in overly dependent behavior in order to, perhaps, gain control and attention from others?

To better explain this concept, the clinician may make reference to the Learned Dependency Model proposed by Baltes (1988). In this model, situations, especially in long-term care facilities, there are many possible environmental reinforcers promoting excess dependency. For instance, residents of long-term care facilities are reinforced by the very nature of staff contact, and frequently the social value of patient–staff interaction is more important than preserved independent functioning for some patients. When excess dependency becomes established, patients may gain control over others and they receive a great deal of attention from their dependent behaviors.

In order to appropriately deal with the problem of excess dependency, whether in the patient's own home or in a long-term care facility, environmental circumstances will need modification and caregiver behaviors will need to change. For instance, care providers will want to consciously decrease over care of the patient and insist on more independent functioning while at the same time improving communication with the patient.

One area which can be a source of reinforced excess dependency relates to meal times. The excess dependency may appear when the caregiver is feeding the patient when that person is capable of feeding themselves. To encourage more independence, the environmental interventions may include reducing excess noise or activities during meals and making sure the patient is sitting at a table when eating. The care provider can place finger foods in the patient's hands, place functionally impaired individuals next to self-feeders, focus on using verbal and tactile prompts related to eating behaviors, repeating simple instructions, modeling desired behaviors, and reinforcing attempts at self-feeding.

Next, the clinician can introduce the problem of decreased social interaction and decreased communication. Since some patients withdraw from social interaction, it may be important for their well-being to increase their social participation. One intervention to bring about greater social interaction is conversational intervention.

Conversational intervention is designed to increase social participation and provide a pleasurable reinforcing activity. To implement this intervention, the patient is provided with materials that serve as external memory aids (such as an album of favorite photos) and encouraged to talk with the care provider and others about the materials. Case example: A man who served in World War II was asked about a short memoir he had written several years ago and the friend, after reading the memoir, asked him about details of his life during the war. That interaction was extremely pleasurable to him as he had the opportunity to recall and talk about a very important phase of his life.

The clinician should talk about the depression and adjustment issues that patients with agitation and behavioral disturbances often experience. It is well to point out to the caregiver that aging and increased dependency on others represents a major transition in life. Most often this transition is characterized by significant environmental changes along with multiple losses. Every experience of a loss can serve to reactivate previous losses.

Losses lead to grief issues. Many of the population for which this chapter is relevant are elderly women. These women frequently have multiple medical conditions and often have sustained multiple losses (of spouses, children, and their own loss of independent living status). The changes in their ability to function adequately and capably can represent a loss as well, and can stir up emotional reactions related to previous losses in their life. Many of these patients will be cognitively appropriate for CBT to help them deal with depression and grief.

For patients experiencing significant grief or depression, not only will a referral to CBT be appropriate, but they will benefit from pleasant events therapy as well. What this means is that the caregiver can find ways to increase their engagement in positive and reinforcing activities. The clinician can provide the caregiver a pleasant activities checklist which the caregiver can in turn administer to the patient. This kind of checklist will give the care provider considerable information about prior interests which can be used to help increase their interest and engagement in enjoyable events and activities. Once the checklist has been filled out with the patient, the caregiver can arrange for activities that will help the individual find pleasure in life.

Homework Assignment

The caregiver can be instructed to use what they learned in this session to attempt to decrease excess dependency, increase the patient's social interaction, and to manage some of the depression and grief issues. They should be encouraged to use the Pleasant Activities Checklist with the patient to find out their previous interests and to schedule pleasurable and enjoyable activities and events.

Session Six: Behavioral Contracting and Wrapping Up

Agenda

1. Homework review.
2. Behavioral contracting.
3. Behavioral management plan.
4. Wrapping up.

Materials Needed

Behavioral contract.

Protocol

In this final session, the clinician can begin with a review of the homework assignment. Reinforcement should be provided if the caregiver has attempted to decrease excess dependency, increase the patient's social interaction, and to manage some of the depression and grief issues. They should be given praise if they began to use the Pleasant Activities Checklist with the patient to find out their previous interests and to schedule pleasurable and enjoyable activities and events.

One of the important things to cover in this final session, particularly if the patient is more cognitively intact, is behavioral contracting. The purpose of behavioral contracting is to help address one or more behavioral problems. It is important to point out to the caregiver that behavioral contracting is an alternative approach to some other approaches covered in these sessions, but it can be rather effective at times. However, care providers should be cautioned that while the idea of writing a contract to address a particular behavior problem sounds simple, it is at times a complex and time-consuming process.

The reason why it may be somewhat complicated and time-consuming is because the process often involves several steps. In addition, the patient must be involved in all of those steps and the patient must "buy in" to the contract. A contract is *not* something that is imposed or forced on a patient. A good contract involves a working alliance between caregiver and patient.

However, some patients will be resistant to change and this resistance is best met through skillful negotiation and avoiding a confrontational approach. In discussing the need for change (related to a behavioral problem), it will be essential to help the patient agree that allowing things to go on as they have been is not going to be to anyone's advantage, and that there are positive benefits to some form of change.

Contract of Understanding between
the Caregiver and Mr. Ray Smith

Implemented on _____ (Date)

The goals in providing your care are to manage your health-related conditions and to help you get along well with other people. I hope you share these goals and that you will treat others with mutual respect. As discussed in the family meeting on _____ (Date), we are concerned about your history of displaying the following behaviors:

1. Inappropriate comments and/or verbal aggressive behaviors toward the care providers who attempt to provide your care.
2. Excessive and/or unreasonable demands of other's attention and time.
3. Unwarranted reporting of complaints to family, friends, and police without first seeking appropriate avenues for remediation.

The caregiver and others do all we can to assist you with your medical care, in following the rules of daily living that have been established, and in resolving concerns that you have with your care provider and others. However, you are responsible for your behaviors. We have recommended that you work with Dr. John Gordon for support toward meeting these objectives and addressing your concerns. We also want to remind you that if you continue to engage in the above behaviors you are creating situations which make it difficult for your caregiver and others to provide appropriate care. If we are unable to work with you in maintaining your medical needs within an atmosphere of mutual respect, we may need to discuss with you the benefits of you transferring to a more appropriate setting and consider ending the relationship with your caregiver. We know you are making an effort and believe you are capable of improving in these areas, and we hope you agree. Thank you for your cooperation in these areas.

_____ (Caregiver) _____ (Date)

_____ (Mr. Smith) _____ (Date)

_____ (Family Representative) _____ (Date)

Figure 11.1 Sample Behavioral Contract

Behavioral contracts are *an* approach to managing behavior problems. While a behavioral contract might be the best approach for some patients, perhaps all patients who exhibit agitated, aggressive, and disruptive behaviors should have a *behavioral plan*. A behavioral contract could be part of a behavioral plan. The key components of a Behavioral Management Plan are:

- *Statement of purpose*: This is a brief, positive statement that conveys to the patient and others the reasons why a behavioral management plan is necessary. In this statement, the targeted behaviors can be listed.
- *Rules*: Specific statements of how the patient is expected to behave.
- *Procedures*: A description of the steps or interventions required for the patient to successfully or appropriately complete certain daily routines (e.g., going to the restroom, taking a bath) or less-frequent activities (e.g., acting appropriately when on an activity, such as a visit to a restaurant).
- *Consequences*: Actions that will be taken to respond to both appropriate and inappropriate patient behaviors. This will include response contingencies, which will be the reinforcements or negative consequences for unwanted behaviors.
- *An action plan*: A method or methods to support the implementation of this behavior management plan.

This final session will conclude with a review of what the caregiver has learned in the previous sessions and verbal reinforcement for the efforts the care provider has made to implement what was taught. They should be encouraged to continue to use interventions that seem to work best for the patient and to try out those that have not been utilized yet.

The caregiver can be reminded that caring for a difficult patient is stressful and they need to remember that and seek support when needed. Finally, they can be told that any time they need support or booster sessions they can contact the clinician.

References

Baltes, M.M. (1988). The etiology and maintenance of dependency in the elderly: Three phases of operant research. *Behavior Therapy*, 19(3), 301–319.

Berglas, S., and Levendusky, P.G. (1985). The therapeutic contract program: An individual-oriented psychological treatment community. *Psychotherapy*, 22(1), 36–45.

Miller, W.R., and Rollnick, S. (2002). *Motivational interviewing: Preparing people for change*. New York: Guilford.

Rosenheck, R.A., and Neale, M.S. (2004). Therapeutic limit setting and six-month outcomes in a veterans affairs assertive community treatment program. *Psychiatric Services*, 55, 139–144.

Chapter 12

Pragmatic Difficulties Protocol

Individuals may say words clearly and use relatively long, complex sentences with correct grammar, but they may still have communication problems. The reason for this is because they may not have mastered the rules for social language. Social language skills are known as pragmatics. And pragmatics difficulty could be the result of a brain injury or stroke or simply because the person has always lacked social communication adeptness.

There are three major communication skills in pragmatics that will be addressed in the treatment protocol that follows:

- using language for different purposes;
- changing language according to the needs of a listener or situation;
- following rules for conversations and storytelling.

With instruction, role playing, practice, and repetition, individuals with relatively intact cognition can learn to overcome their most serious social communication difficulties.

Session One: Social Communication Assessment

Agenda

1. Assessing the social communication deficits.
2. Getting acquainted.
3. Establishing the need for treatment.
4. Increasing the client's motivation.
5. Homework.

Materials Needed

Functional Assessment of Communication Skills (FACS): An assessment tool available from the American Speech-Language Hearing Association that scores

43 communicative abilities in four domains, which are social communication, communication of basic needs, reading, writing and number concepts, and daily planning. In part, this assessment tool examines the effect of the pragmatic disorder on the person's life.

Protocol

Begin the first session with some general information and questions. This will help develop a relationship and rapport. Since the client has pragmatics difficulties, it will be necessary to ask questions that help them to tell more about themselves. Often that means that the questions must be simple, direct, and requesting specific information. For instance, saying, "Tell me about yourself" is unlikely to elicit the kinds of information you will be looking for, whereas asking "How old are you?" will be more productive. Besides asking about basic personal information, ask questions such as "What do you like to do?" and "What do you know the most about?" to find out their areas of interest and knowledge. There is more to this kind of initial foray into treatment besides gathering information. In addition, it helps to show the deficits the person has and it provides initial practice in teaching them to answer simple questions about themselves.

Next, administer the FACS to establish a baseline for the social communication skill level for the client. That then leads to a discussion of his or her specific communication difficulties and their motivation for overcoming some of their skill deficits.

Was the client sent for treatment by someone who recognized his or her pragmatics difficulties? Or was the client aware of their need for help? Are they motivated to improve their social communication skills or are they just coming to satisfy the desires or demands of someone else?

These are questions that need to be addressed in the first session to help determine how the therapist will approach treatment. Obviously, treatment works best if the client is highly motivated. But even if they are not, the motivation can be improved by talking about some of the practical difficulties the client has in their daily life. If you can help them become more aware of some of their difficulties in social situations, then they may recognize that they can benefit from treatment. For example, they may realize that they cannot carry on conversations with others, that they do not know what to talk about in social situations, that others do not like talking to them, or that they do not understand how to engage in conversation when in a group. If they acknowledge any of these difficulties, you can assure them that you can help them get better at these types of skills. And it is important to point out that while some people seem to be born with good social communication skills, others are not. However, by learning about these skills and practicing them, he or she can become much more adept at interacting with others.

You can point out to the client that most of what we do in our day-to-day life involves social skills. And social skills, in turn, involve communicating our thoughts and our needs, as well as listening to others and being able to work together with others to solve problems. If you have good social communication skills, you are more likely to be successful at home, at work, at school, and in the community. On the other hand, if you lack social communication skills, you may not get along with others, may not be able to keep friendships, and may even have trouble maintaining a job.

Goals for this first session are for the client to agree they need to improve their social communication skills and to see that you can help them do this. End the first session by discussing homework.

Homework Assignment

The homework at the end of the first session is to ask the client to keep track of social situations they have during the next week and to make notes about what they notice in those situations. Are they able to engage others in conversation? Or do they feel left out? Do they know what to talk about? Or do they feel like they are at a loss as to how to hold a conversation?

Indicate that Session Two will begin by going over what they noticed during the week in social situations.

Session Two: Reducing interferences

Agenda

1. Review homework.
2. Introduce reducing interferences.
3. Role play and practice.
4. Homework assignment.

Protocol

The first item on the agenda for the second session is to review the homework assignment and discuss what the client observed about themselves during the past week. If they have made a list of observations, that list should be discussed point by point. If no list was made, then the therapist should ask enough direct questions to generate a list in the session. Some of the questions asked and discussed are: Were they able to engage others in conversation during the past week? What were the circumstances that led them to either start a conversation or avoid a conversation? Did they at any time feel left out of social situations? Did they observe that in a social setting they did not know what to talk about? Did they find that on one or more occasions they were at a loss as to what to talk about or how to hold a conversation? By listening to the answers to these questions, you will be better able to understand their communication difficulties. But, the client, too, will begin to pinpoint the difficulties and deficits they have.

To begin with, the therapist should go over what good communication skills require. Some of those requirements include paying attention to others, remembering what others say, expressing your thoughts and ideas, understanding what the other person is saying, and picking up on social cues.

The basic theme for this second session has to do with identifying and reducing interferences to social communication. During the discussion of the homework, some of the barriers and interferences may have been apparent. For instance, during attempts at conversations, they may say inappropriate or unrelated things to the other person, they may use an inappropriate tone or register of their voice, or they may talk excessively without paying attention to the needs or interests of the other person.

Go over some of these common barriers, see which ones the client uses, and then talk about how they can reduce these interferences. For example, cognitive techniques generally can work well in terms of the client reminding themselves what they do to block conversation and telling themselves what they need to do—or refrain from doing. As an example, the individual who talks excessively in social situations needs to remind themselves to stop talking and listen to what the other person wants to talk about or learn what their interests are. The man who has a strong interest in antique automobiles will need to remind himself that very few other people share his interest in old cars, and that he needs to figure out what the other person's interests are.

Furthermore, there may be negative self-talk that is self-defeating. For instance, the client may tell themselves that they are not good at talking to other people and they "never" will be. Or, they may think: "I cannot do this; it is too difficult because I am too shy (or socially inept)." When these cognitions have been identified, help the client develop counter statements. Positive self-talk and positive affirmations ("Other people have learned to do this and I can too") will be added to what they can do to avoid letting the barriers keep them from improving their social skills. With the client, develop three or four reminders that can be used in social situations. The reminders will be written down in the session and then should be transcribed on an index card that the client can carry with them.

Sample reminders to block interferences:

- I will maintain eye contact with the other person.
- I will not talk too much about my personal interests.
- I will ask other people what they are interested in.
- I will not say inappropriate things about other people's interests.
- I will use positive affirmations whenever I am thinking negative and self-defeating thoughts.

In this second session, the therapist and client should role play using the reminders that block conversation. To do this role play, the therapist will start a conversation with the client. With the index card in front of them, the client will during the first role play read the items aloud and then remember those items while trying to carry on a conversation.

In the next and in subsequent role plays, the client will simply look at the reminders and say them to themselves. Then, they will engage in the conversation keeping these reminders in mind. After each role play, the therapist will provide positive feedback and also point out what the client needs to work on. Subsequent role plays can be aimed at working on those areas that need more rehearsal and practice.

Homework Assignment

The homework for this session is to ask the client to carry the index card with them and read it over at least once a day. They are to use the reminders in actual social situations to remember to avoid doing those things that block and interfere with social communication. Ask the client to keep track of those times they were able to remember to remind themselves and then to carry out the reminders. They should also keep track of those situations in which they either failed to remind themselves or, even after reminding themselves, they could not stop themselves from doing those things they wanted to avoid.

Session Three: Initiating Conversation

Agenda

1. Review homework.
2. Introduce: learning how to start a conversation.
3. Rules for initiating conversations.
4. Role play and practice.
5. Homework assignment.

Materials

1. A list of the rules for initiating conversations.
2. A number of conversation starter comments on small slips of paper.

Protocol

Begin Session Three by reviewing the homework. Ask to see the record they have kept for using the reminders to avoid blocking social communication. Were they able to avoid interfering with communication? Discuss their success in using the index card to remember to use reminders. If they were not very successful, indicate that this is common and they should not feel discouraged. Let them know that there will be more role playing and practice in this session.

Introduce the topic for today: Initiating conversations. Discuss how the basis of social communication is talking and talking means carrying on a conversation. The client may be familiar with trying to talk to people and one side or the other is simply carrying on a monologue. That is quite common, but is very frustrating. In order to have a true conversation, both parties need to contribute. But first the conversation must get started.

Go over the rules for starting a conversation.

Rules for Starting Conversations

1. smile;
2. make a comment;
3. ask open-ended questions;
4. listen to what the other person says;
5. take turns in the conversation;
6. use a sense of humor;
7. engage in small talk.

The first step in initiating a conversation is to find someone you would like to talk to. When approaching them, smile. Whether you or both of you are nervous about striking up a conversation with someone who is a stranger or someone you do not know very well, if you are smiling they are more likely to want to talk to you.

A good way to start is to make a comment. There are a million ways to make an initial comment to start a conversation, but here are a few:

- "Are you new here? I haven't seen you here before?"
- "How do you know our host?"
- "You look like you need someone to talk to."
- "I was admiring your tie? Where did you find it?"
- "The weather was frightful today, don't you think?"
- "I don't know about you, but I don't know another person here."

Once the other person responds to your initial comment, you should be prepared to follow up with an open-ended question. For example, you could ask, "How did you meet our host?" or "That's funny. How did you develop such a keen sense of humor?"

Also, be prepared to take turns in the conversation. Of course, a conversation will end if one person stops talking. So, when the other person has concluded their comment or question, you need to take your turn in the conversation. A good way to keep the conversation going is to show an interest in the other person. If, for instance, the person says that they met the host of the party on a cruise, you have several questions you could ask. Certainly you do not want to make your questions sound like an interrogation, but try to display an interest in the other person. For example: "You met on a cruise? That sounds so exciting. Tell me about the cruise you were on." If they give you some details about the cruise, then ask more questions indicating you are interested in their experience: "I've never been on a cruise, but I've been thinking about going on one. What do you like best about cruises?" It does not matter at the moment whether you really want to go on a cruise, but you need to keep the conversation going until it shifts to something you may truly be interested in. When it is your turn, you could say, "I don't know when I'll get to go on a cruise, but a vacation I really enjoy is traveling by train." If they do not ask more about that or comment, you can tell about an experience you had on a train trip: "The worst experience I ever had on a train trip was when I was in Canada and . . ."

Remember to inject humor into your conversation. Hopefully, you are not talking about how angry you are about the economy or about politics. However, people will enjoy talking to you if you are interesting and if you use humor. A great way of using humor is to make fun of yourself ("I am so envious of you because you were able to remodel your house. If I were to do try that, I'm sure I would probably end up building a room without a door—with me inside!") or to joke about your faults ("I'm sure if I went on cruise, I'm so lazy I would probably never get out of a deck chair except to eat six meals a day!").

Finally, a rule about starting a conversation is to start off with small talk. It is not necessary (or advisable) to start off with a heavy subject. For instance, it is better to comment on the weather ("Do you think summer is ever going to get here?") rather than the state of politics in the Middle East ("Don't you think our foreign policy is wretched and that's why the Middle East is so unstable?"). Would you rather talk to someone about the weather or the mess in the Middle East?

At the end of this introduction, give the client the rules for initiating a conversation.

Next engage in role play and practice. With the slips of paper containing some initial comments to start a conversation, place them all in a bowl or dish and ask the client to draw one. Then, he is to use that one to start a conversation with you.

No matter what the comment is, your job is to respond to it in such a way that the client has at least a couple of questions or comments that could keep the conversation going. For example, if the slip of paper that client reads from says, "I noticed you were standing alone over here and thought I would come over and introduce myself," then your response could be, "Yes, I don't know a soul at this party. Thanks for rescuing me from having to stand here all alone." The client could then ask if you came alone, how you know the host, or if you are like him or her in that you feel very awkward when you do not know anyone else.

Encourage the client to take the conversation at least several turns into a discussion. Then, take another slip of paper and have him start a new conversation with you with a different opening line. Do several of these and give him or her plenty of praise and constructive feedback about their efforts.

Homework Assignment

The homework assignment is to ask the client to come up with several comments they could use when they are next in a social situation and need to initiate a conversation. Then, during the coming week, they should read their list of rules daily for initiating conversations and then try to use them once a day to start a conversation with someone. It could be anywhere in their life where they typically have had difficulty starting conversations—at work, at school, at a gym, at church, or at a meeting. They should keep a journal recording each attempt to initiate a conversation, recording what they said and the response of the other person (Table 12.1, see Resource Pack, p. 362).

Table 12.1 Example: Initiating a Conversation Journal

Date	Time & Place Of Conversation	What I Said To Start The Conversation	How The Other Person Responded

Session Four: How to Sustain a Conversation

Agenda

1. Review homework.
2. Introduce new topic: sustaining a conversation.
3. Learn rules for sustaining a conversation.
4. Role play and practice.
5. Homework assignment.

Materials Needed

1. Rules for sustaining a conversation.
2. Homework journal.

Protocol

As in every session, the first order of business is to review the client's success in doing the homework assignment. Did he or she develop a list of comments they could use to initiate a conversation? Did they read their list of rules daily for initiating conversations? How many times were they able to start a conversation with someone? Review their journal with them. After hearing their progress, offer positive reinforcement and constructive feedback.

Introduce the basic concept of conversations. Define a conversation as the exchange of ideas and thoughts between two or more people. Conversations are an essential part of communication and are vital for maintaining friendships. Conversations are composed of words and nonverbal gestures. Both are important to a successful conversation. Most people feel the need to communicate in order to interact with others, learn something, ask for help, or get emotional and psychological support. We all need conversations. They can be seen as the glue of friendships.

Since the client has already learned about initiating conversations, in this session, they will learn more about how to keep a conversation going; that is, how to sustain a conversation. There are rules the client can learn that will help them get beyond openers and keep the give and take of a conversation going.

The basic rules of sustaining a conversation are:

1. initiate a conversation;
2. wait your turn;
3. include others in the conversation;
4. share—just do not ask questions;
5. ask open-ended questions;
6. let others know you are interested in what they are saying: "Interesting. Tell me more";
7. share stories;
8. use nonverbal techniques: have an open posture, learn forward, make eye contact, nod while other person is talking.

While all of these rules are important, perhaps the rule that most often presents difficulties for people with pragmatics problems is turn-taking. Taking turns in a conversation is the grease that makes a conversation a dialogue—not a monologue. And, when one of the individuals does not take their turn—or allow the other person a turn—the conversation ends. This must be emphasized to the client and they must be given pointers in order to learn this important rule. In order to know when it is their turn to speak, a person in a conversation must listen to the other person. If you are too involved in thinking about what you are going to say next (or what you should have said before), you may not be aware when the other person has paused and that you are expected to speak next. So, each must listen and learn to recognize when it is their turn to contribute.

In order to facilitate turn-taking, when it is your turn to talk, you must say something that allows the other person to take their turn. Unskilled conversationalists often make judgmental or inappropriate statements or comments that may stop a conversation. For example, saying, "Anyone who thinks that is stupid" is a conversation stopper. So is "I can't talk to anyone who says what you just said." Instead, if the client is in a conversation and does not agree with something the other person said, a "turn taking comment" would be: "That's very interesting. What led you to come to that conclusion?" This gives the other person a chance to explain their previous statement. Disagreeing with the other person does not have to block the conversation. If you say, "I used to think that but something happened to me to change my mind," the other person can say, "What happened?" This allows the first person to share a story or experience. Stories and experiences enrich and sustain conversations.

Rules for Sustaining Conversations

1. Initiate a conversation.
2. Wait your turn.
3. Include others in the conversation.
4. Share—just do not ask questions.
5. Ask open-ended questions.
6. Let others know you are interested in what they are saying: "Interesting. Tell me more."
7. Share stories.
8. Use nonverbal techniques: have an open posture, learn forward, make eye contact, nod while other person is talking.

The role play and practice in this session has to do with keeping a conversation going. As in the last session, there will be several brief scenarios on slips of paper that can be drawn randomly. The therapist will say the line or the statement on the paper and the client must take his or her turn in the conversation making a comment that will help the therapist take his or her turn in the conversation.

Some examples of statements that might be on the slips of paper are:

- "I can't believe how much traffic there was on the expressway today."
- "I can't believe the president is allowing the war in Iraq to drag on. He should use nuclear bombs and just end it."
- "I think all politicians are crooked, don't you?"
- "If they would just use capital punishment more often, there wouldn't be so much crime."

Homework Assignment

The homework assignment is to instruct the client to read over the rules for sustaining a conversation every day. Then, using a homework journal, he or she should track their efforts to keep conversations going during the coming week. On the journal should be recorded what the client said or did to keep conversations going (Table 12.2, see Resource Pack, p. 362).

Table 12.2 Example: Sustaining a Conversation Journal

Date	Time & Place Of Conversation	What I Said To Keep The Conversation Going	How The Other Person Responded

Session Five: Ending Conversations

Agenda

1. Review the homework.
2. Introduce ending a conversation.
3. Role play and practice.
4. Assign homework.

Materials Needed

Rules for ending a conversation.

Protocol

As in previous sessions, this session begins with a review of the homework assignment. The homework was for the client to read over the rules every day for sustaining a conversation. Then, using the homework journal, the client was to track their efforts to keep conversations going during the week. Go over with the client their efforts to sustain conversations in their everyday activities. Provide positive feedback and help them troubleshoot any problems they encountered. The recording of notes related to their conversations should be helpful in determining what the areas of difficulty were and how they can improve.

Next, introduce the topic: Ending a conversation. Let the client know that after learning how to initiate conversations and how to keep conversations going, they now have to learn the skills related to ending conversations. Often people with social communication deficits feel awkward about ending conversations. One of the reasons for this, besides their general lack of basic skills in holding meaningful and successful conversations, is that they think others will be offended if they end a conversation. They should be reassured that most people understand when one person ends a conversation. That is, they understand as long as the person ending the conversation is not rude or inappropriate.

Perhaps, the best way to end a conversation is to be honest. If you have a good reason to end the conversation ("I need to go to the restroom"; "I'm going to get something to eat while there's still food left"; or "I see someone I haven't talked to in a long time"), most people will be quite understanding and not be upset with you. If you give a lame excuse ("I need to talk to someone else") or a rude excuse ("I am totally bored with this conversation"), they will be much less understanding.

Of course, there are good reasons to end a conversation. For instance, if you are at a party, you may, indeed, want to talk to other people or get some hors d'oeuvres. In other conversations, you may need to stop in order to get to an appointment or take a phone call. Basically, you need to give a short explanation that makes sense to the other person. For example, "I'm sorry to cut short this conversation, but I promised the hostess I would mingle. Maybe we can talk later."

It is also important to look for a pause in the discussion that signals a good time to make your excuse. If the other person has just finished telling a story and they pause, it is a good time for you to say, "That's a great story, I'm going to find my friend and tell them to come over and talk to you so you can tell that story to them." In fact, mentioning someone else is a great way to end a conversation. For instance, you could say, "There's someone else here I'd like you to meet. I know they will find your thoughts as fascinating as I. I'll talk to you later, but I'll send someone over to introduce themselves."

And there is the classic, but entirely acceptable way to end a conversation: "I've got to go. It's been great talking to you and I hope we can do this again" or "I'll talk to you later. I've enjoyed getting to know you."

One last aspect of ending a conversation should be discussed with the client. That has to do with the real reason for wanting to end the conversation. It is a perfectly legitimate reason to want to end a conversation in order to get to an appointment or because the two of you may truly have nothing else to talk about. However, for the person with social communication difficulties, it is not a legitimate reason to end a conversation because they are nervous, shy, or anxious. A major reason for learning how to carry on conversations is to be able to communicate with others without feeling awkward, uncomfortable, or shy. If the client simply wants to end the conversation because talking makes them uncomfortable, it is a good reason to work at keeping the conversation going and continuing to practice social communication skills.

Rules for Ending Conversations

1. Do not feel bad about ending the conversation.
2. Find a natural pause in the conversation.
3. Use a reasonable excuse or reason to end the conversation.
4. Make it short and express something positive about the other person or the conversation.

As with other sessions, the therapist will have a number of scenarios on slips of paper that the client can draw at random and will allow the therapist and client to engage in short conversations and then the client must use a statement to end the conversation. The proposed "conversation ender" will also be on the slips of paper.

As an example, a slip of paper might read as follows:

> Conversation: Discuss your favorite baseball team and how it is expected they will do next season.
> Conversation ender: There is another appointment I need to get to.

So, in this example, the therapist and client will take turns in a conversation for 1 to 2 minutes before the client says, "You know, I really have great expectations for the team next season, but I've got to run because I need to get to my next appointment."

Other scenarios will follow the same format.

Homework Assignment

The homework for this week will be for the client to daily read over the rules for ending conversations. Then, they will keep track in their Ending a Conversation Journal their efforts to smoothly end conversations. This completed journal will be brought to the next session (Table 12.3, see Resource Pack, p. 363).

Table 12.3 Example: Ending a Conversation Journal

Date	Time & Place Of Conversation	What I Said To End The Conversation	How The Other Person Responded

Session Six: Review and Wrap Up

Agenda

1. Review homework.
2. Assessment.
3. Discuss all previous topics.
4. Do final role play and practice.
5. Discuss ending treatment.

Materials Needed

FACS for assessment.

Protocol

Review homework to begin the final session. The homework for this week was for the client to regularly read over the rules for ending conversations. They were also instructed to record their experiences in the journal their efforts to smoothly end conversations. This journal should be reviewed with feedback and opportunities for the client to ask questions.

The major part of this final session will be a review of what has been taught in previous sessions:

- assessment and motivation;
- reducing interfering thoughts and behaviors;
- initiating a conversation;
- sustaining a conversation;
- ending a conversation.

After a review of the rules and guidelines for all aspects on social communication covered in the series of sessions, give the client a chance to ask questions and talk about aspects that still make him or her uncomfortable. Answer their questions and give positive feedback and encouragement.

For the future, suggest that the client review the rules for social communication learned in treatment and to continue to practice their social skills whenever possible. They should be encouraged to practice engaging in conversations in different kinds of social situations so they become more skilled in almost any situation in which they may find themselves.

Troubleshooting

It is likely that during the course of treatment, the client did not find themselves in a sufficient number of social situations so that they did not get in enough practice. One of the usual reasons for this is that in the past, they have avoided many social situations so that they have built their life around avoidance. Consequently, they may continue to do this—even though they have said they were motivated to improve their social skills. Thus, the therapist needs to strongly suggest that they extend themselves to put themselves in new and anxiety-provoking situations in order to be able to practice their conversational skills.

A second problem that may present itself is that if the client has felt like a failure in one or more attempts at conversation, they may have been tempted to withdraw or avoid future possible "failures." They should be taught some cognitive skills to get over labeling themselves as a failure so they can keep practicing.

Booster Sessions

The client should be told that they can come back for booster sessions and for troubleshooting sessions at any time in the future. At any time they feel like they need positive feedback and reinforcement, as well as role play and practice, they can contact the therapist for a booster session.

Chapter 13

The Final Word on Treatment in Medical Settings

It is very common for psychologists and other mental health practitioners to play an important role in providing treatment in hospitals and other medical settings, where they are frequently called on to treat patients with psychological symptoms. What has been provided in this book are cognitive behavioral interventions for effective treatment of nine specific conditions often presented to the doctors and other staff in medical settings. These conditions are:

- Pain
- Sleep Difficulties
- Depression
- Anger Dysregulation
- Anxiety about the Medical Setting and Medical Treatment
- Illness Anxiety
- Panic Attacks
- Agitation
- Pragmatic Difficulties

It is hoped that the protocol chapters of this book are not only practical manuals for cognitive behavioral treatment (CBT) but also clinician-friendly guides to treatment that will help therapists avoid common pitfalls in treatment. For each condition, information was provided regarding its occurrence, assessment of the symptoms, nonmental health interventions, and mental health treatments. In setting forth the treatment approaches for each condition, it was important that each approach has demonstrated success, be goal-directed, and time-limited. The goal in each protocol for each condition was to help the client gain control over their symptoms.

The treatment approaches in this book are focused specifically on CBT, a treatment modality that has demonstrated success, particularly for the types of symptoms seen in the medical setting. Basing the treatment protocols on CBT, each of the nine chapters is a short treatment manual featuring applied principles in treating the nine problem areas. In those "manuals," guidelines for assessment, evaluation of symptoms, and homework assignments were provided.

The authors hope that clinicians will find those chapters useful and will consider those treatment chapters as an initial introduction to the method prescribed, although it was the intent that clinicians can use each protocol to carry out successful treatment.

Another way of viewing the protocol chapters is that they are aspirational. That is, it is expected that a competent clinician will regard these protocols as a preliminary outline with important principles of treatment; however, their application should be specific to the client or patient and to their presenting complaints.

Also, readers may wish to use the principles and procedures in this book to create protocols for similar conditions or for conditions that were not explicitly addressed in the protocol chapters. For example, it might be possible to construct CBT-based treatment protocols for gambling, hoarding behavior, or dental anxiety.

In fact, the authors hope that clinicians apply these principles in their own clinical practice, whether or not they already have a specific protocol for a specific condition. And psychologists, counselors, and therapists are encouraged to continue expanding their protocols by finding other assessment tools that are yet to be developed. Therapists and clinicians are strongly encouraged to keep up with the empirical literature to find such assessments, or fill the void by identifying areas where additional assessment measures are needed.

Furthermore, those readers in the clinical field should be attentive to colleagues in the medical setting who present information about patients who may benefit from this type of treatment. And, finally, consider group supervision with colleagues in discussing such cases and in working together in continuing to refine and perfect existing protocols—whether in this book or found elsewhere.

Resource Pack

All tables and forms used in the thirteen chapters of this volume appear in chronological order. They are identified with their chapter and sesssion number (e.g., C4/S3 for Chapter 4/Session 3). Examples used more than once are placed at the first session in which they are used.

To fit individual table/forms on an A4 sheet please use copy-enlargement: 180%. To fit any double spreads on A4 enlarge to 120%.

Chapters including photocopy resources:

C4/S2

Things that Open My Pain Gate/Increase Pain

Thoughts:	Feelings:	Behaviors: Things I do or don't do:	Physical:

Things that Close My Pain Gate/Decrease Pain

Thoughts:	Feelings:	Behaviors: Things I do or don't do:	Physical:

C4/S1

Short-Term Goals: 10 Weeks

1.					
2.					
3.					
4.					
5.					
6.					
7.					
8.					
9.					
10.					

C4/S3–4

Walking Program

	Week	(walking time in minutes)								
	1	2	3	4	5	6	7	8	9	10
Day 1										
Day 2										
Day 3										
Day 4										
Day 5										
Day 6										
Day 7										

Activity Program

Activity	Time Plan	Day 1	Day 2	Day 3	Day 4	Day 5	Day 6	Day 7

C4/S6

Thought Record

Event	Thought/Image	Feeling	Behavior
Ex: pain increase	Ex: thinking about myself ending up in a wheelchair / Think I hurt myself more	Ex: sad, stressed	Ex: decide to go bed

C4/S8

Activity Plan

Value	Activity (What You Will Do)	Plan (Time, Frequency)
1.		
2.		
3.		
4.		
5.		
6.		
7.		
8.		
9.		
10.		

C4/S7

Thought Record

Event	Thought	Evidence For Thought	Evidence Against Thought	Blended Thought

Worry Worksheet

Anxiety Reduction Exercise
Make a list of problems, worries, concerns, tasks, fears, or other issues that cause feelings of being overwhelmed, racing thoughts, and feelings of anxiety:
1. _____
2. _____
3. _____
4. _____
5. _____
6. _____
7. _____
8. _____
9. _____
10. _____

C5/S3

This I Can Control

Things That I Have Control Over	Things That I Do Not Have Control Over
1.	1.
2.	2.
3.	3.
4.	4.
5.	5.
6	6.
7.	7.
8.	8.
9.	9.
10.	10.
Solutions	

C5/S5

The Thought Chart

Event	Thought	Evidence For Thought	Evidence Against Thought	Blended Thought And New Feeling

C5/S4

Beliefs, Feelings, and Behavior

Event	Belief Thought Image	Feeling	Behavior
Ex: Bad sleep 4 days in a row.	Ex: I have no ability to manage my sleep problem. It is out of control	Ex: Anxious Hopeless	Ex: Wide awake, unable to relax. No pull to sleep Stressed

C6/S2

Thoughts Record

Thoughts/Image	Situation	SUDS Rating (0–100)
1.		
2.		
3.		
4.		
5.		
6.		
7.		
8.		
9.		
10.		

C6/S1

Goals List

Specific Life Areas I Want To Improve	Check Which Three Are Most Important
1.	1.
2.	2.
3.	3.
4.	4.
5.	5.
6.	6.
7.	7.
8.	8.
9.	9.
10.	10.

C6/S2-3

Activities Record

Physical Activities (For Instance, Walking, Biking, Bowling, Climbing Stairs, Etc.)	How Many Days?	How Many Minutes Each Day?
1.		
2.		
3.		
4.		
5.		
6.		
7.		
8.		
9.		
10.		

C6/S3

Thoughts Record

Thoughts/Image	Specific Automatic Thought	Situation	SUDS Rating (0–100)
1.			
2.			
3.			
4.			
5.			
6.			
7.			
8.			
9.			
10.			

C6/S4

Negative Thoughts Record

Thought/Image	Specific Automatic Thought	Is There Evidence To Support This Thought?
1.		
2.		
3.		
4.		
5.		
6.		
7.		
8.		
9.		
10.		

C6/S5

Behavioral Activation Chart

Value Based Activity	Planned Day/Date	Done?	Mood After (0–10)
1.			
2.			
3.			
4.			
5.			
6.			
7.			
8.			
9.			
10.			

C6/S6

Negative Thoughts Record

Thought/Image	Specific Automatic Thought	Is There Evidence To Support This Thought?	Construct A More Realistic Statement
1.			
2.			
3.			
4.			
5.			
6.			
7.			
8.			
9.			
10.			

C7/S1

Anger Log (Week 1)

Day: ....

Incident:
- What made me mad? ....
  ....
- What was my Anger Scale score? ....
- How did I act? ....
  ....
- What was the outcome? ....
  ....

Incident:
- What made me mad? ....
  ....
- What was my Anger Scale score? ....
- How did I act? ....
  ....
- What was the outcome? ....
  ....

C7/S2

Anger Log (Week 2)

Day: ....

Incident:

- What made me mad? ....

- How did I act or behave? ....

- Did I use a strategy? ....

- What was the outcome? ....

Incident:

- What made me mad? ....

- How did I act or behave? ....

- Did I use a strategy? ....

- What was the outcome? ....

C7/S3–8

Anger Log (Week 3–8)

Day: ....

Incident:

- What made me mad? ....

- What was my Anger sclae score? ....

- What were my physical cues? ....

- My thinking cues? ....

- My behavior cues? ....

- How did I act or behave? ....

- Did I use a strategy? ....

- What was the outcome? ....

C7/S7

ANT Chart

Activating EVENT/SITUATION	Belief THOUGHT	Belief (ANT) EXACT THOUGHT (from category above)	Consequence FEELING BEHAVIOUR
1.			
2.			
3.			
4.			
5.			
6.			
7.			
8.			
9.			
10.			

C7/S5–11

Anger Control Plan (Week 5–11)

Immediate Strategies	Preventative Strategies
1.	1.
2.	2.
3.	3.
4.	4.
5.	5.
6.	6.
7.	7.
8.	8.
9.	9.
10.	10.

C7/S9-11

Modified Anger Log (Weeks 9–11)

EVENT ....

CUES ....

STRATEGIES ....

OUTCOME
(rate your anger after using anger control strategies) ....

EVENT ....

CUES ....

STRATEGIES ....

OUTCOME
(rate your anger after using anger control strategies) ....

C7/S9

The Challenging Thoughts Chart

Event	Thought	Evidence For Thought	Evidence Against Thought	Blended Thought & New Feeling

C8/S2

List of Symptoms and Rating Based on SUDS

Situation	SUDS Rating

C8/S2–5

Hierarchy of Exposure (Sessions 2–5)

1. (most distressing)
2.
3.
4.
5.
6.
7.
8.
9. (least distressing)

C8/S3–5

Catastrophic Prediction Chart (Sessions 3–5)

Situation	Prediction/Fear

C8/S2

List of Safety Behaviors

1.
2.
3.
4.
5.
6.
7.
8.
9.
10.

C8/S6

List of Skills to Reduce Fear

Skills That Have Worked To Help Me Reduce My Fear

C8/S3–5

Exposure and SUDS Chart (Sessions 3–5)

Exposure Task	SUDS Before	Sensations	SUDS During	Thoughts	SUDS After

C9/SI

List of Factors that Decrease Symptom Intensity

Physical	Behaviors	Feelings	Social	Thoughts

List of Factors that Increase Symptom Intensity

Physical	Behaviors	Feelings	Social	Thoughts

C9/SI

List of Symptoms

1.	
2.	
3.	
4.	
5.	
6.	
7.	
8.	
9.	
10.	

C9/S2

List of Activities to Do Again

Activities that i'm not doing anymore and would like to do again

1.
2.
3.
4.
5.
6.
7.
8.
9.
10.

C9/S2

Short-Term SMART Goals: 12 weeks

1.
2.
3.
4.
5.
6.
7.
8.
9.
10.
11.
12.

C9/S2-6

Activity Plan Chart (Sessions 2–6)

Activity (Time in minutes)	M	T	W	TH	F	S	SUN

C9/S2

Long-Term SMART Goals: 12 weeks

1.	
2.	
3.	
4.	
5.	
6.	
7.	
8.	
9.	
10.	
11.	
12.	

C9/S2–6

List of Things that Made the Symptoms (Sessions 2–6)

	Things That Made My Symptoms	
	Better	Worse
Physical		
Behaviors		
Feelings		
Social		
Thoughts		

C9/S2–6

Walking Chart (Sessions 2–6)

	Week	(walking time in minutes)								
	1	2	3	4	5	6	7	8	9	10
Day 1										
Day 2										
Day 3										
Day 4										
Day 5										
Day 6										
Day 7										

C9/S4

Situations, Feelings and Rating Your Emotions Chart

Situation Symptom (who, what, where, when)	Feeling (List emotion and rate intensity 0–100)	Thought (What are exact thoughts, circle most upsetting thought)	Specific ANT (What category of ANT does this fall into?)	Alternate Thought (In response to challenge questions)	Re-rate Feeling (emotion 1–100)

C9/S3

Thoughts Record Chart

Automatic Thoughts I Had Which Relate To My Illness Symptoms	Circumstances When I Had This Thought	How Many Times I Had This Thought
1.		
2.		
3.		
4.		
5.		
6.		
7.		
8.		
9.		
10.		

List of Safety Behaviors

My Safety Behaviors								
1.								
2.								
3.								
4.								
5.								
6.								
7.								
8.								
9.								
10.								

C9/S5

Exposure and SUDS Rating Chart

Exposure Task	SUDS Before	Sensations	SUDS During	Thoughts	SUDS After

C9/S6

Sympton Hierarchy Rating Chart

My Symptom Hierarchy Based On SUDS Rating
1. (most distressing)
2.
3.
4.
5.
6.
7.
8.
9. (least distressing)

C9/S6

Identifying and Rating Physical Symptoms

Symptoms	SUDS Rating

C9/S7

Situations Exposure Predictions Chart

Situation	Prediction/Fear	Was Prediction Correct?

C9/S6

Symptoms Predictions Chart

Recreated Symptoms	Prediction/Fear	Prediction Correct (Y/N)?

C9/S7

Situational Exposure Practice Results Chart

Exposure Situation	SUDS Before	Sensations	SUDS During	Thoughts	SUDS After

C9/S9

Rating My Stress Chart

Stress Rating Before (1—10)	Relaxation practice time	Stress Rating After (1—10)

C10/S2–3

Situations, Feelings and Rating Your Emotions (Sessions 2–3)

Situation Symptom (who, what, where, when)	Feeling (List emotion and rate intensity 0–100)	Thought (What are exact thoughts, circle most upsetting thought)	Specific ANT (What category of ANT does this fall into?)	Alternate Thought (In response to challenge questions)	Re-rate Feeling (emotion 1–100)

C10/S1

Panic Attacks and Panic Attack Fears Chart

Panic Situation (who, what, where, when)	Rate Panic Severity (0–100)	Duration of Panic Attack (minutes)	Physical Feelings (body sensations during panic)	Behaviors (What did I do when I had my panic attack)

C10/S4

Identifying Situations and Rating Symptoms

Symptom/Situation	SUDS Rating

C10/S4

Symptom Hierarchy Rating Chart

My Symptom Hierarchy Based On SUDS Rating
1. (most distressing)
2.
3.
4.
5.
6.
7.
8.
9. (least distressing)

C10/S4, 6

Situational Exposure Practice Results Chart

Exposure Situation	SUDS Before	Sensations	SUDS During	Thoughts	SUDS After

C10/S4

Symptoms Predictions Charts

Recreated Symptoms	Prediction/Fear	Prediction Correct (Y/N)?

C10/S6

Panic Attack Avoidance Chart

Activities and Location that Fear of Having a Panic Attach Have Made Me Avoid
1.
2.
3.
4.
5.
6.
7.
8.
9.
10.

C10/S6–7

Situation Hierarchy Rating Chart (Sessions 6–7)

My Symptom Hierarchy Based On SUDS Rating
1. (most scary)
2.
3.
4.
5.
6.
7.
8.
9. (least scary)

C10/S6–7

Situations Exposure Predictions Chart (Sessions 6–7)

Recreated Symptoms	Prediction/Fear	Prediction Correct (Y/N)?

C10/S6–7

Rating My Stress Chart

Stress Rating Before (1—10)	Relaxation Practice Time	Stress Rating After (1—10)

C10/S9

Skills I have Learned to Deal with My Panic

Skills That I Have Learned That Make My Symptoms Better	
Thoughts	
Behaviors	
Situation	
Social	

C10/S7

Coping Card Statements

Solutions to Address the Worst-Case Fears

What are things I can do, that I can say to others, or that I can say to myself in this situation?

1.	
2.	
3.	
4.	
5.	
6.	
7.	
8.	
9.	
10.	

C12/S2–3

Initiating a Conversation Journal

Date	Time & Place Of Conversation	What I Said To Start The Conversation	How The Other Person Responded

C12/S2–3

Sustaining a Conversation Journal

Date	Time & Place Of Conversation	What I Said To Keep The Conversation Going	How The Other Person Responded

C12/S2–3

Ending a Conversation Journal

Date	Time & Place Of Conversation	What I Said To End The Conversation	How The Other Person Responded	

Index